THE CULTURAL PSYCHOLOGY OF SELF

'a remarkable work'

Rom Harré, *Georgetown University*

'It is a most provoking book – thoughtful, scholarly and distinctive in point of view.'

Jerome Bruner, *New York University*

The Cultural Psychology of Self is an exciting and challenging exploration of how people navigate human worlds. It offers a powerful understanding of 'self' as the system through which we became capable of locating ourselves in our worlds, and of finding our ways around them.

Ciarán Benson introduces the exciting field of cultural psychology specifically as it relates to 'self', and applies this understanding in a distinctively original way to themes of great moral and aesthetic importance. These include explorations of responsibility and childhood, pitilessness and compassion, suffering and guilt, visual art and the chang engagement of the spectator, connections between national and personal identi critical analysis of psychological ideals of human development. The volu wide range of cultural psychology, which is in dialogue with disciplin neuroscience and history, while at the same time reaching for an econom based on the ideas of location, dislocation and relocation. In the latter Benson makes extensive use of literature on the Holocaust and on aesth ct to recall. the visual arts to contrast phenomena of self-diminution with tho While not neglecting the centrality of neuroscientif this book speaks particularly to the historical, mor historical psychology.

The Cultural Psychology of Self is an original, far-reac part of physical and social worlds makes of us, and of be understood as a means of navigating them.

Ciarán Benson is Professor of Psychology at University College Dublin.

THE CULTURAL PSYCHOLOGY OF SELF

Place, morality and art in human worlds

Ciarán Benson

London and New York

First published 2001
by Routledge
11 New Fetter Lane, London EC4P 4EE

Simultaneously published in the USA and Canada
by Routledge
29 West 35th Street, New York, NY 10001

Routledge is an imprint of the Taylor & Francis Group

© 2001 Ciarán Benson

Typeset in Perpetua by
RefineCatch Limited, Bungay, Suffolk
Printed and bound in Great Britain by
MPG Books Ltd, Bodmin

British Library Cataloguing in Publication Data
A catalogue record for this book is available from the British Library

Library of Congress Cataloging in Publication Data
Benson, Ciarán.
The cultural psychology of the self : place, morality, and art in human worlds
/ Ciarán Benson.
p.   cm.
Includes bibliographical references and index.
1. Self psychology.   2. Culture – Psychological aspects.   I. Title.
BF697.B458   2000
1552 – dc21   00–055313

ISBN 0–415–08904–2 (hbk)
ISBN 0–415–08905–0 (pbk)

FOR FRANK AND SINÉAD

CONTENTS

Preface   ix

Acknowledgements   xv

PART I

The centrality of place for selfhood   **1**

Introduction   3

1 Selves and the need to navigate human worlds: a cultural
   psychological approach   16

2 The brain's work in locating selves   31

3 Placing oneself in personal time: the narrative structure of self   45

4 Moral identity and cultural-historical locations for self   59

5 Self-creation as self-location   73

6 Pronouns placing selves: 'I' and its associates   88

7 Feeling your way: emotions as self's pathfinders   103

PART II

Location, dislocation and relocation: responsibility,
caring, art and changing prospects   **119**

Introduction   121

8 Childhood, responsibility and acquiring powers to place oneself
   as a moral agent   130

9   Pitilessness and compassion: caring where others are   146

10 Suffering, radical dislocation and the limits of moral responsibility   161

11 Being moved: art, self and positive absorption   176

12 Points of view and none: visual art and the location of self   192

13 Individual and national identity: analogy, symbiosis and artistic process 206

14 Psychologies of maturity: development or destination?   222

CONCLUSION   **237**

Navigating human worlds   239

Bibliography   244
Index   255

PREFACE

> The self is a location, not a substance or an attribute. The sense of self is the sense of being located at a point in space, of having a perspective in time and of having a variety of positions in local moral orders. It is not having an awareness of some kind of being, particularly not an awareness of an entity at the core of one's being.
>
> (R. Harré, *Social Being*, 2nd edn., 1993, p. 4)

'Who' and 'what' you are is a function of 'where' you are. This book is a series of reflections on this theme of selfhood, location and ways of being placed in and displaced within human worlds. The word 'location' rarely appears in the index of a psychology book, and yet it seems to me to be an idea capable of being a very efficient organiser of much contemporary thinking – philosophical, psycho-logical, anthropological and aesthetic – on the nature of 'self' and 'identity'. In discussions of 'self' the ideas of being in place, having a place, losing one's place, changing one's place are ubiquitous, as are the correlative concep-tions of the types of space or place in which these processes of place-gaining and place-changing occur. In the essays that follow I want to articulate an understanding of location and human space not simply as necessary conditions for 'self', but also as a way of encapsulating a primary *raison d'être* of self as a human universal.

It is often surprising how insulated writers on this topic seem to be from the work of other thinkers, and from other disciplines with cognate concerns. Sheer volume of publications as much as the apparent incommensurability of perspec-tives and languages add momentum to the formation of these intellectual islands. It is a matter of some chance as to which island you find yourself on for your initial socialisation into thinking about human experience, self, identity, mind, consciousness and so on. The need for synoptic attempts at organising our under-standing of 'big' issues like self and identity is compelling. Jerome Bruner has a point when he says that psychology 'seems to have lost its centre and its great integrating questions.'[1] The rationale for mapping a federation of interests is often visible only when we raise our eyes to a wider horizon.

Evolutionist
& vs.
cultural ψ

Despite the jadedness of the old nature–nurture construct and its controversies, its influence continues to be evident in contemporary debate, particularly in the thinking of some evolutionary psychologists. Their polemical intent (Steven Pinker comes to mind[2]) is to stimulate discussion and confront what they think is the woolliness of those who argue for the powers of 'culture' to constitute 'human being'. For the culturalists, the polemic of much from the side of evolutionary psychology, artificial intelligence, and neurology misses the points they think they are making and fails to appreciate the nature of the social construction of 'the real' and the questions which this opens up. Bruner's contrast between culturalist concern with specifically human meaning making and computationalist preoccupation with information processing in all and any systems, including human systems, is helpful.

How we navigate our spatial world is obviously dependent upon our brains and perceptual-motor systems, which in turn are the polished tools of a long evolutionary process. Things are much less clear-cut when it comes to the navigation of human worlds, fabricated as they are with meanings. Undoubtedly our genetic structure, courtesy again of evolutionary processes, is foundational. No body, no world, no need to find our way. But evolution did not produce scripts for writing, maps, signposts, laws, codes of manners, moral codes, political organisations for the distribution of power and privilege, and so on. Culture did. Once again I find Bruner compelling when he suggests that 'Culture is probably biology's last great evolutionary trick. It frees *Homo sapiens* to construct a symbolic world flexible enough to meet local needs and to adapt to a myriad of ecological circumstances.'[3]

My understanding of the emerging perspective of cultural psychology is that it can be a sufficiently broad church to accommodate the powerful understandings emerging from both the neurosciences and the social sciences as they relate to human experience. Calling the book *The Cultural Psychology of Self* is not an attempt to consolidate an opposition to naturalists but instead an attempt to contribute to an inclusive framework within which the findings and perspectives of both might find a meaningful place.[4]

Against
txtbks
(& trad'nl
PhD write
ups)

This is emphatically not a textbook on the cultural psychology of self. All too often, a textbook can become a dead hand lying heavily on its topic. Textbooks record findings, refer to methods and 'organise' chapters in analytic sequence. They remind me of those faces used in studying infant perception where the eyes, nose and mouth are jumbled up on the two-dimensional face, and where all hint of the powers that organise and animate the meaningful use of the face as an instrument of relationship are necessarily excluded. In self-defence, Jacques Lacan once spoke of academic texts as being 'like the amber which holds the fly so as to know nothing of its flight'.[5] Of course, the style of Lacan's own texts can make a reader grateful for the stilling powers of amber. But there is a justifiable complaint here.

If textbooks distort their fields by removing the uncertain, kinetic energy of questioning in order to present a static map for reference purposes, then in this book I would like to sacrifice some of that tidiness in order to appreciate how a cultural psychology might think about how being placed in the world lies at the heart of being a self. It is in essence a series of essays, each short enough to be read at one sitting and designed to take the reader on a journey without the interruption of sub-headings or references. Taken together, the fourteen essays and two introductions cover a great deal of contemporary work relevant to the idea of self as being a primary means for navigating human worlds.

I have divided the book into two parts, each of which has an introductory essay and each of which contains seven essays. Part I introduces my understanding of some key contemporary work on the cultural psychology of self, but slanted towards illuminating an understanding of self as, what I call, a 'locative system'. The focus is on the centrality of being located for self. Part II applies that understanding to a range of issues in the psychology of morality and art which I take to be central to questions of the good life. The themes centre on the issue of change approached under the headings of location, dislocation and relocation.

The essay introducing Part I advances the idea that self is primarily a psychological system of location designed by evolution and culture for negotiating our ways through human worlds. Filling out the details of this claim takes us on a journey through a whole range of contemporary work in psychology, philosophy, neurology, history and aesthetics. It involves exploring the idea that having a sense of self requires the idea of being 'in place'. I believe that a cultural psychology which is sympathetic to neuroscience, and which knows its own boundaries and proper domain, is particularly well placed to advance a synthetic understanding of self.

A primary task of the central nervous system is to constitute an organism's world and position in that world. This is true for human beings also, so the brain's work in locating the person needs to be outlined. The idea of self-as-a-story-told, as a narrative structure, functions to place oneself as a moral agent in and across personal time. Kinds of moral and symbolic placement also depend on the repertoires of cultural-historical options which are available to people and their communities. Powers of self-creation and self-responsibility need to be considered as do linguistic ways of placing ourselves in the conversation that is human life. And the role of feeling and emotion in guiding us well or badly through human worlds also needs review.

These are the themes of Part I. In exploring them I draw on the work of many thinkers but particularly on the recent work of Edward Casey, George Lakoff and Mark Johnson, Antonio Damasio, Jerome Bruner, Charles Taylor, Julian Jaynes, and Rom Harré, among others.

Part II deals with some aspects of how we locate ourselves among other people, and particularly with the ideas of choice, responsibility and related feelings. Since the general claim of cultural psychology is that our worlds are largely the constructions of social groups, how do we go about locating ourselves in relation to ourselves and to other people? The essay themes in Part II reflect personal interests of my own. How do we become the sorts of people who believe we should accept responsibility for what we do? Why is it that so many people act pitilessly and without sympathy? Why is it that victims often feel unreasonably guilty? What is the connection between what I call the negative absorption of agony (as in torture) and the positive absorption so associated with aesthetic experience? What happens to our senses of inside and outside, and to our own personal boundaries, when artists deploy different types of point of view and none? How do psychologists think about where human development should lead? These are large questions on which I offer some reflections.

This second set of essays will take us on a journey through childhood, accounts of the perpetrators of the Holocaust, the stories of some former victims of torture and survivors of the Holocaust, aesthetic experience and 'I', light and Ganzfeld Spheres in the work of James Turrell, issues to do with the relationship of individual and national identity, and a critical look at ideals of psychological development. The thread uniting them all continues to be the thread of location, dislocation and relocation and its significance for the processes of self as a locative system.

The story of this book could be said to be part of the millennial *Zeitgeist*, where the acceleration of technological-cultural change, and the interaction of globalising and localising tendencies, must be linked to the emergence of interest in mapping, navigating, searching, revaluating. The remarkable adaptability and versatility of human beings, young and old, must be linked to basic processes of constituting ourselves as we situate and re-situate ourselves in our incessantly reconfiguring worlds. Only a generously spirited cultural-historical psychology can, I believe, face the challenge of describing what is going on at the level of selfhood and the person.

My hope is that, despite the wide-ranging nature of these essays, the power of the idea of location as an underlying dynamic of self will serve to link them together to prove its cogency and their coherence. The American philosopher Edward Casey is right to claim that 'If limits have to do with distinctions between nature and culture, orientation takes us to the point of their merging.'[6] The means and purpose of that merging should be a focus for the cultural psychology of self.

Notes

1 J. Bruner, *The Culture of Education*, Cambridge, Mass., Harvard University Press, 1996, p. 167.

2 S. Pinker, *How the Mind Works*, London, Allen Lane The Penguin Press, 1997. I find myself agreeing with Michael Tomasello when he writes: 'In all, the tired old philosophical categories of nature versus nurture, innate versus learned, and even genes versus environment are just not up to the task – they are too static and categorical – if our goal is a dynamic Darwinian account of human cognition in its evolutionary, historical, and ontogenetic dimensions.' See his *The Cultural Origins of Human Cognition*, Cambridge, Mass., Harvard University Press, 1999, p. 217.

3 Bruner, op. cit., p. 184.

4 Clifford Geertz doubts that such a rapprochement can be easily achieved or even, perhaps, that it should be. See his *Available Light: Anthropological Reflections on Philosophical Topics*, Princeton, NJ, Princeton University Press, 2000, Chapter IX.

5 A. Lemaire, *Jacques Lacan*, trans. D. Macey, London, Routledge & Kegan Paul, 1979, p. xv.

6 E. S. Casey, *Getting Back into Place: Toward a Renewed Understanding of the Place-World*, Bloomington, Indianapolis, Indiana University Press, 1993, p. 33.

ACKNOWLEDGEMENTS

I am grateful to my university, University College Dublin, for the award of a President's Fellowship which enabled me to devote the whole of 1999 to writing this book. My gratitude also to the National University of Ireland for their award to me of a Publication Grant. My colleagues Eilis Hennessy, Tom Garvin, Aidan Moran, Geraldine Moane, Jean Quigley and Mick O'Connell expertly directed my reading at crucial stages and I am most grateful to them. Toni Johnson, with her always cheerful efficiency, helped me prepare the final manuscript. My initial Senior Editor at Routledge, Richard Stoneman, was wonderfully supportive and patient in awaiting the delivery of his book. His successor Tony Bruce, and Muna Khogali, have also been most helpful. Finally I would like to thank Vivienne Roche for her steadfast interest and insight in this project, and especially for her permission to use an image of part of her sculpture *Wave Shadow* (1998–99) for the cover design, as well as for her work on that design.

Professor Hanna Damasio for permission to use and adapt her Figure 10.1 from Antonio Damasio, *The Feeling of What Happens: Body and Emotion in the Making of Consciousness*, New York, Harcourt Brace & Co., 1999, p. 310.

Excerpt from *The Reader* by Bernhard Schlink, London, Phoenix House, 1998.

Part I

THE CENTRALITY OF
PLACE FOR SELFHOOD

INTRODUCTION

Where we are – the place we occupy, however briefly – has everything to do with what and who we are (and finally, *that* we are).
(E. S. Casey, *Getting Back into Place*, 1993, p. xiii)

Just as you cannot fully understand human action without taking
account of its biological evolutionary roots and, at the same time,
understanding how it is construed in the meaning making of the
actors involved in it, so you cannot understand it fully without
knowing how and where it is situated. For, to paraphrase Clifford
Geertz, knowledge and action are always local, always situated in a
network of particulars.
(J. Bruner, *The Culture of Education*, 1996, p. 167)

By the time we can first think about it we have already become the sorts of beings
who live in human worlds. Our particular world will have shaped us in specific
ways for its own needs. It will have taught us some of the paths worth following
and how to find our way within what, at that point, will be 'our' world. It may or
may not have given us the adaptive skills necessary were the configuration of our
being in this world to change radically, or were we to find ourselves in new
worlds. Either way, whether embedded in deeply traditional worlds or in transition between new fast-changing ones, a fundamental problem confronting every
one of us, and indeed every sentient creature, is how to position ourselves in the
worlds we inhabit and how to find our way around them. Skills in navigating
human worlds are primary requirements for successful human being. Location is a
basic ontological category for psychology.

In this book I want to explore the idea that a primary function of the psychological system which is commonly called 'self' is to locate or position the person
for themselves in relation to others. I want to suggest that *self is a locative system*
with both evolutionary and cultural antecedents.

We cannot imagine being nowhere. We can visualise ourselves being lost, but
that is to be somewhere unfamiliar to us, possibly without the means of getting
back to a place we know. Where and when, place and time, are the conditions of
existence. Being nowhere is quite simply a contradiction in terms. Without being

3

placed or located I would not be, and where I find myself implaced influences not just the fact of my being but also its nature. Where, when and who are mutually constitutive. Lives, selves, identities are threaded across times and places. Who you are is a function of where you are, of where you have been and of where you hope to arrive. There cannot be a 'here' without a 'you' or an 'I' or a 'now'. Self, acts of self-location and locations are inextricably linked and mutually constructive.

'Self' functions primarily as a locative system, a means of reference and orientation in worlds of space–time (perceptual worlds) and in worlds of meaning and place–time (cultural worlds). This understanding of self as an ongoing, living process of constant auto-referred locating recognises the centrality both of the body and of social relations. The antecedents of bodily location are well understood in evolutionary terms, whereas those of personal location among other persons are best understood culturally.

Selfhood and mentality are the most sophisticated synthetic achievements of body and culture in the universe known to human beings. In addition, as Jerome Bruner reminds us, 'Perhaps the single most universal thing about human experience is the phenomenon of "Self".'[1]

There is a forceful view that some ultimate account of 'self' will be adequately framed in neural and computational terms alone. I don't share this position. I do believe that the body is a primary and necessary condition for selfhood but also that the additional sufficiency for selfhood has to be supplied by culture. My belief is that a cultural psychology of self offers the most satisfying prospect of integrating the currently far-flung accounts of self and identity.

The field of self studies is now vast, and its creators as cosmopolitan a mix as any in contemporary thought. Philosophy, psychology, neurology, psychiatry, sociology, anthropology, cultural studies, gender studies, geography, literary theory and political science all lay claim to concepts of self and identity in one form or another. Attempts at synopsis are needed for reasons of intellectual economy. A synoptic account of selfhood, as with any synthetic enterprise, must be conceptually parsimonious. Parsimony requires superordinate concepts which can be tested for their organisational powers against the various theoretical and empirical claims made about self.

I want to propose the merits of 'location' as one such concept, though not of course the only one. My perspective is cultural-historical but with a strong belief in the constructive powers of the body. I suggest that a primary function of self is to orient the person in human and humanised worlds, and to efficiently stabilise that orientation within the flux of ever-changing experience.

By 'orient' I mean more than merely direct. Perceptual systems orient organisms. For the sake of survival even the simplest creatures must be able to register 'where-they-are'. This generally has to do with some form of evaluation of that

4

with which they are in immediate physical relationship. Senses of touch, of hot and cold, of vibration and movement, of light, and chemical senses to signal the noxious or the nice, are evolutionary solutions of a fairly direct kind to the problem of locating an organism *vis-à-vis* other organisms and relevant environmental features.

Higher up the evolutionary scale, perceptual systems creative of distance, such as visual and auditory systems, multiply the adaptive challenges and powers of those creatures that possess them. In doing so they also fundamentally elaborate the kinds of space or field or frame or ecosystem or world within which the species of creature must incessantly locate itself.

With our powers to create symbolic worlds we human beings face locational problems of an order unknown in the rest of the animal world. Our perceptual processes work symbiotically with our symbolic powers. In human worlds the literal coexists with the metaphorical, the true with the false, the transient with the durable, the real with the imaginary, the actual with the possible, the desirable with the forbidden. New *types* of world (in evolutionary terms) and new *worlds* (in cultural-historical terms) require novel solutions for the perennial problems of orientation and location. What we call 'self' is one such solution to the human problem of location in time and place, in meaning and moral order, in cultural place–time as well as in physical space–time.

With human beings, and possibly with other primates such as chimpanzees, these locational solutions entail a 'doubleness'. At the perceptual level, there is that which is perceived (the objective) and there is what it is like for the perceiving subject to perceive that object (the subjective). Some thinkers like Descartes have dichotomised this doubleness into distinctive worlds, whereas others (most anti-dualists) have insisted that the apparent doubleness is fundamentally a singleness constituted by a relationship that may be considered from different aspects, sometimes from 'my' point of view and sometimes from an 'other' point of view. This doubleness also characterises people's relationships with symbolic objects, in that there is a psychological distinction between the meaning of something and that something's meaning for me.

I am especially interested in the 'subjective' aspects of this doubleness, in the significance for me of the ways and means by which I locate myself and am enabled to do so biologically and culturally which, taken together, constitute a fundamental part of my psychology. The concept of self lies at the heart of this psychology of location.

The language of location pivots on the preposition 'in'. If I ask where I am, all sorts of answers using 'in' might come to mind depending on the context of the question: 'I am in my head, two inches or so behind my eyes', 'I am in my study', 'I am in second place in the competition', 'I'm in the middle of negotiations', 'I'm in love', 'I'm in a mess', 'I'm in disgrace', 'I'm working in the university',

'I'm in the early stages of the disease', 'I'm in the opening months of the twenty-first century', 'I'm in the chat room', 'I was lost in the book', and so on.

We use the word 'in' when speaking about our selves to situate ourselves within the body, to position ourselves geographically as bodies, to place ourselves in time, to locate ourselves within kinship and other social systems, to specify where we currently are on the internet, to identify an organisation we are part of, to specify the degree of our progress in completing a task, to convey the quality of experience within a relationship, or to specify how a powerful process shaping our future and of known stages is progressing.

Corresponding to each of these usages are ideas of the structure of the places/spaces within which the self is said to be contained, enrolled, enmeshed, entangled, enthused, entertained, enraged, engaged, enveloped, enchanted. There are ideas of cosmic space, social space, mental space, personal space, spiritual space, semantic space, cyberspace, pictorial space, evolutionary design space, dynamic phase space, and so on. Some of these spaces are understood as ontologically literal, others as metaphorical. The point is that ideas of space, place and location are recruited and relied upon at every level of human experience.

What ideas are available to enable us to construct a theory of space, place and position? The history of such ideas has been explored with particular phenomeno-logical insight by the American philosopher Edward Casey.[2] His intellectual history of ideas of space, place, time and position is fascinating, and for those interested in it Casey provides one of the most acute accounts, particularly in respect to phenomenological ideas, of the body's role in generating a sense of place. For my purposes I will cherry-pick some of his conclusions which bear strongly on the case I want to make for the significance of the body's structure in the formation of 'place'.

In Western thought, as with so much else, histories of the notion of space are particularly indebted to Aristotle. He held, like Archytas of Tarentum before him, that place precedes all things. Nothing can be without being in place. Place is a condition of existence. Later in the history of the concept there emerges the idea that 'Place situates time by giving it a local habitation. Time arises *from* places and passes (away) *between* them.'[3]

But what is meant by 'place' as against 'space'? My understanding of 'place', and the sense in which I use it, is that place is humanised, personalised space. I use the idea of place–time to indicate that in personal and collective memory certain places are inexorably constituted as those places by their connection with, and embodiment of, certain moments in experiential time. Experiential time is time as a person experiences it and has paces of ebb and flow that don't map onto the rigid regularity with which clock time is arranged to pass. Our sense of the familiarity of places is intimately connected to the idea of place–time. 'When space feels thoroughly familiar to us,' writes the geographer Yi-Fu Tuan, 'it has become place.'[4]

The contemporary scientific conception of space–time is that it is fundamentally impersonal, generally homogeneous, preceding all sentient life, the precondition of all existence. While this may have potent scientific utility as a conception in contrast to, say, a medieval theological conception of the cosmos as heterogeneous and hierarchical with Heaven on top and Hell below, it is quite inadequate as an idea to describe human habitation.[5] Human beings inhabit places rather than occupy spaces. This difference between 'in' and 'in-habit' is definitive. Place is what human beings make of space and time, and it is that making which is of present interest. It is the subjectification of space and time, but a subjectification that has its roots in collective cultural achievements, which are in turn based on basic biological facts about the body.

The morphological consequences for spatial construction of being the sorts of creatures who stand upright, 'face' forward and are bilaterally symmetrical are profound, as Kant realised.[6] The ways in which space is related to our body as the primary reference point, and the manner in which that relation is developed in terms of binaries like front/behind, left/right, above/below, are foundational for our senses of where we are. 'Front' is always where we, or someone else, *face*. Buildings by extension have *facades* which also *look* to the front. Below is beneath the head. Mountains by extension have tops to which you climb by starting at their feet. Our perceptual construction of space and our language for constituting our ideas of it are intimately rooted in the morphology of our bodies.

There is a question about which comes first, dimensions or directions. Length, width and height are the axes by which we think of space and codify it. Add time as the fourth dimension and you have the widely accepted contemporary understanding of space. From the point of view of a person, or of any living creature, finding your way in this three-dimensional temporal world is more a question of knowing how to work out the direction to take and the reasons to take it. Do we go to the left or right, straight a*head* or do we *back*track and retrace our steps? We may use a compass with its north–south, east–west axes to work out our way but we read that compass by aligning the cardinal points with our front/back, left/right bodily axes. Our bodies shape and support our navigational capacities and instrument-assisted strategies in profound ways.

Most fundamental, it seems to me, is a particular primal binary, that of here/there. I suspect that this is the *ur-axis* for all navigational moves, for humans as well as for all living things. The starting point of every journey is here, the point of reference for each and every moment of the journey is here, and its conclusion is when the there of destination becomes the here of arrival. 'Here' and 'point of view' are arguably synonymous, a point to which I will return later.

In the earliest eons of evolution, when macromolecules evolved into the first

7

cells, a condition of the existence of these cells was that they were bounded.[7] There was a containing membrane where the bacterium ended, and an inside/outside binary of the most profound significance was created. In a purely spatial sense the distinction between the organism and what was not the organism was enabled by the evolution of this containing membrane. As the evolution of living creatures proceeded, this containing membrane became ever more important since it was largely on this surface that that which was not the organism, its 'world', was first registered. Sense organs which served to register that which is 'other' than the organism itself evolved on the boundary surface of the organism. In time, capacities evolved to distinguish sensations which were a consequence of movements initiated by the organism 'itself' from perhaps similar sensations which were a consequence of something other than itself. Like when, for a millisecond, a bird passes between you and the sun, and you wonder whether you have blinked. Here perhaps is a phylogenetic root of agency.

In these primal phases of evolution, one could speculate, are rooted primary biological capacities for constructing the binary self/not-self. But also with this differentiation of the organism from what was not itself came the possibility of that foundational construct for registering movement and aiding navigation, the here/there binary. All movement is from a starting position to a resting one, whether it is the movement of a whole organism in a territory or part of its body from one position to another. The start, and each phase of the movement, is, from the organism's 'point of view', always 'here' en route to a resting position, 'there'. This here/there binary is a functional outcome of the fact that living things are bounded bodies. The here/there binary is primaevally mapped onto the organism/not-organism binary.

Clearly the nature of being embodied is central both to the types of place in which creatures can be and to their ways of being in and navigating those places. Phenomenological investigations like those of Edward Casey concur with contemporary empirically based philosophy like that of Lakoff and Johnson that the body is a *fons et origo* of being human.[8] Casey, Lakoff and Johnson owe much both to Merleau-Ponty and to John Dewey so their agreement should not be surprising, but the extent of scientific support for this view grows ever more compelling.

Lakoff and Johnson write that 'The grounding of our conceptual systems in shared embodiment and bodily experience creates a largely centred self, but not a monolithic self.'[9] This idea that the body's very structure shapes our conceptual systems in important ways, and that one of these influences is the creation of a centredness constitutive of self, a dynamic, mobile, flexible centredness, is central to my argument. I have already mentioned how constructs like left/right, front/back, above/below arise from the upright, forward-facing, bilaterality of the human body, and that of inside/outside from our containing skin. The here/there binary is also rooted in the body, but more complexly.

8

In answer to the question 'What does "being here" mean?' Edward Casey offers five related meanings.[10] In the first place, 'being here' means being in part of my body such as being here just 'behind' my eyes in contrast to my feet which are 'down there'. But here can also refer to my whole body as a bounded unit as in 'I am over here'. Our bodies move and there is a meaning of here that is generated by this fact, a mobile here that moves with and by my body. The fourth meaning of 'being here' is the regional here of all the places in which I can effectively move such as my house, my garden, my neighbourhood, my county, my nation. 'A region, therefore,' writes Casey, 'is a concatenation of places that, taken together, constitutes a common and continuous here for the person who lives in and traverses them.'[11] Finally, there is that sense of 'being here' that is rooted in the interpersonal. Casey, using Husserl, says that 'In this circumstance, more than a dialectic of self and other is at play, the other's (t)here is actively resistant to my here, which thereby meets an intrinsic limit of its own range.'[12]

To become oriented, whether in physical or in interpersonal space, I must ascertain the 'theres' of my changing 'here'. Our fields of experience, whether they have to do with the spaces of our senses or those of our interpersonal and social standpoints, are structured by the splitting of the fields into relations defined by the here/there binary. Of course, this binary does not operate in isolation. It combines with others (as in 'up there', 'down here', 'near here', 'back there', 'here inside', and so on) to refine the location of the person in whichever field is in play. Like Edward Casey, I think that this very power of combining with other binaries suggests that here/there may be the most fundamental in structuring the body–place field.[13]

Much more could be said about the structure of here–there relations. 'There', for instance, could be refined using Gestalt psychology's ideas of figure and ground which in turn could be related to the psychological dynamics of attention and foci of attention. But at this point I would like to summarise some of the central ideas underpinning this book, and particularly the idea of self as a locative system which I will elaborate in Chapter 1.

The fundamental division of the experiential field is that of here/there. This directional binary combines with other directional dyads like up/down, near/far to structure the body–place experiential field. The distance perceptual systems (vision, audition) in particular are based on the intrinsic linkages of perceiver–figure–ground. They collaborate with the sensory systems associated with voluntary movement to constitute personal space.

This is because the body is genetically equipped to structure place. The place-constituting directionality of the body precedes space–time dimensionality (our modern conception of space as being three-dimensional combining with time as the fourth dimension) which is a fairly recent historical construction. Place and place–time are intrinsically personal whereas our scientific idea of space–time is definitively impersonal. The body's verticality and symmetry are products of evolution and yield the up/down, above/below, ahead/behind, left/right binaries which are so crucial for our construction of personal place-scapes. It could have been evolutionarily different: a starfish can have no left–right experience, for example. Could an octopus?

When we move on to the level of human being with our symbolic worlds of meaning, there is a quantum leap in the complexity of the constructs with which we make our places, and position ourselves within them. These constructs are rooted in their pre-symbolic precursors. The genesis and organisation of self/other binaries like I/you and us/them are linked, I want to suggest, to the body–place binaries we have discussed above in terms both of construction and of function.

Specifically, it is plausible to suggest that I/not-I partially maps onto here/there. I say 'partially' in recognition of the sense in saying 'I am looking at my hands there on the keyboard' while still acknowledging the distinction between I and me. The organisation of body–place fields grounds the organisation of self–other fields and is assimilated to them. Lakoff and Johnson in both their earlier and most recent work have compellingly analysed the links through metaphor of perceptual and linguistic structuring of human realities.[14]

This is something to which I will return, but for the moment I want to highlight a governing idea of the book. Human selves are substantially linguistic and dialogical in their construction. Two fundamental constituents of self that enable these dialogues are me/you and I/me. These binaries are intrinsically associated with the spatial here/there binary and the temporal now/then one. 'I' can never occur or be deployed without simultaneously and necessarily deploying 'here' and 'now'. However, I can have a sense of here and now without deploying 'I', which, as I will argue in Chapter 11, is a necessary condition for experiences of absorption or fusion characteristic of aesthetic and mystical experiences, as well as intensely engaging intellectual or practical work.

In evolutionary terms, the perceptual binaries precede the linguistic ones, as they also do in individual psychological development. Once developed at the genetic, the cultural and the personal levels, the perceptual and linguistic binaries work symbiotically. One of the contributions of Lakoff and Johnson is to show how this works as a unity in personal and social life. The primary function of these binaries, perceptual and linguistic, is to enable people to locate themselves in the places in which they find themselves, and to navigate those worlds in line with need and desire.

Location is the ontological condition for all human being. Not to be in a place is to be nowhere, and to be nowhere is to be nothing. Therefore it is a *sine qua non* of human personhood, and therefore of human being, to be in place. If here/there, and its associated binaries, together with I/not-I, and its affiliated binaries,

10

[Handwritten margin notes at top: "Func to core of selfhood = locative system – means of navigating perceptible & meaningful world"]

define the core of selfhood, and if the primary purpose of these binaries is locational, the functional core of selfhood would be that it is a locative system, a means of navigating worlds that are perceptible and meaningful.

This understanding of self as a locative system, as a means of navigating humanly created cultural worlds, crucially involves self-reference, the core binary for which is I/me. This, in quite abstract terms, is what it means to say that 'Who I am is a function of where I am.' It is the aim of this book to spell out in more specific detail what this might mean, and to show that much contemporary philosophical, psychological, neurological and anthropological thinking about self can be usefully connected using the idea of self as a locative system.

[Handwritten margin notes: "I/me binary of self/me" ; "Who am I is a func of where I am. PMC"]

I have titled the book 'The Cultural Psychology of Self' and that needs some explanation. It seems to me that a generous cultural psychology capable of embracing all that biology has to offer is better placed to account for the nature of selfhood than is a biological perspective that seeks to assimilate the cultural to itself. Culture is more than biology can handle alone, yet both form a single system.

Cultural psychology as a sub-discipline has been taking shape throughout the 1990s in particular. Work by James Stigler, Richard Shweder, Gilbert Herdt, Jerome Bruner, Michael Cole, Rom Harré, Bradd Shore, Michael Tomasello, and many others, has contributed to the consolidation of its identity.[15] I would also include the work of Lakoff and Johnson in here as extremely helpful for the elaboration of an adequate cultural psychology of selfhood. Cultural psychology has intellectual antecedents which go back far beyond the 1990s, as these and other writers emphasise, and I have no wish to go over ground well-covered elsewhere as to why it had to wait in the wings for so long before being called on stage. I do need, however, to outline some of the distinctive features of a cultural psychology, especially as they inform an inquiry into the locative dimensions of selfhood.

In a sentence, cultural psychology examines how people, working together, using a vast range of tools, both physical and symbolic – tools which have been developed over time and which carry with them the intelligence that solved specific problems – make meaningful the world they find, make meaningful worlds and, in the course of doing all these things, construct themselves as types of person and self who inhabit these worlds. This working description of cultural psychology draws on features which have been systematised by others.

[Handwritten margin notes: "Def of cult. psy."]

Michael Cole, for instance, characterises cultural psychology as emphasising mediated action that always occurs in a context, as always interested in how a particular phenomenon and its context developed, as granting the centrality of everyday life, as stressing how 'mind emerges in the *joint* mediated activity of people', and as assuming that people are active agents in their own development though not usually in contexts of their own making. Its methods, appropriately, are drawn widely and it favours interpretation as a central part of its explanatory framework in contrast to psychology's historical bias towards positivism.[16] Bruner sees the dominant questions for a cultural psychology as having to do with the making and negotiation of meaning, with the construction of self and a sense of agency, with the acquisition of symbolic skills, and with the cultural 'situatedness' of all mental activity.[17]

My own understanding of the proper domain of a cultural psychology of self has been greatly sharpened by Antonio Damasio's neurological theory of self.[18] Using detailed examples of how a wide range of neurological pathologies result in deficits of self functioning, Damasio presents a fascinating and compelling theory of the various levels of operation which neurologically constitute the processes that we call self. I will save comment on his account of feeling and emotion until Chapter 7. Here I want to outline his theory of self in the most cursory fashion specifically to show how an intellectually generous biological account of self helps to define and situate the proper domain for a cultural psychology of self.

Damasio argues for a hierarchically organised understanding of self ranging from the non-conscious integrations and bodily maintenance of the system he calls the proto-self, through 'core' consciousness which deals attentively with the here and now and which generates what he calls the core self, to the forms of extended consciousness which engender the autobiographical self which can situate itself in representations of time ranging from the past to the future. Extended consciousness requires the normal functioning of core consciousness which in turn requires the proper functioning of the proto-self system.

The lower levels can function without the higher but not the higher without the lower. Damasio presents convincing evidence to show how various forms of brain damage knock out different aspects of this self-system. In doing so, he clearly recognises where the cultural enters the picture, notably in the autobiographical dimension of self which 'places that person at a point in individual historical time, richly aware of the lived past and of the anticipated future, and keenly cognizant of the world beside it'.[19] But the roots of ourselves as we know ourselves lie deep in the non-conscious proto-self. The summits of biology on the other hand are, in Damasio's understanding, ethics and law, art and compassion. These are enabled by but not reducible to biology.[20]

As an aid to identifying where, in this scheme of things, a biological understanding of self would hand over the baton to a cultural psychology of self see Figure 1. I have adapted this from Damasio.[21] He uses it to suggest the levels which need to be taken into account in the biological-cultural journey which we all must take every moment of our lives from simple biological wakefulness to the highest levels of conscience and self-responsibility.

Cultural psychology explicitly acknowledges that how one is located in one's community, how that community is situated in its wider society, how that society

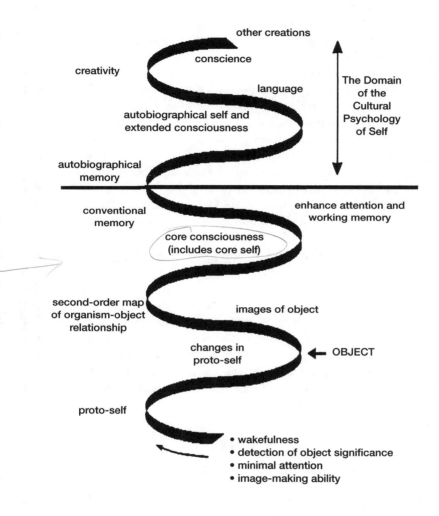

Figure 1 The domain of the cultural psychology of self

Adapted from Figure 10.1 of A. Damasio, *The Feeling of What Happens: Body and Emotion in the Making of Consciousness*, New York, Harcourt Brace & Company, 1999, p. 310.

stands in relation to other societies, and how these relationships are placed developmentally and currently in history, all have profound relevance for the kinds of mind and self that may be formed. Its stress on acts of meaning-making, on the available tools with which the making is done, and on the constraints endemic to the times in which the meanings are made, are also central to understanding the formation of mind and selfhood.

In the seven essays comprising Part I, I lay out what it means to think of self as a 'locative system'. I outline some of the work done by the brain in locating self, and I consider how writers like Jerome Bruner argue that narratives simultaneously constitute and place the autobiographical self in time. I outline Charles Taylor's historical treatment of ideas underpinning the modern Western identity. I then use the work of Julian Jaynes to introduce ideas of self-creation as they relate to personal responsibility, and I review the work of Rom Harré and others on the referential functions of personal pronouns in the psychology of self. I conclude Part I with an exploration of the idea that emotions function as pathfinders in our navigation of human worlds using, among that of others, the recent work of Antonio Damasio.

I make no claim to comprehensiveness in what follows. What I offer is a range of essays reflecting interests I have. They have been written in the spirit of an emerging cultural psychology which takes biology seriously. I don't know if a cultural psychology will have the wherewithal to aspire to some sort of social scientific 'Theory of Everything'. I do know that the potential width of its embrace makes the study of selfhood all that much more interesting, and allows me to consider the work of a disparate range of intriguing thinkers and themes. It will also allow me in Part II to apply some of these ideas in an exploration of themes in the cultural psychology of art and morality which seem to me to be of great importance for quality human lives.

Notes

1 J. Bruner, *The Culture of Education*, Cambridge, Mass., Harvard University Press, 1996, p.35.
2 E. S. Casey, *Getting Back into Place: Toward a Renewed Understanding of the Place-World*, Bloomington, Indianapolis, Indiana University Press, 1993, and *The Fate of Place: A Philosophical History*, Berkeley, University of California Press, 1997.
3 Casey, *Getting Back into Place*, p. 21.
4 Yi-Fu Tuan, *Space and Place*, Minneapolis, University of Minnesota Press, 1976, pp. 72–7. Quoted by Casey, *Getting Back into Place*, p. 28.
5 See M. Wertheim, *The Pearly Gates of Cyberspace: A History of Space from Dante to the Internet*, London, Virago, 1999, for a popular introduction to this history.
6 See Casey, *The Fate of Place*, Chapter 10, for a discussion of Kant's thinking on the significance of bilaterality.
7 For a speculative account of the aboriginal formation of membranes (p.21), but also

for an attempted integration of biology and culture by a mathematician and biologist, see I. Stewart and J. Cohen, *Figments of Reality: The Evolution of the Curious Mind*, Cambridge, Cambridge University Press, 1997. Their knowledge of philosophy and psychology, however, is not to be relied upon. A more sophisticated account is to be found in D. Dennett, *Darwin's Dangerous Idea: Evolution and the Meanings of Life*, New York, Simon & Schuster, 1995.

8 G. Lakoff and M. Johnson, *Philosophy in the Flesh: The Embodied Mind and Its Challenge to Western Thought*, New York, Basic Books, 1999.

9 Ibid., p. 6.

10 Casey, *Getting Back into Place*, pp. 53–4.

11 Ibid., p. 53.

12 Ibid., p. 54.

13 Ibid., p. 56.

14 See G. Lakoff and M. Johnson, *Metaphors We Live By*, Chicago and London, University of Chicago Press, 1980.

15 See J. W. Stigler, R. A. Shweder, and G. Herdt (eds), *Cultural Psychology: Essays on Comparative Human Development*, Cambridge, Cambridge University Press, 1990; R. Harré, *Social Being*, 2nd edn, Oxford, Blackwell, 1993; M. Cole, *Cultural Psychology: A Once and Future Discipline*, Cambridge, Mass., Harvard University Press, 1996; B. Shore, *Culture in Mind: Cognition, Culture, and the Problem of Meaning*, Oxford, Oxford University Press, 1996; J. Bruner, *Acts of Meaning*, Cambridge, Mass., Harvard University Press, 1990 and *The Culture of Education*, Cambridge, Mass., Harvard University Press, 1996; M. Tomasello, *The Cultural Origins of Human Cognition*, Cambridge, Mass., Harvard University Press, 1999.

16 Cole, op. cit., p. 104. Richard Shweder defines the field as follows: 'Cultural psychology is thus the study of the way the human mind can be transformed, given shape and definition, and made functional in a number of different ways that are not uniformly distributed across cultural communities around the world.' See R. A. Shweder, 'Cultural Psychology' in R. A. Wilson and F. C. Kell (eds), *The MIT Encyclopedia of the Cognitive Sciences*, London, The MIT Press, 1999, pp. 212–13.

17 Bruner, *The Culture of Education*, p. x.

18 See especially Antonio Damasio, *The Feeling of What Happens: Body and Emotion in the Making of Consciousness*, New York, Harcourt Brace & Co., 1999.

19 Ibid., p. 16.

20 Ibid., p. 28.

21 Ibid., p. 310.

1

SELVES AND THE NEED TO NAVIGATE HUMAN WORLDS

A cultural psychological approach

> He said the world could only be known as it existed in men's hearts. For while it seemed a place which contained men it was in reality a place contained within them and therefore to know it one must look there and come to know those hearts and to do this one must live with men and not simply pass among them.
>
> (C. McCarthy, *The Crossing*, 1995, p. 134)

> Consciousness is an operation rather than a thing, a repository, or a function. It operates by way of analogy, by way of constructing an analog space with an analog 'I' that can observe that space, and move metaphorically in it. It operates on any reactivity, excerpts relevant aspects, narrativizes and conciliates them together in a metaphorical space where such meanings can be manipulated like things in space. Conscious mind is a spatial analog of the world and mental acts are analogs of bodily acts.
>
> (J. Jaynes, *The Origin of Consciousness in the Breakdown of the Bicameral Mind*, 1976, pp. 65–6)

The world contains my body. My body contains me. I contain my world. Where then is the world and where am I in it if it also is in me? The old man in Cormac McCarthy's novel *The Crossing* who speaks in the epigraph above has understood that the unit of analysis for understanding how it is that the worlds of human beings are meaningful worlds – worlds literally made of meanings – is not the individual in isolation nor the world apart from the individual with which he interacts, but both in serial dialogic transaction. The world contains me and I am a world containing it, and together each expands or constricts the other.

How to find my way about in the world as perceived and the world as known and understood is the problem of navigating humanised worlds and human worlds. We make the world as sensed our own familiar world and thereby humanise it, but we also create symbolic worlds that are developmentally grounded in the world as we perceive and move in it, but for which the metaphor of containment becomes inadequate. These individualised symbolic worlds don't simply contain 'us': they are us. What they are we are. My 'me' is 'me and my world'. My 'self', as I come to understand it, plays a very particular role in my world. It charts my course, finds my way, navigates *the* world through the template of *my* world. My 'self', more coldly stated, is, among other things, a locative system. As such it is organised with parts, dynamics and functions.

There are two general senses to the idea of location as it refers to selfhood. There is the ontological sense of 'being in place' which I introduced in the Introduction to Part I, the idea that without the conditions for being implaced self could not be. There is also the idea of location that saturates how we talk and think about self, and the extent to which ways of thinking and talking about self create the reality of self as it is considered and talked about. It is this second sense that I want to concentrate on in this chapter, and for that I will draw on the recent work of Lakoff and Johnson. In a powerful synthesis of linguistics, cognitive science and philosophy, they lay foundations for understanding the pervasive influence of being embodied, and hence of being implaced, on how we conceptualise mind and self, and the constituting metaphors that enable us to do it.[1]

Before that, and to develop the idea of a cultural psychological perspective on self as a locative system as compared to a computational perspective, I want to follow the path of a particular cognitive approach to self, Ulric Neisser's, to show both its limitations and its potential for incorporation into a cultural psychological framework. Historians of psychology pick 1956 as the year when the Cognitive Revolution began in psychology.[2] The intellectual fertility of this perspective quickly bore fruit and in time came to play a key role in the emergence of cognitive science. Central to it has been the idea of information-processing and computation. In time, the information-processing perspective began to feel unduly restrictive and writers like Jerome Bruner, who had been a key player in the first Cognitive Revolution, Rom Harré and many others began to formulate what some called the Second Cognitive Revolution. The latter has been a seedbed for cultural psychology.

Bruner distinguishes 'culturalism' from 'computationalism'. The former focuses on meaning-making whereas the latter centres on information-processing.[3] Meaning-making and information-processing are not necessarily discontinuous, but the directions for how we understand cognition which are implied by an exclusive focus on one or the other are quite divergent in contemporary practice. The culturalist emphasis on the making of meanings involves looking exclusively at human beings and specifically at such processes as narrative thinking and interpretation, whereas the computationalist orientation is interested in all information-processing, both human and non-human, and is predominantly logical-scientific in approach.

Ulric Neisser played a major role in the development of cognitive psychology understood from an information-processing perspective. He also has explored the idea of self and self-knowledge from within this framework and so serves as a reliable guide to its utility and limitations.[4] The conclusion I draw from what follows is that while the information-processing approach adopted by Neisser is strong on the pre-linguistic locative functions of the emerging self, it becomes quite inadequate to account for the locative functions of the emerging linguistic or autobiographical self. The post-linguistic autobiographical self requires a framework based on the idea of negotiated meaning-making within a context of pre-existing meanings. In short, it invites a cultural psychological approach.

Neisser bases his theory of self on findings from the psychology of cognition and perception, and he anchors these findings in the concept of information. Information can mean something objective that specifies the properties of objects and events according to physical principles which can be 'picked up' by perceivers. It can also be thought of as something stored in the brain. Neisser's strategy is to analyse what he calls the types of information on which self-knowledge is based and to use these to develop his theory of self. What he claims to find are different kinds of information, each specifying a different kind of self. His conclusion is that there are essentially five different kinds of self. They originate at different times, develop differently, go wrong differently, and contribute distinctively to the experience of being social. They are the ecological, interpersonal, extended, private and conceptual selves.

Neisser's description of each draws heavily on developmental psychology for which a most important question is whether a newborn baby has a sense of self, or could in principle have one. By definition a baby could not have a developed self but is there evidence that the roots of later self, or elements of self, are present at this early stage and, if so, the roots of precisely what? Most theorists would agree that a watershed for self-development and for the construction of a personal world is the acquisition of language and that the pre-linguistic period of life (*infans* means 'unable to speak') contrasts radically with post-linguistic psychological life. Pre-linguistically we are looking at precursors of self, or are we?

Infants exist in space–time, or to use my preferred concept, place–time since familiarity already plays a key role in infant life. They see, hear, taste, smell and move in a visible, sound-filled, tasty, odourful and mobile world. But psychologists differ in what they grant to the infant as a subjective being. Some like Freud, Piaget and Margaret Mahler argue that the infant exists in a state of undifferentiated fusion with the world and therefore could not possibly know herself.[5] Until

18

a substantial portion of the infant's first year has passed, it is argued, the child lives in an unsettled world without permanent objectivity and without any idea of herself as one among other durable objects in the world.

Others, like Margaret Donaldson, speculate that infants develop a sense of self much earlier than this.[6] For evidence she points to studies which can be interpreted as indicating that babies in the first six months can quickly learn to exercise effective control, as when playing with a mobile, and can be visibly pleased in doing so. Furthermore, once they become competent in doing something like this, infants tend to do less of it, as though the incentive was in establishing control rather than in the consequences of that control. Within Damasio's theory we could grant that the infant has a functioning proto-self, a rudimentary core self, but that an autobiographical self founded upon them must await the development of extended consciousness.

Neisser's first two selves, what he calls the 'ecological' and the 'interpersonal', relate to this same question. Take the ecological self first. Neisser comes down firmly on the side of those like Donaldson when he writes:

> Certainly by 3 months of age (and probably from birth), the infant perceives much the same sort of world that we do: a world of distinct, solid and permanent objects of which she herself (or he himself) is one. . . . The old hypothesis that a young infant cannot tell the difference between itself and the environment, or between itself and its mother, can be decisively rejected.[7]

If a precondition of self is a boundary between self and other, or not-self, as many like Daniel Dennett have pointed out, then the claim would be that this precondition is established very early in infancy.[8] This supports the idea mooted in the Introduction to Part I that the here/there binary is a primal construct for the formation of self.

Moving on a bit developmentally to verbal two-year-olds, Neisser takes the results of some research conducted by John Flavell and his colleagues to make an interesting point about perception and the ecological self.[9] It also indicates something about the development of the conviction that we are located behind our eyes. Children were told to cover their eyes and asked whether the experimenters could see them. Most two- and three-year-olds said No. When they were asked different questions like 'Can I see your head?' or 'Can I see your leg?' the answer was Yes. When initially asked 'Can I see you?' the answer was No. Neisser's point is this: the child's 'I/me' to which the question 'Can I see you?' refers seems to be somewhere near the eyes. He concludes that 'children locate the self at the point of observation, as specified by the optical flow field'.[10]

As further supporting evidence he refers to Selma Fraiberg's work with congenitally blind children which suggests that they are relatively slow to develop an adequate sense of self, and that they master the pronouns 'I' and 'you' later than sighted children. This question of pronoun mastery lies at the heart of Rom Harré's theory of self and I will return to its developmental psychology in some detail in Chapter 6 where evidence like Fraiberg's may be interpreted as being more relevant perhaps to Harré's than to Neisser's account of self.

Optical flow is central to Neisser's claim that the ecological self is 'the self as perceived with respect to the physical environment'. Here again the idea of location and the division of the perceptual field into here/there is implicit but central. The visual system is anchored to its environment by a continuous flow of optical information. Every change in point of view (here) systematically changes the flow pattern in the visual field. Such flow patterns help to locate the ecological self and to specify how it is moving. Another aspect of this may be the sort of pleasure in being an agent mentioned by Donaldson, a sense of agency being a crucial aspect of a sense of self.

Neisser's ecological self is thus defined in terms of two distinguishable kinds of information: the perceiving being has its location specified by the optical flow field (and also by those of touch and hearing) and, related to this, the existence of a bounded controllable body which can be specified by sight, feeling and action. Neisser maintains that a definite, directly perceived form of awareness accompanies the ecological self in both adults and infants. Although he does not make this point, one could speculate on whether the here/there binary is the foundational construct of the ecological self.

His next self is the 'interpersonal self' and this relates to the idea of a self located and anchored in a social world. The interpersonal self is engaged in 'immediate unreflective social interaction with another person' and, like the ecological self, appears in earliest infancy. His evidence for this comes from the detailed research on mother–child interactions, particularly that of Colwyn Trevarthen and the research reported by Daniel Stern. Such phenomena as the infant's early seeking of eye-contact, smiles in response to expressive signals from the mother, complex coordinations of actions and reactions between the two, the coordination of expressed feeling, and so on were described by Trevarthen as constituting a 'primary intersubjectivity'. The interpersonal self lies within this intersubjective world, we might add, which both contains and shapes its makers, and directs the sequencing of their meaning-making.

The ecological and interpersonal selves are similar, argues Neisser, in that both are based on information that is available to be perceived. They differ in that the interpersonal self involves a specific, biologically given capacity to relate to other members of the human species. We are genetically programmed to be social.[11] Neisser suggests that in the preverbal infant there is a simultaneous awareness of the ecological and the interpersonal selves, and correspondingly of

20

physical and social objects. Each self is, in addition, rooted and located in present time.

So far so good. It is when we come to Neisser's descriptions of the 'extended self', the 'private self' and the 'conceptual self' that the water muddies both for him and for us. Here we approach the utility limits of an exclusive reliance on the idea of information-processing, and we begin to see the value of the cultural psychological idea of meaning-making. Neisser has less to say about these three 'selves', but what he does identify as important are precisely those dimensions of selfhood that are elaborated by culturalists.

His extended self is the one made possible by the capacity to remember, and therefore to transcend the present moment by our ability to represent the world temporally. It is located in sequences of memory and anticipation. Neisser writes: 'Most adults develop a more or less standard life-narrative that effectively defines the self in terms of a particular series of remembered experiences.'[12]

As we will see in Chapter 3, this understanding of self as narrative is precisely that developed by Bruner. Neisser sees the extended self as linked to the conceptual self, but interposed is the idea of private self whose existence Neisser construes from the unavailability of certain experiences to other people. This is the 'what-it-is-like-for-me' self, to borrow Thomas Nagel's formulation for subjectivity, and Neisser has least to say about this particular 'self'. Harré, as we will see, sees it as definitive of personal identity.

Neisser's fifth and last self, the conceptual self, is that concept of themselves as particular sorts of person which people hold and act upon (woman, husband, mother, accountant, and so on). In other frameworks this would be called a social identity. The concepts which people have of themselves are part of a unifying theory. Neisser believes that the theories defining the conceptual self differ from 'the other four aspects of the self' (his formulation) in being social in origin. Furthermore, all the other four 'kinds of self-knowledge' are represented in the conceptual self. He then talks of conceptual selves as 'meta-selves'.

In his declared attempt to clear up confusions in the psychology of self by offering 'a set of clear distinctions' Neisser fails, but does so instructively. The structure of his own narrative account shows why. His initial claim is that the five different kinds of 'self-specifying information', each establishing a 'different aspect of self', are so distinct as to be 'essentially different selves'. He presents these five selves as distinct, but when he comes to the post-linguistic ones his step falters. The reason for this is that his cognitive-perceptual perspective, while intrinsically valuable, simply cannot match the problem he has posed for himself, namely the challenges of self considered as 'a unitary object'.

Even the word 'object' here, rather than 'subject', is revealing. Neisser confuses the issue by treating the ideas of 'self-specifying information', 'self-knowledge', 'aspects of the self' and 'selves' as synonymous. His possible awareness of these difficulties may be evident in the load he makes his conceptual self carry. It must also be said that he does this without any reference to the now vast field of literature on the philosophy, psychology, sociology and anthropology of self.

Without a theory of the constitutive powers of language, coupled with a theory of the social foundations of individuality and privacy, orthodox cognitive psychology simply has not got the tools to account adequately for the stability and felt unity of the autobiographical self. To offer an account of the structure of self, conceived either as a singularity or as a kind of federation, without highlighting the central role of language and the unifying powers of narrative thought, is like describing the structure of Concorde without mentioning the wings. However, while Neisser's analysis does reveal the deficits of the information-processing approach as against the potential of the meaning-making perspective, his idea of the ecological dimensions of self does reinforce the claim that the body must lie at the centre of any account of self as a locative system.

No one stated this more clearly than William James when he wrote that

> The world experienced . . . comes at all times with our body as its centre, centre of vision, centre of action, centre of interest. The body is the storm centre, the origin of co-ordinates, the constant place of stress in all that experience-train. . . . The word 'I', then, is primarily a noun of position, just like 'this' and 'here'.[13]

The idea of centredness lies at the heart of accounts of self, not as some sort of entity, but as an organising locus of reference within constantly flowing fields of experience. These fields are both perceptual and semantic. James's metaphor of the body, and by extension of the self, as the 'origin of co-ordinates' links with Husserl's account when he writes that

> All worldly things there for me continue to appear to me to be oriented about my phenomenally stationary, resting organism. That is, they are oriented with respect to here and there, right and left, etc., whereby a firm zero of orientation persists, so to speak, as absolute here.[14]

For both James and Husserl, the metaphor for self as the constant origin or zero within changing fields of experience comes easily to mind. Again the here/there binary lies at the heart of bodily experience.

Merleau-Ponty's conclusion affirms much the same thing: 'There is, therefore, another subject beneath me, for whom a world exists before I am here, and who marks out my place in it. This captive or natural subject is my body.'[15] My body is here before I am and prepares a place for me as subject. Edward Casey, referring

22

to forms of brain damage and disorientation such as were exhibited by Brenda Milner's famous patient H. M.,[16] concludes that 'It follows that even when we become acutely disoriented, *so long as we have at least a residual sense of where we are bodily* [his emphasis], we are never entirely unoriented in space, . . . never without some vestigial hereness.'[17]

We could draw further support from Heidegger and others but the point is already strongly made: the sense of hereness enabled by the body is the ground for the development of I as, in James's term, 'a noun of position'. That sense of hereness of the body, together with skills in correctly deploying deictics like 'I', lies at the heart of the idea of self as a locative system. 'I' am a flowering shrub grafted onto the stock of bodily 'hereness'. Chapters 2 and 6 in particular will elaborate some of these ideas.

To recap, my sense of self is fundamentally conditioned by my embodiment and physicality. My eyes are in my head and it is here, as Neisser rightly points out, where my point of view on the world seems centred despite the ever-changing patterns in the visual flow of information, that I intuitively locate 'my' position as subject. I might say 'This is where I operate from.' James also locates the 'centre of action' in the body as he does the centre of desire and interest. All informational flows in the lived world of a person, whether visual, auditory, tactile, olfactory, kinaesthetic and, more complexly, sexual, converge on the experience of the body. No account of the sense of self can ignore this basic fact of incarnation.

But how are we to speak of this? How does the 'wordiness' of our being cohabit with its physicality? At this point I want to note some of the ways in which language creates social meanings and realities, including dimensions of self, as a prelude to later discussions of how a person's linguistic skills can be used reflexively to create and transform self. Specifically I want to introduce the idea that our ways of speaking of our selves are ineradicably metaphorical. It makes all the difference how I describe a person or an event for the nature of that person and event, at least among those who share my description.

Take, for example, a problem of taxonomy, of how to classify a behaviour. To the passer-by on the street ignorant of neurological disorders the agitated man shouting obscenities at shoppers is extremely bad-mannered and probably drunk. Under a neurological description he is neither of these but is suffering from Tourette's Syndrome. The consequences for judgement and action in each case are very different because the 'same' behaviour illustrates very different 'facts' according to which scheme of description is available to the onlooker.

If I see him 'as' drunk and disorderly I take a moral stance as a citizen and am not unhappy when he is arrested, charged and held responsible for his actions, including those of getting drunk in the first place. However, once it occurs to me that he should be understood 'as' a case of Tourette's Syndrome then I think an unfortunate mistake has been made, that medicine not law is the proper forum, sickness not guilt the proper judgement. The accuracy of my language of description and its relevance to the present situation can literally transform one situation into another kind of situation.

Take another dreadfully real case where the description is metaphorical but where the metaphor becomes literally genocidal. On 7 August 1942 Goebbels wrote: 'The Jews have always been carriers of infectious diseases. One must either crowd them together in ghettos and leave them to it, or else liquidate them, failing which they will always infect the healthy civilized populations.'[18] On 20 August 1941 he had written that 'It is outrageous and a scandal that the capital of the Reich still has 70, 000 Jews, mostly parasites, spoiling not only the looks of our city but its atmosphere.'[19] Later, at the Posen Conference of 6 October 1943, when Himmler explicitly told the Nazi hierarchy of the Final Solution so that that knowledge would implicate them all, he said that they had lasted through the war so far because they had removed 'this destructive pestilence'.[20]

Here we have one of the most historically awful examples of a root metaphor describing an entire race of people. Jews are a pestilence, parasites, infectious of the healthy, polluters of the atmosphere. The shift into the metaphor of disease carries with it by association forms of remedy appropriate to disease, namely quarantine and eradication. If language creates ideas which can be realised, among these realities are formulae for action, for dealing with the realities created by the particular descriptions. Just as a whole people can be lethally imaged so too can individual persons, both by themselves and by other people. Metaphorical imaging can, of course, be positive as well as negative. Either way, people's sense of themselves, like that of a whole people, is intrinsically linked to the descriptions of themselves which they believe. Descriptions are constitutive rather than merely reflective.

Such descriptions define people as they are, and influence how they act and hence what they may become. The point of all this is not to avoid metaphors since most language use and abstract thought is inherently metaphorical. Rather it is to be aware of their power and to be wary in one's choice of generative metaphors. The idea that 'reality' is 'out there' waiting to be described by the language which we have 'in here' is one description to lay quickly to one side. What is 'out there' might begin 'in here' and what is 'in here' may begin 'out there'. How we describe ourselves and others, the associative networks into which our thinking is tracked by virtue of the metaphors we use or have used about us, has obvious implications for the sorts of selves we are and for how we navigate our social and intimate worlds. The metaphorical armature of our ideas about 'the world' and about ourselves has powerful existential consequences at every level for our own and for others' lives.

All of us, as individuals, are enmeshed in constantly shifting social networks and webs of meaning. Finding our way within them is greatly facilitated if they are the sorts of webs we are familiar with, webs we have grown up with, webs which have shaped us more or less to be their own vehicles for reproducing themselves.[21] Within these webs and networks, 'here' means where I am, where I stand, and 'there' is where I might or might not want to be. Getting from here to there in social networks, as in physical space, is a function of what I am and of where my current 'here' lies in reference to the desirable 'there'. Understanding the navigational strategies of people in symbolic worlds means understanding the local topographies of meaning of their communities and culture. This is especially pressing in the moral domain, in what we think of as good and desirable or as bad and repulsive.

Just how profound for our conceptions of self are ideas of location can be seen in Lakoff and Johnson's elaboration of the metaphorical structure of the concepts of mind and self, and of many other phenomena and ideas such as time, causation, events and morality. It is the nature of all neural beings, as they point out, that they must categorise. Categorisation is an intrinsic part of the organisation of living things. Also determined are the kinds of categories living creatures can have and the structure of those categories. For example,

> We have a visual system, with topographic maps and orientation-sensitive cells, that provides structure for our ability to conceptualize spatial relations. Our abilities to move in the ways we do and to track the motion of other things give motion a major role in our conceptual system.[22]

When we think about categories themselves we tend to use the spatial metaphor of a container with an interior, an exterior and a boundary. Some categories are bigger containers than others and contain them, and so hierarchies of concepts elaborate. Lakoff and Johnson argue that 'Spatial-relations concepts are at the heart of our conceptual systems.'[23] The complexity of our reasoning, which takes place largely unconsciously, can be nicely illustrated with one of their examples centring on the spatial word 'in'. What does it mean to say 'The butterfly is in the garden?' To understand this, which we do effortlessly, we actually have to think of the garden as a three-dimensional container with an interior that extends up into the air. The butterfly is then related to that conceptual container and judged to be inside it. Just how high above the garden it would have to fly to be out of the garden is another question!

When we think of our selves, we use spatial-relations concepts and also concepts with the structure of a motor-control system such as our bodies exhibit. Lakoff and Johnson develop the idea of 'primary metaphor' to show just how much of the way in which we conceptualise the world, and ourselves, reaches deep into our sensorimotor make-up, and hence into our own evolutionary and ontogenetic histories. Reason, they argue, is not transcendental. It is rooted in and grows out of our sensory and motor systems. Piaget, of course, shared a similar understanding of reason.

Metaphor allows the rich inferential structure of sensorimotor knowledge to be used in the creation and elaboration of subjective experience. Primary metaphors like 'categories are containers', 'similarity is closeness', 'states are locations', 'intimacy is closeness', 'actions are self-propelled motions', 'relation-ships are enclosures', 'happy is up', 'more is up', 'purposes are destinations', 'change is motion' and 'linear scales are paths' are all rooted in the sensorimotor domain of space and the body's movements and orientations in space.[24]

I select these only because they relate to the idea of self as a locative system and to my themes of being-in-place and human navigation. There are hundreds of other primary metaphors that combine in wonderful ways, as Lakoff and Johnson show, to form complex metaphors such as 'love is a journey'. Primary metaphors are key constituents of the cognitive unconscious.

Our ideas of time, and of our location in time, are also profoundly meta-phorical. They draw from our orientation and motion in space. In what is called the 'Time Orientation Metaphor', for example, our location as observers is the present, the space in front of us is the future and that behind us is the past. 'I've left the past behind me and am looking forward to the future!' is a common statement. The 'Moving Time Metaphor' is based on the notion of times as locations in space. It draws on our sense that objects that move past us from front to back have fronts in the direction of their motion. These objects map on to 'times' and the motion of these objects past the observer maps on to 'the passage of time'. 'The summer just flew by' would be an example.

We also think of events and causes metaphorically in terms of spatial locations, movements, journeys, destinations and obstacles. Lakoff and Johnson show how what they call 'the location branch of the Event-Structure Metaphor' is a pro-foundly important metaphor. This metaphor grounds how we conceptualise such basic concepts as states ('I'm in love' or 'I was on the edge of a breakdown'), changes ('I eventually emerged from my depression'), causes ('The sight of the little street-child moved me to tears'), actions ('It's plain sailing from here on'), difficulties ('He's between a rock and a hard place'), freedom of action ('Her smile opens doors'), and purposes ('I can see light at the end of this tunnel'). Motion through space, as they illustrate so well, forms the basis of a vast metaphoric system for our understanding of events, causes and purposive action.[25]

Metaphors of location and movement in space are also fundamentally import-ant for our conceptualisation of mind. Mind is often thought of as a body and, following from this, thinking is understood as moving, ideas are locations, not being able to think is being unable to move forward, lines of thought are followed as paths, communicating is guiding, understanding is following, and so on. Thinking might also be thought of as perceiving and again locational aspects would be evident in the idea that trying to know something is 'a search', knowing from a standpoint is knowing from a point of view, directing attention is pointing, and so on. If primary metaphors are the stuff of abstract thought in general, they are powerfully so when it comes to thinking abstractly about self and location.

In the cultural psychological framework, the idea of 'self' involves the notion of a subject who can reflexively engage with other aspects of personhood, usually conceived as possessions, such as my body, my reputation, my family, my beliefs, and so on. G. H. Mead's primary distinction of I–me catches this meaning.[26] Within that framework the key elements of selfhood include the idea of centredness, of self being the pivotal point of reference within various flowing fields of experience. It also includes the idea that action is centred on or sourced to self as the author or agent of the action. And, crucially for the task of unifying these dimensions of selfhood, it encompasses the function of self as maker and narrator of one's own story or autobiography.

These are themes to which we will return throughout the book. For the moment, I want to map Lakoff and Johnson's discussion of the metaphoric structure of our ideas of self onto this framework, not as an exposition of their argument as such, but to further emphasise the pervasiveness of ideas of place and location in our conceptualisations of self.

They identify a hierarchy of special instances within the single general 'Subject–Self Metaphor'. This metaphor recognises the key fact about us that we experience ourselves as 'split'. The 'Subject' is the locus (from the Latin meaning 'place') of thinking, perceiving, feeling, acting. I as subject exist in the here and now. 'Self' includes all those aspects of personhood not picked out by the 'Subject' such as the body, social roles, relevant past experiences and so on. Whereas there may be many selves, there is only one subject. In the Subject–Self Metaphor, the Subject is always conceived of as a person whereas selves may be metaphorically conceptualised as a person, an object or a location.[27]

Lakoff and Johnson's reference to 'The Locational Self' is not the same as my idea of self as a locative system, but would be included in it. Their 'locational self' is focused on the idea that self-control has to do with our experiences of 'being in a normal location' whereas not being in a familiar place is metaphorically correlated with being out of control. Refinements of this primary metaphor are the idea of self as a container and of being out of control as being out of the container ('I was *beside* myself with rage'), or the idea of 'being on the ground' as being in control and vice versa ('I felt *the ground falling from under me*').

Throughout the rest of their analyses of self as scattered ('She's *all over the place*'), as involving the capacity to get outside of oneself ('I need to *take a good look at myself*'), as evaluating myself as a social type ('I *saw myself as* a bad son'), as engaging 'The Multiple Selves Metaphor' ('I keep *moving back and forth* between my managerial and my academic selves'), as projecting on to someone else ('*If I were you* I'd pack my bags and leave him'), as 'essential' or 'true' ('The slightest opposition and he *retreats into himself*'), we can everywhere see the pervasiveness of the idea of spatial location and of movement between locations in the ways we have of constituting our selves.

Neisser's analyses of the formation of the prelinguistic selves (particularly the 'ecological' and 'interpersonal' selves), and those of many other theorists of self, can be understood within Lakoff and Johnson's account as being continuous with the linguistically constructed selves and, most interestingly, with the linguistically constructed subject. The locational nature of the ecological and interpersonal dimensions of early selfhood fuses with the spatial armature of the general Subject–Self Metaphor. This metaphor, and its myriad instances, help to consti- tute self as we know it. That the structure is metaphorical does not imply that it is illusory or ineffectual. Quite the contrary. Most of what is distinctive, interest- ing, laudable and awful about human beings resides in their symbolic powers and in what they do with them.

If my world is my self, and my self-world is part of the wider world of other networked self-worlds, we can see how the dynamics of self are substantially composed both of skills for the literal navigation of sensorimotor space–time and of capacities for metaphorical meaning-making and interpretation which help us to navigate human worlds. The embodied realism of Lakoff and Johnson, building on the naturalism of John Dewey and the phenomenology of Merleau-Ponty, argues for the unity of both types of capacity. This is part of what I mean to convey by asserting that self is a locative system.

The three essays to follow flesh out some contexts for these ideas. We will need to say something more about the brain's capacities for dealing with spatial locations of self, specifically in relation to the ideas of centredness and continuity of the self-world. The stories that we construct about ourselves are also of fun- damental importance for locating ourselves across our representations of time and in relation to other self-worlds. Narrative impulses have their own roots. Daniel Dennett sees the urge to tell stories, our own story included, as bio- logical. 'Like spider webs', he writes, 'our tales are spun by us: our human consciousness, and our narrative selfhood, is their product, not their source.'[28]

These strands only knit together with the acquisition of language and all that that enables. This knitting together is not an isolated individualistic happening. As Bruner stresses, 'It can never be the case that there is a "self" independent of one's cultural-historical existence.'[29] It may be better perhaps to think of larks rather than spiders when thinking about our narrative capacities. Telling stories is as natural for human beings as singing songs is for larks. But larks need other larks from which to learn the full lark song, and we too learn from others the general methods of storytelling with local forms of emphasis and embellishment. That is why we must also outline the idea of formative cultural-historical legacies for our deep-seated ideas about how the world is and should be, and how we should aim to be within it.

Notes

1 G. Lakoff and M. Johnson, *Philosophy in the Flesh: The Embodied Mind and Its Challenge to Western Thought*, New York, Basic Books, 1999.

2 H. Gardner, *The Mind's New Science: A History of the Cognitive Revolution*, New York, Basic Books, 1985.

3 J. Bruner, *The Culture of Education*, Cambridge, Mass., Harvard University Press, 1996, Chapter 1.

4 U. Neisser, 'Five Kinds of Self-Knowledge', *Philosophical Psychology*, 1, 1, 1988, 35–59. For subsequent developments see U. Neisser and D. A. Jopling (eds), *The Conceptual Self in Context: Culture, Experience, Self-Understanding* (Emory Symposium on Cognition, 7), Cambridge, Cambridge University Press, 1997.

5 For a fuller discussion see C. Benson, *The Absorbed Self: Pragmatism, Psychology and Aesthetic Experience*, London, Harvester Wheatsheaf, 1993, Chapter 3.

6 M. Donaldson, *Human Minds: An Exploration*, London, Allen Lane The Penguin Press, 1992, Chapter 3. Jerome Kagan writes that 'There is no evidence requiring the positing of a concept of self before the middle of the second year. Scientists who believe that infants possess such a structure must either provide more convincing evidence or create a persuasive theoretical argument that renders this idea necessary.' See his 'Is there a self in infancy?' in M. Ferrari and R. J. Sternberg (eds), *Self-Awareness: Its Nature and Development*, New York, The Guilford Press, 1998, p. 146.

7 Neisser, op. cit., p. 40.

8 D. Dennett, 'The Origin of Selves', *Cogito*, 1, 1989, pp. 163–73.

9 J. H. Flavell, S. G. Shipstead and K. Croft, 'What young children think you see when their eyes are closed', *Cognition*, 8, 1980, pp. 369–87.

10 Neisser, op. cit., p. 38.

11 See Lynne Murray and Liz Andrews, *The Social Baby*, London, The Children's Project, 2000.

12 Neisser, op. cit., p. 49.

13 W. James, *Essays in Radical Empiricism*, London, Longman's, Green & Co., 1912, pp. 169–70.

14 E. Husserl, 'The World of the Living Present and the Constitution of the Surrounding World External to the Organism', trans. F. D. Elliston and L. Langsdorf, in Husserl, *Shorter Writings*, eds P. McCormick and F. Elliston, Notre Dame, Ind., University of Notre Dame Press, 1981, p.250. Quoted in E. S. Casey, *Getting Back into Place*, Bloomington, Indiana University Press, 1993, p. 332 n. 26.

15 Quoted in Casey, *Getting Back into Place*, p. 47.

16 B. Milner, 'The Memory Defect in Bilateral Hippocampus Lesions', *Psychiatric Research Reports* 11, 1959, pp. 43–58.

17 E. S. Casey, *Getting Back into Place*, p. 52.

18 G. Sereny, *Albert Speer: His Battle with the Truth*, London, Macmillan, 1995, p.261.

19 Ibid., p. 262.

20 Ibid., p. 390.
21 P. Bourdieu, *Outline of a Theory of Practice*, Cambridge, Cambridge University Press, 1977.
22 Lakoff and Johnson, op. cit. p. 19.
23 Ibid., p. 30.
24 Ibid., pp. 50–3.
25 Ibid., Chapter 11.
26 G. H. Mead, *Mind, Self and Society*, Chicago, University of Chicago Press, 1934.
27 Lakoff and Johnson, op. cit., Chapter 13.
28 Dennett, 'Origin of Selves', p. 169.
29 J. Bruner, *Actual Minds, Possible Worlds*, Cambridge, Mass, Harvard University Press, 1986, p. 67.

2

THE BRAIN'S WORK IN LOCATING SELVES

> At each moment the state of self is constructed, from the ground up. It is an evanescent reference state, so continuously and consistently *re*constructed that the owner never knows it is being *re*made unless something goes wrong with the remaking.
>
> (A. Damasio, *Descartes' Error*, 1996, p. 240)

> To note that the thing I call my individuality is only a pattern or dance, that is what it means when one discovers how long it takes for the atoms of the brain to be replaced by other atoms. The atoms come into my brain, dance a dance, and then go out – there are always new atoms, but always doing the same dance, remembering what the dance was yesterday.
>
> (R. Feynman, *What Do YOU What Care What Other People Think*, 1988, p. 244)

Societies, selves, bodies and brains are all of a piece, albeit a very big piece. Challenges over time, as both biological and cultural evolution teach us, supply the momentum for their interdependencies. Self, considered as a locative system, could not exist without the extraordinary navigational machinery of the brain in its body, nor could it be without the hugely complex range of route maps for surviving and thriving supplied by culture.

At the perceptual-motor level most of this neural and bodily machinery operates silently and unconsciously, swiftly supplying solutions to the persons who are the subjects of these acts of perceiving and moving, and who count themselves as their authors or owners. The same is true at the level of symbolic navigation through worlds of meaning and webs of relationship. Symbolic navigational capacities are profoundly indebted to perceptual-motor ones, though not reducible to them. Both shape self and the places within which self emerges, lives and quests. Consider first the relationships of brain and space at the perceptual-motor level.

I am watching a master stone builder at work. He is rebuilding an old Irish stone cottage. His materials are field-stones thrown up by centuries of ploughing, and gathered to make ditches and walls. They are of all shapes and sizes and many colours, and were the building materials of the poor. His skills in using them well are highly sophisticated and require a subtle design sense. The walls are in fact double walls, the space between them filled with rubble. Each stone must be chosen according to the space left by the ones already set, by whether filling or capping is needed just here, and by the visual balance of mass as the pattern of the wall emerges. He works according to a plan of height and openings for doors and windows, but within the area of the wall itself each judgement is contingent on what is already there but is also a creative judgement setting up succeeding contingencies. It is labour that requires all sorts of spatial abilities.

His general plan is a traditional one, learnt from others, yielding a standard floor layout, a set of functional spatial requirements determining domestic life and a particular 'look', that of a traditional Irish cottage. All of his decisions are governed by this armature. Traditional builders would rarely have worked from drawings. They would negotiate the building on site and would face each and every constraint and opportunity as problems to be solved there and then. They visualise how it will look when finished. In this way the process of building is hierarchical in its psychological requirements.

Today, the stones are randomly spread on the ground. He places them one at a time, flicks in the mortar, turns to survey what is on the ground, chooses a stone, twists and bends to pick it up, matches it to the space, rotates and positions it, and mortars it in. Rarely does he reject a stone he has chosen. The space for the stone and the stone chosen are wedded easily by his visual perceptual and kinaesthetic judgement. A new space opens up, a large stone is split with a sledgehammer, its inside is purple. When placed this can be seen to balance another purple stone already in place below to the left. A pleasing look emerges. And so it goes on.

The perceptual, motoric, memory and aesthetic skills so effortlessly deployed are impressive. The skilled body at work is a fluent unity of self and not-self, a dance whose choreography is never fully determined in advance but which nonetheless relies on memory. Our understanding of that unity is being rapidly deepened by contemporary neuroscience and especially, from the point of view of this book, by cognitive neuroscience.

A strong everyday belief about the brain is that its organisation will be found to be supremely logical with its parts in place like those of a well-engineered machine. Industrial spies steal the completed products of their competitors and then take them apart to see how they have been made. These espionage agencies become highly skilled in the craft of reverse-engineering. But what the object dismantled in this way will not easily reveal is what problems a particular combination of components may have been intended to solve. Was it a problem within the object's own construction or was it perhaps a problem to do with some function of the object? Reverse-engineering the brain has shattered any expectation that it is like some sort of well-engineered machine. Borrowing from François Jacob, Jacques Paillard writes that 'evolutionary mechanisms are not a product of the logical brain of an engineer but are more likely to be the result of a 'bricolage genial' – the work of a tinkering genius'.[1] Acknowledgement of nature's tinkering engineering style is also evident in the work of Antonio Damasio.[2] As a biological system carrying with it the history of its innumerable evolutionary adaptations, the brain epitomises our conception of a growth that is 'organic'. Its organisation seems to be modular with many different systems evolving to work together in constructing and adapting to the world as found, and to worlds as made.

What? and where? problems are central concerns of the brain. What stone should the builder place where in the emerging wall, for instance? How much of the work of that judgement is done consciously by the builder and how much is done unconsciously by subsystems of the brain? What frames of reference are being used? Do they rely on the relationship of the builder's body to the stone or on the stone's relationship to the wall? How is the repertoire of motor patterns comprising the builder's skill linked to his visual perception of space?

All of the builder's actions require frames of reference, or perhaps centres of rotation. There is a frame generated within the retina, a frame for the movements of the eye in its socket in combination with the retinal frame, a frame for movements of the head in combination with the oculo-retinal frame, proprioceptive-motor frames to do with the space occupied and generated by the fingers, by the arm in relation to the fingers, by the shoulder in relation to the arm, and so on. These sorts of frame are hierarchically organised. For example, if the task was one of pointing at a target then the articulation moves from shoulder to arm to wrist to finger in synchrony with the visual positioning of the target.[3]

Many different types of orientational and navigational problem need to be solved by our builder. The position of the target of an action, say the space for a stone, needs to be encoded. The distances involved need to be calibrated via various reference frames. His movements need to be visually guided and controlled using feedback from successive stages of movement. He needs to mentally rehearse certain actions without actually carrying them out in order not to make costly mistakes. He must coordinate his actions and plans with assistants who are negotiating their own spaces. Other space-structures generated by senses of hearing, balance, touch, proprioception and so on may also form part of what ultimately is a single fluent coordinated action.

Paillard writes that 'there must be as many sensori-motor mappings as there are associations between existing sensory channels and motor path structures' but that these many regional spaces must be integrated into 'a superordinate system of space coordinates.'[4] His view is that gravity plays the central role in this superordinate system which he calls a 'geotropic statural referential'. This would allow for the organisation of 'body-centred egocentric space coordinates' to which the position of objects and their changes in physical space can be referred. This distinction between personal egocentric frames of reference and impersonal allocentric frames recurs in the literature on brain and space. In the egocentric frame, spatial relationships are organised with reference to the viewer. In the allocentric frame, spatial relationships are perceived to hold between objects independently of the viewer. Experiments to induce the feeling that you are moving, for example, can pull either egocentric or allocentric frames of reference into play. Surrounded by a moving visual scene the subject can either see a visual scene rotating around his fixed body, or can sense his body itself to be moving in an immobile space.[5]

This links to another distinction made by Stephen Kosslyn between categorical and coordinate representations of space in memory.[6] Categorical representations are familiar linguistic ones such as that my computer lies to the right of my desk-lamp, and that my desk is situated on the left-hand side of the room in front of the window. These categories capture basic relationships between objects but they are imprecise. They are also, as we have seen earlier, indexed to a viewer. Coordinate representations are much more precise and are essential for actions such as reaching for the switch on my lamp to the left of my computer. Kosslyn proposed that the left hemisphere forms categorical spatial representations whereas the right forms coordinate representations.

It appears that, so far as is known, no distinct map of space exists in a particular location of our brains.[7] Michael Arbib suggests that the coherence of the brain's multiple maps comes not from some over-arching mathematical definition of space but rather from their connections to repertoires of movement. 'For the animal,' he writes, 'space is the measure of movement.'[8]

There is much in the results of contemporary neuroscience to support Merleau-Ponty's view that there is a basic internally represented 'body-scheme' within which synthesis of all the elements of spatial positioning occurs. Antonio Damasio uses a similar idea as a possible neural basis for subjectivity.

Despite the complexity of the neural mechanisms underpinning our sense of being and moving in space, as conscious subjects we effortlessly feel ourselves to be part of a seamless space in which we see and hear, touch and move. We can appreciate that that unified space is the outcome of enormous and constant unconscious neural work. It is also, if Lakoff and Johnson are right, the ground for many of the primary metaphors with which our psychic lives are constructed.[9]

For instance, the source of the conviction that as conscious subjects we are located a few inches behind our eyes may be related to our registrations of gravity. Stein wonders whether all the different spatial metrics are reduced to a common coordinate system centred on a point midway between the eyes, and often called the egocentre. He writes that 'personal space' is that occupied by our own body. Its coordinates are defined by the body's orientation with respect to gravity, and the position of our heads and limbs. It provides the datum point for 'egocentric localization . . . . [I]t is probably modelled and served by the superior parietal lobule.'[10] This supports Paillard's contention that the 'geotropic statural referential' is the basic integrating framework for the variety of sensorimotor spaces. Our sense of self may turn out to have an innate *gravitas*!

Antonio Damasio insists that the brain not be considered separately from the body when considering the big ideas like reason, feeling, self and mind. I will return to his ideas on emotion and reason in Chapter 7, but now I want to move up the scale of abstraction and focus on the role of the brain in anchoring the self as a unity over time. Specifically, I want to consider the significance for self of the brain's constant renewal of the body image and of autobiographical memory. Both relate to our sense of ourselves as the same owners and knowers of our experience over time. Psychologists tend to emphasise the latter but I think that Damasio's more inclusive approach is compelling. 'I imagine this perspective,' he writes, 'to be rooted in a relatively stable, endlessly repeated biological state. The source of the stability is the predominantly invariant structure and operation of the organism, and the slowly evolving elements of autobiographical data.'[11]

To illustrate the importance of both, consider the consequences for selfhood of two forms of brain damage, complete anosognosia and anterograde amnesia. The first illustrates the brain's role in constantly renewing its representation of the body and the importance of this for self. The second reveals the brain's role in constantly updating its representations of self-in-its-world, and the consequences for autobiographical self of losing this capacity. Consider first the phenomenon of complete anosognosia as discussed by Damasio.

Lakoff and Johnson's 'Time-Orientation Metaphor', as we have seen, refers our location as observers to the present, the space in front of us to the future and that behind us to the past. This metaphor recurs throughout many of the world's languages and profoundly influences the ways in which we construct and place self in time and place.[12] It is well to remember that there is a neural limit to this metaphor as it applies to our psychological sense of the present. Damasio puts it like this: 'What is happening to us *now* is, in fact, happening to a concept of self based on the past, including the past that was current only a moment ago.' He goes on to say that 'The present is never here. We are hopelessly late for consciousness.'[13] Nonetheless, the ubiquity of the Time-Orientation Metaphor is part of its utility. What happens when the brain is damaged in such a way that what is now in front of us is what is behind us, when the past is the future, when the conditions of change which determine psychological time itself are irrevocably stultified?

Anosognosia, as its name conveys, is a disease of knowledge.[14] An anosognosic person is profoundly damaged but blissfully unaware of the fact. Certain rare types of major stroke leave their victims completely paralysed on the left side, unable to move hand, arm, leg, foot, or the left side of the face. Functionally, the victims can neither stand nor walk. In addition they believe everything is fine and as before. Even when forcefully told that they cannot walk or move their arms they remain unperturbed. This inability to register the catastrophe that has befallen them does not happen to stroke victims paralysed on the right side. They know the full awfulness of what has happened to them. What the anosognosic person has lost, apart from the ability to move and sense their left half-body, is something we take absolutely for granted; their brains no longer receive automatic, rapid, internal updates of their body scheme.

Damasio makes a fundamental theoretical point about the neural basis of self using the evidence of this condition. What is absent from anosognosics is the ability to update internally the representation of their body. When something about the state of their bodies changes they won't know it through the normal internal automatic channels. The image of their bodies with which they work is the representation in play just at or before that particular set of brain systems was irrevocably damaged. This inability to feel the current state of their bodies, especially their unawareness of present background bodily feelings, profoundly alters their selfhood. Linguistically, they still know who they are and what their personal and social world comprises. In crucial ways, however, they cannot update that linguistic knowledge about themselves and others. 'Our individual identity', writes Damasio, 'is anchored on this island of illusory living sameness against which we can be aware of myriad other things that manifestly change around the organism.'[15]

Damasio's view is that in an anosognosic person what has been destroyed is the 'substrate of the neural self'.[16] Their neural self, or proto-self as he subsequently calls it, is forever frozen at the point of damage, and that grows more disabling with every passing day since the world as it should be registered by their bodies moves always onwards. The 'neural self', on this view, is grounded on the continual reactivation of at least two sets of representations. There are the primordial representations of the person's body, not just representations of what the person perceives nor representations of the body's responses to this perception, but crucially the representations of the person in the act of perceiving and responding to what is perceived. It is in this third type of representation that Damasio locates the neural source of subjectivity. As a neural process, this 'third-party' representation builds 'a *dispositional* representation of the self in the process of changing as the organism responds to an object'.[17] This is a non-verbal neural narrative incessantly being told to the brain by the body. It is the voice of that 'other subject beneath me, for whom a world exists before I am here' of whom Merleau-Ponty spoke. Descartes' error, if I am to summarise Damasio's argument, is that the order of his famous dictum is wrong; *Cogito ergo sum* should be *Sum ergo cogito*.

There is, however, another narrative which is linguistic and which forms the second set of representations whose continual reactivation and updating grounds the neural self. These are representations of key events in the person's own story, autobiographical elements continuously reconstructed and forming narrative identity, the story that is me. If anosognosia as a form of brain damage teaches us by absence the importance of the constantly renewed representations of the body for selfhood, anterograde or retrospective amnesias perform the same function for our understanding of the role of the brain in supporting narrative identity and autobiographical self.

There are many case-studies of unfortunates who have lost the capacity to lay down new long-term memories of the world, of themselves, and of themselves-relating-to-the-world. Their memories of what happened to them at or sometime before their brain damage remain intact but they cannot remember anything new, other than for the few minutes at most allowed by their short-term memory systems. Oliver Sacks offers a particularly illuminating story of a man he calls 'The Last Hippie'.[18]

Greg was born in the early 1950s in New York. During his teens he rebelled against his parents and teachers, and became part of the hippie culture of Greenwich Village. Allen Ginsberg and the Grateful Dead formed a key part of his imaginative world. His search for some ideal led him from the drug culture into the Hare Krishna organisation in 1969, a move which greatly satisfied him. Here he was compliant, pious and popular.

Sometime in 1970 he complained that his vision was growing dim. His swami interpreted this as the growth of 'inner light'. Greg accepted this, and although his sight grew dimmer he complained no more. Furthermore, his intermittent contacts with his parents ended almost completely when he moved in 1971 from Brooklyn to the temple in New Orleans. Within the Hare Krishna community he became ever more serene, with a strange smile on his face, and slowly he came to need ever greater care from his confrères. For them he exemplified the achievement of enlightenment.

In 1975 his worried parents gained permission to visit him. What met them was horrifying. The lean, hairy truculent Greg they remembered as their son was gone. The Greg they met was fat, hairless, smiling 'stupidly', bursting into bits of song and verse, making strange wisecracks, 'scooped out, hollow inside' as his father noted. He was also totally blind, but utterly unaware of it. His ability to walk was very seriously impaired. Shocked, his parents removed this embodiment of enlightenment to hospital. Greg was found to have a massive but benign tumour of the pituitary gland.

This had destroyed the adjoining optic chiasm and tracts thus causing irreparable blindness. It had also extended on both sides into the frontal lobes thereby destroying crucial neural substrates of identity and personal being, and also preventing an awareness of being blind and ill (another form of anosognosia). It had extended backwards and destroyed large parts of the medial temporal lobes, notably the hippocampus and adjacent cortex, which resulted in a profound amnesia and inability to transfer present experiences into long-term memory. The tumour had extended downwards to damage the forebrain or diencephalon undermining his emotional capacities and contributing to his pervasive blandness. As a result of damage to the diencephalon, the regulator of basic functions, Greg expressed no sexual interest, exhibited no desire for food unless it was brought to him, and in the absence of stimulation fell into a somnolent daze. Finally, it had destroyed his pituitary gland which resulted in his Buddha-like weight gain, his hairlessness, and the replacement of his hormonally driven aggressiveness by its absence, an abnormal placid submissiveness.

Far from achieving a Krishna ideal of serene enlightenment, Greg was massively and avoidably brain damaged. At twenty-five years of age he entered a hospital for the rest of his life, and it was there that Oliver Sacks met and came to know him over the next fifteen years or so. Sacks' account of Greg's observable abilities and inabilities over the years illuminates both the neuropsychological and the discursive psychological operations of narrative.

To begin with a general comment, the failure of Greg's swami to consider any alternative explanation for Greg's dramatic transformation – his startling physical transformation into a semblance of an iconic cliché of enlightenment, his blind 'gaze' and his bland placidity – other than 'enlightenment' is a cautionary tale for anti-scientific mentalities and their interpretive frameworks. Achieved enlightenment is not to be confused with catastrophically imposed 'innocence' or 'absence'. Letting self go is something quite different from having self dispossessed or diminished, and the wisdom of the injunction to 'live in the present' applies only to those who can live elsewhere in the past or future. Paradoxically, profound self-possession is necessary for self-relinquishment. Having lost the grounds for full selfhood, Greg lost the grounds for enlightenment of any kind. That is his tragedy.

From the perspective of narrative, what are the signs of Greg's loss, or at least gross diminution, of selfhood? Let me start with the observation that without stimulation Greg's consciousness seemed to idle in neutral gear. During such periods he showed no spontaneous activity, and originated nothing from 'within' himself. The understanding of selfhood as having 'depths' suggests that Greg had become all surface, but a surface to be written upon by others and not by himself.

Self-reflection involves consciously intending some idea of oneself as an object of reflection and interrogating it. But what if both the capacity to intend and the pool of ideas, feelings and memories towards which consciousness can be directed are diminished to the point of obliteration? In terms of the three blended colours of selfhood – perspective, agency, autobiography – agency has been almost bleached out of Greg. Showing no normal sign of self-initiated activity, the selflessness of his Krishna ideal has had the selflessness of his brain damage super-imposed on it. He sits blankly for hours until some stimulation from outside kick-starts him into action. Greg's autonomy has been replaced by something closer to 'automatony'.

This arousal has different aspects to it depending upon what the situation demands of him. Socially, Greg presented as a very likeable, easygoing young man without a trace of anger or distress at what, to others, was his appalling fate. To the untutored eye this could easily have been construed as a 'philosophical acceptance' of the inevitable or as an instance of the power of 'detached enlightenment' to cope with even the most extreme of life's adversities. But this would be a total misconstrual.

What would be the conditions of true acceptance of adversity? Knowing that you were the victim of it, that things had once been better and will for evermore be worse, feeling the horror of this, coping with the fear and blame that this entails, running the real risk of failing to come to terms with the enormity of the loss, but wanting to overcome it. These conditions involve a developed sense of the temporal context of events. Without a sense of one's past, present and future all personal events are adrift and self is dislocated. They involve an understanding of responsibilities which in the case of those who failed to take early action on Greg's behalf would give rise to the conditions of anger and blame and, in his own case, would involve taking responsibility for what is left of his life. This assumption of personal responsibility would give rise to conditions for feeling hope and despair, and would be a source for the energy necessary to make the very best of what he has by self-reflectively shaping his attitude towards his losses.

In Greg's case none of these conditions were fulfilled because the neurological requirements for meeting them were gone. Most dramatically impaired was his memory. This type of damage, where present percepts and thoughts never more become part of long-term memory, and therefore part of the narrative and narrating of self, is disastrous. For those sufferers aware of the loss it is awful for all concerned. For those unaware, it seems like a blessing but at the same time onlookers may feel that without the suffering person's own awareness the loss of the person is all the greater. The case of Clive Wearing as presented by Jonathan Miller is a graphic example of the first situation.[19] Other well-known examples in the literature are Brenda Milner's case of H. M., Oliver Sack's Korsakoff Syndrome patient, Jimmie, and Antonio Damasio's David.[20]

The consequences of anterograde amnesia for social and personal life are dramatic. In my own acquaintance, F. H. was damaged in this way. Physically he looked as fit as he always was, and socially as friendly and pleasant. He could find his away around the town he knew so well before his brain damage, but change the routes or place him in a previously unknown environment and he became totally lost. He was blissfully unaware of his loss. Conversation with him, while initially amusing, quickly became frustrating since every three minutes or so he had forgotten everything and the cycle began again as new conversation for him but as part of an endless repetition of sameness for his interlocutors. Things were most difficult for his family. At the time of his injury his son, for example, was a teenager. Eight years later he was a grown man with his own life but not for F. H. For F. H. his son was still a boy who 'should speak to his mother with respect'.

In Irish mythology there is a mythical land called *Tír na nÓg* which is a land where no one grows old. F. H., Greg, Jimmie, David and all other sufferers from anterograde amnesia are citizens of a psychological *Tír na nÓg*. For F. H. all his emotional relations will be frozen in the remembered state in operation at the cut-off point of the amnesia. His son will forever remain an adolescent boy in F. H.'s emotional consciousness and relational dispositions. Not just sufferers themselves but their loved ones, as they exist for them, become trapped in time despite the manifest signs of ageing.

When after many years of visiting him daily in hospital Greg's father died in 1990 Oliver Sacks was away. On return he went straight to Greg and said: 'I guess you must be missing your father.' Greg replied that he saw him when he came every day. When Sacks told him his father had died the previous month he observed that Greg looked shocked and ashen. He commented that his father must have been around fifty to which Sacks replied 'well up in his seventies'. A few minutes later he had totally forgotten the conversation. But the incident revealed something else of significance. In his continuous present with all its ancillary complications Greg showed signs of a capacity for love and grief, but without memory how could he mourn? Greg got on well with fellow patients in his ward but once gone he never mentioned them again. Without memory had he the capacity for friendship? Early in his acquaintance with Greg, Sacks wrote that 'He seemed to have no sense of "next", and to lack that eager and anxious tension of anticipation, of intention, that drives us through life.'[21]

This idea of 'drive' is most interesting when teamed up with that of narrative. In the next chapter we will see how our urge to discursively string things together in narrative form is, as Bruner argues, a distinctive type of human thinking and, as Dennett surmises, a biological imperative. A peculiarly vivid example of this drive to make narrative sense of experience, I believe, can be found in a distilled form in a phenomenon that is occasionally observed in clinical practice, whether psychiatric or neurological. It is called 'confabulation'.

Greg supplies an example. Months after his father had died, if Greg was asked where his father was he might say 'Oh, he went down to the patio' or 'He couldn't make it today'. Why did he answer like this? Why did he not simply say:

'I don't know'? The answer may have to do with what we might call the rules of rationality at work in a discursive situation. This is not a point about confabulation that one encounters in its literature but it seems curious to me that people with certain forms of brain damage still respond to questions, however bizarre those responses might be to the listener, as though it was important to *be plausible*.

If the adequacy of self depends upon the constant neural renewal and updating of the sort of body scheme representation that is damaged in anosognosia, or of the autobiographical representations that are damaged in anterograde amnesia, and if certain types of frontal lobe damage curtail our relationship to the future by contaminating our ability to plan and make decisions, as we will see in Chapter 7, then confabulation tells us something about the brain's capacity to weave narrative coherence at the point of present telling and answering.

The brain like nature, it seems, abhors a vacuum. Why do people damaged like those above not experience voids or gaps in the telling of their stories? Of course, some people with other sorts of damage are distressingly aware that something is not right in the narrative trajectory of their lives. But still there is something to be learned from the urge to fill the gaps, albeit confabulatory in kind. From a narrative perspective I would offer the following brief speculations.

Our present thought, as William James observed, has an appropriative function with regard to our previous thoughts. It owns the previous thought and is itself owned by its successor. This supplies a sense of continuity and stability to our stream of consciousness. 'I' am always the subject of my present thought. That thought, and all that conditions its constitution and dynamics, and of whose structures it is a part, influences my stance towards those other thoughts and perceptions which it appropriates to itself.

This stance of the present thought towards that which is being appropriated is a selective process which governs relevance, and is therefore the axis of what is included or excluded in the narrative being woven. As long as the conditions governing the operations of present thinking remain stable, then *stance, relevance,* and *appropriations to the ongoing narration of self* will remain much the same.

If, however, the conditions governing the present thought and its functions change radically, thereby changing the sense of the present thought – crises of loss, for instance – then *stance* changes which in turn changes the *rules of relevance* which in turn changes what is chosen or excluded from the present narrating of self. The felt purpose of that narrative will also change, perhaps from being a narrative of self-congratulation to being a narrative of guilt or exoneration or victimhood or self-pity.

Disorders like confabulation show how, even when functioning badly, there is an effort after meaning, plausibility and coherence on the brain's, and hence on the person's, part. This idea links with that of a left-brain interpreter, a specialised brain system whose function is to carry out interpretive syntheses.[22] It seeks explanations for internal and external events and seems tied to our ability to see how contiguous events relate to each other. Its functioning is largely unconscious but it is believed to do much of the work in threading together our personal story into a coherent narrative.

Evidence supporting the existence of this system comes from experiments with patients whose brains have been split (severing the corpus callosum which links the two hemispheres together to reduce intractable epilepsy). Two pictures were shown to a patient. One was presented exclusively to the left hemisphere and one exclusively to the right hemisphere. A set of pictures was then presented in full view to the person and they were asked to choose which ones were associated with the ones presented to the left and right hemispheres.

In one case, pictures of a chicken claw were presented to the left hemisphere and a snow scene to the right. Included among the set of pictures then given in full view was one of a chicken and a shovel. 'Chicken claw' should obviously associate with 'chicken' and 'shovel' with 'snow'. One subject chose 'shovel' with his left hand (the left hand is controlled by the right hemisphere) and 'chicken' with his right (the right being controlled by the left hemisphere which is the main seat of language). When asked Why? he — that is his speaking left hemisphere — answered: 'Oh, that's simple. The chicken claw goes with the chicken, and you need a shovel to clean out the chicken shed.' Gazzaniga and his colleagues interpret this as indicating that the left hemisphere, observing the left hand's choice of 'shovel' — which was directed by the non-speaking right hemisphere to which the 'snow scene' was presented — then interprets this in such a way as to maintain coherence with what it knows about 'chicken' since it knows nothing at a level of verbal consciousness about 'snow scene'.

Cognitive science is showing how the brain, organised on a modular basis, conducts most of its operations outside the person's awareness. The results of this work connect directly to executive systems, such as the motor systems of the skilled stone-builder with whom we started. Some results become conscious cognitive states. It is the task of 'the left hemisphere's interpreter module', on this view, to keep pace with the implications of all this non-conscious processing and to formulate such mental constructs as 'beliefs' which can in turn liberate their holders from the automaticity of the stimulus-response aspects of our everyday lives. 'In many ways,' write Gazzaniga et al., 'it is the system that provides the story line or narrative of our lives.'[23]

This is a crucial point. Our present thoughts are in some ways like spiders at the centre of the webs of self always tying what knots they have to tie at the point of the present and of its demands. To what extent this 'interpreter system' provides the story-line of our lives, and to what extent we *are* that narrative-supplying system or more, is what we will next consider. What is absolutely clear is that our genetic inheritance does not determine all of the organisation of our developing brains nor of their working. Each person's history and circumstances are reflected in individual and unique circuitry in his or her brain. That poses major obstacles in the path of any account of self and mind that seeks to reduce these processes just to neural computations.

'To understand in a satisfactory manner,' writes Damasio, 'the brain that fabricates human mind and human behavior, it is necessary to take into account its social and cultural context. And that makes the endeavor truly daunting.'[24]

Notes

1 J. Paillard, 'Knowing where and knowing how to get there' in J. Paillard (ed.), *Brain and Space*, Oxford, Oxford University Press, 1991, p. 474.

2 A. Damasio, *Descartes' Error: Emotion, Reason and the Human Brain*, London, Papermac, 1996, p. 137.

3 A. Berthoz, 'Reference frames for the perception and control of movement' in Paillard, (ed.), *Brain and Space*, chapter 6.

4 J. Paillard, 'Motor and representational framing of space' in Paillard (ed.), *Brain and Space*, p. 167.

5 Berthoz, op. cit., p. 83.

6 M. Gazzaniga, R. B. Ivry, and G. R. Mangun, *Cognitive Neuroscience: The Biology of the Mind*, New York, W. W. Norton, 1998, pp. 355–61.

7 J F. Stein, 'Space and the parietal association areas' in Paillard (ed.), *Brain and Space*, p. 186.

8 M. A. Arbib, 'Interaction of multiple representations of space in the brain' in Paillard (ed.), *Brain and Space*, p. 379.

9 Neurological support for Lakoff and Johnson's claim comes from Damasio who argues that 'you never would have formed a dispositional representation without first forming a topographically mapped perceptual representation: there seems to be no anatomical way of getting complex sensory information into the association cortex that supports dispositional representations without first stopping in early sensory cortices. (This may not be true for noncomplex sensory information.)' Damasio, op. cit., pp. 106–7.

10 Stein, op. cit., p. 210.

11 Damasio, op. cit., p. 238.

12 G. Lakoff and M. Johnson, *Philosophy in the Flesh*, New York, Basic Books, 1999, p. 140.

13 Damasio, op. cit., p. 240.

14 For details of the particular areas of the brain damaged in anosognosics see Damasio, op. cit., p. 65.

15 Ibid., p. 155.

16 Ibid., p. 237.

17 Ibid., p. 242.

18 O. Sacks, 'The Last Hippie', first published in *The New York Review of Books*, XXXIX, 6, 26 March 1992, 51–60, and now available in *An Anthropologist on Mars: Seven Paradoxical Tales*, London, Picador, 1995, pp. 39–72.

19 J. Miller, *Prisoner of Consciousness*, BBC Film, November 1988.

20 See O. Sacks, *The Man Who Mistook His Wife for a Hat*, London, Picador, 1986, and also A. Damasio, *The Feeling of What Happens: Body and Emotion in the Making of Consciousness*, New York, Harcourt Brace & Co., 1999.
21 Sacks, *An Anthropologist on Mars*, p. 46.
22 Gazzaniga, Ivry and Mangun, op. cit., pp. 542–8.
23 Ibid., p. 545.
24 Damasio, op. cit., p. 260.

3

PLACING ONESELF IN PERSONAL TIME

The narrative structure of self

Yet even so there is but one world and everything that is imaginable is necessary to it. For this world also which seems to us a thing of stone and flower and blood is not a thing at all but is a tale. And all in it is a tale and each tale the sum of all lesser tales and yet these also are the selfsame tale and contain as well all else within them.

(C. McCarthy, *The Crossing*, 1995, p. 143)

A human being pondering the nature of language is not unlike a snowman pondering the nature of snow, for a snowman's instruments are no less snowy than the human beings are wordy.

(S. Heaney, Address to Reading Association of Ireland, 1982)

A story is an answer to a question. Who are you? Where do you come from? What do you do? Why did you do it? What happened? What happened next? And so on. There is no complete story of a life or an event, nor can there be since there is always something more to be said, another angle to be taken. Just bigger stories that can contain smaller ones, as the wise man in *The Crossing* observed. The conditions shaping the act of asking the question, and the freedoms and fears of the person asked, give substance to the story told.

A doctor asking me about the history of my symptoms is meant to be on my side and, notwithstanding embarrassment on my side, it is in my interests to make the story I tell as near as possible to my understanding of events. A secret police interrogator asking me to account for myself and my friends is a 'whole other story' as we say. Third parties evaluating the veracity of stories need to be very perspicacious. The subtle analyses of literary critics and the incisive probing of good lawyers and historians are skills of story assessment. The story or stories of myself that I tell, that I hear others tell of me, that I am unable or unwilling to tell, are not independent of the self that I am: they are constitutive of *me*. This is a central claim of the cultural psychology of selfhood.

How much of me is in the telling? Is there a 'me' apart from a telling? Is the story I tell of myself or hear told of myself a record of what I am and have been or is it a fabrication or construction which can never really hit the mark? These are the sorts of question asked by philosophers and psychologists interested in narratives. The identity of an individual or of a community is the answer to the question, 'Who did this?'. The answer comes in the form of a proper name which designates a life which is the same life from birth to death. But what justifies us in thinking that this life is 'constant' or the same throughout its existence? A narrative identity says Paul Ricoeur. He writes that 'this narrative identity, constitutive of self-constancy, can include change, mutability, within the cohesion of one lifetime. The subject then appears both as a reader and the writer of its own life, as Proust would have it.'[1]

This understanding of identity as a woven narrative has focused attention on the nature and processes of autobiography and on the ways in which the shape of a life is made and remade by the stories a person tells of herself or himself. Foremost among the thinkers developing ideas on autobiography as part of a new cultural psychology is Jerome Bruner who writes:

> To look at a life as if it were independent of the autobiographical text that constructs it is as futile a quest for reality as the physicist's search for a Nature that is independent of the theories that lead him to measure this rather than that phenomenon. . . . it is the culture . . . that provides the formulae for the construction of lives. . . . I persist in thinking that autobiography is an extension of fiction, rather than the reverse, that the shape of life comes first from imagination rather than from experience.[2]

This idea of 'shape' as it is applied by each of us to our lives is revealing. From one point of view you might think that the shape of your life is there to be found. You were born on such a date to this mother and father, lived in this area and moved to that, attended this school and that college, were close to one brother but not another, were in love with so-and-so but he married someone else, achieved this in your career but experienced loss in some other part of your life, felt yourself to be changed by events like A and B, and so on. Put like this, the chronology of your life might seem to be its shape. The 'facts' of your life might seem clear but the significance of even straightforward facts like 'being seriously ill when I was six' for my life as it subsequently developed can be very subtle and itself subject to metamorphosis.

So in what sense might it be claimed that such a shape is made rather than found? In the discussion on the urge to be plausible, albeit bizarrely to an onlooker, which is exhibited by those who confabulate, I suggested that ideas of stance, relevance and appropriation were features of the ways in which 'present thoughts' wove their patterns of meaning. Stance can be understood as the point(s) of view which I adopt towards what I want to say or write, the structure of my attitudes towards what I represent and express in symbolic terms. Stance determines relevance, tells me what I should put in and what leave out, keeps very much in mind how what I say or write will be heard or read by my ideal public. Appropriation has to do with how what I say or write, the objectification of some aspect of my life, is rewoven into the ongoing fabric of my life to give it that narrative continuity and gel to which Ricoeur refers. The choreography of normal selfhood is an endless dialectic of fixed forms and uncertain improvisation. That is the dynamic in which the possibility of self-creation resides.

If I review my life at a certain stage in order to understand its shape over time, then I will always do so from a particular perspective, the viewpoint of that time in my life from which I choose to look back and re-view the things I have done or those that have happened to me. I am likely to think of my life in terms of a metaphor like 'a journey' leading eventually to some goal of fulfilment, or 'a path' which destiny has chosen for me much as Alan Bullock has shown to be a crucial similarity between Hitler and Stalin, or I may think of my life as wasted and of myself as the innocent victim of malign forces.[3] However I do it one thing is inescapable, I must make choices. I must select what to tell and what to leave unspoken and I must do so now in the particular moment of its telling. I must have a felt sense of what is relevant. As it unfolds discursively over time the tale told is the result of a rich succession of choices and selections governed and shaped by the dynamics of the many nows and 'present thoughts' which make up the stream of experience which is my particular life. My 'life' will always be an edited version.

This of course assumes that 'I' have the necessary powers to know what is there to be selected in my life and to choose among them as I wish. But there is much psychological evidence to show that the patterns and forces at work in shaping my experiences, and my ability to know and control them, can often be more apparent to other people than they are to myself. Psychologists invoke concepts like 'the unconscious' to name this territory of personal ignorance. In the Freudian sense this unconscious system has a major say in shaping my subjectivity, the ways in which it feels as it does to be me. At the base of my warm personal life is a strong, often destabilising, impersonal base which in Freud's original sense was 'the It' (Das Es). How then will I ever know that what I say of myself is not grossly distorted by the means by which the unconscious defences do their work in protecting 'me' from anxiety by censoring or twisting what I find myself thinking it is important to say? Such defences are, in cultural psychological terms, reticences about how we speak to ourselves about ourselves.[4] For even this to be a consideration in my telling my story I must think it important not to deliberately or unintentionally distort my narrative. I need to be sophisticated enough to realise that there is more to 'me' than meets the 'I'.

The answer to this dilemma, whether or not you are sympathetic to psycho-analytic formulations of mind and selfhood, has to be by some sort of checking. From a cultural psychological perspective such checking is best understood as a way of negotiating meaning within a specific social context. That context may be an intended relationship with a current public, as with a prominent figure like Henry Kissinger using memoirs to negotiate favourable regard for past actions;[5] or it may, perhaps, be representations of key people who are integral parts of the person's self and who, even though long dead, retain an influence still powerful enough for them to be the primary people with whom the meaning of the person's life is being negotiated.

Telling stories requires many skills and these, while locking into neural pre-dispositions for narrative continuation, must be learnt and refined in the course of individual and collective development. All autobiographies are constructions, fabricated with the tools of storytelling which a culture makes available to its members. Personal narratives depend on the person's skill in using these tools and on their abilities to innovate and invent new narrative tools thereby enabling new experiences of hearing or reading. These expressions of self also depend on the reasons why the person feels they want their story told and on the particular circumstances giving rise to those reasons.

The urge explicitly to narrativise oneself in an effort to 'take stock' frequently occurs when people are in deep personal pain, often bereaved, and desperately seeking to re-assume control of their lives in order to start living satisfyingly again. Much psychotherapy can be understood as a process leading to a satisfactory narrative of one's selfhood where 'satisfactory' means enabling the next phase of self-construction to proceed. Stuart Sutherland's account of a disintegration in his own life, *Breakdown*, uses his critical tools as an experimental psychologist in an act of autobiographical writing to restore himself to a control of his own life. Similarly, Lewis Wolpert uses his skills in scientific argument to begin with his own experience of depression in *Malignant Sadness* and to analyse contemporary understandings of that affliction, in part as a means of understanding what happened to himself. William Styron deployed his skills as a writer in *Darkness Visible* to offer an account of his depression.[6]

Of course it may also be that the autobiographer is luxuriously self-satisfied, publicly honoured, and wishing to copperfasten public support for that private self-satisfaction. Many memoirs are written with the clear idea of where on the shelves of the Library of History this particular life should be filed. The legion of politicians' and soldiers' memoirs include many of this type. On the other hand they may, like Albert Speer, be anxious to remake the story of their lives so that it will be more palatable to themselves and others after an early career that attracts odium and condemnation.[7] The Irish writer Francis Stuart wrote his 'auto-biographical fiction' *Black List, Section H* after a turbulent career which included spending most of the Second World War in Berlin. It becomes, as Colm Tóibín writes in his introduction, 'a quest for revelation and redemption in a time when revelation and redemption are no longer possible'.[8]

Even more interesting from a psychological perspective are those auto-biographical accounts which are written by people who clearly know how the process of making up one's own story is a process of making up one's self, and that that self always eludes a complete telling precisely because it is always in the process of being made. Marcel Proust and Simone de Beauvoir come to mind.[9] The means of expressing oneself narratively, whether it involves unfolding expressively in real time as in conversation, or in the more controlled and revi-seable medium of writing, is highly significant. Again take Albert Speer as an example.

I mentioned above that cultural psychology is interested in pursuing the idea that the Freudian unconscious might be reinterpreted as forms of reticence and privacy. There is an incommunicable core to personal identity but much that remains private does so for reasons of cultural norms rather than for reasons of mystery. People learn the things to feel private about, as historians have shown us.[10] Privacy is also a choice and a preference. It can depend on the *means* of communicating which suit a person's make-up. Albert Speer was a remarkably able, ambivalent, self-absorbed, controlling, disciplined, intensely reticent and private man. During the nearly twenty years he spent in Spandau prison he wrote thousands of letters to his family and friends which were smuggled out by friendly prison officials. These were warm, informative and lively.

Face to face, however, prison visits were painfully mute, formal, ungiving. He himself offered a very insightful explanation to Ulf, his new son-in-law, who had just experienced this painful contrast between the letter-Speer and the talking-Speer. For an illustration of the relationship of privacy and the availability of a preferred means of self-disclosure it is worth quoting Speer at some length. It should be remembered that you have immensely more control in acts of letter construction than you have in face-to-face speech construction. For one thing you have more time for consideration and revision. For another, your addressee as you write is actually an imaginary being partly of your own construction whose reactions you can anticipate and subsequently shape by the ways in which the letter is written. Speer wrote:

> I use letters and writing – as Hess uses fantasizing – to produce 'feeling'. But what is not possible is to transmute one into the other. It means that I, who am by nature reserved, can abandon this restraint and come alive in letters – sometimes I fear even sounding exalted, which is also against

my nature, as you may already know — but what I can't do is apply this 'letter' dimension of being above my self-enforced sub-temperature to normal intercourse. This is what you saw, and no doubt found yourself surprised by when we met in person. But it is not really alarming. It will become difficult when I have to return to living in 'normal temperature' one day.[11]

It did, exactly as Speer predicted. In this particular discursive situation Speer noticed the disappointing impression he made, and using another letter brokered the gap which he recognised, and Ulf felt, between his letter-expressed and his talk-expressed self to repair any possible damage to his relationship with his new son-in-law. This act of explanation depended on one communicative means to justify the failure of the other. Speer explains and thereby protects his self-presentation as private and reserved, and his sense of himself as unable to be more expressive. He does this by using letters as his controlled outlet for the expression of feeling to diminish the pressure to be otherwise which he would feel if Ulf proved lastingly disappointed and distanced from the taciturn Speer he had just met face-to-face. Privacy is a complex social phenomenon.

As an autobiographer himself, Jerome Bruner is intimately aware of the complexities of autobiography as a psychological process.[12] It is extraordinarily complex. In some ways all the strands of psychology integrate in the act of telling one's story or, better still, the series of stories which may make up an individual human being's life as *a* self. Since a cultural psychological conception favours an understanding of self as a continuously self-integrating process negotiating its stability through all the changes of location and demand that make up a human life, it should come as no surprise that this problem of achieving stability of self should present itself as a core problem for psychology.

William James formulated this with his metaphor of consciousness as a stream. How do I know I am the same self today as I was yesterday? I have after all lost consciousness for about eight hours between then and now while I slept. And what about the links between me as I am now and me as I was twenty years ago? What is the nature of that linkage? As we have seen, James thought that this had to do with each present thought appropriating its predecessor, *owning* it, as it were, and blending it into the ongoing flow of consciousness. In this way the stream has the subjective quality of being all of a piece, of being a single stream, *my* stream.

Bruner identifies this problem as lying at the heart of the psychology of autobiography. Notwithstanding what he calls the 'robustness' of selves over time, they also exhibit an instability when observed over extended periods. Selves change. Sameness and change must both be accounted for. The universal changes of ordinary human development (infancy, childhood, adolescence, young adulthood, middle adulthood and old age), the particular changes of individual lives (personal successes and failures, griefs and joys), and the structural changes of the societies to which people belong (periods of peace and stability, war and terror and dispossession, growths and collapses of economic/moral/religious systems) must all be accounted for in an adequate psychology of autobiography.

Bruner endorses and develops William James's idea that abilities of narration are a distinct mode of cognitive functioning. They contrast with and complement the abilities of another mode which he calls paradigmatic or logico-scientific thinking which 'attempts to fulfill the ideal of a formal, mathematical system of description and explanation'.[13] The way of checking whether or not an argument is true and therefore convincing in the paradigmatic mode of thinking is by appealing to established procedures which if properly applied lead to formal or empirical proof.

Narrative thinking, on the other hand, functions differently and does so to quite a different end. As Bruner puts it, if arguments are about truth, stories are about verisimilitude or lifelikeness. Each involves a different kind of causality. Paradigmatic thought aspires to establishing universal truth conditions whereas narrative thought looks to likely connections between particular events. The one is concerned with verifiability and replicability within high-level abstractions of the world, the other with plausibility and convincingness within the particular worlds of living engaged individuals. Bruner argues that story making is 'the mode of thinking and feeling that helps children (Indeed, people generally) create a version of the world in which, psychologically, they can envisage a place for themselves – a personal world.'[14]

This has powerful implications for a psychology of autobiography. Bruner himself has spelt out many of them. Thinking about your life comes naturally if narrative thinking is a natural part of human psychology. But you don't have 'a life' apart from your thinking about it, since it is thinking about it that singles it out as *a* life. To think about your self and about your life as the way in which you have become yourself is a creative act. What it creates *is* your self and its life. Bruner's conclusion that 'autobiography is life construction through "text" construction' follows from the identification of narrative abilities as a natural mode of human thinking, albeit much neglected until recently by psychologists.[15] Cognitive neuroscience's ideas on a 'left brain interpreter', as we have seen, support this idea of a distinctive form of narrative thinking.

It is the application of this type of thinking to one's own life that ensures its sense of being continuous as the story of my life. Both these ideas, that of 'story' and that of possessing, as in 'my story', need further comment. Let me take the idea of ownership first and acknowledge a debt to Nicholas Humphrey's perceptive discussion of its nature and primitive origins.[16]

The everyday concept of ownership is social and involves the idea of a 'right'. Owning something means having the right to do with it as one wishes including allowing someone else to use it, or giving it away. Humphrey extends this idea by suggesting that the idea of owning private property is a metaphorical extension of the sense of 'my body'. Owning my body is my primary sense and sphere of ownership. The violation of this sense is one reason why slavery is so abhorrent. How does this basic sense of ownership arise? Humphrey argues that what I as a voluntary agent indubitably own are my volitions. I come to own my body to the extent that I come to control it. My limbs are mine because I can move them when I wish. Even if I were motorically paralysed, but not I think sensorily paralysed, I may still own them if Humphrey is right in arguing that sensation is a form of activity. On this view control, either by way of socially legitimated rights or by way of more foundational acts of coming to own one's own body in infancy, is a key part of ownership.

The manner in which a narrative becomes 'my story' will itself be a history of control, as will the struggle over the rights to history-making of any group or community wishing to be the tellers of 'their own story'. One way in which Bruner addresses this issue is *via* his use of the category of metacognition of which meta-narrative is an instance. In everyday language this has to do with the ways in which a person comes to reflect upon why her life or some aspect of it has come to be as it is. It also has to do with the resources available to her to pull the diverse accounts of segments of her life together under the umbrella of a single story, *the* story of *her* life.

So far we have assumed the idea of a story. But what is 'a story'? Theorists in various fields have offered analyses of the structure of narratives as they find them in history, literature, medicine or law. Kenneth Burke, Hayden White, Vladimir Propp, Tzvetan Todorov, Roman Jakobson, Paul Ricoeur and Amelie Rorty are among those called upon by Bruner to lay bare the nature of narrative as it applies to the autobiographical construction of self. What Bruner does to support his view that we *are* the stories we tell of ourselves is to draw out the analogy between the structure of a typical story, on the one hand, and the criteria we use to identify the presence of a self in any human activity on the other.

First the structure of a story. His simplified account of the structure of a narrative is this:

> An *Actor* with some degrees of freedom;
> An *Act* upon which he has embarked, with
> A *Goal* to whose attainment he is committed;
> *Resources* to be deployed in the above, with
> A presupposition of *Legitimacy,*
> Whose violation has placed things in *Jeopardy*.[17]

The other part of this analogy is the answer to this question: When we listen to other people talk about themselves, or when we read what they write about their lives, what are the signs we look for to establish the presence of a self? The following are the 'indicators of self' which we use to answer the question: An *agent* with some freedom to choose, who shows *commitment* to a line of action (rather than just reactiveness to momentary demands), who has *resources* to further this commitment, who *refers socially* to other people in the process, who can *evaluate* how things are progressing, who *feels* (*qualia*) and has a personal subjective sense of the situation, who can *reflect* (*metacognition*) on himself and the context, who *positions* himself in the social order, and who integrates all the relevant elements of his life into some sort of *coherence*.[18]

Bruner notes a striking similarity between the elements that compose the core of a narrative and those indicators which identify the presence of a self. They seem to be isomorphic or homologous. Are they convertible into one another? Is self actually a narrative? Bruner's view is that it is. With Kalmar he writes: 'Self, then, is a narrative construction, and as such, operates under the same constraints as narrative constructions in general.'[19] This is a view that would, I think, find support from other thinkers who have seriously addressed the complexities of 'self' as a psychological problem. When Rom Harré speaks of self as a 'theory' and the development of self as the process by which the theory that is self is acquired he would be happy, I think, to have Bruner's concept of self as story in mind.[20] For Harré autobiographical skills are a crucial element in the construction and maintenance of self. Ken Gergen would similarly find much to agree with in Bruner's arguments, as does Charles Taylor whose work I will introduce in the next chapter.[21]

Would this view of self as narrative lead us to think differently about the theoretical significance of self in and for psychology? This question implies a wider claim still. A cultural psychological view of self should insist on the foundational importance of biology, and the evolutionary context of that biology, while at the same time arguing for the central role of culture in the development of selfhood. But the wider claim concerns culture's rootedness in self:

> Perhaps it is this combination of properties that makes Self such an appropriate, if sometimes uncomfortable, instrument in the dynamism of human culture. For without the malleability (or 'rewriteability') of Self, the human cultural adaptation that makes our species unique would probably not be possible.[22]

Here we have the idea that selves are the building blocks or, better still, the cells that compose the living adapting mega-organism that is human culture, this great network or web or conversation of endlessly symbolising, continuously remaking and ceaselessly communicating minds.

With this comes the notion of cultural evolution and ideas of cultural adaptability and failure to adapt. Richard Dawkins most forcefully proposed the idea that we are the vehicles for the transmission of genes, and not the other way round.[23] In parallel, he also argued that human beings are transmitters of 'memes' (ideas, beliefs, values, attitudes, melodies and so on) and that there was a dynamic cultural evolution analogous in interesting ways to biological evolution. Selves form, whether inadvertently or not, the lines of transmission for ideologies, beliefs, ideas and values from one generation to the next. Daniel Dennett argues that

> The invasion of human brains by culture, in the form of memes, has created human minds, which alone among animal minds can conceive of things distant and future, and formulate alternative goals . . . . In particular, it is the shaping of our minds by memes that gives us the autonomy to transcend our selfish genes.[24]

In a Lamarckian-type way, the changes experienced and taken account of in the lives of one generation are passed on to the next by forms of tutoring and apprenticeship. In this context the Self with all its freedoms and constraints is a crucial arena for cultural formation and for cultural adaptability and change. Narrative processes are the intellectual meeting ground for theory of self and theory of culture. This is the wider implication of Bruner's work. He, like Harré and others in this tradition, acknowledge Lev Vygotsky as an inspiration.

This is where the idea of meta-narrative as a form of metacognition comes into play. As the link between culture-now and culture-next, Self will be shaped *by* culture in Self's own formation and in the shaping *of* culture through its nurturing of the next generation. Every culture has its own world-view, and stories are the threads with which that *Weltanschauung* is woven. One has only to listen to the Bosnian Serb leader, and indicted war criminal, Radovan Karadic's interpretation of Serbian epic poems of oppression to see how the self-righteousness of Serbian aggression is rooted in narratives of historical oppression and resistance. Serbian nationalism is far from being alone in this as any self-critical Irish nationalist will know. The point is that each society and sub-culture will have its own self-constituting stories and story genres. Primary makers and purveyors of such narratives will be poets, writers and other artists. A pool of narratives and narrative-types (memes) will be available for the formation of all new selves in a society. Built into them will be the values, hopes and fears which will suggest the 'ideal self' of that society as well as positioning the society in relation to its past and its future, and incorporating its stances towards other societies.

It is in this sense that life will imitate art and that Bruner can suggest that the shape of a life can come more from the fiction of imagination than from the stuff of first-hand experience. In his earlier work on narrative thinking he asked what it was that a story must 'be' in order to be a story and he concluded that 'narrative deals with the vicissitudes of intention.'[25] When someone hears or reads a story they are led and guided by the story on a search for meaning. Psychologically this will involve the activation by the story of a 'presuppositional background' for its own interpretation, a coming to grips with the 'subjectification' whereby the narrated realities are filtered through the consciousness of the protagonists which in turn involves a narrative reality that is composed of many perspectives.

For all this Bruner coins the phrase 'subjunctivizing reality' which is intended to convey the indeterminacy of the realities created by and in stories.[26] Story worlds are worlds of open-ended possibilities, unsettled and contingent worlds always open to another interpretation. Their readers must, as Roland Barthes and Wolfgang Iser argue, become themselves virtual writers of a virtual story-world since they must imaginatively fill in all the gaps absent from the story told or written but required by it for more complete takes on its meanings.[27]

In asking how reality is made 'subjunctive' by language Bruner turns to Todorov and the idea of 'transformations' which change the action of a verb from being a given to being more subjunctive, indeterminate, psychologically in process. He adapts Todorov to show how a very definite statement of 'fact' can be unsettled and made more open and porous by applying transformations of modality, intention, result, manner, aspect or status to it. Bruner suggests that it is in specific ways like this that language, spoken or written, subjunctifies reality and deals with the ups and downs of intention.

For stories like autobiographies, these indeterminacies of narrative fuse with the particular intentions of autobiographers to tell 'the truth' of their lives. Apart from narrative mould-breakers, most autobiographies big or small rely on conventional narrative models. Whether I tell my story – by far the most common path – or write it, there are certain definite and stringent requirements if the job is to be done any way well in a public sense. I must be linguistically competent, have available to me a repertoire of narrative forms, and have developed the skills of narration. It is these abilities which will allow me to reflect upon the various accounts I can give of the different parts of my life so that I can pull them together into the coherence of 'my story'.[28] This is the meta-narrative task whose goal is the integration of self.

My story may emphasise certain key elements of the *ur-narrative* and not others so that a different self may emerge from each. Here is how Bruner and Kalmar put it:

. . . we would propose that the various genres of narrative are specialized to highlight the different types of Self-indicators referred to earlier. Emphasis on Agency signals an adventurous Self; a focus on Commitment signals a dedicated Self; specialization on Resources signals either a profligate or a miserly Self; too much social referencing reveals the in-grouper and/or the snob; preoccupation with *qualia* is the self-contained aesthete.[29]

Of course more than one of these sub-species of oneself may co-exist in the story, albeit problematically. The life of self is after all a life fraught with conflict and contradiction. The available stock of acceptable narrative/self types may favour one or other sub-type as the ideal one to achieve. Either way there is the task of unifying them into some sort of 'omnibus meta-narrative' which may find favour with oneself and with those others whose opinions matter.

From everything said so far a number of points will be clear. Autobiography will always be specific as to time and place. There never can be a definite end to the narrative which is a self, and there will always be other ways to do the telling and construct what is told. Bruner agrees with Henry James that adventures happen only to those who know how to tell them. Significant adventures in the trajectory of a life may often be troublesome and disruptive. This is a point of great significance. Often what gives rise to the impulse to reflect upon oneself and one's life is trouble and pain. Empirical studies of the accounts people give of their lives find that these are organised around what are often referred to as 'turning points' or crises. It is when that element of narrative which throws open the direction of the whole game occurs – *jeopardy* – that the reflective or meta-cognitive powers of the person are called upon to pull the life together again and to rechart its course. Telling one's story, especially to oneself, is a key navigational strategy in turbulent times. And to follow the same maritime theme, in our most troubled times it is not unlike rebuilding the boat while at the same time having to stay afloat.

In ordinary social life, the occasions for producing omnibus accounts of self are normally to do with the requirements of others, a clinician for counselling, a priest for confession, a lawyer for litigation. Each demands a partial, specialised story. In most personal lives, however, options are kept open perhaps by *not* completing the omnibus edition of self until the world as it is known is thrown out of kilter and reappraisal becomes an urgency. At that point narrative 'organises the travails of jeopardy', as Bruner and Kalmar put it. Large individual differences in narrative ability are evident here as they are in other forms of problem-solving. For those adept in it narrative reconstruction is intrinsically linked to the stabilisation and further integration of self. The integrity of self is the integrity of its story as lived. 'Nothing matches turning points,' writes

Bruner, 'for generating identity maintaining maneuvers, especially metacognitive self-admonitions about how you should and shouldn't think about yourself.'[30]

Finally, a comment on the development of this ability. When Isabelle at two and a half years of age begins a sentence with 'When I was a lickle baby . . . ' can we assume that she has a sense of 'having a past'? There is no reason why a two-year-old cannot metacognitively represent herself as a person with an already personalised past. The roots of narrative lie deep and early. At a far more primitive level still, if Nicholas Humphrey is right, even sensations are self-characterising. To use his description, 'Sensations tell their own story or give away their characteristic properties, so that the subject is directly and immediately aware of them.'[31]

Studies show that self-accounting, which is a species of autobiographical narrative, begins very early in a child's speaking life. One study by Bruner and colleagues recorded the monologues of a two-year-old alone in her cot after lights out.[32] In the course of these she was heard structuring her world, binding her own intentional states with newly acquired words like 'because', distinguishing between what 'is' and what 'should be', and using such locutions as 'I wish that . . .' and 'I don't know whether . . .' as the means of adopting stances towards the people and the events in her life. Even at this early stage of normal development there is an impetus towards the elaboration of a 'reflective self'.

Where and when you are born and reared matters hugely for the skills of selfhood that you acquire, and for the sort of self you become. The contingencies of historical phase, cultural type and economic status will shape the world in which a child has to find a place, determine the scope of the actions that will compose his or her sense of agency, and prescribe the type of story that she will be permitted and enabled to tell and be. A Pathan girl in the mountains of Pakistan is formed in ways radically different from a girl of the same age in prosperous Los Angeles. Selves are saturated by history and culture. If the work of Bruner and others on the constitutive powers of narrative opens up our understanding of how individual selves are narratively constructed, then that of Charles Taylor shows the importance of understanding the history of the formative ideas that shape individual lives.

Notes

1 P. Ricoeur, *Time and Narrative*, vol.3, translated by K. Blamey and D. Pellauer, London, The University of Chicago Press, 1988, p. 246.

2 J. Bruner, 'The Autobiographical Process', *Current Sociology*, 43, 2/3, Autumn 1995, p. 176. See also A. G. Amsterdam and J. Bruner, *Minding the Law*, Cambridge, Mass., Harvard University Press, 2000.

3 A. Bullock, *Hitler and Stalin: Parallel Lives*, London, Fontana, 1993, p. 382.

4 J. Bruner and D. Kalmar, 'Narrative and metanarrative in the construction of self', in

M. Ferrari and R. Sternberg (eds), *Self-awareness: Its Nature and Development*, New York, Guilford Press, 1998. See also M. Billig, *Freudian Repression: Conversation Creating the Unconscious*, New York, Cambridge University Press, 1999.

5 See, for example, H. Kissinger, *The White House Years*, London, Weidenfeld and Nicolson, 1979.

6 S. Sutherland, *Breakdown*, St Albans, Granada, 1977. See also L. Wolpert, *Malignant Sadness: The Anatomy of Depression*, London, Faber and Faber, 1999, and W. Styron, *Darkness Visible*, London, Picador, 1991.

7 A. Speer, *Inside the Third Reich*, London, Cardinal, 1975.

8 F. Stuart, *Black List, Section H*, London, Penguin, 1996, p. x.

9 M. Proust, *Remembrance of Things Past*, New York, Chelsea House, 1987. Also S. de Beauvoir's *Force of Circumstance*, London, Penguin, 1968 is an example.

10 A. Prost, and G. Vincent, *A History of Private Life: Vol.5 Riddles of Identity in Modern Times*, Cambridge, Mass., Belknap Press, 1991.

11 G. Sereny, *Albert Speer: His Battle with the Truth*, London, Macmillan, 1995, p. 653.

12 J. Bruner, *In Search of Mind: Essays in Autobiography*, London, Harper & Row, 1983.

13 J. Bruner, *Actual Minds, Possible Worlds*, Cambridge, Mass., Harvard University Press, 1986, p. 12.

14 J. Bruner, *The Culture of Education*, Cambridge Mass., Harvard University Press, 1996, p. 39.

15 Bruner, 'The Autobiographical Process', p. 176.

16 N. Humphrey, *A History of the Mind*, London, Chatto & Windus, 1992, Chapter 18.

17 Bruner and Kalmar, op. cit., p. 319. See also J. Bruner, *Acts of Meaning*, Cambridge, Mass., Harvard University Press, 1990.

18 Bruner and Kalmar, op. cit., pp. 310–13.

19 Ibid., p. 322.

20 See for example R. Harré, *Personal Being*, Oxford, Basil Blackwell, 1983.

21 K. Gergen, *Realities and Relationships: Soundings in Social Construction*, Cambridge, Mass., Harvard University Press, 1994. Also see C. Taylor. *Sources of the Self: The Making of the Modern Identity*, Cambridge, Mass., Harvard University Press, 1989.

22 Bruner and Kalmar, op. cit., p. 326.

23 R. Dawkins, *The Selfish Gene*, Oxford, Oxford University Press, 1976.

24 D. Dennett, *Darwin's Dangerous Idea: Evolution and the Meanings of Life*, New York, Simon & Schuster, 1995, p. 369.

25 Bruner, *Actual Minds, Possible Worlds*, p. 17.

26 Ibid., p. 26. See also P. J. Eakin, *How Our Lives Become Stories: Making Selves*, Ithaca, Cornell University Press, 1999.

27 See R. Barthes, *A Barthes Reader*, ed. Susan Sontag, London, Cape, 1982, and W. Iser, *The Act of Reading: A Theory of Aesthetic Response*, London, Routledge & Kegan Paul, 1978.

28 C. Linde, *Life Stories: The Creation of Coherence*, Oxford, Oxford University Press, 1993.

29 Bruner and Kalmar, op. cit., p. 320.

30 J. Bruner, 'Self Reconsidered: Five Conjectures', Paper presented to the Annual Meeting of the Society for Philosophy and Psychology held at the State University of New York at Stony Brook, 8 June 1995, p. 16.

31 Humphrey, op. cit., p. 122.

32 J. Bruner and J. Lucariello, 'Monologue as narrative recreation of the world' in K. Nelson (ed.), *Narratives from the Crib*, Cambridge, Mass., Harvard University Press, 1989, pp. 73–97.

4

MORAL IDENTITY AND CULTURAL-HISTORICAL LOCATIONS FOR SELF

It would seem a warranted conclusion, then, that our 'smooth' and easy transactions and the regulatory self that executes them, starting as a biological readiness based on a primitive appreciation of other minds, is then reinforced and enriched by the calibrational powers that language bestows, is given a larger-scale map on which to operate by the culture in which transactions take place, and ends by being a reflection of the history of that culture as that history is contained in the culture's images, narratives and tool kit.

(J. Bruner, *Actual Minds, Possible Worlds*, 1986, p. 67)

We should note that the memes for normative concepts – for *ought* and *good* and *truth* and *beauty* – are among the most entrenched denizens of our minds. Among the memes that constitute us, they play a central role. Our existence as us, as what we as thinkers are – not as what we as organisms are – is not independent of those memes.

(D. Dennett, *Darwin's Dangerous Idea*, 1995, p. 366)

With each look at self we have moved higher up the slope of abstraction. Now, beyond narrative identity we ascend to a new level. Before us are great patterns of hills, valleys, fields and rivers which are largely invisible to those who live in or near them but which contain and shape their lives in profound ways. This is the territory of the intellectual historian, the cartographer and tracker of ideas (memes) across time and place.

Charles Taylor is one such map-maker and in his *Sources of the Self* he brings us on a long winding journey through the history of some of the ideas that have come to be central to how we think about the modern Western identity.[1] So close are we to this organisation of self – after all it *is* us – that only something like a sharp contrast with people from a quite different culture, or an account of the ways in which people thought of themselves in more distant historical times, will provide the necessary foil for us to realise how we think about ourselves.

Such comparisons enable us to go some way towards understanding how changing ways of thinking about self might alter people's sense of themselves and of the landscape of their subjectivity. If Bruner is right and if different ways of narrating self produce different selves, then this is precisely what should happen if the story of what self is and does changes significantly from one period to another.

In *Wild Swans* Jung Chang tells of her father's complete and utter identification with the Chinese Communist Party from his boyhood, even when this meant behaving appallingly, if sorrowfully, towards his wife.[2] Late in his life, during the Cultural Revolution, disaster befell the family when he was disgraced by the young Red Guards. Jung Chang, herself a teenage Red Guard, writes of coming to hate the government but not her idol and inspiration Mao. The whole meaning of her life had been 'formulated in his name'. Although his magic power had 'vanished from inside me' she says that Mao was 'sacred and undoubtable', and that but a few years previously she would willingly have died for him.

Notice the metaphors of containment 'in' and 'inside' which doubly enclose her. Later in a different world and a different time she writes a bestselling story of her life and that of her mother and grandmother. The compelling story she tells would have been inconceivable to the young Red Guard she was some decades previously. It is not simply that she is older and wiser. The very basis of her life has changed and with it her self. The moral shape of the young Jung Chang is now scrutinised by the changed moral perspective of the later narrating Jung Chang. She has been dislocated and relocated in a series of ways and has been transformed. It is the significance of such moral sources for the making of an identity that lies at the heart of Charles Taylor's work on self.

Taylor's viewing point allows for a panoramic, if partial, grasp of Western intellectual formulations of ideas of self, identity, and the sources from which these ideas draw their meaning. This allows him to chart the changes in these ideas over millennia and to show what is distinct and new in modern conceptions of identity. This provides a salutary warning to any naive psychology which seeks to understand self outside of an intelligently informed historical and cultural perspective. The pedigree of many of the meta-narrative capacities which Bruner believes create the 'regulatory self' of people in the modern Western world should be identifiable in an historical project like Taylor's.

Centredness, agency and autobiographical narrative as aspects of self find their meaning in worlds that are not initially of the self's making. This is not to deny that such worlds are made part of self by psychological means of construction and reconstruction; it is to say that these worlds also make individual selves part of their own fabric and put them to their own uses. It is from such worlds that neophyte selves acquire the skills of thinking about and locating themselves, and this in turn determines the extent to which the subsequent range of possibilities for self-creation will be drawn, as we will see again in Chapter 5.

Like Jerome Bruner, Rom Harré also argues that self should be studied as part of the anthropology and history of morals. For this a distinction must be made between 'a mechanism' and 'a practice'. Harré writes:

> It makes sense to conduct experiments if you believe that there is a mechanism behind what happens. In much of human conduct there are no mechanisms, only practices. . . . The source of a practice must be looked for in the customs and forms of life of a culture; that of a mechanism in the microstructure and internal processes of an active agent. Contemporary academic psychology is shot through with confusions between mechanisms and practices. A mechanism is activated: one is trained in, inducted into . . . practices.[3]

Taylor's concern is also with the cultural evolution of practices that constitute selves, but with this caveat.[4] He is not offering an historical explanation for the rise of the modern identity. This would need to examine the evolution of modern political structures, economic practices, military and bureaucratic organisations, scientific and artistic developments, geography, climate, companionate marriage, child-rearing practices and so on. What Taylor contributes is different but relevant to this far wider project. He asks how people in the Western world interpreted identity such that they found it convincing. He asks about the ideas governing the evolution of interpretations of self, interpretations which in fact give rise both to notions of self and senses of being particular sorts of self. For this he looks mainly to writings in philosophy, religion, psychology, poetry and art.

At the heart of Taylor's analysis is the idea that the psychological and the moral are inextricable. To be a self, in Taylor's view, is always to be in association with some notion of 'the good'. This is not the association of self as an isolated island loosely federated to an idea of what it thinks is good for it. It is a connection to some notion of 'the good' which actively makes that self what it is and wants to be. The relationship, in other words, is constitutive rather than merely connective. We develop and live in a 'web of interlocution' and must locate ourselves among the questions that make up this web, notably questions of what is valuable and worth living for. Specifying this relationship with 'the good' is as important when describing self as accounting for the ways in which its centring and self-locating, its sense of its own powers and its self-narrating work. Being centred, active and self-narrating are living elements of this relationship with 'the good,' whatever that good might be. What psychology needs to explain, according to Taylor, is how people live their lives within the terms of those lives.

Like Bruner and Harré, Taylor is very critical of those versions of psychology which presume that self can be treated mechanistically as a scientific object and he outlines some obstacles to this being a successful programme. My self cannot be taken 'objectively' as some entity on its own detached from its meaning for me or for other people; it cannot be described without reference to the social worlds in which I live and have lived; what 'I am' is directly related to the ways I have for describing and interpreting myself; and since I am always an incomplete project, to use an existentialist phrase, 'I' elude explicit and final description. I am always in relationship with 'the other' and this relationship and its terms change endlessly within the stream of experience until, that is, the stream of consciousness itself dries up. These are reasons why self cannot in principle be the sort of object that a positivist psychology could study successfully.

Self is about meaning and is, to use a term much borrowed from Bakhtin, dialogic in structure.[5] It emerges from relations with others and continues to be maintained by them even when representations of these others have become internalised players in the ongoing conversational structure that is self. Consequently, because self is essentially relational in organisation, describing it adequately must always include those aspects of the world towards which self has been or is selectively directed. 'Interested', 'desiring', 'valuing', 'believing', 'avoiding', 'hating', 'envying', 'resenting', 'trusting' and so on are words to describe aspects of such directedness towards the other.

'How do I know who I am?' is a central question for an account of self and Taylor answers in unequivocal moral terms:

> To know who I am is a species of knowing where I stand. My identity is defined by the commitments and identifications which provide the frame or horizon within which I can try to determine from case to case what is good, or valuable, or what ought to be done, or what I endorse or oppose. In other words, it is the horizon within which I am capable of taking a stand.[6]

These terms need some explanation. Taylor uses the word 'horizon' to indicate the particular framework of meaning which shapes the world for a person or a society. Others might use a word like ideology or *Weltanschauung*. A 'good' means anything that is considered valuable, worthy or admirable. Goods have sources, and a 'moral source' is 'something the contemplation of which commands our respect, which respect in turn empowers'.[7] This is an important and illuminating idea.

Take an extreme example, one which in another possible world could have been Jung Chang or her father. I am a young man or woman who loves life and looks forward to my future. Imagine my community is troubled and feeling oppressed, and within it arises a movement which tells a story of its oppression in which individual acts of retaliation against the oppressor are glorified, brutality justified and the 'heroes' who commit these 'deeds' are assured certain 'glory' and 'honour' when as 'martyrs' they pass into 'Heaven' while also becoming everlastingly memorialised in some earthly 'Pantheon of Heroes'. My sense of my own 'courage' or lack of it is challenged and I join this movement whose tactics include strapping explosives around the bodies of young volunteers who then blow themselves to pieces together with others whom they have never met, except as a type.

Every war, every invasion and every defence recruits such feelings of self-abnegation in favour of the greater good, be it Nation or People or Creed. 'Germany, I have not yet used this word, you country of big strong hearts. You are my home. It is worth one's life becoming a seed for you', a young German soldier wrote home from Stalingrad.[8] And, as if in echo, a young Russian tank commander made this diary entry: 'Our aim is to defend something greater than millions of lives. I am not speaking about my own life. The only thing to be done is to lose it to some advantage for the Motherland.'[9]

Leaving aside all question as to whether this is by other standards a good and desirable thing, how are we to explain how the young woman or man finds the power to destroy or accept the destruction of their own lives in the course of destroying others? Part of the answer can be given in terms of Taylor's formulation of a 'constitutive good'. A constitutive good is 'a something the love of which empowers us to do and be good'.[10] The powers enabling such extreme voluntary actions as those above can only be understood in terms of the 'good' which has become an integral part of that person's identity, a good which both directs their actions and empowers them to carry them out.

The particular path of meaning upon which that person embarks is constituted to a large degree by the good with which they have now fused, a set of beliefs which now forms a key part of their regulatory self. Things I may never have thought of wanting to do, nor of myself as being capable of doing, become possible when my identity locks into such a moral source which then becomes a defining part of a redefined 'me'. If I am loosed from such a source and become redefined by my stance towards some other good (various examples of 'reform' or 'redemption' or 'seeing the light' come to mind), I may equally wonder how I was ever capable of doing or wanting to do the things I did in the past. I might say that 'I was a different person then'. To use more traditional and often static psychological terms, 'context' or 'situation' could be usefully described in terms of the constitutive goods that operate as part of their dynamics. The effects of incorporating a good into the organisation of self include alterations in the orientation of attention and action, the formation of different habits and action scripts, and changes in the ways in which emotion and feeling operate in the making of decisions.

The notion of a constitutive good is a crucial but neglected idea for the psychology of self and one on which Taylor rests much weight in his account of the modern identity. Indications of its influence would be given when a person's 'ideals' are discussed. It relies on an understanding of language as itself creative of new realities, and of narrative as an organising structure of language. Taylor insists that 'this sense of the good has to be woven into my understanding of my life as an unfolding story. But this is to state another basic condition of making sense of ourselves, that we grasp our lives in a narrative.'[11]

Taylor's discussion of the moral bases of self therefore connects four areas: our notions of the good, our understandings of self, the kinds of narrative with which we make sense of our lives, and our concepts of society. Morality, identity, narrative and politics are intimately intertwined and mutually constitutive. How do these interrelate and how have they changed to give rise to the modern Western identity? Taylor's very extensive answer to this question is even still a sketch, given the complexity of the question. Paler still by far is the synopsis of some of his conclusions that I want to give here. That selection is nonetheless sufficient to strengthen my claim that a cultural psychological understanding of self and identity must acknowledge how they locate inescapably in specific moral horizons.

Individualism and subjectivism are keywords describing the modern identity. The composition of these terms includes the notion of the 'inwardness' of self, the idea of there being an 'inside' or interior of self with its own 'depths', and an 'outside' or objective world. This in turn involves the 'stance' which the modern self habitually adopts towards the world, a stance of distance and disengagement. This disengaged stance allows it to use 'reason' as an instrument for controlling and using its world, and its self as part of that world. This scientific attitude and its technological children dominate the modern world, including the modern identity.

This distancing stance gives rise to an understanding of self as autonomous, responsible for itself, looking inside itself for its own moral sources, and capable of actually creating and recreating itself through language. Exploring oneself and especially one's 'feelings' is deemed to be important, as is the idea that a vision of the good life requires self to commit itself to that life. The creative powers of language loom large in this account and with that comes a recognition of the central importance of the arts in the modern world. It is from the modern novel, poetry, theatre, film, the modern autobiography and so on that patterns of narrating oneself are made publicly available as models for self-narration and for the construction of the 'private' or individual self. The artist becomes an ideal for self as one who creates and realizes herself through her work. Self-expression, individualism and the rise of the artist as an ideal are symbiotic.

Related to this is the egalitarianism characteristic of the modern world, with

64

its respect for ordinary lives and its widespread feelings of repugnance at the infliction of suffering by one person or group on another. Finally, the horizons bordering the modern world and the frameworks of meaning to which citizens of the modern world appeal to justify these dimensions of self increasingly include no God or Providence or concept of a metaphysical Presence.

The fabric of the modern self is many-coloured and its patterns, as we have just listed them, are to be understood as dominant rather than total and exclusive. Many others contend with them, some of ancient lineage defending an apparently eroding position and some currently emerging and struggling for notice. But the features above are sufficiently widespread as habitual aspects of the modern Western sense of self to justify weaving them into this general pattern and naming it the modern self or identity. Self was not always so, as we will see from another angle in Chapter 5. Historically, where did the constituting themes of Taylor's modern self come from? The stories of their various developments are the stories told by Taylor. He constructs, as it were, a geneology or family tree for the elements coalescing to form the modern self.

Take, for instance, the idea of a moral source and specifically *types* of moral source which although ancient still find themselves pallidly present in the modern world. An historically early source is the honour ethic associated with warrior cultures. Here the most esteemed social position, more than that of farmer or merchant or scholar, is that of the warrior. It is exclusively male and intensely hierarchical. Fame and glory as honourable fighters are the highest goods. What makes the man of honour is precisely his willingness to risk his life in the service of an ideal. The worst that can happen is for dishonour to befall the warrior in which case suicide may remain the only option. Homeric tales and those of medieval knights exemplify this elitist ethic where the goods of ordinary life, peaceful domesticity and work, are distinctly second best.

This code still characterises many military cultures and criminal gangs. In a recent description of lethal infighting among Scandanavian Hell's Angels and their rivals the Bandidos, a Finnish member was quoted as saying that the war would continue 'until the Angels admit they've lost. It's a matter of honour and nothing else – we're the meanest mothers up here now, and everyone, including the police, had better understand it.'[12] This is of course a much-diminished version of the ancestral honour ethics but recognisably of the type. The nature of the honour involved and the associated ideas of virtue and generosity would be much less sophisticated or admirable. A feature of all such honour ethics, however, is the degree to which regard is traded in the public arena. It is there that self-regard has its source and it continues to depend for its value on the regard of others.

Religions have always been major moral sources. Their great empowering narratives tell how goodness in the form of God or gods or a Way can be followed in a manner that will bring peace of mind and some form of salvation.

These narratives describe the providential order of the universe and of self's place in it. Those for whom this is a moral source of themselves willingly submit to the demands of the narrative, and yield their own powers of choice to follow the moral path laid down by the religion.

This may mean engaging in practices designed to free it from what is taken to be the illusory reality of self itself, as with Buddhism. It appears that religious perspectives developed early in the evolution of human culture and continue to be primary moral sources for billions of human beings today. In the Western world the social power of the dominant religions of Christianity is much less than it was. Secular moral sources are a strong feature of Western societies and have rendered the Churches less powerful as moral sources. But the antecedents of contemporary secular sources of the good are significantly shaped by religious sources.

Christianity, and the Puritan tradition of Protestantism in particular, played a central role in establishing the family and the working lives of ordinary people as ideals of the 'full life'. This is a major story in Taylor's account. Whereas for Aristotle the full life was one of contemplation and political involvement for the eligible few, and for the honour ethic it was fame and glory for the male elite, in the newly emerging order of modernity the full life came to include the home and work lives of the many.

The Protestant belief in companionate marriage was very significant, as was the Puritan belief that the most menial of work can be transmuted when offered to the glory of God. 'God loveth adverbs,' he quotes the Puritan writer Joseph Hall as saying, 'and cares not how good, but how well.'[13] Family and work came to be understood as expressions of the religious life. Political ideologies such as communism and nationalism have also served as potent moral sources in the modern world, as has the idea that sources of the good can be found deep within the person, an idea to which I will return below.

Taylor also charts the development of that aspect of modern sensibility which finds the infliction of pain morally and emotionally repugnant. Not wanting to cause suffering is a value which he identifies as being unique among higher civilisations. The infliction of barbarous punishment is widely felt and agreed to be repugnant, and when it occurs somewhere in the world it elicits deeply felt condemnation. It is only in the last few hundred years, since the Enlightenment, that the Western inconceivability of bringing young children to the spectacle of gruesome public executions has evolved.

As well as committing themselves to the ideal of reason as responsible for itself, and to the inherent values of ordinary life, the thinkers of the Radical Enlightenment (Smith and Bentham in England for example, and Voltaire, Diderot, Rousseau et al. in France) also espoused the ideal of universal and impartial benevolence. The utilitarians put the relief of suffering, animal as well as human, at the centre of the social agenda for the first time and this also has become a defining feature of the modern identity.[14] Taylor reflects that

> This sense of the importance of the everyday in human life, along with its corollary about the importance of suffering, colours our whole under-standing of what it is truly to respect human life and integrity. Along with the central place given to autonomy, it defines a version of this demand which is peculiar to our civilization, the modern West.[15]

Particularly noteworthy is how the concept of 'a right' has become a major influence in the recent history of the modern Western identity. This is a key part of modern legal systems and is a cornerstone of attempts to construct a world order such as is envisaged in the concept of the United Nations. Moving from a time when such rights only applied to select elites (rights to govern, assemble, tax and so on), the modern world speaks of universal human rights and some-times acts accordingly. 'Human rights', observes Michael Ignatieff, 'has become the major article of faith of a secular culture that fears it believes in nothing else.'[16]

It is worth remembering that the Universal Declaration of Human Rights is barely fifty years old. Taylor emphasises that, from the point of view of identity, this change in the conception of the person as a carrier of rights has also involved a change in the understanding of the person as free, autonomous and deserving of respect. This further entails the modern demand for individuals to have the freedom to develop their personalities in their own way. What are sometimes forgotten are the correlative responsibilities that are paired with rights.

A major part of Taylor's effort has been directed towards describing the evolu-tion of what he calls 'inwardness' and the modern self. The construct inside/outside is central to our modern languages of self-understanding. We think of our selves as having their own inner spaces and we take it for granted that our capacity to 'reflect' upon ourselves is an important route to taking control of 'our' lives and shaping them as we think we ought to. In Bruner's terms this is what metacognition and metanarrative is all about. This construct lies at the heart of many of the elements of the modern self which I listed above.

From the point of view of when, historically, words start being used as part of a discourse of self-understanding, the *Oxford English Dictionary* tells us that it is only during the seventeenth century that words like self, self-knowledge, self-made, self-knowing, self-deception, self-determination and so on entered the English language for the first time. Taylor emphasises that the partitioning of the world into 'inner' and 'outer' is not universal, whether historically or culturally. It is a mode of self-interpretation which has developed as a feature of the modern Western world and which has for some time been spreading to other parts of the globe. It has had its own beginning in time and space and may have its own end. For now, however, it is a central part of the modern identity, one whose lineage he traces out in some detail.

The idea that self has inner depths is closely connected to the notion of mastering the self. Taylor looks to Plato in the first instance for an early formulation of the idea of self-mastery. He tracks the history of the ideal of self-mastery, and its associated ideas of self as having 'depth', from Plato through Plotinus and St Augustine to Descartes and into the modern era.

In Plato's scheme, 'reason' should be the master of self. Reason is the ability to give 'reasons' or 'accounts'. To be ruled by reason is to be ruled by the correct vision of the natural cosmic order. Plato's moral doctrine in *The Republic* is that we are good when reason rules and when we are self-possessed, but bad when we are in the grip of our desires and passions. Reason should dominate desire.

Taylor argues that Plato's view requires some conception of the mind as a unitary space. The soul is the single source of thinking and feeling. Taylor speaks of the unification of the moral self in Plato's thinking as a centring. This idea of a unified, centred self becomes, in his view, a precondition for the development of the modern notion of interiority with its subsequently developed construct of inside/outside.[17] For Plato the good life concerns not what happens in the soul but rather where the soul faces in the metaphysical landscape. The order of our souls and that of the eternal order of the cosmos are intimately connected. Becoming rational on this view means connecting up to the larger cosmic order rather than establishing an order within oneself.

The inner/outer dichotomy comes into more serious play with St Augustine. For St Augustine the principal path to God is not through the objects of the external world but through the very activity of knowing itself. This focus on the workings of our own subjectivity, on the ways in which things are for us, rather than on what objects we are attending to, shifts attention inwards. This now requires a conception of self as an interior place with its own dimensions. Taylor calls this focus of attention on myself as the agent of experience 'radical reflexivity'. It stresses the uniqueness of my presence to myself, as someone who can speak in the first person as 'I'. But whereas for St Augustine the path inwards is also the path upwards to God, the changes in modernity truncate that path and leave the modern mind to create its own alternatives.

The crucial move towards 'internalization' occurs when, notably with Descartes, the idea of being dominated by reason is transformed into another idea. In this early modern formulation the order of reason is made and not found; with the Platonic model it was there to be found rather than made. Quite a different understanding of self is now required for an idea of the world of which human minds are co-creators. The first-person standpoint, which is so central to modern identity, begins to assume its powerful role.

Evil, for St Augustine, is when reflexivity becomes closed in upon itself; good is when it opens out and acknowledges that it depends on God.[18] But what happens when God has ceased to be for the self, as for so many in the modern world? Where is the inwardness of self to be redirected? With Descartes comes the argument that the moral sources we need are within us. A further elaboration of the powers of self now begins which underpins modern conceptions of identity.

Finding meaning in the world by correctly representing the given structure of the world – the Galilean view – or making the world meaningful by the construction of representations themselves – the Cartesian view – become competing options for emerging modern science. Descartes' dualism of mind and body involves the person realising his immaterial nature by objectifying the body and the world. These must now be understood as mechanisms whose workings are to be unravelled by science. The standards to be met by this mode of inquiry must derive from the thinking activity of the knower.

This theory had moral and political implications far beyond what Descartes himself could have imagined. To conceive of the world as a mechanism carries with it the possibility of controlling that mechanism. No longer does the cosmos supply us with providential order and meaning which is there to be accepted and obeyed. Instead we have a prototype of the modern notion of the universe as impersonal and there to be used by the instrumental reason of man for the benefit of man. With this view also come the seeds of the widespread agnosticism and atheism so characteristic of Western civilization.

At the moral and psychological level men and women must now look within themselves for the sources of their meaning. Where we look for a sense of our own worth also shifts inwards; we look to maintain our worth 'in our own eyes'.[19] An ideal develops of self as capable of systematically creating and recreating itself. This idea of 'working on yourself' is now a modern-day commonplace. What opens up the idea that it is possible to remake self is the radical disengagement of self from what it thinks about. This is a view developed in the philosophy of John Locke.[20]

Such a disengaged Lockean self is what Taylor calls 'the punctual self'. This punctual self identifies itself with the power to objectify and remake, and by this act of identification distances itself from all that is open to change, not least in oneself. The essence of self is the 'I' that changes rather than the 'me' that is open to being changed. In Taylor's view this 'perfectly detachable consciousness' is an illusory shadow cast by the punctual self, yet it is one that pervades contemporary psychological thought. Freud's mature conception of the ego, for example, is at root a disengaged agent of instrumental reason and in this sense a successor of Locke's punctual self. Taylor concludes that 'Disengagement demands that we stop simply living in the body or within our traditions or habits and, by making them objects for us, subject them to radical scrutiny and remaking.'[21] It is not an idea he favours but he recognises its influence.

By the eighteenth century the form of the modern identity was taking shape. The idea that the psychological – ideas and feelings – are now understood as being confined to minds where in previous systems of thought they were conceivable as parts of the world is firmly rooted. This strengthens the idea of self's 'inner nature'. The writings of Montaigne reveal a self intensely engaged in his personal life. The instability and impermanence of his inner life deeply unsettled Montaigne. 'Constancy it selfe is nothing but a languishing and wavering dance', he wrote in his *Essaie*.[22] Montaigne is one of the first who undertakes in writing the inward search for his own originality. If Descartes classified, Montaigne particularised. In a very modern way he knew that the means by which he did so shaped his own account of himself: 'I have no more made my booke, then my booke hath made me.'[23]

A particular feature of the modern identity is one for which Taylor offers his own term, 'poietic' powers. This refers to the new importance in mental and moral life of understanding the creative and constructive powers of language. In the twentieth century the preoccupation with these 'poietic' powers has become intense. The arts have themselves become moral sources with the artist as an exemplar of a desirable form of self. The rise of the modern novel is especially important for ways in which people find identity through self-narration.

With the onset of modernity and the growth of individualism it becomes more difficult to take over readymade story-models for the purposes of forming one's narrative identity. The particular, disengaged modern self needs a way of narrating his or her life which both combines the events which causally make up that life, and also recognises that the meaning of those events unfolds through them. This pattern of narrativity is what emerges in modern autobiographies such as those of Rousseau, Goethe and Jung Chang. The shape of a life as it emerges from its constitutive events become the theme of the story. More generally, the Protestant culture of introspection 'becomes secularized as a form of confessional autobiography' (Bunyan, Pepys, Boswell, for example) while also shaping the new form of the English novel in the eighteenth century.

Alternative moral sources to theism become available. One could rely on one's dignity as a rational agent or, like the Romantics, one could turn to nature itself whose principles are accessible within ourselves. Kant argues that the responsibility and the means for generating moral laws lie within ourselves. As Taylor observes, this is one of the most direct and uncompromising formulations of a modern stance. The sources of the good lie within self. Along with this Enlightenment ideal of the growth of rationality comes the belief that it will also bring a growth of universal benevolence. Taylor suggests that our growing difficulty in holding on to this ideal reflects a spiritual crisis for our civilisation.[24]

This brings us to a final important source of meaning for modernity and for the modern identity, a source much neglected by psychology. Bruner recognises the significance of 'the left hand' as does Taylor. The source is art, the creative imagination, the idea of 'expression' and 'poietic' powers.

Take the idea of 'expression' first and remember Montaigne's recognition above that he and his book were 'consubstantiall' where each made the other, and you have the general idea of expression in art. What is revealed depends upon the means available to reveal it. The medium is a vital part of the meaning rather than simply a means to make visible or audible something – the artistic 'idea' – which was already there. I define my own nature, on this view, in the act of formulating it. The act of formulating is essential to shaping it. This is the same idea as that of a metanarrative not just describing a self's life but constructing that same self. This expressivism led to ideas of new ways of becoming an individual and, in the late eighteenth century, to the idea that each individual is different and original. We each have our own nature but we can only know what that is by realising it.

If this is so for self, it is so for nationalism and art also according to this view. The nature of each nation and artistic impulse is formulated and shaped only when it is expressed. Art and artist begin to assume a new and exalted status in Western life. With the passing of the idea that art imitated life and nature, and its replacement with the idea of creation, artists begin to be seen as 'creator gods', seers, priests, revealers of the familiar, an image which connects back to a more ancient one but on completely different foundations. 'Nature', 'life' and art begin to be thought of as sharing a common source in the artist's creativity. This expressive power is tied to the idea of having 'inner depths'. As long as there is always something more to say and express there is depth, and art is the emblem of this endless fecundity. But the call is always towards some completeness of self-expression. It is in this sense that the Romantic ideal of self-completion through art has become so powerful a moral source.

Cultural critics have long commented upon the ways in which art has come to supplant religion in contemporary life. James Joyce's idea of an 'epiphany' is an emblem of this incorporation of religion by art. This is the idea that the work of art ushers us into the presence of something which would not otherwise be accessible, something of great moral significance. For Taylor 'realizing an epiphany is a paradigm case of what I called recovering contact with a moral source'.[25] In the late twentieth century this is one account of the modern identity and some of its ancestry. If Taylor is even broadly correct then self, narrative and art, as with *Wild Swans*, fly in formation.

71

Notes

1 C. Taylor, *Sources of the Self: The Making of the Modern Identity*, Cambridge, Mass., Harvard University Press, 1989.

2 J. Chang, *Wild Swans: Three Daughters of China*, London, Flamingo, 1993.

3 Harré, 'Language Games and Texts of Identity' in J. Shotter and K. Gergen (eds), *Texts of Identity*, London, Sage, 1989, p. 27. Harré cites cognitive science here and the mistaken idea that rule-following is a rigidly constructed mechanism rather than an inculcated practice. Cognitive science will never be able to construct 'adequately mental working mechanisms' because this can't be done. I am also reminded of Paul Feyerabend's reflection that 'Meaning is not located anywhere. It does not guide our actions (thoughts, observations) but arises in their course. Meaning may stabilize to such an extent that the assumption of a location starts making sense. This, however, is a disease and not a foundation.' See his *Killing Time: The Autobiography of Paul Feyerabend*, Chicago, The University of Chicago Press, 1995, p. 118.

4 Taylor, op. cit., Chapter 12.

5 M. Bakhtin, *The Dialogic Imagination: Four Essays by M. M. Bakhtin*, ed. M. E. Holquist, trans. C. Emerson and M. Holquist, Austin, University of Texas Press, 1981.

6 Taylor, op. cit., p. 27.

7 Ibid., p. 94.

8 A. Beevor. *Stalingrad*, London, Penguin, 1999, p. 77.

9 Ibid., p. 28.

10 Ibid., p. 93.

11 Ibid., p. 47.

12 *The Guardian*, 1 August 1996, supplement p. 7.

13 Taylor, op. cit., p. 224.

14 Ibid., p. 331.

15 Ibid., p. 14.

16 M. Ignatieff, 'Human Rights: The Midlife Crisis', *The New York Review of Books*, 20 May 1999, p. 58.

17 Taylor, op. cit., Chapter 6.

18 Ibid., p. 139.

19 Ibid., p. 152.

20 Ibid., p. 171.

21 Ibid., p. 175.

22 Ibid., p. 179

23 Ibid., p. 183.

24 Ibid., p. 367.

25 Ibid., p. 425.

5

SELF-CREATION AS SELF-LOCATION

Self-creation depends on the beliefs we have about what we are now like: on the stories we tell about ourselves.

(J. Glover, *I: The Psychology and Philosophy of Personal Identity*, 1989, p. 139)

We have the power to defy the selfish genes of our birth and, if necessary, the selfish memes of our indoctrination . . . . We are built as gene machines and cultured as meme machines, but we have the power to turn against our creators. We, alone on the earth, can rebel against the tyranny of the selfish replicators.

(R. Dawkins, *The Selfish Gene*, 1976, p. 215)

Beliefs are central components of selfhood. To think of them as mere bloodless propositions about the world is to ignore the fact that our system of core beliefs is the central nervous system of our identity. How we deal with ourselves and with what we encounter on our journey through life depends crucially on what we believe about ourselves, about our world, and about the worlds of others. Jonathan Glover notes how our beliefs about the world cohere 'like a mental map of a city too large to be known'.[1] He reminds us of the English philosopher Frank Ramsay's idea of a belief as 'a map of neighbouring space by which we steer'.[2] Beliefs are not there at birth: they are acquired as part of the development of skills for living. The efficacy of living skills in turn depends upon the challenges and demands of the times in which we live. The practices of living which make up the lives of persons and societies are underwritten by systems of belief.

Theorists like Rom Harré cautiously propose that 'people are what they believe they are'.[3] Being and becoming follow from beliefs. We learn our core beliefs by learning grammar in the Wittgensteinian sense of learning the rules for the use of words that constitute particular beliefs. Harré emphasises Wittgenstein's insight that the ways in which modern Europeans use psychological terms indicate that they generally do so as 'part of physiognomic language games'. Words are used instead of, or as an extension to, feelings which naturally accompany states of the body.

This lies at the heart of the belief that I have the power to make myself, a belief that is endemic to certain cultures and to certain recent phases of human history. Many – perhaps most – of the forces that shape us are outside our control. A Jewish child who survived the Holocaust, or a Rwandan who survived the genocide, did not choose to be born in that awful formative time. Yet the qualities of the times in which we live make a vast difference to the sort of people we become. Nor can I do much about the genetic unfolding of my life with all its implications for how I look, what I can and cannot do well, and the span of my life. But some peoples in certain places and certain times have come to believe that they can influence what they become by dint of their own choices and, moreover, that they can be held responsible or accountable for those choices.

Seeds of extraordinary personal and cultural power and consequence are sown by this belief. They involve key moral aspects of human being such as freedom and responsibility, respect, dignity, and authenticity as that relates to the idea of self-fulfilment. 'Our inner story lets us get our bearings when we act. Without it,' writes Jonathan Glover, 'all decisions would be like steering at sea without a map or compass. It is not surprising if those without a story are driven to invention.'[4] What are the antecedents of this concept of an inner story, and from where does it derive its powers for self-creation? This essay introduces some further themes for that story.

In 1976 an intriguing book was published which should be a text of considerable interest for cultural psychology but which rarely gets a mention in that literature. This was Julian Jaynes's *The Origin of Consciousness in the Breakdown of the Bicameral Mind*.[5] Read in conjunction with work like that of Charles Taylor, for example, Jaynes's theory helps to elaborate a framework for a cultural-historical account of the sort of human subjectivity that favours the belief that we have powers, with all sorts of qualification, to create aspects of ourselves. Even if invalid, Jaynes's speculative account of the psychology of early historical man allows us identify the absence of certain key psychological dimensions which seem necessary for processes of self-creation.

In evolutionary psychological language, work of this sort on the history of embodied psychological ideas, and what they enable, is like an archaeology of memes. But this is an excavation of great import. 'Let no one think,' writes Jaynes, that 'these are *just* word changes. Word changes are concept changes and concept changes are behavioral changes.'[6] The concept changes in focus here are none other than elemental concepts of subjectivity coalescing to form key constituting ideas of self which, over millennia, evolved to shape modern subjectivity and identity, as Charles Taylor has shown. By way of a rather densely phrased reminder, this concept of the modern identity involves powers of self-making and self-transcendence, and has as key elements the idea of an embodied autonomous subject, 'I', understood as a dynamic, linguistically constituted, accountable centring within its own metaphorical, interior 'mind space' which incessantly locates, renews and narrates itself as more-or-less focused, coherent and continuous.

Jaynes argues that there has been a profound transformation of 'mentality' in human beings the evidence for which can be largely found in extant written texts from the early periods of recorded history. The cusp of this transformation is the second millennium before the common era, that is between three and four thousand years ago. In a sentence, Jaynes proposes that a form of mentality which he calls 'the bicameral mind' transmutes into the type of mentality which today we take to be ordinary human subjectivity. He argues that developments in the characterisation of the sources of human action within the ancient written texts of the Greeks and Hebrews in particular reveal this revolutionary change in human psychology. This is an engaging piece of speculative theorising and Jaynes disarms his critics by referring to his 'sometimes flamboyant' theories.[7] His theory of the history and fate of the bicameral mind is flamboyant and even if it is overstated, or even wrong, it is a striking foil against which to consider the possible connections of self-responsibility and self-creation.

The story told by Jaynes is in effect a story of how human beings came to think of themselves as being responsible for their own actions, and consequently of being in control of them. Such self-responsibility is a psychological prerequisite for the powerful modern idea that I can, within definite limits, choose what sort of person I want to be. Jaynes begins by making a point that, twenty-five years later, has been greatly amplified by cognitive science, namely that the greater part of psychological functioning, including thinking, takes place unconsciously. Being conscious of what it is we are doing is a matter of indifference to our performance of many activities, and is sometimes a hindrance as when, for example, I consciously analyse what I am doing while I am walking, or playing the piano. The related idea that consciousness is located 'inside' my head is also problematic. Jaynes writes:

> When I am conscious, I am always and definitely using certain parts of my brain inside my head. But so am I when riding a bicycle, and the bicycle riding does not go on inside my head. . . . In reality, consciousness has no location whatever except as we imagine it has.[8]

If this is true, then it is conceivable that there could be a race of men who could function perfectly well in all sorts of psychological ways (speaking, thinking, feeling and so on), and be capable of a high level of reactivity to their world, and yet not be conscious in the way we feel ourselves to be.

But what would 'not being conscious' imply? Jaynes places language, and especially its metaphorical powers, at the root of consciousness in a way that has since been elaborated by Lakoff and Johnson, among others. Consciousness is an operation, not a thing nor a place for things. In the terms of Damasio's theory of consciousness, Jaynes's use of the word would refer to the developed ranges of extended consciousness. Jaynes argues that

> It operates by way of analogy, by way of constructing an analog space with an analog 'I' that can observe that space, and move metaphorically in it. It operates on any reactivity, excerpts relevant aspects, narratizes and conciliates them together in a metaphorical space where such meanings can be manipulated like things in space. Conscious mind is a spatial analog of the world and mental acts are analogs of bodily acts.[9]

This is obviously in line with my earlier proposal that self be considered as a locative system, and it supports the claim that extended consciousness is a substantially cultural achievement. Not to be conscious in Jaynes's sense, therefore, would imply not having the linguistic-conceptual means to create this 'metaphorical world' with its 'analog I' inhabiting its own 'mind-space'. If consciousness in this sense follows such linguistic developments, then in evolutionary terms that must have been quite a late development. So when might it have arisen? This is the background for Jaynes's subsequent argument about the existence and demise of the bicameral mind and the emergence of its successors, the various phases in the development of modern subjectivity.

We are familiar with the idea of 'inner speech' as developed by Lev Vygotsky (curiously unused by Jaynes). It is part of our consciousness that we 'talk to ourselves', urging ourselves to do or not to do something, hearing what we have to say. One of the huge benefits of this linguistic consciousness, Jaynes speculates, is that our ancestors became capable of sustained work over time.

> A Middle Pleistocene man would forget what he was doing. But lingual man would have language to remind him, either repeated by himself, which would require a type of volition which I do not think he was then capable of, or, as seems more likely, by a repeated 'internal' verbal hallucination telling him what to do.[10]

Verbal hallucinations, in this sense of voices advising, urging, ordering us what to do next are crucial constituents of the 'bicameral mind'. They are its control systems.[11]

As a consequence of the pressures of tasks that take time to be accomplished, Jaynes theorises that speech began to be lateralised in the left hemisphere, leaving the right hemisphere free for the development of these 'voices of control', thereby giving rise to a two-chambered 'bicameral mind'. These voices would have originated in the actual voices of chiefs or leaders or parents ordering or urging the person to do something. They would in time be internalised, much as Vygotsky suggests is true for us. But there is this key difference: we are instances of a type of subjectivity that has developed over the last three millennia, to take Jaynes's theoretical time-scale, which allows us to metaphorically construct our own mind-space occupied by ourselves as self-conscious subjects who hear and respond to such voices in our own inner speech. Our early ancestors, and later bicameral man, had not developed this subjectivity or self-consciousness. They received the instruction of the voices in direct ways unmediated by an interpreting, distancing subject or 'I'. This is the meaning which Jaynes wishes the 'bicameral mind' to have. The bicameral mind is a mind in two parts, one an admonitory voice or 'god' and the other the follower or 'man'. What evidence is there for this?

About 5,000 years ago writing was invented. Speech became visible in markings on clay and other materials, and thereby became capable of travelling beyond the confines of its initial utterance.[12] These earliest writings are our best evidence for imagining what the mentality of early historical man (that is man as represented by writing in recorded time) might be. In the canon of early Greek writings the *Iliad* is centrally important. The *Iliad* is an epic poem which is thought to have been developed orally by a tradition of bards (collectively known as Homer!) from about 1230 BCE to about 850 BCE when it is thought to have been first written down. By examining the terms for mental life in the *Iliad* and the ways in which they are ascribed to characters in the story, it is argued, one can reconstruct how the authors of the epic construed mental life and human action. This in turn helps us understand the makeup of their own psychology. This is Jaynes's method.

There are in general no words for consciousness or for mental acts in the *Iliad*. There are words like *psyche* and *noos* which later come to have meanings like soul or mind, but in the *Iliad* their meanings are particular and concrete. *Psyche* in the epic means life-substances like breath or blood and only later evolves to mean soul or conscious mind. *Noos* (spelt *nous* in later Greek) which afterwards comes also to mean conscious mind, conveys the idea of perception or recognition or field of vision in the *Iliad*. *Thumos*, which in time comes to mean something like emotional soul, here simply means motion or agitation. So when a warrior stops moving, the *thumos* leaves his limbs. It can also tell a man to eat, drink or fight. *Phren* is localised in the midriff and is used most often in the plural to mean something like 'catching one's breath in surprise'. There is no word for 'will' and it is only in subsequent Greek thought that this concept develops. The *soma* which in later thought comes to mean body is used plurally in Homer to mean dead limbs or a corpse. Jaynes calls these mind-words 'preconscious hypostases'. They are the causes of action as action was then construed, pivots of reaction and responsibility. Whereas parts are referred to, there is no reference to the body as a whole. Jaynes then asks what initiates behaviour in Iliadic man if there is no construal of subjective consciousness, mind, soul or will.

His answer is 'the gods'. The characters never ponder what to do: the gods tell them what must be done. A god tells Achilles to strike Agamemnon for stealing his mistress just as the gods caused Agamemnon to steal her in the first place. But who are these gods? 'They were voices whose speech and directions could be as distinctly heard by the Iliadic heroes as voices are heard by certain epileptic and schizophrenic patients, or just as Joan of Arc heard her voices,' according to Jaynes. They are persistent

> amalgams of parental or admonitory images. The god is a part of the man, and quite consistent with this conception is the fact that the gods never step outside of natural laws. Greek gods cannot create anything out of nothing, unlike the Hebrew god of Genesis.[13]

These voices or 'gods' advise, order, urge, admonish and lead. This relationship of imperative 'voice' to obedient actor is analogous to the relationship between ego and superego in Freud, or of self to 'generalized other' in the thought of George Herbert Mead. These voices or gods are what today might be called hallucinations.

Some neurological evidence which adds to the plausibility of 'voices' having a neural basis comes from the work of Wilder Penfield who electrically stimulated posterior parts of the right temporal lobe in some of his patients. These patients often reported hearing voices which were felt to be quite other than themselves. Jaynes interprets this evidence to indicate 'hallucinations that distill particularly admonition experiences, and perhaps become embodied or rationalized into actual experiences in those patients who reported them on being questioned'.[14] He emphasises that the plasticity of the brain is such that it is more capable of being organised by the environment than was previously supposed. Consequently such changes as would be entailed by a transition from bicameral mentality into a culturally shaped modern consciousness could be achieved by learning, without requiring the sorts of neural change that would need biological evolutionary periods of time.

The Mycenaean Greeks, on the linguistic evidence of the *Iliad*, had no internal mind-space within which to introspect, no equivalent of an 'analog I' which self-responsibly initiated action, and no sense of themselves as self-conscious authors of their own actions. Instead they had 'bicameral minds' in which volition, planning and initiative were processed unconsciously and then 'told' to the character by a voice of some sort. The voice or 'god' rather than the person was the responsible author of the action. It is against this 'bicameral' psychology, according to Jaynes, that the later form of consciousness develops in which, so to speak, we become our own gods, pondering options within ourselves, initiating action, and taking responsibility. The *Iliad* is interpreted in this view as standing on the cusp of a revolutionary transformation in human consciousness and hence in human being. The revolution is cultural rather than biological.

The various sources of human action in the *Iliad* can be linked back to the Wittgensteinian idea that words are used instead of or as an extension to feelings which are natural accompaniments of states of the body. What Jaynes is suggesting, as I understand him, is that from a time when there was no sense of the person as a unified agent, when actions were separately sourced to feelings in various parts of the body, there followed a synthesis of these various sources or mind-words or 'preconscious hypostases' into a concept of 'one conscious self capable of introspection'.[15]

Intimately connected with this was the expanding metaphor of these elements as containers or spaces within which things could be located (for example, *menos* or vigour was 'put into' a warrior's *thumos* during the fighting), and of this container metaphor then being more abstractly applied to the whole person as a containing space. These would be antecedents of the modern idea of self as a subject in his or her own 'mind-space'. The problem of dualism is also created in the sixth century BCE when *psyche* becomes soul and *soma* becomes body. Jaynes supplements his argument from Greek texts with equivalent observations of transformations of the use of psychological terms in the historical sequence of the Old Testament from the Book of Amos to Ecclesiastes.

If the bicameral mind was a form of social control 'which allowed mankind to move from small hunter-gatherer groups to large agricultural communities'[16] then its elaboration into more modern forms of subjectivity was fundamentally a shift towards forms of individual self-control. Or to put it another way, it was a shift from an internalised but impersonal control of action to a personal, private form of psychological control in which an 'I' operates within its own 'internal space'. 'Like the queen in a termite nest or a beehive, the idols of a bicameral world', writes Jaynes, 'are the carefully tended centers of social control, with auditory hallucinations instead of pheramones.'[17] These auditory 'gods' of the bicameral mind were a consequence of the evolution of language and *were* man's volition. The neural basis for this was probably within the right hemisphere, and its social origin was the stores of admonitory and advisory experience accumulated within stable social hierarchies which 'told' the person what to do in any of the situations which he would encounter in his stable routinised world.

What would break the adaptiveness of this rigid psychological organisation and force reorganisation would be a shift from a stable predictable world to a turbulent one charged with novel survival demands. This, according to Jaynes, is precisely what happened between three and four thousand years ago, a millennium of profound and unprecedented upheaval. The increasing use of writing at governmental level eroded the auditory authority of the bicameral mind. But the real cause of its breakdown was, Jaynes argues, the spread of social chaos in which the gods could not tell people what to do since the problems confronting them were without precedent. The second millennium BCE, with its earthquakes and wars of unprecedented ferocity, with its collapse of civilisations and great movements of refugees, provided the awful challenging conditions which forced the development of a new mentality.

Deceit, for instance, which depends upon being in one's own 'internal space' in ways which are at variance with the face presented to an oppressor, aids the development of this inner space. The bifurcation of private and public ways of being a self becomes possible. 'Subjective consciousness, that is, the development on the basis of linguistic metaphors of an operation space in which an 'I' could narratize out alternative actions to their consequences, was of course the great world result of this dilemma,' asserts Jaynes.[18]

At the core of our consciousness is the metaphor of *time as a space* within which people and events can be located, where 'in front' and 'behind' give rise to ways of constructing and thinking about past, present and future. On the basis of changes in the content of inscriptions on Assyrian buildings, Jaynes speculatively dates this profound development to around 3, 300 years ago.[19] This metaphor of time as space opens up the very possibility of narrative. In the new post-bicameral mentality, this narrative power becomes the basis for imaginary positionings of myself as a subject within an idea of time that empowers me to shape myself in line with an anticipation of what I might be, and of enabling me to imagine the steps necessary to achieve this. Conceptions of interiority, privacy, reflectiveness, a sense of myself as a responsible subject capable of initiating my own actions, and a sense of unrealised but realisable possibilities for myself, are all features of the post-bicameral mind, as is the idea of personal responsibility. Jaynes, with engaging assurance, suggests that 'the true beginning of personal responsibility' can be seen in one of the fragments of Solon of Athens – 'the morning star of the Greek intellect' – who at the beginning of the sixth century BCE warns his fellow Athenians not to blame the gods for their woes but themselves.[20]

The transition from the bicameral mind, where the sources of action were centred in social locations but embodied in the proxy voices of 'gods', to the new consciousness where sources of action are now centred in the 'interior spaces' of self, was not absolute or clear-cut. Traces of bicamerality are still widespread in our times and in our cultures. They coexist with but are largely subservient to the universal elements of the succeeding consciousness, self-reference, mind-space, and narrative thinking. This new mentality is still evolving and one of its striking characteristics is the extent to which the taking of responsibility is increasingly individualised. 'We, we fragile human species at the end of the second millennium A.D.,' concludes Jaynes, 'we must become our own authorization.'[21]

It seems that self-creation is a consequence of holding the belief that I must assume responsibility for what sort of person I am to be. If I live in a culture where the idea that the best achievement of 'the good' is for me to absolutely obey those authorities who are taken to be the legitimate voices of that good, then self-creation will be understood as undesirable and discouraged. At the end of this century of totalitarian political systems and fundamentalist religious ones we should be quite familiar with what such a situation would look like, especially in the thrust of its educational and artistic policies. What I ought to be is what they say I ought to be. This would be a social climate favouring residual aspects of bicameral mentality such as a sort of moral automatonism among their citizenry, which is another way of saying that the central psychological forces controlling actions are located 'outside' self. But even if I felt myself to be free, that idea is itself an idea not of my own making. Is this a paradox? Does this mean that even here I am merely a vehicle for the transmission of some sort of *free choice meme*, perhaps fostered by the dynamic of consumerist capitalism, and to that extent 'occupied' by that free choice meme and therefore unfree?

There is no such thing as absolute freedom. We can be more or less free, but are always constrained by physical or social factors. Equally, the idea of 'creation' inherent in the idea of 'self-creation' is more Greek than Hebraic in the sense that it is relative; it is not the notion of making something out of nothing, but of changing what *is* into more or less of what it is. It may be original but it does not arise *ex nihilo*. Jaynes observes that 'History does not move by leaps into unrelated novelty, but rather by the selective emphasis of aspects of its own immediate past.'[22] It is similar with personal history and self-creation. Iliadic man as a type of bicameral man could not be said to be capable of self-creation; any change in the operations of an Iliadic warrior would be a consequence of what he heard himself instructed to do and the consequences of trying to do it. The prevailing beliefs of that culture did not nurture the sorts of psychological organisation that favoured or engendered self-responsible choosing. The historical emergence of the modern idea of self-creation, it seems to me, is the history of the emergence of the idea of self-responsible choosing understood as a good and desirable way of being.

This forms a backdrop for Charles Taylor's narrative of the modern identity as we encountered it in Chapter 4, and specifically for six aspects of that story: the developing idea of the 'inwardness' of self, the capacity for radical reflexiveness (an instance of metacognition in contemporary psychological parlance), the intrinsic creativity of language where meanings are made rather than found, the centrality of narrative for self-construction, the ideal of 'fulfilling' one's self, and the emergence of the idea of the artist as an exemplar of the modern ideal of self-fulfilment as self-creation. These are all interconnected constituents of the concept of the modern identity. Consider the ideal of the artist as a model of self-creation.

'Artistic creation', writes Charles Taylor, 'becomes the paradigm mode in which people can come to self-definition. The artist becomes in some way the paradigm case of the human being, as agent of original self-definition.'[23] The reason for this is that with the development of the sense of our selves as having 'interior depths', and with the decline of the moral authority of religious institutions or of elitist hierarchical political systems, the search for moral sources turns inwards. This intersects with a profound change over the last two hundred years or so in the nature of art, from a conception of art as mimetic to an idea of art as expressive. Mimetic art depended on an idea of the relationship of art to the world in terms of correspondence, with ideas of imitation and resemblance to the fore. Nature and the world were the sources of art. Expressive art depends on an idea of the relationship of the world to art in terms of constitution. Art comes to be about that which it makes, rather than about that which it imitates.

The mimetic idea of art changes alongside the growing sense from the eighteenth century onwards that 'each individual is different and original, and that this originality determines how he or she is to live' and, further, that these differences 'entail that each one of us has an original path which we ought to tread; they lay the obligation on each of us to live up to our originality.'[24] To fulfil this originality we must give it form, but that form is not independent of the means available to us to formulate it and make it manifest. Symbol and symbolised are integral and inseparable. I make my original nature in the act of giving it voice; I realise it in the act of articulating it. Nature is now 'within' self and our 'inner depths' become a profound source of meaning. 'We can only know what realizing our deep nature is when we have done it.'[25] As Taylor shows, this idea of 'expressive individuation' has become a hallmark of modern culture, not simply in terms of the centrality of individualism and subjectivity but politically at the level of, for instance, nationalism where the nation also has its own 'nature' struggling to find fulfilment in expression.

With the growing dominance of this expressivist idea in modern culture, art begins to compete with and, increasingly, to supplant religion as a moral source. 'The artist doesn't imitate nature so much as he imitates the author of nature . . . . By analogy,' writes Taylor, 'the work of art now doesn't so much manifest something visible beyond itself as constitute itself as the locus of manifestation.'[26] Encounters with art now carry the potential for revelatory or 'epiphanic' experience. If the shift from the mentality of the bicameral mind meant becoming our own gods by developing the sort of subjectivity whereby we could claim the 'admonitory voices' as elements of ourselves — as part of the internal conversation that is our stream of consciousness — then this was greatly augmented by subsequently incorporating and becoming governed by the idea that we are in crucial respects the authors of ourselves. This double divinisation underpins our modern belief that we are responsible for the creative realisation of our natures. Our own inner admonitory voices shape potential ideals for ourselves, and cajole, encourage and sustain us in the work necessary to realise them – 'you should . . .', 'why don't you . . .', 'wouldn't it be great if you succeeded in . . .', and so on.

We make ourselves in the act of making sense of ourselves. This is what Jonathan Glover means when he identifies self-creation with the stories we tell about ourselves, and, as we saw in Chapter 3, this is why Jerome Bruner sees self-narration as creative of the self we are and that which we wish to become. Of course, other conditions must be in place for even this partial self-creation to occur. I must believe that what I want to become is possible to achieve and I must want to do it; but I must also be enabled and allowed to do so or at the very least not prevented from doing it. Positive and negative freedom, in Isaiah Berlin's sense, are both necessary for self-creation, notwithstanding their potential for becoming dangerously antagonistic.[27] Such permissions to believe that I am free enough to make more or less of what I already am can be given by myself to myself, or by others to me. Ideas of self-creation work hand-in-glove with notions of freedom.

William James, for example, endured a deep depression in 1870 when he was 28 years old. One root of his depression lay in doubts about the possibility of free will. This is part of his diary entry for 30 April 1870:

> I think that yesterday was a crisis in my life. I finished the first part of Renouvier's second 'Essaies' and see no reason why his definition of Free Will – 'the sustaining of a thought *because I choose to* when I might have other thoughts' – need be the definition of an illusion. At any rate, I will assume for the present – until next year – that it is no illusion. My first act of free will shall be to believe in free will.

James goes on to write that he 'will go a step further with my will, not only act with it, but believe as well; believe in my individual reality and creative power.'[28]

Although never finally banished, this act did alleviate James's depression. Committing himself to incorporate his much-respected Renouvier's idea of free will into his sense of himself, albeit tentatively at first, empowered him at least to some extent to hold his depressive tendencies at bay.[29] Renouvier's formulation of the idea of free will, and James's embodiment of that belief, created a new location from which James could view the world, and with that shift of perspective came a change in his sense of himself within his world. This formed part of, in Taylor's words, a constitutive good since it commanded his respect and believing it empowered James to act and be in ways that were not otherwise possible. Self-belief has potential as self-fulfilling prophecy.

At a wider cultural level, not every culture includes a belief in the desirability of self-fulfilment as self-realisation. Many patriarchal, authoritarian cultures are actively hostile to this idea, particularly where girls and women are concerned. What is clear is that freedom, understood as what one can or could do, is, culturally, a moveable feast. Some cultures actively give their members the tools and permissions to make the sorts of choice which, in other cultures, would be judged totally unacceptable. Personal agency which incorporates the empowering ideal of self-creation tends to be cut from the same cloth as ideals of social and political freedom. Change the rules that people have to structure their psychology and you change that psychology, and with it the scope of the people to participate in its creation. How free people are, therefore, depends upon their positions within the ongoing conversation of their culture, and the skills at their disposal, rather than on some innate, aboriginal freedom. Change their location and self-interpretation, engender new skills, and you change the powers of a person as an agent.

There can be no creation or making without the expenditure of energy, without work. 'Consciously shaping our characteristics', observes Jonathan Glover, 'is self-creation.'[30] Conscious shaping of self involves forming an idea or image of the sort of person I want to be. This idea and my commitment to it influence the decisions I make about what I commit myself to, the activities on which I expend my energies. Of course many things that happen to us change us, but the question of self-creation is concerned with the sorts of effort that a person voluntarily makes to realise an idea of himself or herself. This notion of 'working on yourself' has become commonplace in Western culture, and it intersects with the ideal of the creative artist which, as we have seen, has become a moral source in our time.

Expressive work in the arts has as a key characteristic that it is dialogical in a particularly interesting way. Consciousness, as phenomenology emphasises, is always consciousness *of* something. When I think or feel or perceive, there is always an object for my thinking, feeling or perceiving (even if I cannot identify it, as in certain 'free-floating' phenomena). For most people most of the time what they are conscious of is something already available to them in some form or other and not of their own making.

In creative work, especially in good art (and we should remember that, like every other human activity, much art is of poor quality), the structure of artists' consciousness *as they work* is dynamically shaped by that on which they are working. That on which they are working, however, is not independently in existence. Work and worker here are mutually constitutive in an emergent process quite unlike that of routine, repetitive work. The materials with which artists work, the moment-by-moment decisions they make in shaping those materials, or in following newly apparent accidents of shape or form or feeling, influence the oncoming decisions in ways that do not pre-exist that particular temporal phase in the work. Maker and material (and that material can be almost anything) flow and change dialogically until that mysterious moment arrives when 'the work' is 'finished'. How the artist knows when that moment of 'completion' has arrived is another story.

This type of work where, on completion of the process of working, the doer is significantly changed as a consequence of doing, where the objective product somehow contains the producer in a way that is now publicly available ('That is a Hockney!'), is a highly valued and aspired-to ideal in the contemporary Western world. Optimally, artists' lives unfold to public esteem and, in parallel, their private lives grow ever richer with each objectification. With each successful 'work' they become 'other' to themselves, and therefore visible to themselves in a way that would not otherwise be possible. John Dewey was right to argue that the 'work of art' should not be taken to be the object as work, but rather the dynamic *relationship* of maker and made, and of receiver and made.[31] The ideal of self-creation, drawing on the ideal of creative art, has in the modern world become the ideal of a life understood as an unfolding project which only comes to personal conclusion with the death of creative consciousness. It is an ideal, in Marx's sense, of human labour.

Given the right conditions, and recognising that there is a continuum of potential, an ideal of self-fulfilment which involves powers of self-creation can become a universal aspiration within a framework of human rights. Even so, as Alan Gewirth reminds us, 'One's best is never finalised, but it can be more fully approached.'[32] That 'best', of course, is variable; to believe otherwise is to risk travelling along a path to one or other form of tyranny. I sympathise with Isaiah Berlin's assertion that pluralism 'is more humane because it does not (as the system-builders do) deprive men, in the name of some remote, or incoherent, ideal, of much that they have found to be indispensable to their life as unpredictably self-transforming human beings.'[33] This unpredictable creativity of self as both source and object is the hallmark of Jaynes's post-bicameral consciousness as it has evolved into the modern self.

Notes

1 J. Glover, *I: The Philosophy and Psychology of Personal Identity*, London, Penguin Books, 1989, pp. 154–5.

2 F. Ramsay, 'General Propositions and Causality' in *The Foundations of Mathematics and other Logical Essays*, London, 1931, p. 238. Quoted in Glover, op. cit., p. 154.

3 R. Harré, 'Language Games and Texts of Identity' in J. Shotter and K. J. Gergen (eds), *Texts of Identity*, London, Sage, 1989, p. 22.

4 Glover, op. cit., p. 152.

5 J. Jaynes, *The Origin of Consciousness in the Breakdown of the Bicameral Mind*, Boston, Houghton Mifflin Company, 1976. I chose to focus on Jaynes in this chapter specifically to highlight the idea that there is a history to the ways in which people think of themselves as being responsible. For more recent and compelling accounts of the origins of the modern mind as such see, for example, M. Donald, *Origins of the Modern Mind: Three Stages in the Evolution of Culture and Cognition*, Cambridge, Mass., Harvard University Press, 1991.

6 Jaynes, op cit., p. 292. Daniel Dennett forcefully argues for the power of ideas in cultural evolutionary terms: 'Our *selves* have been created out of the interplay of memes exploiting and redirecting the machinery Mother Nature has given us . . . . [W]hat makes a person the person he or she is are the coalitions of memes that govern – that play the long-term roles in determining which decisions are made along the way.' See *Darwin's Dangerous Idea*, New York, Simon & Schuster, 1995, p. 367–8.

7 Ibid., p. 431.

8 Ibid., p. 46.

9 Ibid., pp. 65–6.

10 Ibid., p. 134.

11 For more recent work on this idea of language as controlling and maintaining work over time see A. Clark and A. Karmiloff-Smith, 'The Cognizer's Innards: A Psychological and Philosophical Perspective on the Development of Thought'. *Mind & Language*, vol.8, 1994, pp. 487–519.

12 For a fascinating account of the psychological consequences of writing see David Olson, *The World on Paper*, Cambridge, Cambridge University Press, 1994.

13 Jaynes, op. cit., pp. 73–4.

14 Ibid., p. 112.

15 Ibid., p. 260.

16 Ibid., p. 126.

17 Ibid., p. 144

18 Ibid., p. 236.

19 Ibid., p. 250.

20 Ibid., pp. 287–8.

21 Ibid., p. 438.

22 Ibid., p. 228.

23 C. Taylor, *The Ethics of Authenticity*, Cambridge, Mass., Harvard University Press, 1991, p. 62.

24 C. Taylor, *Sources of the Self: The Making of the Modern Identity*, Cambridge, Mass., Harvard University Press, 1989, p. 375.

25 Ibid., p. 376.

26 Ibid., pp. 377–8.

27 I. Berlin, 'Two Concepts of Liberty' in Henry Hardy and Roger Hausheer (eds), *The Proper Study of Mankind: An Anthology of Essays*, London, Pimlico, 1998.

28 J. J. McDermott (ed.), *The Writings of William James*, New York, The Modern Library, 1968, pp. 7–8.

29 G. E. Myers, *William James: His Life and Thought*, New Haven, Conn., Yale University Press, 1986, p. 47.

30 Glover, op. cit., p. 131.

31 J. Dewey, *Art as Experience*, New York, Capricorn Books G. P. Putnam's Sons, 1958.
32 A. Gewirth, *Self-Fulfillment*, Princeton, NJ, Princeton University Press, 1998, p. 227.
33 Berlin, op. cit., p. 242.

6

PRONOUNS PLACING SELVES

'I' and its associates

We are a grandmother.

(Mrs Thatcher)

But reference to self and to the states of self requires far more than a lexicon of self-reference, even more than the shifter requirements that govern pronominal discourse (I am 'I' when I am speaking; I am 'you' when you are). For self is also defined and delineated in situated speech by its location in discourse and by the role it plays in the social world in which the participants believe themselves to be operating.

(J. Bruner, *The Culture of Education*, 1996, p. 109)

Personal pronouns – 'I', 'you', 'us', 'them' and their siblings throughout world languages – are universally felt to be somewhere at the 'centre' of self. Julian Jaynes, as we saw in Chapter 5, identifies the metaphorical creation of a mind-space within which the 'analog I' could metaphorically move as the revolutionary step on the way to consciousness, self and subjectivity as we know it. Without the development of language, of course, and the possible social relations that its uses enable, none of this could happen. 'Language may not be the source of the self, but it certainly is the source of the "I"', writes Antonio Damasio.[1] This is another way of saying that the social and psychological fact and use of pronouns as key elements of self have to be understood culturally. Bearing in mind that James Strachey translated Freud's 'I' as 'ego', Freud concluded that 'Where id (It) was, there ego (I) shall be. It is a work of culture – not unlike the draining of the Zuider Zee.'[2]

The primary function of pronouns, like that of names, is locative. Knowing who you are and where you stand at any point in time are the most important tasks of selfhood. In answer to the question 'Who are you?' you are likely to offer your name. 'I am Vivienne Murphy,' you might say, 'and I am the sister of Kate who is giving the party. I am also your daughter's teacher.' With each answer you locate yourself in a network of relations in such a way as to say something significant about your social identity. You might go on to speak about your family, your political activities, your views on particular issues, your interests and dislikes, and so on. For your interlocutor, your identity clarifies with each additional piece of information. You might feel that, even with all the information you have given, he has not grasped your identity in the way you would have liked: you have not, you might feel, *impressed* him. 'Nice meeting you,' he might say and walk away having lost interest in you. What you are, you might think, does not sum up who you are.

Most of the issues of self with which Rom Harré has engaged are contained in this simple introduction. The focus is on issues of identity. My personal identity, who I am for myself, is different from my social identity, who I am for others. Until recently psychology has focused mainly on social identity but Harré is particularly interested in personal identity.[3] Social identity is about what *sort* of person I am, my social class, position in the family, job, attitudes, relative level of self-esteem and so on. Psychological ideas of self-concept are in practice mostly ideas of social identity, albeit my own version of my social identity. Personal identity is about what it is like to be uniquely me as I am for myself.

'Self' is used in a variety of different ways by psychologists and social scientists and it is important to distinguish them. It is closely connected to the concept 'person'. Harré distinguishes three categories of use of self, as part of what he calls the 'standard model' of personal identity. 'Person' means me in my unique, embodied, unanalysable, public, singular being, as I am for myself and for other people. A person is a distinctive, physical entity, and clearly identifiable as such. Being treated as a person is what gives rise to the development of 'self'. But 'self' is not an entity like 'person'.

The uses of the word 'self' show that it refers not to some thing but to various processes, 'to attributes of the flow of personal action, and to the skills, powers and dispositions a person must have so as to act'.[4] Harré speaks of Self 1, 2 and 3 when indicating which process is the focus of attention. If the spotlight is on *how the world seems to me* from my point of view, situated as I seem to be at the centre of a web of relationships that make up my world, then he calls this 'Self 1'. Thomas Nagel's description of subjectivity as 'how things are for me' is very close to this and allows us to think of Harré's 'Self 1' as referring to the subjective dimensions of self in this Nagelian sense.[5] A concern with the nature and uses of 'I' would to a large degree be an interest in the 'Self 1' process. 'I' and subjectivity are symbiotic. But self is also about what we know, think, believe, value about ourselves as persons. 'My' qualities and characteristics, 'my' self-concept, my 'story', 'me' with all my attributes, are processes encompassed by 'Self 2'. 'Self 3' refers to the characteristics which I present to other people, and to what other people take me to be.

These aspects of self are all quite different, if interlocked. It is the nature of the questions being asked that picks out one or other of them and makes that particular process of self salient at that time. One of the uses of this taxonomy is that it clarifies whether 'self' should be thought of as singular or as potentially multiple. As a human being you can normally be only the one person, perceiving and acting from one position in space and time, with your own distinctive life trajectory. But there could be more variety and diversity from time to time and place to place in the make-up of 'me', and then it might be reasonable to argue that a person could have more than one 'Self 2'. And clearly there may be many 'Self 3s' given that we all have changing repertoires for how we present ourselves to other people, and the ways in which other people interpret those presentations of self may be volatile and vary greatly from one circumstance to another. Harré's governing understanding of selfhood is this:

> We create our minds *ad hoc* in the course of carrying on our lives. Stabilities and unities in these creations create the illusion of inner selves, but they have no more independent existence than the selves we produce *ad hoc* for others, which they may or may not confirm, and so bring more concretely into existence. At most this array of selves has the status of a vortex in the flow of the river.[6]

What these metaphorical vortices rotate around, we might say, are *pronouns in use*. What they rotate in is the ongoing stream of experience (in John Dewey's relational sense) or of endless conversation (in Harré's sense) that is the flow of human life. How is our understanding of selfhood advanced by observing that 'I' am a pronoun *in use*? First of all, we need to avoid the idea of 'a user' as some entity if we want to escape the trap of dualism. Instead we can follow the idea that the conditions of pronoun usage are essentially *social* conditions. The locus of agency when 'I' is deployed in its various ways is not to be found in proto-agents such as a shadowy Cartesian ego. Agency, instead, is substantially rooted in social processes, of which the relevant psychological processes, it is argued, are derivatives. These are uniquely human, linguistically based processes of questioning, ownership, and authorship. They are the social foundations for such powerful convictions as that these are *my* thoughts, that *I* am the owner of my body, and that the ultimate source of these actions is *me*. The neurological basis for this conviction of ownership may well be that form of representation hypothesised by Damasio as connecting the organism in change to the object changing it.

This description helps explain why it is only intermittently that I am self-conscious as a subject who is a questioner, owner or author. It is only from time to time that I am called upon, or call upon myself, to answer questions that require locutions like 'I think that' or 'I believe that', or to acknowledge ownership of relationships, desires, possessions, or to claim responsibility or authorship of some object or action. These processes of questioning, ownership, and authorship arise from within social relationships and are at the heart of personal psychology. Each is a fundamental way of positioning its speaker/thinker in social, moral, intellectual, or legal spaces and of identifying her or him as a person of a certain kind. They define personal and social identities.

To say that 'I' am a pronoun in use, then, is to say that 'I' denotes processes rather than entities. It is to argue that these processes are those of ownership and authorship which are called into play in the first place by acts of questioning. 'I have' and 'I do' are the mainstays of all kinds of identity and selfhood. They give rise to their contraries such as 'I have not' and 'I don't do' and also to moral elaborations like 'I cannot have' or 'I must do' as well as to elaborations of desire like 'I want' or 'I wish'.

Only in symbolic fields of intersubjectivity can elaborated subjectivities of ownership, authorship, morality and desire arise. Only by being adept in skills of positioning, of which forms of pronoun use are primary, can I come into being *as* an owner, author, moral agent or location of desire for future possibilities. Contrariwise, it is only within social worlds that I can change or leave one kind of ownership, authorship, responsibility or desire for another. Forms of selfhood come in and out of existence in dialogue with forms of intersubjective demand. The corollary is that forms of subjectivity transform themselves in parallel with changes in ambient intersubjectivity. This is why it is so important to understand the micro-development of skills in pronoun use and to follow the micro-analyses of pronoun usage in the analyses of various discourses. Subjecthood, agency, responsibility and desire all pivot on such skills.

Let us return to our opening scene at the party and pursue some of the issues raised by Harré and his work on self. That scene begins with talk and a question which presupposes a questioner, an 'addressee' and a social context in which such a question is legitimate. The tools enabling the question to be asked and answered are linguistic and already within the repertoire of most three-year-olds. Names and pronouns like 'I' and 'you' are central as are the acts in which they find their meaning, *speech acts*, such as 'questions' and 'answers'.[7] Vivienne Murphy's sense of herself as real and uniquely herself and no other person is unquestionable. Her interlocutor is passingly interested in her social identity (self 2 and 3) but not in her personal identity (self 1). Murphy's feeling that there is more to her than her uninterested interlocutor allows may make her feel peeved. Finally, there is the seemingly obvious fact that if she or her questioner had no language at all to use, then this brief interlude simply could not have *been*. It is, however, in the unmasking of the obvious that really productive questions come to be asked.

Harré is frequently misunderstood as saying that self is a mere wraith and that viewing it as he does eliminates what we feel to be the most important aspects of ourselves. This misunderstanding can be summarised in a series of questions: If self is merely a product of discourse, fabricated in and through people's joint uses of language, and if my sense of myself as a 'real entity' is only a shadow cast by the grammar of the language of self, then am 'I' not simply a shadow without solidity or 'real' existence? Does this theory of self not imply that self is merely an evanescent product of language, a shadow shorn of autonomy which could not then be held responsible for its actions? If so, wouldn't this account simply remove that freedom which is the ground of human dignity and leave the field open to a relativistic nihilism where anything goes? None of these conclusions flow from Harré's theory.

In fact, one could understand what he is trying to do as a concerted effort to show how cultural practices of making selves, through narrative discourses, differ in the real powers that they enable individuals, as partial authors of their own lives, to have. Some societies value the individual as a responsible co-creator of her own life and work to give her the skills and values to do this, thereby building in her powers of autonomy and choice. Others require and produce selves that largely reproduce what they have become without the sense of need or the ability to change the model.

Harré's work addresses some of these issues. His theory of self is rooted in the work of Lev Vygotsky and Ludwig Wittgenstein. To Vygotsky he attributes an understanding of how language moves *into* the person by showing how learning one's mother tongue helps to organise the private 'inner' discourse which is mind.[8] Vygotsky took seriously what is obvious to every parent, namely that the incessant stream of talking which characterises most two-year-olds is in fact the doing of their thinking 'out loud' and publicly. By the time they get to four years of age they have developed the ability to do much of this silently and privately. Outer speech has become inner speech, and the shape of mind is greatly influenced by the structure of the conversation in which the child has been immersed. The private is structured, at least in key higher level respects, publicly.

From Wittgenstein Harré takes his framework for understanding how language allows us to move *out* of ourselves.[9] Wittgenstein's 'Private Language Argument' shows how our language for private feeling must in principle be established publicly, and this public source of subjectivity enables apparently isolated minds to know each other. Wittgenstein also showed how psychology makes mistakes by failing to notice how psychological terms are used in many different senses in everyday speech. One common error, which we have already noted, is to assume that because you have a name or other noun ('self', for example) there must be some thing or entity to which it refers. Psychological words find their meaning in specific contexts of human conduct. Wittgenstein called these activities-in-context 'language games'.

This combination of approaches to language and self, the Vygotskian and the Wittgensteinian, provides the foundation on which Harré builds his idea of self as

a product of discourse. It allows him, especially when asking questions about the development of self, to suggest how the private structures of subjectivity arise from and are shaped by public discourses (where 'discourse' means the intentional and jointly coordinated use by people of language). The 'inside', so to speak, begins 'outside' and always retains the dynamics of its public origins. Even in solitude the person is essentially social. These dynamics are those of conversation with its own speakers, voices, positions, stances, intentions, agendas and histories. Unifying such complex living conversations, as we have seen with Bruner, is the challenge to autobiographical narratives.

Pronouns entail location. Who you are is a function of where you are, where you have been and where you want to be. You can occupy positions by circumstance of birth, say, or by your own choice. Understanding this means adopting a different sort of ontology – a different set of conceptual building blocks for the idea of 'the psychological' – than that assumed by traditional scientific psychology.[10] This new ontology sees 'the psychological' as being significantly located in arrays of people in which the units are speech acts. The relations to be unravelled by psychology would then be, to a large extent, conventional rules and storylines.

The sorts of 'place' that selves can meet and be are always places of meaning, meaning which is social in origin and symbolic in form. We need some sort of image to pull together what is involved here, what Susanne Langer called a generative metaphor. One that crops up regularly is that of a 'network' or 'web'. 'Each link created by a meeting', writes Theodore Zeldin, 'is like a filament which, if they were all visible, would make the world look as though it is covered with gossamer.'[11] There is this vast conversation going on, its now unimaginably complex webs wrapping the globe. It is made by individuals, used by them, maintained by them, developed by them, but greater than them. Users of the internet come into being *as users* and as *persons* at intersections in the networks. They key in, gain access to a section of the web, communicate, and exist for those others who are part of this particular communication. Portions of the net become visible and audible for them –' real' – and they for it. Then they log off and exit the conversation and are no longer in the network. Now they are somewhere else, talking to their family perhaps, located at the intersection of another conversational web made by and binding together another array of people.

Using the image of a 'web' or 'net' or even 'a swarm' to understand the symbolic worlds of humans, and understanding that individual people occupy different and varying positions in these webs, gives rise to the idea that to be a 'person' is to be a location at an intersection of discourses. Being a 'self' is a 'skill' in occupying such positions. Harré is not saying that we are nothing but complex ciphers temporarily and unstably existing at various nodal points of cultural networks. Of course, for those that think self is substantial in a Cartesian sense then, short of abandoning that position, the idea that self has its being in 'a web of interlocution' will remain implausible. For the non-Cartesian, this view of self gains in cogency as we answer this question: Do newborn babies 'have a sense of self'?

Self involves a combined sense of centredness, agency and autobiography. One needs language to develop the sort of sense of self that involves these skills of self-consciousness. There are precursors of these elements of self very early in infancy, but there is no sense of being centred as an 'I' with agentic powers nor with powers of reflection which focus on represented aspects of oneself. Without skills in the use of 'I', without self-consciousness, without a narrated sense of continuity we can say that newborns *have* no sense of self. Personal identity is the outcome of a long period of socialisation and development. Does this mean that newborn babies are not *persons*?

Because newborn babies cannot be said to have a sense of self this does not imply that babies are not persons. Personhood is a moral attribution not a psychological category. Babies, like the rest of us, are granted the status of personhood by other people. With personhood, as modern understanding has it, come rights and responsibilities. Personhood is a social-moral category which concerns how we are positioned or located in the array of other people, and it is one which is crucial for the developmental psychology of self.

In normal circumstances what happens when a baby is born? It is 'taken over' by its parents and minders. Right from the beginning, it is treated *as* a person. It is addressed face-to-face, talked to, handled, and generally *included* in the family and its world. Very quickly, for example, it is named. The choosing of a name is not done lightly by parents who implicitly know the subtle semiotic powers that are attached to names. They know that it is by one's name that one is *called* and located in human networks for the rest of one's life. Names carry information about all sorts of social positions such as sex, nationality, class, parental sense of familial history, parental sense of national history, parental attitudes to conventional naming practices, and so on. Vivienne Murphy, for example, would not expect to be mistaken for an Egyptian woman just as Fatima El-Hitami is unlikely to be an Irish man; Fifi-Trixibell Murphy is a different sort of parental statement than Mary Murphy; and Karl Marx Murphy positions a son in a different associative network than would John Paul Murphy.

From the beginning babies are addressed by personal names and treated as though they possessed personal psychologies. Quickly, we believe, they emerge from a fog of sensation into the ever-clarifying light of perception. And all the time they are surrounded by talk and have their names spoken as they are being *called to attention*. Following Vygotsky, Harré's argument is that it is by virtue of being treated as a person that one develops self; that the developing intrapersonal world of the private is fashioned along the lines of the interpersonal world of the public; and that the materials and methods by which private and public psychologies are fabricated are symbolic.

A concept from René Spitz, psychological symbiosis, which describes a permanent interactive relationship between two people in which one supplements the psychological attributes of the other, comes into play here. The effect of this symbiosis with parents and others is that the baby appears as a complete and competent social and psychological being.[12] This is similar to the sort of tutoring that Vygotsky envisaged occurring in his 'zone of proximal development' and for which Bruner uses the idea of 'social scaffolding'. What this means is that mothers don't simply talk about their babies' wishes, feelings, intentions and so on. They *supply* them for the infants, and then relate to them as though it were the babies who possessed them, as though they 'liked', 'wanted', 'asked for', 'intended', 'disapproved', 'changed their minds', and generally 'understood'.

This is the currency of adults' 'baby-talk'. The 'as though' nature of this sort of talk in which infants are treated as though they were persons with a clear social position and a developed psychological being, is what creates for them the experience of being just such persons. In this milieu, although their personhood begins as a very large outsize, they grow into it by developing just those competencies which they have been treated as having. A sense of self is the most sophisticated of these competencies and one which allows for a very adaptive organisation of experience, one anchored by the various processes comprising 'self'.

A developing awareness of the world needs a means of locating and stabilising one's own position in it. For reasons of adaptive economy alone this is necessary. William James rightly insisted that an awareness of the body and its boundaries lies at the heart of all such locational efforts. It is by our bodies that others recognise and identify us. Courts of law depend on it, as the belated trial in Israel of John Demianjuk, and many other alleged war criminals, graphically illustrates. But if the body always had to be present and perceptible for identification of a person to occur this would greatly restrict communication. This may be fine in the world of cats or horses, but it is not in the world of humans. In a symbolic world other indices of personal presence and responsiblity are needed to locate and track people.

Names are the first of these. More complex and articulate are the system of words that stand in for names, pronouns. The length of time it takes a child to master the skills of pronoun use is a clear indication of the complexity of the social skills involved. There is nothing much in the phonetic difference between 'eye' and 'I', but it takes much longer to master the use of the latter. That is because language acquisition is much more than vocabulary and syntax. It is also about the pragmatic use of language, its rootedness and functions in society. The reason autistic children have such difficulties with personal pronouns like 'I' is that it is probably an associated feature of their difficulty in forming a view of other people's minds. Uta Frith was one of the first to observe that

> pronoun use improves when reciprocal social interactions improve. This relationship suggests that autistic children's difficulties in pronoun use are not specific but have the same root as their other difficulties in social interaction. This root could well be a poor conceptualization of their own and others' mental states.[13]

Blind children's apparent slowness in acquiring pronoun skills, as was mentioned before, may have to do with the amount of visual information that goes into specifying the positioning that underpins pronoun use. The sign language of deaf people suggests this. American Sign Language, for example, uses the bodies of the speakers as 'sign spaces' and different spatial positions locate different pronouns. 'You' is front-centre, a third person is signed to the right, another to the left, and others to the space between. Once a person is assigned a space in a conversation it continues to be reserved for that person for the duration of the conversation.[14]

This introduces visually the idea of indexicality. Indexicals are words of position, and derive from the Greek *deixis* meaning 'pointing'. Roman Jakobson called them 'shifters' because their meaning is tied to the context in which they are used and so can shift with a change of context.[15] 'There' can become 'here', 'now' can become 'then', 'this' can become 'that', 'you' for me becomes 'I' for you. These words are indexed to the situation. Personal pronouns, more specifically, are indexed to speakers and their interlocutors.

In addition to indexing position they can index relative status and distance in social relationship. 'Vous' and 'sie' in French and German indicate respectful formality, 'tu' and 'du' familiarity and friendship. When Mrs Thatcher appropriated the royal 'we' for the 'We are a grandmother' pronouncement there was in Britain a national knowing nod. When Clint Eastwood says 'I wouldn't do that' we know he is not talking of himself. When I have repeated a stupid mistake I might 'hear myself' saying 'Idiot! You've done it again.' And when a concentration camp survivor says 'After about three weeks I began to think of myself in the third person' we know the awful depersonalisation to which he was subjected. At a more abstract but psychologically important level there is the idea of 'One' as in 'One doesn't do that!' George Herbert Mead, another important predecessor of cultural psychology, calls this 'the generalized other'. It is implicit in a sign on the lawns of a country hotel near Dublin which reads 'Ladies and gentlemen will not and others ought not pick the flowers!'

> The Japanese, it seems, have the most elaborate indexical system such that if two Japanese people used all the pronouns and verb inflections

available to them in their language they could represent something like 260 different social relations between them.[16]

In English there is a developmental sequence in which first-person personal pronouns are typically acquired. Initially young children are likely to label themselves as 'baby' ('Baby want') but by 21–24 months most can use their own names. Somewhere in the middle of the second year they begin to use personal pronouns. By three years of age most children refer to pictures of themselves using their own names and the appropriate personal pronouns. If we include the possessive pronoun, a typical sequence of use would be 'mine', 'me', 'I', which itself suggests a move from the public to the private. With the ability to organise experience in terms of 'I' as 'subject' and 'me' as object comes the scope for 'I–me' relationships, for self-consciousness. This enables Harré's Self 2 and Self 3 to develop, as it does Damasio's autobiographical self.

It is not by instruction that the child achieves mastery of the use of 'I' in the third year. A moment's thought will show the knots you would tie yourself in trying to formally teach this: '*You* should say *I* when *you* want *me* – that is *you* to *you* but *I* to *me* – to know that *you* are speaking . . .!' The child is always addressed by her name or as 'you', but by age three most children know the difference between 'I' and 'you', 'my' and 'yours', and can use them appropriately. They become competent in the use of first-person pronouns ('I', 'me', 'my') earlier than second-person ones ('you', 'your').

The reason for this is probably, as Maureen Cox suggests, that the child first *understands* the pronouns which other people use to address her ('you', 'yourself', 'yours') and later comes to understand those by which she refers to herself ('I', 'me'). But when she comes to *use* them herself, it is those that refer to herself that she uses first, and only later those that refer to other people. This asymmetry between understanding and use may have to do with the number of referents. When spoken to as 'you' the child is the only referent, but 'I' as used refers to many speakers. But when she comes to use 'I' she is the only referent and 'you' refers to many people.[17]

Learning how to use pronouns is also learning about other minds, other selves. Charlotte Linde puts it like this:

> To understand the shifter nature of *I* is to come to comprehend that others exist in one's world who have the same nature and who must be seen as separate but fellow beings. This is an important step forward into humanity. Pronouns are thus a central linguistic resource for establishing the self.[18]

In time the child also develops the ability to detach the meaning of words in general from the situations to which they apply. This meta-linguistic awareness in which a word can be liberated from its referent is evident around eight years of age. But what referent can 'I' be liberated from? If 'I' has no entity as a referent but is instead a 'noun of position', to use William James's phrase, then what would be involved in liberating 'I' from its context and position?

After this excursion into the developmental psychology of English pronoun acquisition (there are huge differences between the pronoun systems in world languages with corresponding consequences for local psychologies of self[19]) we are now ready to see how Harré places personal pronouns at the centre of his theory of self as a discursive production. His argument is this:

> Since 'myself' is not a thing I could discover, it seems I cannot first experience myself and then attach the personal pronoun 'I' to that experience. I must be learning the pronoun system as a whole through the ways in which and the means by which I am treated as a person by others. So that, by being treated as 'you', or as a member of 'we' I am now in a position to add 'I' to my vocabulary, to show where, in the array of persons, speaking, thinking, feeling, promising, and so on, is happening.[20]

This of course depends on my having a recognisable physical identity, my body. Harré's conclusion is that since self is not something I find but rather a very complex *idea* which I acquire in the course of my social development and tutoring by other more competent people, like parents, then its status is that of a *theory*. Key elements of this theory include unifying constructs like 'myself', and 'I' as source of action and viewpoint. Once the child masters the complexities involved in correctly using 'I' she has achieved a new and lastingly efficient way of organising experience.

Just as a sentence has a subject and a predicate, with 'I' as the key construct in the now completed pronominal referencing system, the child is at this point truly a subject capable of predicating everything else to herself. 'I think', 'I see', 'I move', 'I want', 'I feel', 'I was', 'I will be', and so on become skills constantly deployed in the moment-by-moment episodes of conscious life, both intraper-sonal and interpersonal. Every thought, as Kant and James point out, has 'I think' as part of it. Once mastered as a skill 'I' becomes omnipresent. It is always part of 'here' and 'now' and it is to 'I-in-the-here-and-now' that all other thoughts and perceptions are invariably referred, however implicitly. All the many threads of life are knotted *at* the point occupied by 'I' and all stories told are told *from* this moving vantage point.

This is how 'I' become the centre of my own life and my own story. That this point incessantly changes right up to the demise of the ability to use 'I' – as, for example, in the tragedies of dementias like Alzheimer's Disease – and that people still maintain a sense of their own stability is a marvel of human psychology, and a marvellous challenge to students of that psychology. No wonder people, assuming that 'I' as a noun refers to an entity of some kind, come to believe that such an entity as 'myself' is omnipresent and 'behind' and 'separate from' every thought, perception and feeling. 'I' is always present not because it is a thing but because in the course of individual development every thought, perception and feeling, to be part of the system of experience that is 'mine', must be allocated to it by the symbolic skills of 'I think'. Part of the task of every 'present thought' in James's view is, as we noted earlier, to appropriate its predecessor and so maintain continuity and the sense of my ownership of experience.

The source of the belief that 'I' is an entity is the shadow cast by the grammar of 'I'. It is in this sense that Harré points to the significance of where in the intersection of communication you find yourself, and it is in this sense that he proposes thinking of self as a skill of the highest complexity, rather than a substance of some kind. The development of the capacity to correctly use 'I' marks the emergence of that 'privileged center of reference within the field of givenness' which for William James also is self.

Self and location can be seen, once again, to be inextricably and intrinsically connected. 'To have a sense of one's personal individuality,' in Harré's view, 'is to have a sense of having a place or places in various . . . systems of location.'[21] Key systems of location are those to do with where I am in space (my point of view), where I am in unfolding time (including my sense of the present moment and of my life as a continuity through time), where I am in the moral universe of other people and living things (my responsibilities, mutual obligations, commitments), and finally my social place (my status, age, occupation, reputation).

My sense of who I am is tied to where I am since it is from such places that I perceive and act, and also where I am perceived to be. I can of course occupy places in a number of locative systems simultaneously. For any particular episode of experience, I occupy a position in place–time. Depending on the discourse I will speak or think from a social position as a teacher or son or defendant. Finally, as we saw from Charles Taylor's work, I speak from some moral position where my identity is further defined by what I am committed to and responsible for.

This question of my positioning as a moral person brings us back to the mistaken view of Harré's work as potentially nihilistic. If we are not to think of ourselves as substantial beings whose freedom somehow attaches from the beginning of life to the nature of that mental/spiritual substance, but rather as symbolic beings who emerge in the course of individual development partly under the aegis of an unfolding biology but largely by occupying positions in the various social-symbolic orders of discourse, how are we to account for the sense of freedom to which everyone, to a greater or lesser degree, can attest?

Julian Jaynes, Daniel Dennett and many others warn us that it is a mistake to think that theoretical ideas like 'self' are powerless simply because they are abstractions. All ideas, selves included, are part of much wider systems, and derive their powers from the positions they occupy and roles they play in these systems. Dennett puts this well:

> The fact that these abstract selves seem so robust and real is not surprising. They are much more complicated theoretical entities than a centre of gravity. And remember that even a centre of gravity has a fairly robust presence once we start playing around with it. But no one has ever seen or ever will see a centre of gravity.[22]

Human freedom is always constrained. The field of choices available to people varies enormously, and many of us are lucky that we have not had the limited menu of choice available to other less fortunate people, and which has shaped the entire moral bases of their lives. In the cultural psychological view, freedom is not some mysterious given but rather a consequence of skills one has developed, and these skills further depend on the beliefs and commitments which help constitute one's personal identity. Human freedom, on this view, is not something one has but something one can do and is allowed to do. And what you can do depends on your resources, your skills in deploying them and the possibilities available for deploying them.

Far from removing the idea of freedom from self, cultural psychology is actively trying to account for what it takes to be free, for the fact that people believe they are free to lift their arms or not, or to accept this evaluation of themselves or not. Harré and Gillett explicitly assert that

> The task for discursive theories of agency is therefore to reinsert the agent into the story, the one who initiates the action, the one who, in some way, is significant in giving meaning to what he or she does and who they are.[23]

This is achieved by analysing the ways in which people acquire the rules by which to shape their conduct, the nature of these rules, how they vary from time to time and place to place, and the ways in which individuals come to apply them to regulate and shape their own actions. It is an inquiry into human powerfulness rather than into human powerlessness.

The ideal psychological life from the cultural psychological perspective of the present time is one with the character of an artistic project where the meaning of a life is no more summarisable in words than a symphony or a painting but which is nonetheless discernible to connoisseurs of living. Which is why it is appropriate to conclude this essay with a comment from an artist. In his last piece of writing before he died of AIDS the American novelist Harold Brodkey wrote: 'My identity is as a raft skidding or gliding, borne on a flux of feelings and frights, including the morning's delusion (which lasts 10 minutes some-times) of being young and whole.'[24] Towards the end of the piece he writes of himself

> standing on an unmoored raft, a punt moving on the flexing, flowing face of a river. It is precarious. I don't know what I am doing. The unknowing, the taut balance, the jolts and the instability spread in widening ripples through all my thoughts.[25]

Being moored, learning to moor oneself and being unmoored is a good summary of the trajectory of self and the problem of navigating a human life.

Notes

1 A. Damasio, *Descartes' Error: Emotion, Reason and the Human Brain*, London, Papermac, 1996, p. 243.
2 S. Freud, *The Complete Introductory Lectures on Psychoanalysis*, trans. and ed. J. Strachey, London, George Allen & Unwin, 1971, Lecture 31, p. 544.
3 See R. Jenkins, *Social Identity*, London, Routledge, 1996.
4 R. Harré, *The Singular Self: An Introduction to the Psychology of Personhood*, London, Sage, 1998, p. 148.
5 T. Nagel, *Mortal Questions*, Cambridge, Cambridge University Press, 1979.
6 Harré, op. cit., p. 178.
7 For this Harré is indebted to J. L. Austin, *How to Do Things with Words*, Oxford, Clarendon Press, 1962.
8 L. Vygotsky, *Thought and Language*, Cambridge, Mass., MIT Press and Wiley, 1962.
9 L. Wittgenstein, *Philosophical Investigations* (2nd edn), eds G. E. M. Anscombe and R. Rhees, trans. G. E. M. Anscombe, Oxford, Basil Blackwell, 1958.
10 R. Harré and G. Gillett, *The Discursive Mind*, London, Sage, 1994, p. 29.
11 T. Zeldin, *An Intimate History of Humanity*, London, Minerva, 1995, pp. 465–6.
12 R. Harré, *Personal Being*, Oxford, Basil Blackwell, 1983, p. 105. See also R. Spitz, *The First Year of Life*, New York, International Universities Press, 1965.
13 U. Frith, 'A New Look at Language and Communication in Autism', *British Journal of Disorders of Communication*, 24, 1989, p. 136.
14 D. Crystal, *The Cambridge Encyclopedia of Language*, Cambridge, Cambridge University Press, 1989, p. 222.
15 R. Jakobson, *Russian and Slavic Grammar: Studies, 1931–1981*, eds L. Waugh and M. Halle, The Hague, Mouton, 1984.
16 Harré and Gillett, *The Discursive Mind*, p. 105.
17 M. V. Cox, *The Child's Point of View*, Brighton, The Harvester Press, 1986, p. 74.

18 C. Linde, *Life Stories: The Creation of Coherence*, Oxford, Oxford University Press, 1993, p. 112.
19 P. Mühlhäusler and R. Harré, *Pronouns and People*, Oxford, Basil Blackwell, 1993.
20 Harré, *Personal Being*, p. 211.
21 Harré and Gillett, *The Discursive Mind*, p. 103.
22 D. Dennett, 'Why Everyone is a Novelist', *Times Literary Supplement*, 16–22 September 1988, pp. 1016, 1028–9. For an extended treatment of this idea see D. Dennett, *Consciousness Explained*, London, Allen Lane The Penguin Press, 1991.
23 Harré and Gillett, *The Discursive Mind*, p. 117.
24 H. Brodkey, 'Passage into non-existence', *Independent on Sunday*, 11 February 1996, p. 10.
25 Ibid., p. 11.

7

FEELING YOUR WAY

Emotions as self's pathfinders

At their best, feelings point us in the proper direction, take us to
the appropriate place in a decision-making space, where we may
put the instruments of logic to good use. We are faced by
uncertainty when we have to make a moral judgment, decide on
the course of a personal relationship, choose some means to pre-
vent our being penniless in old age, or plan for the life that lies
ahead. Emotion and feeling, along with the covert physiological
machinery underlying them, assist us with the daunting task of
predicting an uncertain future and planning our actions
accordingly.

(Antonio Damasio, *Descartes' Error*, 1996, p. xv)

Feelings tell us where we are and what is happening to us. They are also the
traces of where we have been and of what has happened to us there. If we advance
gropingly we do so with the aid of our feelings. Whether we are moving through
the worlds of perception or through the infinitely rich symbolic worlds of meaning collectively created by ourselves – our cultures – we must have systems of
navigation in place if we are not to lose our way and become disoriented or lost.
Sometimes the paths forward are already there to be found, but some of the time
we must simultaneously assist in the making of new territory and in the construction of novel paths through it. Some of the best contemporary work on emotion
can be understood as elaborating the ways in which feeling and emotions act as
self's pathfinders through human landscapes both familiar and unfamiliar. The
concept of 'the familiar' is a good place to start in reviewing some of this work.

Spatially, the shift from the unfamiliar to the familiar is a shift from space to
place. The geographer Yi-Fu Tuan, as we noted earlier, considered place to be
that transformation of space effected by familiarity.[1] Edward Casey writes of the
ways in which Eskimos navigate featureless spaces like the Arctic wastes, or of the
ways in which the Puluwatan people of the Caroline Islands find their way across
the often featureless Pacific Ocean, or of how the Bedouin or the Australian
Aboriginal peoples traverse vast open deserts. Navigating such difficult territories

can be further complicated by blizzards, fogs or sandstorms which diminish the powers of visual and auditory perception.

These conditions transform 'feelings of familiarity' (which constitute place-scapes and placetimes) into 'feelings of disorientation' because the reference system of 'my marks' and 'landmarks' is made inoperable by the absence of recognition. 'Feelings of familiarity' involve 'feelings of recognition' upon encountering marks of either kind. Familiarity is signalled by feelings of recognition. Past encounters are neurally encoded as dispositions to re-construct and re-present themselves as feelings of recognition. Landmarks in geographical places, together with man-made marks in cultural ones, are rooted in the 'somatic markers' of feeling and emotion.

In these circumstances people 'find their way' on the back of the methods by which they negotiated previous routes. The Puluwat system of navigation, for example, systematically exploits the collectively accumulated wisdom of how the body moves and senses on the open sea (including, it seems, feelings in the testicles), of how horizons form common edges of sky and sea, and of the ways in which places can be located in relation to the stars.[2] 'Feelings of familiarity' are also what help us to successfully find our way through the subtle worlds com-posed of human meanings. What then is 'a feeling', and what is involved in our having 'familiar feelings' or 'feelings of familiarity'? Synthesising the developing neuroscientific work on feeling and emotion with relevant work in psychology, philosophy, sociology, and anthropology is a task for a cultural psychology of emotion.[3] This is because the final, most efficacious, most morally accountable points of view on emotion are those of the developed, culturally constituted subject 'I', or subjects 'we'.

It is a pity that knowledge of the work of Susanne Langer remains restricted largely to those interested in aesthetics. The range of her three-volume *Mind: An Essay on Human Feeling* presages many of the conceptual issues which are routinely part of contemporary thinking on feeling and emotion. Feeling, for Langer, was the basis for a philosophy and, by extension, for a psychology of mind:

> The study of feeling – its sources, its forms, its complexities – leads one down into biological structure and process until its estimation becomes (for the time) impossible, and upward to the purely human sphere known as 'culture'. It is still what we feel, and everything that can be felt, that is important. The same concept that raises problems for natural science takes one just as surely into humanistic ones: the differences between them are obvious, but not problematical.[4]

Langer deploys a number of ideas which are useful to bear in mind when reading what follows. Like Wittgenstein and others she notes how 'feeling' as a noun unhelpfully seduces some into thinking of feelings as entities of some kind, rather than as the processes that they are. She emphasises the distinction between what is 'felt as impact' and what is 'felt as autogenic action' as being the most important in the domain of feeling.[5] The former seems to come inward from outside, whereas the latter appears to arise within. This distinction between feelings which are taken to be responses to stimuli, and feelings which arise as a result of some action for which I take responsibility, or know myself to be the author, is one which Antonio Damasio's theory develops well. A third idea is that of a limen or threshold 'in the rise and abatement of cerebral processes,' such processes being threaded along time in phases, some of which may be known consciously and some not, some of which originate in locations 'outside' self and others of which emerge from 'within'.[6]

The neurologist Antonio Damasio, as I have suggested, presents one of the best contemporary analyses of feeling as a key part of human decision-making.[7] His is a theory that restores and advances William James's idea that emotions are our feelings of the bodily changes that occur when we perceive or comprehend some event that excites or moves us. In a way that significantly advances Langer's thinking on its biological structure and cultural location, Damasio places feeling at the root of consciousness and, by extension, at the core of self. Implicitly, this situates feeling at the heart of our abilities to navigate human worlds. Emotions are key parts of our selves as oriented, incessantly adapting, guided and self-guiding subjects.

Our emotional navigational systems have been designed in general by our common evolutionary past, but calibrated in particular by our own unique, culturally saturated, personal pasts. Every significant decision we make is partly made in light of the inclinations or disinclinations which we viscerally feel. This is what writers like Carl Rogers mean by emphasising the importance of 'organismic feeling' and of our need to create the conditions necessary to trust it. These urgings and recoilings are voices of past personal experience speaking from our various forms of memory. In this sense, our embodiment is crucially an embodiment of what has been, of pasts both ours and mine.

By developing a clear and detailed neurobiological theory of feeling, and of its significance for self, Damasio, it seems to me, offers the necessary contrast for the proper delineation of a cultural psychological account of emotion just as he does for a cultural psychology of self. This is what he argues.

If Micronesian sailors or nomadic Bedouin find their way with the guidance of landmarks and 'my marks', then individuals find ways through their personal worlds with the aid of 'somatic markers'. Navigating human worlds is a form of planning which relies on feelings to select and emphasise what in our past has been marked as important or significant for us. Our past forms us to care about some things and not about others. That significance can be in terms of what is pleasurable and approachable or painful, dangerous and repulsive, and anywhere in between. Indeed the metaphor of a circle rather that of a line may be more appropriate given how pleasure and attraction can sometimes link to the dangerous and the forbidden. The ways forward are guided by the ways behind. How this is neurologically and neuropsychologically instantiated is the focus of Damasio's theory of emotion. He is guided by the losses in personal guidance systems that occur with certain forms of brain damage, notably damage to the prefrontal cortices.

All living things must behave selectively if they are to survive. At its most primitive, that selection occurs in terms of approach or withdrawal. The more sophisticated the organism the greater and more complex are the behavioural selection processes. In modern Western cultures, the concept of rational selection, of placing maximal value on the role of 'Reason' when making decisions, occupies the dominant position in our common understanding of good decision-making.

The belief that 'Reason' is somehow opposed to 'emotion' – the latter often contaminating and distorting the former – is identified as a major misconstrual by those who wish to argue against the validity of this dichotomisation of experience, and for an integrated 'felt-thinking' which is more appropriate to actual human behaviour as it occurs in normal, real-life situations. This is not to say that systems of emotion cannot sometimes negatively determine individuals' judgements as to how best to act. Anxiety and panic attacks, anger, fear and infatuation can have real impact on the capacity to behave well. These exceptional cases, however, also have strong cognitive components and should not distort our understanding of the role that feeling and emotion routinely play in the guidance systems shaping human conduct.

A further problem is the variety of ways in which emotion is defined. For a cultural psychology of emotion which is fully open to the findings of neuroscience, definitions of emotions which restrict them to what might be called the 'subjective phase of experience' are a further obstacle to advancing description and explanation. From a cultural psychological perspective, emotions are processes which include that subjective phase – what is felt and reported by a particular person when they are happy, sad, fearful, angry, surprised, disgusted, embarrassed, ashamed, guilty, remorseful, envious, jealous, resentful, anxious, proud, and so on – but only as part of a larger story. This larger story must include the 'world' inhabited by that person, and the elements of that world which the person cares about. It involves the ways in which certain aspects of that world induce emotion and the intensity with which the emotion is felt. It is linked to how their culture interprets, emphasises and legitimates some patterns of decisive action rather than others, and to all of the other ways in which those elements and these forms of caring and concern are shared with, and shaped by, others.

From this perspective it makes sense to trace the course of an emotion as frequently beginning in people's physical or social worlds. From there the emotion-inducing person, object or event engages their concerned attention, arouses and shapes what they feel (the subjective phase to which many restrict the range of the concept of emotion), activates memories and associations, guides actions, incurs consequences, and presents the person with new challenges to feeling and decision-making. This much broader framework is that favoured by cultural psychology because it respects the biological and cultural complexity of emotion.

Of course, the process of feeling can also begin 'within' a person, triggered by a thought or by an imagined scenario or memory, and can then move through guided action into the vicissitudes of a communal world. That 'beginning within', however, once examined will be found to have its own history which inevitably will involve the world with which the person had previous contact. In short, emotion includes subjective feeling but is much larger than it. Furthermore, emotions are cognitive in that a central element of their being (with some possible exceptions) is thought in the form of appraisal, interpretation and integration into one's own personal narrative.

Consequently, conceiving of the psychological process of emotion as separate from or as opposed to thought is quite simply unhelpful. When people talk of emotion 'distorting' rational thinking, cultural psychology reformulates this as one kind of informed caring coming into conflict with another. The basis of the conflict would then be understood as residing in conflicting ways of making meaning, each in the service of different interests, rather than with one 'primitive' system – emotion – contaminating a more advanced one, 'Reason'.

With the famous nineteenth-century case of Phineas Gage, and his own more recent example of Elliot, Antonio Damasio introduces his idea of the key role of somatic marking in effective and efficient human decision-making. Gage and Elliot suffered similar forms of frontal lobe brain damage. Elliot had a orange-sized tumour which pushed the frontal lobes upwards against the skull causing severe damage. The tumour was successfully removed along with the damaged sections of the frontal lobes. While retaining high-level cognitive abilities, Elliot lost the capacity to feel his way forward. This had catastrophic, if instructive, results. Whereas normally functioning people have available to themselves, as part of the information with which to make decisions, certain autonomic, emotional responses to arousing stimuli, unfortunates like Phineas Gage or Elliot with their forms of prefrontal cortical lesion do not.

From the perspective of an observing scientist, for example, their galvanic skin responses to emotionally disturbing stimuli are flat compared to the peaks and troughs of non-injured people. From their own points of view, stimuli and decisions are not accompanied by feelings which might incline them to make one choice rather than another. The emotional value of each stimulus or of each option in their decision-making space is effectively the same. In normal people, their feelings help them to anticipate which is the best route to take in a problem. Not having the assistance of such anticipatory feelings leads to irrational behaviour.[8] Phineas Gage and Elliot continued in their ability to know, but lost a certain capacity to feel, and that loss showed itself in the extremely bad decisions they made and continued to make after their injuries, decisions with catastrophic results for their personal, social and vocational lives.

A *caveat* is necessary here. It is not that Gage and Elliot lost all forms of feeling. What they lost were aspects of what is sometimes called secondary or social emotion. These are emotions which are vital for the proper navigation of social and personal worlds. They include embarrassment, pride, guilt, jealousy or envy. People like Gage and Elliot suffer, according to Damasio, from 'a disturbance of the ability to decide advantageously in situations involving risk and conflict and a selective reduction of the ability to resonate emotionally in precisely those same situations, while preserving the remainder of their emotional abilities'.[9]

Being able to know while not being able to feel might suggest that these are people approaching the ideal of the rational chooser since the absence of distracting feeling should mean that the field is clear for the untrammelled operation of reason. Their choices should be highly rational with the benefits this is expected to entail. Unfortunately for sufferers like them, this is not what happens. Without the benefit of 'somatic markers' — gut feelings that help us favour one rather than another option — our abilities to plan, choose and navigate our incessantly changing and demanding worlds would be hugely handicapped. We would have no fast track to the best decision based on how we feel from previous experiences, and without feeling components or somatic markers being laid down on the basis of our current experience, we would not embody the type of past which would help guide us in the future. A personally disadvantageous downward spiral would be set in train.

Phineas Gage, Elliot and others like them are radically adrift, but in subtle ways. Feelings and emotions anchor us to what our personal and social pasts have come to mean for us. Without these types of feeling we would be severely handicapped in making real-life choices. Our senses of responsibility and obligation would be severely diminished. Our ability to plan and navigate the future would be severely disrupted. This is what happened to Phineas Gage and Elliot. Their lives took on a disaster course after the damage to their prefrontal cortices.

From being reliable, responsible, competent men prior to injury, each was a noticeably different person afterwards. The common parts of that alteration pivoted around an inability to plan for the future, to competently decide between different courses of action, and to manage interpersonal relationships. Sustaining a marriage, holding down a job, deploying resources to good advantage all proved too much for them. What Damasio and his colleagues eventually found to be a common thread between their relatively unimpaired cognitive abilities, as addressed by standard tests of cognitive ability, and their radically impaired competence in the realm of everyday life, was the absence of an ability to feel in particular ways. Damasio was led to conclude that this absence of feeling from Elliot's reasoning had made 'his decision-making landscape hopelessly flat.'[10] A crucial dimension of familiarity — his feeling of it and its shaping of his anticipations — had been bleached from that landscape. Elliot had lost the services of these emotions as pathfinders for self in specifically human worlds. That loss, with its dramatic consequences, alerts us to the subtle role of feeling and emotion in the rationality and reasonableness of everyday life.

There is clearly a problem with the traditional ideal of neutrality as a defining feature of rational decision-making, and its compatibility with real-life decision-making. The neutrality ideal lies at the heart of the natural scientific 'view from nowhere' and has yielded enormous intellectual and technological dividends. This, however, is not how individuals live their everyday lives. We tend to judge those who attempt to incorporate this model as an ideal for their own personal lives as cold misguided fish. The biological and psychological point of emotion is precisely its constituting role in the non-neutral engagement of the living, experienced person making a way in the life-world. The world as it is to be navigated by human beings is one that has already got all kinds of claim on our cares and concerns.

The non-neutral intentionality of our feelings subsists biologically in Damasio's processes of 'somatic marking', and psychologically in the ways in which a person's meaning-making selectively identifies and values some aspects of the common intersubjective world as worth caring about, and others as not. When it comes to caring or not caring, emotion and cognition, body and culture are all of a piece. Prompted by cases such as Phineas Gage and Elliot, Damasio has developed a theory for the role of the body and emotion in the making of consciousness. Like Susanne Langer's, this theory does not render the relationship of the biological and cultural accounts of feeling problematical, just different in level and phase.

If we take 'feeling' as referring to the subjective phase of emotion, and 'emotion' as the wider process which includes feeling but coupled with other, often publicly observable, inducers and responses, then we can widen our understanding of emotions as pathfinders. This we can do by introducing the further idea that the basic mechanisms of emotion do not require consciousness even though they eventually help guide its focus and shape its quality.

Take, for instance, Damasio's patient David, a man with an even greater handicap than Brenda Milner's famous H. M. Having suffered severe damage to both his temporal lobes, including damage to the hippocampus and amygdala, David cannot remember any new facts and has forgotten many that he had remembered prior to his injury. He is a prisoner of the present moment. His extended consciousness, and hence his autobiographical self, is severely narrowed and irreparably frozen. After less than a minute he remembers nothing of what happened during the previous minute. Curiously, though, David was observed by those caring for him to consistently prefer some people and to avoid others. How could this be if every time he met them it was as though for the first time since, having met them, he almost immediately forgot them? Out of sight out of mind is the apparent condition of his existence. To explore this phenomenon, Damasio and his colleagues carried out the following experiment.

Over a week the experimenters engaged David in three different kinds of interaction. One was with a person – a good guy – who was always pleasant and rewarding to David. The second 'neutral guy' was emotionally neutral and engaged David in tasks that were neither pleasant nor unpleasant. The third – the bad guy – was brusque, refused any request made by David, and engaged him in extremely tedious, boring psychological tasks. David was known to like women, so to further test the impact of the negative interaction the 'bad guy' was actually an attractive young woman. The interactions were randomised and in accordance with good experimental design.

To test the effects, David was subsequently presented with two tasks. In one he was presented with a series of four photographs, each of which included one of the three people who had engaged him in interaction. He was asked to whom he would go if he needed help or a friend. Remembering nothing, all the faces would now be strangers to him. The 'good guy' was chosen over 80 per cent of the time, the 'neutral guy' no more than by chance, and the 'bad guy' almost never. Chance cannot account for this. His decisions were being guided, but not for reasons of which he was conscious. When asked to look at the faces of the three individuals together and say which was his friend he consistently chose the good guy. 'David's brain', concludes Damasio, 'could generate actions commensurate with the emotional value of the original encounters, as caused by reward or lack thereof.'[11]

On one occasion Damasio was present when David turned a corner and saw 'the bad guy' in front of him. He flinched and stopped for a moment. Damasio asked if anything was the matter. David denied that anything was. He had experienced an emotion but without any sense of its cause. Lacking memories which could explain this feeling to himself, its effect remained isolated and unknitted into David's narrative of himself. Nonetheless, even though *he* did not author this emotional reaction favourable to his own well-being – that is to avoid an unpleasant encounter if possible – his body did. If these experimental conditions were repeated over a longer period of time Damasio is sure that David's *organism*, given its available design and dispositions, would have homed in on such behavior. He would have developed a tropism for the good guy as well as an antitropism for the bad guy, in much the same manner he had developed such preferences in the real-life setting.[12]

Here we have a very clear example of the ways in which feelings function as pathfinders to the advantage of the person, even if the person himself cannot give an account of why the object of the emotion seems to matter to him, or even a recognition that it does indeed matter to him.

This navigational language suffuses Damasio's theory of emotion. Emotions *lead* in the creation of circumstances which are advantageous to the organism which feels them. Their expression, and the meanings given them, can be greatly influenced by culture but they depend, in Damasio's view, on 'innately set brain devices' produced by evolution which are part of those systems which regulate and represent body states.[13] The variety of emotional responses profoundly alters the *body landscape* and the *brain landscape*. It is these changes which eventually become emotional feelings. Emotions supply organisms with automatic action-sequences which assist their survival based on past experiences, both phylogenetic and ontogenetic. Their regulation becomes ever more complex with increasing consciousness, culminating eventually in the kind of consciousness that allows objects to be known, including the objects of emotion.

Feeling and emotion are intimately connected to normally functioning consciousness, notwithstanding the abnormalities we witness in the likes of David. To reiterate the key elements of Damasio's theory of consciousness, self and emotion, there is the non-conscious proto-self which is that ensemble of brain devices which continually represents the state of the living body and works to maintain that state within the range of functioning necessary for survival. If this system is knocked out, so too is core consciousness. Core consciousness arises

> when the brain's representation devices generate an imaged, nonverbal account of how the organism's own state is affected by the organism's processing of an object, and when this process enhances the image of the causative object, thus placing it saliently in a spatial and temporal context.[14]

Again we can see how, in this hypothesis, the locative function of core consciousness and core self is to the fore. To place an object in a spatio-temporal context is to simultaneously place oneself as its knower in a spatio-temporal frame. A premise of this account is that the mental images that describe the relationship between the maps of the organism – as they are altered by maps of the object – and the second-order maps which represent the relationship of object and organism, *are* feelings.[15] The biological roots of knowing and feeling are thus intimately connected. So also are those of self and feeling.

Knowing that you are from one conscious moment to the next is a species of feeling. This is a central idea elaborated by Damasio. This feeling is supplied within the stream of consciousness by the hypothetical second-order maps of the organism in the act of being changed by an object. Early in an infant's development this is the dominant, non-verbal narrative supporting core consciousness. Later, with the advent of language – a third-order level of representation – the narrative structure of the autobiographical self incorporates the presentations of the ongoing non-verbal narrative, and fuses the moment-by-moment feelings underpinning the conviction that-I-am with a linguistically constructed sense of who I am. On the emergence of this nonverbal subject Damasio writes:

> Looking back, with the license of metaphor, one might say that the swift, second-order nonverbal account narrates a story: *that of the organism caught in the act of representing its own changing state as it goes about representing something else.* But the astonishing fact is that the knowable entity of the catcher has just been created in the narrative of the catching process.[16]

We emerge as subjects within, and continue to be located within, these processes of representation which underpin the different levels or dimensions of consciousness. On this understanding, there is an essential bodily feeling of selfhood that is the core of our later developed, narratively constructed self. Culture is biological just as biological knowledge is cultural. They are of a piece. My feeling that I am most myself when I can say and think 'I' is a linguistic development of 'a feeling which arises in the re-representation of the *nonconscious protoself in the process of being modified* within an account which establishes the cause of the modification.'[17]

The conclusion that knowing is itself a feeling echoes that of Susanne Langer whose work also suggests that thinking is the brain's way of feeling. A profound feeling of familiarity results from the constancy of normal bodily functioning underpinning core consciousness and core selfhood, and is caught in the complaint when something goes wrong that 'I don't feel myself today!' Illness or injury renders taken-for- granted body maps unfamiliar.

The feeling that I am is a given part of core consciousness. Knowing who I am in the sense of being able to correctly use 'I' and experience myself as a subject is also a part of normally functioning core consciousness. There is a condition in which patients are temporarily deprived of a memory of what has happened in their immediate past, and consequently they are deprived of plans for the immediate future. This disorder of extended consciousness is called transient global amnesia. Damasio discusses this as a perfect example of the continuing operation of core consciousness during the temporary suspension of extended consciousness and autobiographical self.[18] Episodes of transient global amnesia usually last for a few hours and less than a day.

From our focus on the locative functions of self, what such cases isolate are the ways in which forms of consciousness and forms of location are linked. Damasio observes that sufferers from this syndrome anxiously repeat the same questions: 'Where am I? What am I doing here? How did I come here? What am I supposed to be doing? The patients tend not to ask who they are'[19] The fascinating diary entries of a very mild sufferer in the middle of a brief global amnesic episode shows how she continues to know where she is spatially (at her desk in the office), and that she can still find her way about (to the rest room and to the restaurant), although one senses an uncertainty even here.

The radical dislocation is evident in her sudden loss of familiarity with what she was doing as an editor. She writes of being 'intensely centered on self' but of not recognising the page of the manuscript she is editing, nor of knowing what she is doing, nor of recognising the lines she knows she has just written. 'Felt unsure of identity of old friends in the hall,' she writes.[20] Without extended consciousness her world is suddenly de-familiarised, and she feels at a loss as to what to do next. Without the assistance of autobiographical memory for what has just happened she is handicapped in her ability to make happen what should happen next. The past provides the moment of present consciousness with the means to move forward into the future. The phenomenon of global amnesia fills out our understanding of the details of this. It shows what a certain kind of loss of position in extended conscious experience feels like.

It also illustrates again how intimately connected are feeling, emotion and consciousness. 'The secret of making consciousness', writes Damasio, 'may well be this: that the plotting of a relationship between any object and the organism becomes the feeling of a feeling. The mysterious first-person perspective of consciousness consists of newly-minted knowledge . . . expressed as feeling.'[21] The memory of feeling such feelings, experiential memory, enables us to form patterns of caring and not caring, and these in turn form the armatures for our plans.

Planning and navigating are similar processes. Keith Oatley and Philip Johnson-Laird have related emotions to the relevance of patterns of caring to goals, and to the management of action.[22] Lazarus condenses ideas concerning the types of emotion we feel when we experience an event, the relevance of that event to our goals, whether the event promotes or hinders those goals, and the degree of our investment in achieving these goals, into a decision tree based on our appraisals of the event.[23]

If the event has no relevance to any of our goals then we feel no emotion. If it has we do. If the event moves us on towards the achievement of that goal we will experience a positive emotion. We may feel happy. If the event enhances our esteem for ourselves then pride may be the emotion, and if it furthers mutual affection with a desired person then love may be the ensuing emotion. If, on the other hand, the event thwarts our goals then the emotional consequences will be negative. We will feel angry if it damages our self-esteem, fearful or anxious if it threatens us, and sad if it involves a loss of some kind.

Emotions, positive and negative, argue Oatley and Johnson-Laird, entail distinctive sequences of action designed to further goals.[24] Correlating emotions with action patterns in this way emphasises once again their central, pathfinding role in human affairs. Attachment love, for example, encourages the person feeling it to talk and keep contact with the caregiver, whereas caregiving love guides the person to help, nurture and support those in his or her care. Sexual love, on the other hand, shapes courtship and sexual activity. Disgust leads to rejection and withdrawal from the source of contamination. Contempt leads the person feeling it to treat the other person without consideration. The anger we feel when our goals are thwarted can lead us to try harder or to attack the cause of the obstruction; the happiness we feel when successes along the way promise ultimate achievement assists us to continue with the plan, to cooperate or be affectionate. Fear makes us vigilant, freeze and want to escape. Built into each pattern of emotion is a strong inclination towards an appropriate form of action based on the lessons of the past. 'What emotions really are, therefore,' write Oatley and Jenkins, 'are the guiding structures for our lives – especially of our relations with others.'[25]

Culture and civilisation are the products of large numbers of conscious persons, diversely organised, actively working together to create meaningful ways of existing, coping, thriving. Intersubjectivity is simultaneously the outcome and the condition of inter-consciousness. A cultural psychology of mind, consciousness, emotion and self is a psychology which tries to account for the ways in which human consciousnesses, as enabled by human bodies, blossom into the full glories and appalling horrors of collective human life. When and where the neuroscientific baton of understanding emotion is passed to the cultural psychological is an issue of contemporary debate. That both must work towards a synthesis is widely agreed.

Within certain limits, the plasticity of the brain favours the idea that the structure of a developed human brain is to a considerable, if partial, degree a cultural outcome. Luria's insight that learning new ways of doing things actively restructures the brain and nervous system enables one to understand the mutual influences of brains, bodies and societies.[26] The exquisitely intricate and highly variable maps of social worlds are instantiated in and reproduced through the embodied minds of their inhabitants. These social maps form a vital part of their selves and are constantly used to devise ways of acting that enhance those selves and avoid dangerous, embarrassing or otherwise disadvantageous courses of action. These brain-reshaping practices are constitutive parts of the culture. For any new member, such as a child or immigrant, these are the rules for ways of behaving and caring that will optimise the quality of their lives within that particular cultural world.

This is a deeply influential idea for those cultural psychologists like Harré and Parrott who look 'at the way patterns of social control enhance the natural human responses and develop specific cultural action patterns, thereby creating the neural basis on which those very responses and patterns depend'.[27] The ways in which emotions function as agents of social control is a central part of any understanding of emotions as navigational devices for selves trying to find the best way forward in human worlds. Embarrassment, modesty, guilt, shame, remorse, and regret, for example, are each forms of feeling that powerfully regulate human action. An un-embarrassable, immodest, shameless person who is incapable of feeling guilt, remorse or regret would be regarded as a difficult and probably dangerous person in any society unless there was a stock role available to contain them – some examples of 'The Leader' come to mind!

Of course, the rules governing that which is embarrassing, shameful, or morally wrong vary greatly from one culture to another. Historians of culture can identify such differences. For example, early New England Puritans, according to John Demos, with their emphasis on constant self-examination and self-abasement under the ever-present gaze of God, placed huge value on reputation as a good and public derision as an evil.[28] Their forms of punishment – stocks, pillories, badges of infamy – exemplified the punitive nature of adverse public exposure. Over a period of about a century and a half, New England culture slowly moved away from an emphasis on shame and towards a concentration on guilt. The controlling structures of feeling, within the practices of personal and public control, shifted as the ways in which New England society made sense of itself changed. Punishment by one's own conscience rather than by the scorn of others came to seem more appropriate. Becoming a New Englander would thus entail the construction of differently felt moral understandings from one period to the next.

Ways of feeling, particularly in relation to their commonly understood appropriateness in social, moral and aesthetic situations, vary distinctively across time and place, even if their biological underpinnings remain more or less constant in kind. As constituents of self, feelings select, guide and energise individual and social actions. They function at the core of what makes us behave most humanely or inhumanely.

Reductionisms, whether biological or social in hue, obscure this key fact about human being: that at our best our self-meaning is open-ended and generous.

Certain ways of feeling lead in this direction, whereas others block those possibilities by felling every wonderful tree along the way. It is refreshing to find a deeply empirical neurologist like Damasio construing the best of culture as continuous with, and a flowering of, biology. This is what John Dewey also believed and struggled to articulate, especially in his aesthetics.[29] 'Still, consciousness', writes Damasio, 'is a sunrise, not the midday sun, and a sunset even less.'[30] Conscience is the zenith.[31] In Part II, I turn to some quintessentially cultural aspects of moral and aesthetic experience, which fulfil or fail the illuminating promise of individual and collective consciousness.

Notes

1 Yi-Fu Tuan, *Space and Place*, Minneapolis: University of Minnesota Press, 1976, pp. 72–3 and quoted by Edward Casey, *Getting Back into Place: Toward a Renewed Understanding of the Place-World*, Bloomington, Indiana University Press, 1993, p. 28.

2 Casey, op. cit., pp. 27–8.

3 For recent work which works towards formulating such a synthesis see Rom Harré and W. G. Parrott, *The Emotions: Social, Cultural and Biological Dimensions*, London, Sage, 1996 and also Keith Oatley and Jennifer Jenkins, *Understanding Emotions*, Oxford, Blackwell, 1996.

4 Susanne Langer, *Mind: An Essay on Human Feeling*, Volume 1, Baltimore, The Johns Hopkins University Press, 1970, p. 32.

5 Ibid., p. 23.

6 Ibid., pp. 30–2.

7 Antonio Damasio, *Descartes' Error*, London, Papermac, 1996, and *The Feeling of What Happens: Body and Emotion in the Making of Consciousness*, New York, Harcourt Brace & Co., 1999.

8 Damasio, *Descartes' Error*, p. 53.

9 Damasio, *The Feeling of What Happens*, p. 41.

10 *Descartes' Error*, p. 51.

11 *The Feeling of What Happens*, p. 46.

12 Ibid., p. 46.

13 Ibid., p. 51.

14 Ibid., p. 169.

15 Ibid., p. 170.

16 Ibid., p. 170.

17 Ibid., p. 172.

18 Ibid., pp. 202–9.

19 Ibid., p. 203.

20 Ibid., p. 206.

21 Ibid., p. 313.

22 K. Oatley and P. N. Johnson-Laird, 'Towards a cognitive theory of emotions', *Cognition and Emotion*, 1987, vol.1, pp. 29–50.

23 R. S. Lazarus, *Emotion and Adaptation*, New York, Oxford University Press, 1991 and reproduced in Oatley and Jenkins, op. cit., p. 101.

24 Ibid., p. 256.

25 Ibid., p. 124.
26 A. R. Luria, *Human Brain and Psychological Processes*, New York, Harper and Row, 1966.
27 Harré and Parrott, op. cit., p. 2.
28 J. Demos, 'Shame and Guilt in Early New England,' in Harré and Parrott, op. cit., pp. 39–56.
29 J. Dewey, *Art as Experience*, New York, Capricorn Books G. P. Putnam's Sons, 1958.
30 Damasio, *The Feeling of What Happens*, p. 28.
31 Ibid., p. 230.

Part II

LOCATION, DISLOCATION AND RELOCATION

Responsibility, caring, art and changing prospects

INTRODUCTION

It [Pragmatism] tells us that we are as friendless, as much on our
own, as the panda, the honeybee or the octopus – just one more
species doing its best, with no hope of outside assistance, and
consequently no use for humility. The best we can do is to take full
advantage of our ability to use language by becoming ever more
social animals, banding together in ever more complex ways for
mutual support.

(R. Rorty, *London Review of Books*, 25 July 1991, p. 6)

I have argued in Part I that the fact of being located is central to the concept of
selfhood. Self is a locative system endlessly working to situate the person advantageously within his or her world. Ranging through various levels of being, from
the non-conscious processes of biological homeostasis to the highest forms of
moral, intellectual and artistic-aesthetic consciousness, each requires, evolves or
creates appropriate systems of navigation. These are intricately interconnected.
Each system of navigation has some dimension of self as its anchoring reference
point, working within the demands of a current situation. Depending upon the
level of question and analysis, that point of origin, to borrow a phrase of William
James, might be the proto-self in one of its momentary instantiations, or a stabilised
teller of his or her own story if the focus is on whom?

Everything of significance in human psychology is tied into the system of self as
an auto-referring navigational system. That is why describing it demands that we
range from the neuroscientific to the cultural-historical, and all the time be aware
of the philosophical dimensions of our cultural psychological questions. So far we
have asked about the nature of place and space and have suggested that being the
sorts of creatures we are, we transmute space into place, space–time into place–
time, as the milieux we inhabit. Every contact we make, every relationship we
form, every thing we touch like more blessed Midases, we try to turn into the
familiar. The stability of our individual and collective lives inheres in this familiar-
ising touch. It is from this sanctuary of the familiar that we venture out into the
new and unknown.

Our feelings of bodily familiarity, I have suggested, ground our feelings of
familiarity with ourselves as 'I' or 'we', but not in a way that crudely reduces the

cultural to the psychological nor the psychological to the biological. The political, military, economic or intellectual stability or instability of the times in which we live out our lives hugely influences who we think we are and where we think we ought to be going. All of us have been formed to include beliefs which we reflexively apply to ourselves as means of control and guidance, and have applied to us and our actions by others. These vary greatly. One system of belief that enables the idea of self-creation is that which includes central beliefs about personal responsibility and personal powers to choose one's own moral and intellectual path, subject of course to certain constraints. I have discussed this as a form of self-location within the ambient discourses of our – mainly Western – lives.

The stability of human lives is, however, a precarious thing. The twentieth century was from that point of view an awe-full and an awful one. It began with a world population of about a billion and a half and ended with one in excess of six billion and set to double within the first half of the twenty-first century. It started out with empires whose vast colonies subjugated most of the world, and ended with a single superpower and a greatly increased number of nations. Imperialism lost ground to nationalism, political imperialism yielding to the imperialism of the market. The century commenced with the thunderous black furnaces of heavy industry as the emblem of advancement, and ended with the quiet whiteness of microchip manufacture. It saw the worst wars in the history of the known universe, the worst scale of atrocity, the ascendance of various new forms of barbarism. It witnessed vast movements of people as refugees or migrants whose human face we can see in the work of the great photographer Sebastiao Salgado.[1] Like that period of 4,000 to 3,000 years ago which was identified by Julian Jaynes as being so crucial to the emergence of modern forms of subjectivity, the twentieth century was one of the most profound dislocation.

This dislocation is much more than physical. The meanings of the world, and of ourselves within it, changed dramatically. The altering status of world religions and of totalitarian ideologies, changing concepts of democracy, the promotion of human rights and human responsibilities, our advancing understanding of the universe and of ourselves as evolutionary products of it, and the extraordinary transformations of ordinary human lives by technology and the consumer economy, have all impacted on the nature and functioning of the psychology associated with extended consciousness and contemporary self-interpretation. It should be a function of a developed cultural psychology to articulate an understanding of the consequences of such personal and collective dislocations and relocations both for subjectivity and for the inter-subjectivity that is culture.

This concept of dislocation, with its associated dynamics of relocation, are background themes of Part II. Casey, Lakoff and Johnson, Bruner, Taylor, Harré, Jaynes, Damasio, and many others were called upon in Part I to amplify our understanding of the locative dimensions of selfhood with a view to clarifying the nature and domain of a specifically cultural psychology of self. The range of issues to which we could apply this sketched position is vast. Selection is unavoidable. In Part II, I have chosen to focus on a few issues which seem to me to be of particular interest. Readers will, I am sure, think of many others that could, or perhaps should, have been addressed.

A few themes underlie the following essays which build on the significance of location for an understanding of the import of dislocation and relocation. Relocation may be forced on people, and therefore have to be coped with. It may also be actively chosen with a view to the beneficial ends which a new way of being located may bring with it. Trauma and aesthetic experiences have the general fact of significant relocation in common. How they differ is my point of interest.

An overarching, if implicit, theme of this whole book is the changeability of self. We have seen that at the non-conscious level the perimeters of change allowed to the proto-self are relatively tight and invariant over the life of the organism. The internal bodily landscape must, if it is to ensure health, range within fixed parameters. The core self, as grounded on the proto-self, is also relatively unvarying in its operation even if the objects of attention sustaining it are constantly changing.

Consciousness, core and extended, is twofold in structure. It comprises subjectivity and intentionality. Subjectivity concerns what it is like to be me experiencing something. Intentionality concerns the something I am experiencing, the object of my attention. Each constitutes the other as a unity of experience within the ongoing flow of consciousness. If during the transient states of core consciousness the object of attention changes, then my subjectivity – what it feels like to me at that time attending to that object – also changes. Core self is changeable in that sense. The greatest scope for changes of self, however, lies within its autobiographical form.

Autobiographical self is narrative self. It depends on the extended consciousness which memory systems make possible. These capacities for remembering are enormously elaborated when they are formed by linguistically competent members of a community. At these higher – for which read normal everyday – levels of selfhood, language, meaning and self are intimately interwoven. This is the domain of Bruner's narrative self, Harré's self-placing pronoun user, Taylor's moral cultural-historical subject and the linguistically constructed selfhood of social constructionists, psychoanalysts and anthropologists. Feeling and emotion, as we have seen, play a foundational role in personal navigation at both conscious and non-conscious levels.

It is at this level that changing beliefs about self and self's capabilities have their impact. Changes in self-meaning entail changes in the autobiographical self of extended consciousness. The sources of such shifts in self-interpretation could be deliberate attempts by individuals to reshape or redirect their lives such as would occur, for example, if they underwent a period of intense self-exploration in psychotherapy. They may also cultivate their capacities to experience those expansions of being which creators of various sorts enable in the arts, or in fields of understanding like science, philosophy, history or law. On the gradient of active, sought-for self-change, yielding oneself to temporary reshaping during successful aesthetic experiences can be a particularly interesting, if neglected, locus of self-change.

We can also locate occasions for self-change along a gradient of passivity. A person might, for example, have a Road-to-Damascus experience and undergo some kind of conversion experience. Further along that gradient lies the dark territory of trauma, the space where awful unwished-for things happen to people. A life-threatening illness, a permanently disabling physical injury, the loss of some intensely loved person, possession, or social position, these can all act as turning points in individual lives where a person can honestly say that they are significantly different afterwards.

The problems confronting those who become permanently paralysed through spinal injury or disease, for instance, show how challenging adjusting to this form of initial dislocation and subsequent relocation can be. As Wendy Seymour correctly observes in her discussion of the rehabilitation process:

> To hang on to the past, though understandable as a protective strategy in the early stages of the crisis, is ultimately counterproductive because it prevents the person from exploring new subjectivities that relate to his or her new body, and to the world within which the person will now live.[2]

Traumatic events of their nature catch people unprepared. They must cope using what skills they already have. To the extent that the nature or scale of the event is unprecedented, to that extent are its victims unprepared. The violence of trauma may be a deliberate strategy of oppression. Speaking of Poland's state of mind in 1939 after the savagery of the German onslaught and the Soviet invasion on its other borders, Alan Bullock writes:

> Defeat and occupation had gone a long way to shake its foundations. Instead of allowing it to recover, the activities of both the occupying powers were directed to replacing it with disorder, insecurity, disorientation, turning upside down the normal world in which the population existed. A vacuum was deliberately created in which everything familiar disintegrated, and millions of people found themselves at risk, naked, without protection from the law or authority, many separated from their

families, deprived of their place in society, unsure any longer of their identity.[3]

The experience of the various classes and groups of Poles in the face of this dismantling onslaught is one that many have been condemned to throughout the world. What I want to emphasise is how identity depends for both its stability and its changeability on the stability and mutability of its anchoring conditions. As Stewart and Cohen put it, 'In this view, organisms change because the geography of the surrounding space-of-the-possible makes change inevitable.'[4] This changing space-of-the-possible, with its implications for the next moves to be made by a person faced with the inevitable need to navigate it, is an idea with which all who have found themselves in a new situation can resonate. A few examples will suffice to suggest some of the feelings involved.

The Palestinian writer Edward Said, describing his unhappy stay in his new American school, Mount Hermon, writes:

> The fact that I was never at home or at least at Mount Hermon, out of place in nearly every way, gave me the incentive to find my territory, not socially but intellectually.[5]

Said's strategy in the face of dislocation – the move from Egypt and his familiar Middle Eastern world to a new country and new world in the United States – was to seek control of his own means of imaginative understanding and to create his own territory. Many writers will understand this move. For others, the sequence of dislocation and relocation has been different. In such cases it may move from normality to profound curtailing abnormality and back again to what might be thought to be familiar. In this case, the ostensibly familiar is in fact novel and challenging to the skills of coping which the person has developed into some sort of normality during the abnormal period.

Our normal lives are largely composed of the fluent interplay of skilled habits in flows of mutual experience. These are enormously complicated, but because we are so adept in knitting together our many social and practical skills we find the demands on us to make decisions, and to initiate and navigate our own daily paths to attain what we want, relatively easy and routine.[6] Crises break that routine and show us how much we take these accomplishments for granted. The American journalist Terry Anderson was held for seven years as a hostage in Beirut. He spent up to a year, in various stretches, in solitary confinement. The rest of the time he spent with other hostages, chained, often blindfolded, frequently beaten or otherwise humiliated. Writing after his release, he described the difficulties he faced just dealing with ordinary human living:

The first weeks found me late for every appointment, and incredibly disorganised. I'd lost the skill of managing all the small things that make up a day – when to shave, where I put my wallet, what I'm supposed to do next. Most of all, I've been bemused by the sudden onslaught of choices – from where and what to eat to what will we do when this vacation is over. I've been a journalist nearly all my adult life, and most of that for the AP. Twenty of the last 25 years I've been out of the country. Do we go back overseas? Where? Do I change careers? I'm 44. This is the last chance I'll have to make major alterations in my life. What should they be?[7]

Anderson also asserted that, in the face of his humiliating treatment, 'The only real defence was to remember that no one could take away my self-respect and dignity – only I could do that.' Does this apply to even more extreme situations like those of the Nazi concentration camps, or those of the Muslims in Bosnia, or in situations of extremely cruel torture? In what does the development of self-responsibility and self-respect consist? What maintains it? What destroys it?

These are big questions and the best I can do in Part II is to nibble at them. But they are, it seems to me, crucial questions for human beings and consequently for a cultural psychology that seeks to take seriously the ways in which human beings take themselves seriously. The essays in Part II fall into a tripartite pattern. The first three focus on questions of responsibility, especially in extreme situations, and on ways in which the perpetration and impact of cruelty works to the diminution of self. The second three explore ways in which art works to redefine experiential boundaries and, in doing so, to assist expansions of self, including elaborations of collective self such as national identity. The final essay returns to the role that the field of psychology itself plays in delineating desirable ways of developing. All seven essays ramify this book's governing idea that self is a loca- tive system, and that the constant supply of navigational metaphors to be found in the work of those writing on all aspects of human psychology is suggestive evidence for this.

Without wishing to overly anticipate what is to follow, it may be helpful to signpost in a general way a few ideas which I want to develop. The first is the idea of responsibility and its centrality for a developed sense of self and conscience. Morality is an inescapable condition of selfhood, as was argued in Part I, just as it is for a peaceful, tolerant, pluralistic society. This type of society is itself just one of a number of possible societies, but it is one to which I would commit myself. Dominant figures of the twentieth century like Hitler, Lenin or Stalin would not, nor would the many petty dictators who litter the political, economic and cultural landscape.

I mention this because part of the requirements of the claim that self is moral is that I myself must also occupy moral and political positions. Adam Smith identified empathy, sympathy and pity as the moral sentiments which make human society possible.[8] After a century of experimentation in which pitilessness became the hallmark of many regimes, we would qualify Smith's claim in cold hindsight and say that compassion and tolerance characterise some types of desirable society. Societies with antithetical qualities exist, and persist horribly for those who inhabit them.

In the first three essays, I examine aspects of moral responsibility. I ask how human beings become morally responsible, how we do awful things for which we don't accept responsibility, and how we suffer awful things for which we sometimes accept crippling, but arguably unreasonable, responsibility. The locative theme is reprised in thinking of childhood as a placement in a particular culture, and then construing the process of becoming morally self-responsible as involving the acquisition of powers to place oneself as a moral agent. Both pitilessness and compassion are functions of the process of caring or not caring where other people are in a common world, namely inside it or outside it. The recriminations which survivors visit upon themselves after extreme suffering might, I suggest, be illuminated by considering the consequences of simultaneously occupying two utterly antagonistic moral universes, before relocating to a subsequent one.

The link between the first and the second set of three essays is that suffering is a form of contraction whereas art can be a form of expansion. Artists of all kinds invent worlds which have borders and points of entry, and which require certain cognitive passports. Their entry requirements can be very strict in terms of background experience, understanding and the open, felt structure of selfhood. But granting these complex demands, the experiences that art can enable are among the best that human beings can have. In Chapters 10 and 11, I counterpoint two forms of absorption. Negative absorption characterises extreme pain, both physical and psychological. The probable risk of self-diminution is very high. Positive absorption characterises aesthetic experiences of art – but can also accompany kinds of understanding and types of physical activity – where self-expansion is the likely consequence.

I interpret the idea of 'being moved' in terms of the consequences of positive absorption where I temporarily cede responsibility for the construction of my feelings to the dynamics of the work of art. In Chapter 12, I explore in some detail the role of points of view in the visual arts in order to introduce what I think is a particularly interesting phenomenon. I call this the 'no-point-of-view-phenomenon' and note how it dismantles our felt sense of our boundaries such as inside/outside and here/there. For this I use the work of the American artist James Turrell, and I speculate that he has maybe isolated a way of experientially accessing some aspects of Damasio's hypothesised third form of representation in which, Damasio argues, subjectivity inheres.

I referred above to how the twentieth century has seen a great growth in the number of nations. This has been accompanied by an equivalent expansion of nationalisms. It is striking how the language of national identity utilises the language of personal identity. Given our now familiar emphasis on the ways in which language creates social reality, it is interesting to reflect on the relationships between the two. I suggest that that relationship is twofold: one is analogical and the other symbiotic. I also highlight the importance of art, especial writing, in the construction of ideas of national identity. Again, this parallels our discussion in Chapter 3 on the sources for a narrative construction of self. It exemplifies this idea of Jerome Bruner:

> Insofar as we account for our own actions and for the human events that occur around us principally in terms of narrative, story, drama, it is conceivable that our sensitivity to narrative provides the major link between our own sense of self and our sense of others in the social world around us. The common coin may be provided by the form of narrative that the culture offers us. Again, life could be said to imitate art.[9]

It is in the dynamics of narrative that the role of art in the construction of both national and personal identity, and their symbiotic relationship, is to be found. Finally, the stories of the good life, as understood in psychologies of maturity, are the theme of the last essay. The argument here is that the stories of good development offered by psychology are not those of a neutral disinterested observer but rather those of an active participant in the conversation that makes human lives fully human. Here, it seems to me, is one point where cultural psychology can, for good or ill, become cultural critic. The pertinence of that criticism will be a function of the astuteness of the psychology's self-awareness. Inescapably, though, it will have a moral dimension for which it can and should be called to account.

A final point of context for Part II needs mention. One could argue that the building blocks of mind and culture are ideas. Ideas are ways of noticing and thinking about the world. They are symbolic formulations that guide our attention and shape our actions. Key ideas make us before we become conscious of ourselves. We are authored by them in crucial ways. The most important ideas constituting self are those, as we have suggested, that make some actions and ideals desirable and thinkable, others abhorrent and unthinkable. Some ideas with which we think ourselves into novel ways of being – ideas that ground our self-creative capacities – are particularly powerful. Potent, identity-forming ideas have their own lives, histories of reproduction and consequences. I cannot see how a cultural psychology of self and identity can be successful without a deep concern for the historical sources and trajectories of key ideas that constitute self.[10] Cultural evolutionists with their concept of memes share this belief about the importance of ideas. Without such concerns, where would a cultural-historical psychology be? This belief is an important source for some of the arguments in Part II.

Milton wrote of

> A Mind not to be chang'd by place or time.
> The mind is its own place, and in itself
> Can make a Heav'n of Hell, a Hell of Heav'n.[11]

He could equally have written that place can make of mind a heaven or a hell since, in the bigger picture, mind and place are one.

Notes

1 S. Salgado, *Migrations: Humanity in Transition*, New York, Aperture Foundation, 2000.
2 W. Seymour, *Remaking the Body: Rehabilitation and Change*, London, Routledge, 1998, p. 42.
3 A. Bullock, *Hitler and Stalin: Parallel Lives*, London, Fontana, 1993, p. 702.
4 I. Stewart and J. Cohen, *Figments of Reality: The Evolution of the Curious Mind*, Cambridge, Cambridge University Press, 1997, p. 78.
5 E. Said, *Out of Place: A Memoir*, London, Granta Books, 1999, p. 231.
6 R. C. Schank and R. P. Abelson, *Scripts, Plans, Goals, and Understanding: An Inquiry into Human Knowledge Structures*, Hillsdale, NJ, Erlbaum, 1977.
7 T. Anderson, *The Observer*, London, 15 March 1992, p. 13.
8 A. Smith, *The Theory of Moral Sentiments*, Oxford, Oxford University Press, 1976.
9 J. Bruner, *Actual Minds, Possible Worlds*, Cambridge, Mass., Harvard University Press, 1986, p.69.
10 For a fine example to illustrate this see D. N. Robinson, *Wild Beasts and Idle Humours: The Insanity Defense from Antiquity to the Present*, Cambridge, Mass., Harvard University Press, 1996.
11 J. Milton, *Poetical Works*, ed. D. Bush, London, Oxford University Press, 1966, p. 218.

8

CHILDHOOD, RESPONSIBILITY AND ACQUIRING POWERS TO PLACE ONESELF AS A MORAL AGENT

> The academic disciplines that study the child are increasingly inclined to view the child not as a natural object but as a social object, not as the product of developmental, biological forces alone but as a fiction constructed just as much by social and historical forces located in time and space.
>
> (E. Cahan et al., *Children in Time and Place*, 1993, p. 192)

> [The] apparently unique features of human imagination, human creativity, and human morality are 'emergent' features of complex processes such as evolution and culture: they have *not* been developed gradually from small beginnings and many important features cannot sensibly be traced back to precursors. The crucial trick has been our development of specific cultural 'Make-a-Human Kits', which arrange that our juveniles pass through a succession of experiences which result in the kind of adult that supports the society that produces that kind of human being. It is, of course, another recursive process.
>
> (I. Stewart and J. Cohen, *Figments of Reality: The Evolution of the Curious Mind*, 1997, p. 28)

The use of spatial metaphors to articulate dimensions of self and action continues into philosophical and psychological explorations of morality. The concept of a 'moral self' has come to have a higher profile since the early 1980s. Writing of those who are developing this idea, Noam and Wren observe that they 'have tried to show that morality is at once a cultural field within which we live our lives and an interior psychological space at the center of our personal being'. They go on to say that there is more than one way to 'chart this space'.[1] Another prominent researcher in this area, William Damon, in addition to identifying an awareness of our own and others' feelings and their interrelations as essential elements for a mature understanding of justice, adds this as a fourth core requirement: 'an internal "moral compass" that enables the child to make the critical choices about when to veer towards the self's reactions and when to veer towards those of the other'.[2]

Our insertion as infants and as children into pre-existing worlds of meaning and obligation centrally influences the sorts of selves we become. This implacement ensures that we come to notice and care about the things our family and community notice and care about, and to ignore what for them is insignificant. Of particular importance for the development of self as a moral agent is how we come to think about ourselves as we acquire skills and habits of attributing responsibility to ourselves ('self-responsibility') or to other people ('other-responsibility').

These skills and habits come with and are favoured by the patterns of caring and ignoring of those who rear and school us. By 'care about' I include both 'good' and 'bad' aspects of the world, aspects which are stitched into the community's self-understanding and identity. The description of morality as having to do with 'a cultural field' into which we are inserted, 'an interior psychological space' which is core to our identity, and the possession of 'a moral compass' which enables us to know when to turn towards our own feelings and when towards those of other people for guidance in the making of moral choices, suggests the tasks of childhood in shaping the moral dimensions of self.

Among the most sophisticated challenges confronting us as persons are those to do with navigating our moral worlds in ways that harmonise with the sense we have developed of ourselves as persons of a particular kind, the kind of person we would ideally like to be. More than that, identities are, as anthropologists like Dorothy Holland and her colleagues argue, 'key means through which people care about and care for what is going on around them. They are important bases from which people create new activities, new worlds, and new ways of being.'[3] With Charles Taylor we saw that our identities are constituted in varying ways according to the 'goods' in relation to which we stand. In this context we can understand how our selves, understood locatively, function as 'moral compasses'. How we feel plays a key role in calibrating how we orient ourselves in the space of moral choices and demands, and it shapes our concerns and action.

Our system of feelings, which includes our cognitions about the sources and objects of our feelings, is the self's moral compass. These cognitions involve how we categorise aspects of the world, the nature and intensity of our cares about them, and the concepts available to us to reflect on our own relationships to these categorised realities. Behaving morally entails reasoning or intuiting our way through moral landscapes signposted with feelings. These signposts are simultaneously part of our selves and part of our world, part of the enveloping 'cultural field' and the 'interior psychological space'. These 'culturally figured worlds' or moral territories that are our social lives are densely and unstably populated with those people — and kinds of people — whom we know and trust and those we don't.[4] They are often difficult to describe and traverse since both trust and mistrust can be misplaced. Knowing that this can be the case impels the need for skills in 'reading' or interpreting our own feelings about aspects of our worlds, as well as imagining how other people's worlds might look to them.

The dichotomisation of our selves into 'inside/internal' and 'outside/external', while retaining a certain utility, loses value the closer we come to understanding the relational dynamics of moral action. Moral spaces include us and us them. The trajectory over time of self-development is dialogical, our 'interior' subjectivity arising in large part from our interactions with what is not initially ourselves and therefore 'exterior'. Subjectivity and intentionality are mutually, dialogically constitutive, two abiding aspects of one transforming personal consciousness.

Over time our understanding of what is 'outside' comes to depend on our internalized maps and models of the world as we construct and know it. What 'matters to us', good and bad, becomes part of our selves. The metaphorical 'boundaries' between inside and outside, between self and other, are moveable feasts and are drawn and redrawn according to the questions we ask of ourselves and the demands made upon us both currently and in the past. The location of these boundaries becomes particularly salient when describing the dynamics of moral actions and conduct, and notably when considering the appropriateness of self-responsibility as against other-responsibility.

Self-responsibility — acknowledging and holding myself accountable for the consequences of actions initiated by myself — seems to lie at the heart of moral agency. Julian Jaynes's theory of the origins of (self-) consciousness in the breakdown of the bicameral mind, as we saw in Chapter 5, can be read as a theoretical account of our historically developing capacities for self-responsibility in the face of profound historical and cultural changes. The significance of acquiring skills in pronoun use for the construction of self, as we then saw in Chapter 6, includes recognising how these skills enable us to constitute ourselves as subjects capable of self-placement within the ongoing conversation of our world, especially within situations that call for the location and allocation of responsibility.

Self-responsibility entails a compelling feeling that I should or should not do something because it is 'right' or 'wrong', because it is how 'I' should act if I am to be authentically 'the person I am'. It further involves the understanding that if I do or don't do what I feel I ought to, then the consequences for how I regard myself are of my own making and, at this deep personal level, not ultimately attributable to or blameable on anyone else, even though others may force me to make agonising choices I would prefer not to have to make. Finally, those consequences affect the core of my identity and include such emotional after-states as guilt, self-blame, pride, sense of personal dignity or honour, and self-esteem or self-hate.

We need a theory of moral agency, of self as morally constituted, both to understand how to frame productive questions for research into moral and immoral conduct, and for interpreting the results of what research is currently available. Self-responsibility, identity and ideals are intrinsically connected. The philosopher Harry Frankfurt, in analysing how intimately a part of us ideals are, speaks of their 'necessity'.[5] His argument is this.

There is an intrinsic tension between freedom and individuality. One can only exist as an individual within limits or boundaries, whereas the thrust of freedom is to erase these limiting, 'self' containing boundaries. Individual identity would be impossible if total freedom reigned. Without individual identity, on the other hand, what point is there to freedom? The key to understanding this dynamic of self and freedom is to focus on what people 'care about', to ask what they consider important to them.

A person's caring about something he considers important 'consists . . . in the fact that he *guides* himself by reference to it'.[6] He identifies with what he cares about, so that his well-being is partly dependent on its well-being. Because of this identity of the person with what he cares about, necessity enters the picture. There are certain things he simply cannot do because of the sort of person he is, which in turn has to do with how what he cares about constitutes him as that sort of person. In terms of understanding and capacity he may well be capable of doing them but he cannot because he has not the 'will' to do so. In these circumstances, he simply cannot deploy the capacities he has for doing something that is utterly at variance with what he cares about, with being the sort of person he 'is'. Such actions would be, as people say, *unthinkable*. Observing that Andrei Sakharov seldom if ever comments on himself as morally courageous in his *Memoirs*, for instance, Colby and Damon remark that 'It is as if he assumes that he has no choice in matters of principle.'[7]

Such a person's conduct is limited by this powerful aversion to acting in certain kinds of way. This is a real, viscerally felt aversion. It matters to the person that he endorses this aversion, that he thinks it right that he should continue to think like this. He values his incapacity to act in this way. Caring about something in this way is a very different sort of constraint than other limits on choice such as addiction or terror. The morally compelled person does not feel his incapacity as a constraint, unlike the addicted or terrorised person. His aversion to doing 'the unthinkable' is, we might say, harmonious with the person he 'is'.

Of course, the structure of who we are and of what we care about is subject to shaping by all sorts of circumstance such that the unthinkable can in time become quite thinkable, and vice versa. People do change. But the fact is that at a time when the person is so structured as to find the prospect of doing something unthinkable, he cannot alter this by a direct effort to 'change his will'. 'He is', as Frankfurt says, 'subject to a necessity that, in this sense, defines an absolute limit. And this necessity is unequivocally constitutive of his nature or essence as a volitional being.'[8]

Once again the navigational or locative functions of self are central to understanding the nature of characteristics that we identify as 'personal'. The higher-order reflexive features of a person's will pertain, in Frankfurt's words, 'to a person's efforts to negotiate his own way among the various impulses and desires by which he is moved, as he undertakes to identify himself more intimately with some of his own psychic characteristics and to distance himself from others'.[9] People try to guide their actions according to what they care about. Being a person entails being able to adopt an evaluative stance towards dimensions of oneself, favouring some motives and wishing to change others. The boundaries of one's will, seen in what one finds unthinkable, are boundaries of the nature of one's self. These boundaries are what make us who and what we are.

Is it possible to have no ideals, for there to be nothing that it is unthinkable for me to be willing to do? Obviously this is a key question for the next chapter where I want to open up the question of the relationship between self, responsibility, pitilessness and compassion. The implication of Frankfurt's analysis is that a man or woman without ideals, for whom there are no boundaries formed by the unthinkable, is himself or herself amorphous and without fixed identity. Without ideals, on this analysis, there is nothing such a person can be said to be. Any consistencies in how he behaves will be the product of impersonal causal influences rather than personal ones of his own choosing. He is other-shaped rather than self-created. What he is at any point in time is what he accidentally happens to be. He is literally without integrity because he is without the boundaries required for integrity.

Of course not all ideals that serve this containing, self-constituting function are moral ideals in a narrow sense of 'moral'. Many different notions of the good across history and culture supply ideals, as we saw in Chapter 4. Charles Taylor also draws on earlier work by Frankfurt on 'second-order desires' to elaborate his understanding of the nature of moral agency and self-responsibility.[10] This involves a person taking responsibility not just for what he does, nor simply for the degree to which what he does is in conformity with his own evaluations and ideals, but also for these evaluations themselves. It is through the act of endorsing or espousing personal evaluations and ideals that responsibility arises. The capacity for evaluating our desires, for placing some higher than others is essential to human agency, as is the idea of the necessary limiting of freedom for the establishment and maintenance of identity. Taylor uses Sartre's idea of 'radical choice' to show how freedom without limits is incoherent, which is also Frankfurt's conclusion.

How we interpret ourselves, including how we evaluate ourselves, constitutes both our selves and our experience. There are many ways in which this can occur. An implication of Frankfurt and Taylor's analyses of ideals and agency is that the study of individual biographies will reveal the richest examples of how self-interpretations constitute moral selves, how types of self-evaluation are rooted in cultures, and how self-evaluations empower people to do things that other self-interpretations would never make possible. Anne Colby and William Damon's idiographic studies of people who stand out for the level and intensity of their moral commitments provide examples of how this works.[11]

A *leitmotif* of their study is the coincidence of personal identity and moral goals. 'Who I am is what "I" am able to do and how I feel all the time – each day, each moment. It's hard for me to separate who I am from what I want to do and what I am doing,' said one of Colby and Damon's moral exemplars, Cabell Brand.[12] For such people moral goals are central to or constitutive of who they are. Their identities are moral identities, their selves moral selves. They interpret and evaluate themselves from explicitly moral perspectives. Their 'vocabulary of worth' we might say, using a Charles Taylor phrase, is in fluent play. These people are exceptions, and Colby and Damon argue that from a developmental psychological perspective 'early in life, morality and self are separate conceptual systems with little integration between them'.[13] It is during childhood and ado- lescence that integration occurs, that self-interest coalesces with moral interest, that 'I' become what 'I care about'.

There is great variation among individuals in the extent to which this occurs, and presumably therefore in the extent to which their actions are governed by moral, reflective, second-order desires. From their empirical work in this area Damon and Colby conclude that, in addition to there being a wide range of individual difference, what is more important for this unity is the person's sense of self rather than the particular nature of the moral beliefs. A key quality is 'the place that morality occupies in the person's life' and this can only be gauged by exploring individuals' self-understanding or self-interpretation, to use the language of Frankfurt and Taylor above.

Are moral ideals constitutive of a particular person's identity in a strong sense or are they merely ancillary to it in a weaker sense, we might ask? We might also ask what the empowering potential, so to speak, of particular moral ideals might be. What is it that people can and will do as a consequence of incorporating a particular set of ideals into their identity that they would not otherwise be capable of or willing to do? Answers to these latter questions would help us to predict how someone identified with this 'good' is likely to behave in relevant circumstances. There are of course many different moral ideals and they may favour or diminish the prominence of self-responsibility as against obedience to acknowledged higher authorities in a person's self-constituting interpretations.[14] Whatever the nature of these ideals, how people act and conduct themselves morally is intimately connected with how important for themselves, for their identities, these ideals are.

There is a concordance on this issue of identity and ideals between the thinking of moral philosophers like Frankfurt and Taylor and the empirical work of psychologists of morality like Damon and Colby. In their study of 'moral exemplars' Damon and Colby found that despite variation in the nature of the moral beliefs held, there was a unity between morality and self which firmly linked moral judgement to action and conduct. One consequence of this was that uncertainty and self-doubt about the rightness of what to do was not widespread among their subjects. Virginia Durr, a prominent participant in the American Civil Rights movement, remembering those who accused her of being self-righteous, could say 'I knew I was right' and mean in the most literal sense that in essence *she-was-right* since, so far as being committed to the justice of civil rights, that was the sort of self she was.[15] Other correlates of these exemplars were a relative lack of concern about the dangers for them of acting in these ways, the absence of an experience of moral courage, a positive attitude towards life and a deep enjoyment in doing what they did. Research by the English psychologist Helen Haste produced parallel results.[16]

All normally functioning adults begin their lives powerlessly and malleably, inserted into the 'figured worlds' of others more competent than themselves who expect and demand things of them. The chance circumstances of that implacement, and the range of experiences it enables, are crucially important for the development of moral agency and self-responsibility. To take responsibility is to take possession of and to 'own' one's actions, their meanings and their value. That is what speaking of my 'own' actions means. Owning them may be an act of pride or of shame, with beneficial or awful consequences. Our disposition to assume responsibility for our actions and their consequences, to be self-responsible, develops from our own positioning as children. This in turn depends upon how our community constructs its version of 'childhood' and therefore on its own particular 'make-a-person' practices.

Historians of childhood have, since the pioneering work of Philippe Aries and others, shown how the nature of 'childhood' has varied historically and culturally.[17] The concept of 'the child', the expectations of what children should and could do, patterns of child-rearing (which is to say person-making), ages of legal and criminal responsibility, rights to education, requirements to work, degrees of choice offered and responsibility encouraged, ideals of good and desirable outcomes of childhood, all are known to vary from time to time, from place to place, from class to class, from gender to gender, from race to race, from religion to religion. There is dispute as to the respective roles of biology and culture when the development of some of a child's abilities are at issue, but as far as self-responsibility is concerned it is cultural psychological perspectives that are most illuminating since responsibility is essentially a socially constructed phenomenon.

Locating oneself morally is more than a question of judgement. It is a question of practice. The development of moral conduct is the development of moral practices, including the sort of self-reflection that engenders moral awareness and enables the sort of self-interpretation that constitutes the moral identity. This sort of self-reflection includes not only the ability to 'read' one's own feelings but also the ability to interpret those of one's own feelings that tell us about the psychological states of others. It also includes the ability to have feelings that are a response to those we find in others but have not yet perhaps felt ourselves. 'Feelings' or emotions are guides formed by experience which enable us to decide what paths to follow through whatever moral maze we happen to find ourselves in. Underpinning the relationship of identity to moral feelings of these kinds are facts of responsibility and ownership.

Damon concludes that 'There is no more effective facilitator of moral development than fostering children's willingness to take responsibility for good and bad deeds.'[18] The ability and readiness to take responsibility for what you have initiated yourself lies at the core of this ideal of 'moral character'. Damon goes on to say that 'Neither the most empathic emotional response, the sharpest awareness, nor the best of intentions can do very much for the social good if one lacks the strength of character necessary to take responsibility for one's actions.'[19] This idea of 'strength of moral character' relates to that aspect of identity wherein a core belief constituting self is the desirability and perhaps the necessity of self-responsibility, of declaring to yourself, and if appropriate to others, that you take ownership of the consequences of an action initiated by yourself. This may mean accepting just punishment and possibly making restitution. The ability and the belief that one should be willingly self-responsible serve a powerful role in moderating a person's social conduct.

Self-responsibility is a social ideal, and as such may or may not be favoured by a particular culture or family. It is developed when young people are given opportunities to assume responsibility and are expected to take them. This in turn depends on trusting that the young are competent to rise to the expectations held for them. These expectations carry with them the sorts of beliefs and values that enable young people to think that it is good to assume responsibility, and to come to think of themselves as responsible people. Self-responsibility becomes part of their identity. Beliefs in the competencies of young people and in what it is appropriate to expect of them vary widely. Western urban societies have relieved children of many of the responsibilities routinely expected of them in more traditional agrarian societies.

The span of 'childhood' as a period of economic dependence on parents, and as a period without major responsibilities for the care of others, has in Western societies expanded substantially in the twentieth century. Of course there are all sorts of exceptions to this, especially in times of war and unrest. Huge numbers of adolescents fought the horrifying battles and wars of this last lethal century, and huge numbers of children coped with their barbaric consequences. But in ordinary peacetime conditions the economic and moral requirements of education in particular have fuelled the chronological expansion of childhood.

Children in many non-Western rural societies assume greater responsibilities within the family than do their counterparts in urban, Western societies. They look after younger children, work in the fields, and help with the washing and cooking. It is reported that children in Philippine, Kenyan and Mexican rural societies, for instance, behave more altruistically than children from cities in the United States or India.[20] The assumption of family responsibilities by young children in these rural societies, including caring for the sick and elderly, is simply expected. A consequence is that cooperative, prosocial conduct is more likely to become habitual for them.

In Western urbanised societies, children assume very little responsibility within the family. Requiring them to do so would be regarded as inappropriate, unfair or even irresponsible of the parents. This, it would seem, is not without its consequences. There is research suggesting that such urban children are more competitive, conflictual and attention-seeking than children in rural societies.[21] The dynamics of child-formation, and the informing ideals for childhood of the culture, clearly play a role in this.

How parents enact expectations also differs. Some family cultures simply expect certain types of behaviour of their children, and only react when it falls below par. Praise is not generously dispensed because the expected behaviour is a taken-for-granted part of life. This has been found in certain African studies and contrasts sharply with middle-class American patterns where praising and complimenting good behaviour is the norm. This, it is argued, increases attention-seeking which is itself part of a culturally favoured assertiveness. Such assertiveness is a valued behavioural commodity in an achievement-oriented society. Tendencies to sacrifice oneself in favour of a greater communal good, however, may find it hard to cohabit with individualistic, economically required, achievement-motivated self-assertiveness.

There is no doubt that in terms of potential competence, children can rise to very exacting demands. Unfortunately for them the circumstances in which these occur are often negative, hostile and potentially traumatising. Millions of children throughout the world now live abandoned lives on the streets, surviving on their wits. They face daunting challenges and hardships that would cause most adults to despair, and yet they manage to survive, albeit at great cost and to a low level. Competencies and responsibilities, however, can be synchronised in many ways.

Until 1929 girls in England could legally marry at 12 years of age, or perhaps more accurately 'be married'. Women's legal rights to vote, however, had in the twentieth century to move from no vote at all through the right to vote at 30, then 21 and then 18. In the United Kingdom young people cannot vote or join the police until they are 18 but they can be recruited as soldiers at 16 and trained to kill for their country. Contemporary campaigns against paedophilia and child soldiers reflect the changing concept of 'a minor'. The changing idea of a minor or of 'a child' is part of an ongoing reinterpretation and reconstruction of their responsibilities by adults and nations to protect current ideals of the best interests of children.

There is a tension here between politically determined ages of consent and individual children's abilities and competencies. For the purposes of the UN Convention on the Rights of the Child (ratified by all the states of the world except the United States of America and Somalia) the cut-off age for childhood is 18. Moral and legal responsibilities such as the right to vote or sign a contract generally come into play around this age in Western-style democracies. For large swathes of the world, however, this is an as yet unattained ideal of childhood.

Children have features which can make them lethal. A 1999 document from the International Secretariat of Amnesty International on child soldiers reports that a

> recent trend – notably in Liberia, Sierra Leone and DRC [The Demo-cratic Republic of Congo] – has been the deliberate recruitment of children in preference to adults because of their greater malleability and willingness to commit atrocities and because of the greater destructive-ness to the community and its values when the perpetrators are children.[22]

The Khmer Rouge genocide in Cambodia also ranked children among its most pitiless killers.

This raises questions about the age of criminal responsibility and the extent to which children as young as 10 can have any real understanding of the consequences of their actions in killing and maiming others. The July 1998 Statute underpinning the proposal to establish an International Criminal Court precludes it from exercising jurisdiction over any person who was under the age of 18 at the time the crime was committed. On the other hand, the general consequences for children of having been child soldiers are known.[23] A 1996 report from the World Health Organisation says that

The repeated exposure of children as perpetrators to violence may lead to persisting patterns of problematic behaviour and functioning. Many children may be withdrawn, depressed and display difficulties in social relationships and at school. Others, particularly the 'successful' child soldier, are likely to adopt an active role, becoming the agent of aggressive behaviour rather than becoming its passive victim.[24]

The Coalition to Stop the Use of Child Soldiers estimates that as of September 1999 over 300,000 children under the age of 18 are currently taking part in hostilities around the world.[25] Clearly, children can become what adults want them to become, often far earlier than might elsewhere have been thought possible and far sooner than might be thought good for the child, even by local norms.

There is not a lot of research available on the connections between competency and responsibility in children. Vygotsky's 'zone of proximal development', Bruner's notion of 'scaffolding', Harré's use of René Spitz's 'psychological symbiosis', and others, all describe ways in which children develop competencies under the tutorial guidance of already competent adults. One practical area that has received attention is children's decision-making and consent regarding surgery on themselves. The question here is whether and when children are competent to consent, or to deny consent, to major surgical procedures being proposed for them such as limb-lengthening or amputation. Part of the problem has been the delineation of legal rights of responsibility in making these decisions, and part has been the question of assessing a child's competence and rights to make such an important decision. Competence and responsibility go together. Who should do it and how? Often, this hinges on a legal determination. Priscilla Alderson in her book *Children's Consent to Surgery* presents the issues comprehensively.[26]

A 1914 ruling in the United States by Judge Cardozo formulated what became the legal basis for Anglo-American respect for adult rights to physical and mental autonomy: 'Every human being of adult years and sound mind has the right to determine what shall be done with his own body.'[27] A crucial English case concerning children's rights in this area was the *Gillick Case* in the mid-1980s which gave rise to the concept of *Gillick Competence*.

Mrs Gillick, a Catholic mother of ten, took her health authority to court to ensure that children under 16 could not give consent to certain types of medical treatment, something which the governing 1969 Act had omitted to state. Her primary concern was that children could not have access to advice or treatment for contraception without their parents' consent. The Law Lords ruled that a competent child is one who 'achieves a sufficient understanding and intelligence to enable him or her to make a wise choice in his or her own interests'.[28] It was up to the doctor to decide whether the child was competent. If the child was adjudged to be competent and wished to exclude the parents, then the doctor should advise on including them but not enforce this advice. This is a complex issue and ruling, one subsequently retracted in a 1991 judgement by Lord Donaldson.

The legal issue of the balance between children's maturity, competence and rights to bodily autonomy *vis-à-vis* how long parents have rights over them remains a live one. Psychologically, however, children show a wisdom which also characterises the thinking of adults when confronted by serious medical decisions whose complexity and urgency challenges their confidence in their own powers of decision-making. Alderson contends that

> The only way to become autonomous is to learn to be so through risking mistakes, which are seldom extremely serious or irrevocable. If they are, our interview and survey replies from over 1000 children suggested that children tend to be cautious about how much responsibility in decision making they can cope with.[29]

Children themselves tend to set the 'maturity threshold' for consent at around 14 years whereas professionals tend to put it at somewhere over 10 years of age. The research suggests that children are players in the negotiation of their own competencies to give or withhold consent to surgery.[30] In general, both children and adults negotiate their way towards the construction of the child's moral agency and self-responsibility.

From one point of view, this negotiation depends on sharing and trust, what Damon refers to as 'respectful engagement'.[31] Parents, and other figures in authority like teachers, clergy or older brothers and sisters, focus on domains of meaning and conduct which they want the young to incorporate into themselves while the young would like their feelings and interests to be acknowledged. I want to finish this chapter by considering the significance of some fascinating research on the developmental roots of shared realities since the basis for both compassion and pitilessness, as I understand them, resides in sharing and in the refusal of sharing. Moral selves, with their associated ways of taking and refusing responsibility, can be compassionate or pitiless and anywhere in between.

Simon Baron-Cohen and his colleagues have developed a theory of the roots of 'mindreading' in normal children and of 'mindblindness' in autistic ones.[32] Very briefly, the mindreading system, he claims, is rooted in four mechanisms. These are the Intentionality Detector (ID), the Eye-Direction Detector (EDD), the Shared-Attention Mechanism (SAM) and The Theory-of-Mind Mechanism (ToMM). From birth or thereabouts to 9 months the infant has ID and the basic functions of EDD. ID, according to Baron-Cohen, is probably innate and enables the infant to begin to interpret any self-propelled object as an agent with goals. Evidence that very young infants are sensitive to changes in an adult's goal is adduced for the existence of the ID. The EDD detects the presence of eyes or eye-like stimuli, computes whether they are directed at the infant itself or elsewhere, and infers that if they are so directed the agent sees that thing.

From around 9 to 18 months the Shared Attention Mechanism (SAM) kicks in. The key function of SAM is to build triadic representations which specify the relations between an agent, the self and an object. This is a crucial mechanism in that it enables the computation to occur that you and I are perceiving the same thing. SAM underpins sameness for me and you. From about 18 to 48 months Theory-of-Mind Mechanism (ToMM) comes into play in normal children. ToMM enables the child to infer the full range of mental states from behaviour. It enables them to infer that others are thinking, knowing, pretending, guessing, deceiving, and so on. ToMM is built on the work of the other mechanisms, but particularly on the Shared-Attention Mechanism (SAM). Baron-Cohen's theory argues that autistic children have suffered damage either to SAM or to ToMM. Congenitally blind children obviously have no EDD but their intact ability to share attention enables them to develop ToMM normally. Autistic children have ID and EDD but massive impairment to SAM, and consequently to ToMM. Autistic children cannot infer mental states from behaviour, and are profoundly handicapped consequently as social beings. ToMM obviously is crucial, therefore, to insightful social lives. If Baron-Cohen's modular theory of mindblindedness in those suffering from autism illustrates the consequences of an inability to share attention, then the fascinating research over many years of Michael Tomasello and his colleagues on the comparative and developmental psychology of the ability to share attention lays the basis for his argument that advanced human cognition originates culturally.[33] Unlike Baron-Cohen, and many contemporary evolutionary psychologists, Tomasello argues that

> [T]here simply has not been enough time for normal processes of biological evolution involving genetic variation and natural selection to have created, one by one, each of the cognitive skills necessary for modern humans to invent and maintain complex tool-use industries and technologies, complex forms of symbolic communication and representation, and complex social organizations and institutions.[34]

Tomasello argues instead for 'a single biological adaptation with leverage' which he identifies as the distinctively new ability which human beings evolved for identifying with other human beings and understanding them as intentional beings. This distinguishes us from our higher primate relatives. This radically new ability helps human beings to share and construct social realities in profoundly creative ways in which basic cognitive skills, of a kind which we do share with our primate cousins, can be turned into exquisitely complex cognitive skills which are exclusively our own.[35]

He suggests that around one year of age, soon after infants begin to understand others as intentional agents, they begin to participate in discourse with them. Some years later they come to understand others as mental agents. This takes time

> [B]ecause to understand that other persons have beliefs about the world that differ from their own, children need to engage them in discourse in which these different perspectives are clearly apparent – either in a disagreement, a misunderstanding, a request for clarification, or a reflective dialogue.[36]

The roots of children's abilities to understand social and moral agency lie within the very dynamics of mutual understanding that this primary ability to see other human beings as intentional beings enables. The understanding that other people are intentional agents, with goals like oneself and 'whose relations to outside entities may be followed into, directed or shared', seems to emerge at about nine months when infants begin to engage in joint attentional behaviours.[37] This apparently simple, distinctively human, communicative ability to point to an object solely in order to share attention with someone else, and so influence that person's attention, is a psychological root of culture. This feature of our biology ensures that we live culturally. Non-human primates like chimpanzees are intentional and causal beings but, crucially, they cannot understand their world in intentional and causal terms. We can. Sharing lies at the cultural heart of human being, and is evident in normal children before the end of their first year of life. Such sharing is what underpins the ability to identify with others. We learn not just from others, but through them.

There is this further point, not made by Baron-Cohen, that ToMM understood purely biologically or neurologically or evolutionarily, is not sufficient on its own to account for our ability to know other minds, although it is necessary. A developed and fluent knowledge of other minds such as is needed for social life requires in addition a theory of culture along the lines sketched by Tomasello's 'Ratchet Theory' where modifications in material and symbolic artifacts are accumulated through historical time. Bruner makes the general point succinctly:

> To infer the mental state of another requires more than a theory of mind: it also requires a theory of culture. Lacking the guiding presuppositions required by speech acts, how could we understand what somebody has in mind when they say, 'Would you be so kind as to pass the salt?'[38]

This chapter has been a prelude to wondering whether pity is more than empathy, whether it involves ownership or responsibility for the well-being of others and whether pitilessness has everything to do with not taking responsibility, or not feeling that one should take responsibility, for the suffering of others. Against our understanding of self-responsibility and moral agency as crucial aspects of developed selfhood, we can ask some questions about these quintessentially human phenomena of pitilessness and compassion. Specifically, what is involved in being a sympathetic moral agent or a pitiless one? Is caring about other people generally a function of how we categorise them? How can a cultural-historical psychological perspective make sense of pitilessness and compassion? Do we have innate tendencies to compassion and if so what happens to them in times of cruelty? Was William Blake right when, in 'A Divine Image' he contended that 'Cruelty has a Human Heart'?[39]

Notes

1 G. G. Noam and T. E. Wren (eds), *The Moral Self*, Cambridge, Mass., The MIT Press, 1993, p. vii.

2 W. Damon, *The Moral Child: Nurturing Children's Natural Moral Growth*, New York, The Free Press, 1988, p. 128.

3 D. Holland, W. Lachicotte Jr., D. Skinner and C. Cain, *Identity and Agency in Cultural Worlds*, Cambridge, Mass., Harvard University Press, 1998, p. 5.

4 Ibid., p. 51.

5 H. Frankfurt, 'On the Necessity of Ideals' in Noam and Wren, op. cit., pp. 16–27.

6 Ibid., p. 20.

7 A. Colby and W. Damon, *Some Do Care: Contemporary Lives of Moral Commitment*, New York: Free Press, 1992, p. 16.

8 Ibid., p. 22.

9 Ibid., p. 23.

10 C. Taylor, *Human Agency and Language: Philosophical Papers 1*, Cambridge, Cambridge University Press, 1985, Chapter 1.

11 Colby and Damon, op. cit..

12 A. Colby and W. Damon, 'The Uniting of Self and Morality in the Development of Extraordinary Moral Commitment' in G. G. Noam and T. E. Wren (eds), *The Moral Self*, Cambridge, Mass., The MIT Press, 1993, p. 149.

13 Ibid., p. 150.

14 Regarding trends of change from obedience to autonomy and independence in the United States, for example, see D. F. Alwin, 'From obedience to autonomy: changes in traits desired in children, 1924–1978', *Public Opinion Quarterly*, 1988, 52, 33–52.

15 Ibid., p. 170

16 H. Haste, 'Moral responsibility and moral commitment: The integration of affect and cognition' in T. Wren (ed.), *The Moral Domain: Essays in the Ongoing Discussion between Philosophy and the Social Sciences*, Cambridge, Mass., The MIT Press, 1990.

17 See, for example, P. Aries, *Centuries of Childhood*, Harmondsworth, Penguin, 1973; W. Kessen, 'The American child and other cultural inventions' in F. S. Kessel and

A. W. Siegel (eds), *The Child and Other Cultural Inventions*, Houston Symposium, No.4, New York, 1983; C. Hardyment, *Dream Babies: Child Care from Locke to Spock*, London, Cape, 1983; J. Anderson, 'Child development: an historical perspective', *Child Development*, 1956, 27, pp. 181–96; L. J. Borstelman, 'Children before psychology: ideas about children from antiquity to the late 1800s' in W. Kessen (vol. ed.), *History, Theory and Methods* vol. 1 of P. H. Mussen (ed.), *Handbook of Child Psychology*, 4th edn., New York, Wiley, 1983; E. Singer, *Child-Care and the Psychology of Development*, London, Routledge, 1992; U. Bronfenbrenner, *The Ecology of Human Development*, Cambridge, Mass., Harvard University Press, 1979; R. Stainton Rogers and W. Stainton Rogers, *Stories of Childhood: Shifting Agendas of Child Concern*, London, Harvester Wheatsheaf, 1992.

18 Damon, *The Moral Child*, p. 129.
19 Ibid.
20 Ibid., p. 69.
21 Ibid.
22 Amnesty International. 'Child Soldiers', International Secretariat, 18 November 1999, p. 2.
23 See E. Cairns, *Children and Political Violence*, Oxford, Blackwell, 1996, Chapter 4.
24 WHO Family and Reproductive Health and the Division of Emergency and Humanitarian Action, 'The Impact of Armed Conflict on Children: A Threat to Public Health', Geneva: *WHO*, July 1996, p. 54.
25 http://www.child-soldiers.org/
26 P. Alderson, *Children's Consent to Surgery*, Buckingham, Open University Press, 1993.
27 Ibid., p. 43.
28 Ibid., p. 45.
29 Ibid., p. 195.
30 For a more recent discussion see J. Pearce, 'Consent to Treatment during Childhood: The Assessment of Competence and the Avoidance of Conflict', *British Journal of Psychiatry*, 1994, 165, 713–16.
31 Damon, *The Moral Child*, pp.119–20.
32 S. Baron-Cohen, *Mindblindness: An Essay on Autism and Theory of Mind*, Cambridge, Mass., The MIT Press, 1997.
33 M. Tomasello, *The Cultural Origins of Human Cognition*, Cambridge, Mass., Harvard University Press, 1999.
34 Ibid., p. 2.
35 Ibid., p. 189.
36 Ibid., p. 182.
37 Ibid., p. 61.
38 J. Bruner, *The Culture of Education*, Cambridge, Mass., Harvard University Press, 1996, p. 113.
39 W. Blake, *William Blake: A Selection of Poems and Letters*, ed. J. Bronowski, Harmondsworth, Penguin, 1978, p. 59.

9

PITILESSNESS AND COMPASSION
Caring where others are

> Concern for others emerges from fullness, flourishes in a climate
> of generosity and well-being; but easily withers away, and putrefies
> into egoism and hatred, under conditions of emotional threat or
> scarcity.
>
> (T. Kitwood, *Concern for Others*, 1990, p. 10)

> I wanted simultaneously to understand Hanna's crime and to
> condemn it. But it was too terrible for that. When I tried to
> understand it, I had the feeling I was failing to condemn it as it
> must be condemned. When I condemned it as it must be con-
> demned, there was no room for understanding. But even as I
> wanted to understand Hanna, failing to understand her meant
> betraying her all over again. I could not resolve this. I wanted to
> pose myself both tasks – understanding and condemnation. But it
> was impossible to do both.
>
> (B. Schlink, *The Reader*, 1998, p. 156)

At the end of his book on *The Psychology of Sympathy* Lauren Wispé asks what kind
of a world would this world be without sympathy.[1] Curiously, he then fails to
answer the question, partly, I suspect, because the experimental psychological
cast of his approach is signally inappropriate to the question. The phenomena of
sympathy and compassion, of hatred and pitilessness, are intrinsically cultural and
historical in their make-up. An essentially ahistorical, acultural theorisation of
sympathy such as Wispé's, while well-meaning and correct in identifying the
relative neglect of sympathy by psychology, is rather like trying to analyse cooking without taking account of heat, chefs or recipes. It may tell us something
about the various relationships of the ingredients, but nothing about how they
transmute into a coherent distinctive dish nor about how they could have turned
out differently under other conditions. The absence of any account of 'belief',
self, identity, or distinctive social 'worlds' prefigures the inevitable failure of this
type of psychology when confronting such a complex social psychological
phenomenon as sympathy. The phenomenon is far too complex for the method.

146

The question of what a world without sympathy might look like, however, does not need to be posed hypothetically since it can be answered historically. The catalogue of twentieth-century genocide – Turkey, the Soviet Union, the German Third Reich, Cambodia, Burundi, Rwanda, for example – provides ample material. The most documented of these genocides is the Holocaust. Here we have in graphic awfulness the fullest imaginable answer to the question of what a world without sympathy does look like, down to its smallest, most demeaning brutality. Its scale equalled 600 massacres of 10,000 utterly defenceless people a time – the number '6 million' has blunted our imagination – a massacre a day every single day for a year and eight months. In such circumstances as these we have pitilessness in its purest form. It is in the face of mass societal mobilisations for the purposes of killing an 'outgroup' (racially, religiously, ethnically, ideologically 'other') that a psychology of sympathy must test its descriptive and explanatory power. Only a cultural-historical psychology has the breadth necessary to address pitilessness such as this.

We have many accounts from Holocaust survivors of what it is like to be subject to the pitiless regard of institutions and persons whose aim is to utterly and ineradicably destroy them and everything human about them. I will return to a particular aspect of this in Chapter 10, where people without power assume responsibilities that cause them abiding pain. Here my concern is with people who have total power and responsibility but who seem relatively untouched by the sort of guilt or remorse one might expect given the vile things they did to children, women and men. Until recently, comparable accounts by or about perpetrators of genocide in particular have been notable for their rarity. Among the books which have latterly focused on the motivation of the perpetrators of the Holocaust, and on some of the consequences for them, are Christopher Browning's *Ordinary Men: Reserve Police Battalion 101 and the Final Solution in Poland* and Daniel Goldhagen's *Hitler's Willing Executioners: Ordinary Germans and the Holocaust*.[2] Disgust rather than guilt or shame was an emotion that seemed to characterise these men and women in carrying out their genocidal work, often coupled with a sense of pride in the thoroughness of a job well done. How can pride without guilt or remorse become the companion of pitilessness?

Pride, guilt and shame are emotions of responsibility. You feel proud when something for which you are responsible turns out well. Guilt, on the other hand, is a consequence of taking responsibility for something that turns out undesirably and not, perhaps, having prevented it when you could have. Research on these emotions shows that children's understanding of personal responsibility changes, especially between 6 and 9 years of age, and that with their changing understanding comes corresponding changes in the emotions of guilt, shame and pride.[3] Whereas six-year-olds described themselves as experiencing guilt even though they had little control over the outcome, the older children 'confined their guilty feelings to outcomes that were more obviously within their control'.[4] The change with age is a change that involves understanding that whether one is responsible or not is relevant to the appropriateness of feeling guilty or ashamed or proud. This alone, however, is insufficient to account for these social emotions.

It also matters what other people think. The approval or contempt of others influences whether we feel pride or shame or guilt in certain circumstances. Their emotional state can imbue ours. My feeling of pride can dissipate if other people who matter to me disapprove of what I have done. In that case it is possible for an initial feeling of pride to transform into a subsequent feeling of shame or guilt. Equally, I might be able to resist the attitudes of others to what I do and to supply my own approval or disapproval of my actions and so still feel pride, for example, no matter what they think. Responsibility and norms are core to this, as are the primary emotions of anger and joy upon which those of shame, guilt and pride are probably built. There is a sense in which pride, guilt and shame are negotiable.

The recursive nature of emotional interactions is worth stressing, where, for instance, the next in the sequence of emotions felt by an antagonist feeds off the emotions which he or she causes in the person being victimised. The oppressor's starting emotion shapes the emotion he tries to cause in his victim, which in turn shapes his next emotion upon witnessing that state of his victim. After the *Anschluss*, when Hitler annexed Austria in 1938, Jews were publicly humiliated in front of and by their fellow citizens in Vienna by being compelled to clean the pavements on their hands and knees with ridiculously small brushes. The photographs show the triumphal, contemptuous amusement of their tormentors and the impassive endurance of the victims, so recently fellow citizens. This scene became common throughout the Third Reich, a prelude to infinitely worse atrocities. By humiliating Jews in this utterly demeaning way, especially Jews of obvious social standing, the Nazis – whose identity was partly constituted as Daniel Goldhagen argues by a hatred for the category 'Jew' and other 'racial inferiors' – deliberately made the Jewish people into objects of public contempt. Visibly constructing Jews as 'contemptible' helped ensure that the oppressors' feelings need not be alloyed by feelings of compassion or sympathy given this public evidence of the contemptible nature of the work-shy Jew. What does one do with the contemptible if not sneer at them? The more unopposed their power to abuse became, the more abusive became their behaviour, and the more self-righteously confident their self-justifications. Such mass feelings about outgroups have roots and histories. Their psychology can only be understood in terms of these cultural histories.

Emotional recursion and the location of responsibility are closely linked. Hitler blamed the Jews for his own treatment of them. At its crudest, he asserted that the Jews brought their catastrophe upon themselves, which implied that he was merely the instrument of it. This same process of relieving self of responsibility and shifting it onto the victim threads through all our lives. Criminals often use it. One seventeen-year-old burglar put it clearly: 'If I started feeling bad, I'd say to myself, "Tough rocks for him." He should have had his house locked better and his alarm turned on.'[5] Even if his initial state of feeling was 'bad', by judging that the house-owner deserved it by his lack of security the young burglar could make himself feel better. Projection of blame, shifting of responsibility and self-justification are easy allies.

The developmental psychological roots of understanding others, and caring about how they feel, are particularly evident in the second year. Carolyn Zahn-Waxler and her colleagues showed that during that year most children become sensitive to the distress and anger of other family members.[6] Equally interesting, however, is the work of Judy Dunn and her colleagues suggesting that with the onset of the ability to respond to the distress of others comes the ability to deliberately upset them.[7] From fourteen months onwards, infants understand how to provoke and annoy siblings during a confrontation. This can involve taking their prized possession, or damaging it, or spoiling a game, or frightening them. While one mother was talking to a researcher about how Anny was terrified of a particular toy spider, her sibling got the toy and shoved it towards Anny thereby deliberately making her cry. Verbal teasing becomes common by two years of age. One twenty-four-month-old would infuriate her sister when they were in conflict by maintaining that she was Allelujah, one of her sister's imaginary friends. Very young children also explicitly comment on their own responsibility for transgressions, 'I done it. I done it.'

Children in their second year develop some conception that rules are shared by family members, and they are intensely interested in what is expected and permitted as well as in what is forbidden. The qualities of the family in which the child is placed make a huge difference to the development of their moral understanding and conduct. Dunn and Munn showed that those children at two years of age who exhibited relatively mature conduct when they were in conflict – acts of conciliation, teasing, reference to rules, justifications – characteristically had mothers who referred frequently to social rules, and to the feelings of siblings, when the mother intervened in sibling conflicts.[8] Other work shows that what matters most in how a mother communicates the idea that one should not hurt others is not the explanations *per se*, nor the consequences, but the quality of emotional intensity of the mother's communication.[9] What really matters to the mother, as indicated by the strength of feeling with which she makes herself understood, influences what comes to matter for the child.

The very young child can use his or her sense of how a sibling feels either to alleviate distress or to deliberately cause it. The growing ability in the second year to respond to others' distress is shaped by how the mother's intensity of feeling shapes the child's way of feeling about an issue. A mother's world-view is a major influence on a child's, though not always in obvious ways. Needless to say, it is not just the mother who is influential. Fathers, brothers, sisters and others can play a powerful part in developing the frames of reference by which a child categorises the world and differentially cares about the well-being of some categories, actively wishes ill to others, and is indifferent to the fate of yet others.

The point is that this mapping of the child's world begins very early indeed and is powerfully shaped by the pre-existing maps of the world in which the child is implaced. The 'thinkable' and 'unthinkable' boundaries of personal identity are drawn early and are intricately linked to the thinkable and unthinkable boundaries of the social identities of the group to which the child belongs. The roots of pitilessness are to be found somewhere in this dynamic, and in the fact that empathy does not necessarily entail sympathy and may entail its opposite, even for two-year-olds. Cruelty and compassion are rooted in some of the same cognitive capacities, it appears. What influences the likelihood of their occurrence seems to be the dynamic of 'caring'. Caring and not caring might helpfully be understood as different patterns of emotional recursion.

Fritz Heider presented a useful taxonomy of the ways in which a person might be affected by the emotional state of another person.[10] The crucial factor is the nature of a person's care for another. Care can be negative as well as positive in the sense that it might either please me or upset me that a particular person or type of person fares well or badly. If the person, or category of person, is one to whom I feel positively disposed then I will 'sympathetically enjoy' their state if they do well, whereas if they fare badly I will feel 'sympathy' for them and share to a degree their upset or anguish. If, on the other hand, I start by feeling hostile towards them and they do well then I will be inclined to feel 'envy' whereas if they do badly what I am likely to feel is 'malicious joy' or *Schadenfreude* (literally, joy in the harm of others). Pity or compassion is a function of the type of caring which gives rise to sympathy and sympathetic enjoyment; pitilessness or mercilessness is a function of the type of caring which generates envy and *Schadenfreude*. In the former type of caring people share the fate of others in some way whereas in the latter there is no enveloping common concern. A further point is that the enjoyment of another's misfortune in this scheme of things is generally a feature of the malicious witness, with pitilessness characterising the actual perpetrators of others' pain. These are of course two sides of the same coin in that perpetrators are also witnesses, and malicious witnesses are potential perpetrators and at least accessories in their support and condonement.

Undoubtedly there are biological, evolutionary roots to the facts of categorisation with their accompanying tendencies to approach or avoid. Jerome Kagan has claimed that a finite number of emotional states ground a limited set of universal moral categories, and that these underlie the great variety of moral behaviours and consciously held ideals that we find among human beings.[11] He has in mind feelings like the fear of punishment, social disapproval, concern for those in distress, guilt and so on. The specific content of most social categories, however, with their particular valences of feeling, are likely to be learned and therefore to be culturally constituted.

For these reasons a cultural-historical psychology is needed to explain why specific historical instances of pitiless behaviour by one group towards another occur, and why emotions of pride rather than shame and guilt typify perpetrators who, in other contexts, can genuinely care about the well-being of their animals. The architect of the Holocaust, Heinrich Himmler told his Swedish chiropractor Felix Kersten that 'Nature is so wonderfully beautiful, and every animal has a right to live' and that after the war he would issue strict regulations to protect animals.[12] The commander of Police Regiment 25 – whose men were shooting tens of thousands of Jewish children, women and men, and suffocatingly packing tens of thousands of others into cattle trucks for transport to extermination camps – could on 11 June, 1943 reprimand his men for not adequately obeying the posted regulations on animal protection: 'One should with renewed strength take measures against cruelty to animals (*Tierquälereien*) and report it to the regiment. Special attention is to be devoted to the beef cattle, since through overcrowding in the railway cars great losses of the animals have occurred, and the food supply has thereby been severely endangered.'[13] How can a man shoot children and their desperately protecting mothers in the most brutal manner and simultaneously be a loving father or be genuinely compassionate about animals?

To us this can seem mysteriously inexplicable because it is so chillingly awful. Why though, when history so regularly and globally shows us how ordinary people can behave dreadfully towards those whom they have categorised or re-categorised out of the range of pity and compassion, do we tell ourselves that this is inexplicable? Could it be that the conditions for hatred of the other can come so easily into play that inexplicability and references to Evil are in fact our defences against recognising how close to being such a person each of us could come? What governs the emergence or inhibition of the conditions that lubricate vile behaviour on a large scale? Not, it would seem, individual moral restraint, exceptional exemplars notwithstanding. Socio-political explanations and their histories are by far the more compelling explanations for the sort of genocidal pitilessness that demands explanation. That is why at the beginning of this chapter I identified the concepts of social world, identity and belief as being necessary to explain sympathy and its opposite, pitilessness. Social worlds have distinctive identities which are constituted by beliefs, and these in turn shape the making of individual selfhood. Moral compasses are mass-produced and come with 'Made in X' labels attached.

It is a fact that members of ingroups can show great empathy and kindness to members of their own groups while acting barbarously towards equivalently positioned members of outgroups. This is universally the case. We tend to think of this disparity in the following sort of terms:

a.   There is a universal empathic–sympathetic ability.
b.   It can be *inhibited* when the object of attention is a member of a despised or feared outgroup.
c.   It is fear or disgust which acts to inhibit the operation of these capacities for empathy–sympathy.
d.   The solution is to dilute or eradicate the conditions for the experience of fear or disgust in order to allow fellow-feeling to work untrammelled.

There is an alternative or, better, a complementary possibility. The capacity for sympathy is universal, as is that for empathy, but the objects of sympathy are local in the same way that the capacity for fear or disgust is universal but their objects are local and variable. Worms may disgust us a culinary delicacy but may delight others. Therefore, on this hypothesis, it is not that the natural capacity for sympathy is inhibited, but rather that particular unsympathised objects have not been included in the category of the sympathetic when those categories were being constructed and filled. The connection between empathy and sympathy must be actively constructed, rather than being naturally there already but needing to be revealed through stripping off layers of obscuring, inhibiting feeling. Pitilessness would then be an absence rather than an inhibition. Compassion would be a connection between categories of person and dispositions to help.

In extreme circumstances empathy may be fully in play in that an aggressor or torturer knows full well what it is like to be the victim and understands with a Sadean precision how the world looks to the victim, but that sympathy is simply not in play at that time. Remember our two-year-olds! In other words, it may be morally desirable that capacities for empathy and sympathy are knitted together but that that knitting will not happen, or will not happen well, if it is not explicitly an objective of a socialisation process. The linking of empathy and sympathy is, in this account, a political problem.

On this alternative view, capacities for empathy (imaginatively understanding how the world is from the other person's point of view) and sympathy (feeling what it is like to be the victim in those circumstances so that one would wish that *they* did not feel like that and, consequently, that *we* in our paler sympathetic way did not feel as we do either) are capacities that must be meshed together rather than coming with natural linkages and subsequently being uncoupled or inhibited.[14] From this perspective, the dynamic of sympathy formation would need to be a global political project, yet with enough there naturally on which to culture the sorts of belief that underpin, for instance, the UN Declaration on

Human Rights, and to promote their incorporation as constituents of national, ethnic, religious and personal identities.

Theodore Zeldin reports how the mother of the Russian poet Yevtushenko witnessed the procession of 20,000 German prisoners through the streets of Moscow in 1944. Their well-dressed generals walked in front 'oozing contempt' and superiority. The crowd surged forward in anger and hatred. But when they saw the utterly miserable, ragged, hopeless, wounded condition of the ordinary German soldiers the street, it seems, became silent. An old woman broke through the cordon and offered a crust of bread to one of the soldiers. Others followed with food and cigarettes. Powerless, unthreatening and broken, the enemy soldiers had been re-categorised as people worthy of sympathy, but not their generals whose demeanour neither asked for nor invited sympathy. As Zeldin remarks, however, 'such spontaneous outbursts of compassion have seldom been more than rainbows in the sky; they have not changed the climate; they have not so far stimulated a desire to listen to what enemies have to say.'[15]

The beliefs with which human worlds are fabricated necessarily create divisions between 'us' and 'them', between ingroups and outgroups. This inescapable dividing of the world subsequently carries consequences, some subtle, many gross, for how we feel about the different elements of our partitioned worlds. Henri Tajfel argued that the very fact of grouping entailed discrimination. Social identities pivot on self-categorisations, which in turn underpin the sorts of conflicts that occur between groups. Tajfel highlights this simple point:

> . . . in order for large numbers of individuals to be able to hate or dislike
> or discriminate against other individuals seen as belonging to a common
> social category they first have acquired a sense of belonging to groups (or
> social categories) which are clearly distinct from and stand in certain
> relations to those they hate, dislike or discriminate against.[16]

The work of a cultural-historical psychology includes accounting not just for the specific beliefs and their histories that generate ingroups and outgroups, but also for the scripts of concern and action that these beliefs entail. Beliefs, as ideas, are menus for behaviour whether personal or collective. As explorations of scripting the pitiless treatment of an outgroup, the accounts of Christopher Browning and Daniel Goldhagen on how the 'ordinary Germans' of the Reserve Police Battalions came to become such effortless killers so quickly makes salutary reading for a cultural psychology of pity and pitilessness. I am aware of the criticisms, for and against, of Goldhagen's passionately argued case for the malignant power of 'eliminative anti-semitism'. These are generally beside my point of interest here which is the idea of 'willing' as in *Hitler's Willing Executioners*. How does the unthinkable become thinkable? Goldhagen's re-focusing of attention, following that of Browning, on the perpetrators and their enabling worldview can be usefully juxtaposed with accounts such as that of Ervin Staub on the origins of genocide.[17]

Browning was first in 1992 to offer an account, from the files of the Office of the State Prosecutor in Hamburg, of how one particular group of middle-aged, minimally trained men in Reserve Police Battalion 101 became routinised mass murderers. Over sixteen months between 1942 and 1943 this one battalion of under 500 men shot an estimated 38,000 Jews. The investigation by the Prosecutor's Office between 1962 and 1972 yielded interrogations for 210 of these men, and these formed the basis of Browning's account.

Unlike the killing groups of the SS, these reserve policemen had no specific training to prepare them to be 'hard' killers and that is why they are so interesting. Their first operation involved shooting women and children face to face. Major Trapp, their commanding officer, was visibly upset at his orders and exonerated anyone of his men from the operation if they felt unable to carry out these orders 'from above'. Only about a dozen of the 500 men stepped forward. That first day the remainder shot in excess of 1,500 Jews in awful circumstances. Browning describes their initial disgust, upset and rationalisations for particular choices they found themselves making. One 35-year-old metalworker from Bremerhaven chose to shoot only children while his comrade shot their mothers as they held the children by the hand ' . . . because I reasoned with myself that after all without its mother the child could not live any longer. It was supposed to be, so to speak, soothing to my conscience to release children unable to live without their mothers.'[18]

Browning examines many explanations for how these ordinary Germans became pitiless professional killers and in his very last paragraph lists them before concluding with his stark question:

> There are many societies afflicted by traditions of racism and caught in the siege mentality of war or threat of war. Everywhere society conditions people to respect and defer to authority, and indeed could scarcely function otherwise. Everywhere people seek career advancement. In every modern society, the complexity of life and the resulting bureaucratization and specialization attenuate the sense of personal responsibility of those implementing official policy. Within virtually every social collective, the peer group exerts tremendous pressures on behavior and sets moral norms. If the men of Reserve Police Battalion 101 could become killers under such circumstances, what group of men cannot?[19]

All these explanations and more are needed to explain how particular men or groups of men become merciless. There is nonetheless some order to the dynamic in which each of these influences, and their relative potency, comes into play. Part of that order concerns the ways in which individual consciousness is shaped by collective social consciousness, how personal identity is patterned by group identity, how the concerns of individuals arise from their insertion into pre-existing patterns of social concern, and how the ranges and types of choice confronting individuals are determined by forces not of their own making or choosing.

Ervin Staub's analysis of the roots of genocide recognises its multi-faceted genealogy. Genocide does not occur without warning. Those who kill are likely to have long held negative views of their victims. Beliefs about one's own group and its constituting outgroups – what 'we' are 'not' – have histories. These constitute identities. In the context of my initial proposal that self functions as a locative system, these identities simultaneously constitute social worlds and ways of locating and navigating within these worlds. Staub argues that Germany was a classic example of how genocide 'does not normally *arise* from strong prejudice but *evolves* from it'.[20] Anti-Semitism, on this view, was part of the condition of Germany preceding Hitler's accession to power. Its entailment of genocide, however, was a transformation brought about by the process of Nazification that followed. This is important because Goldhagen's argument is that Hitler's taking total control allowed an already existing 'eliminationist anti-semitism' to operate untrammelled rather than transforming a virulent anti-Semitism into a genocidal one. This is a key difference between Staub and Goldhagen as far as the Holocaust is concerned.

Difficult social conditions are the cauldron in which prejudice transmutes into genocide. Germany lost the First World War and experienced protracted social and economic upheavals in its wake. Such conditions favour scapegoating, and Jews offered such a scapegoat. Their association with other perceived threats to the Nazi ideal for Germany, capitalism and communism, added to their demonisation. From 1933, when Hitler came to power, to 1941, when the genocide began in earnest, the German public had participated in increasingly brutal anti-Semitic actions. These started with boycotting Jewish stores and moved through a progressive denuding of their rights as citizens and persons, and on to their public branding with stars and extreme social isolation and segregation. All of this was laced with a pervasive violence towards them. Anti-Semitic propaganda over those years increased to a virulent torrent. The German public participated to a large extent in each increment of oppression and was, Staub argues, incrementally changed by its participation.

As perpetrators, as willing joiners, as people who simply go along and do as they are told, and even as passive bystanders, people come to distance themselves from victims. They do so to protect themselves from distress through empathy and guilt. They justify what happens to victims by devaluing them more and more, until they exclude them from the human and moral realms.[21]

The emotional costs of sympathising, with the inevitable choices with which the sympathetic person is faced in such extreme circumstances, bear emphasising. Sympathy is a demanding and burdensome relationship which needs the sustenance of beliefs about solidarity, beliefs built into the making of ourselves such that we feel we have no choice but to be sympathetic, otherwise we are not being 'true to ourselves'. The pervasive anti-Semitism of Germany at that time, coupled with the enormously improved quality of life and the resurgence of national pride for ordinary – non-Jewish – Germans made their distancing from the 'parasitic Jew' all the easier. It should also be said that anti-Semitism was widespread outside Germany, reaching its zenith in the United States, according to Staub, in 1938.[22] Most nations refused to allow Jews to escape Nazi Germany by immigrating to their own countries after the Evian conference in 1938. Other internal influences enabling genocide included the threat associated with being a dissident and a deep societal value on respecting authority and obeying leaders.

Staub's view is that the path followed by Germans of that time to genocide was paved with many small decisions and that that is where the responsibility of each is located. Each in his or her own way could have acted differently and that 'could' is what generates the space for responsibility. An extreme social pathology, viewed from a democratic humanist perspective, became a normal worldview in which the unthinkable was just a few further steps along the path and around the corner. This metaphor implies that the path and the corner were already there. Another way of thinking about it might be that the path and its vagaries were being constructed as its travelling-makers went along. This question of inevitability is a controversial part of the argument advanced by Goldhagen and of the ensuing controversy surrounding his book. Pushed to its limits, the alleged propulsive power of 'eliminationist anti-semitism' actually runs the risk of excusing its perpetrators, according to some critics.[23]

Speaking of the range of prejudicial beliefs that have characterised societies over time, Goldhagen says that

> even if many of these beliefs are now considered to be absurd, people once held them dearly, as articles of faith. Because they did, such beliefs provided them with maps, considered to have been infallible, to the social world, which they used in order to apprehend the contours of the surrounding landscapes, as guides through them and, when necessary, as sources and inspiration for designs to reshape them.[24]

His thesis regarding the Holocaust is simply stated: 'no Germans, no

Holocaust'.[25] The central causal agent for the Holocaust was their particular beliefs about the Jews:

> Not economic hardship, not the coercive means of a totalitarian state, not social psychological pressure, not invariable psychological propensities, but ideas about Jews that were pervasive in Germany, and had been for decades, induced ordinary Germans to kill unarmed, defenseless Jewish men, women, and children by the thousands, systematically and without pity.[26]

Goldhagen argues that a particular ideology engendered Germans' willingness to kill the Jews, an ideology that led them to conclude that the Jews ought to die. He argues that such beliefs were constitutive of German identity and its world. In this world a pitiless regard for the Jew was easily thinkable because it was part of their moral order. Germans were led by the dominant construal of the world to think like this. Hence Staub's view that Goldhagen effectively exonerates the perpetrators by arguing so strongly for the inevitability of their thinking in genocidal terms given the nature of the beliefs that constituted their collective and subsequently their personal identity. Culture and cognitive models are first and foremost to blame.

This anti-Semitism preceded the Holocaust by many decades and was enabled by Hitler's assumption of total power. Goldhagen's is the account of pitilessness most radically committed to an etiology of beliefs wherein sympathy is actively discouraged from connecting with empathy (understood as being able to imagine the world from another's point of view) as far as the Jews in particular were concerned. Of course, many other groups also suffered horribly under this merciless regime.

Goldhagen estimates that the killing machine specifically involved in the Holocaust was over 100,000 people, and possibly in excess of half a million.[27] The camp system was without restraint where the Germans 'could give free rein to the Nazi German morality of pitilessness in the application of violence to subhumans'.[28] They turned people there into the very image of the subhumans that they took them to be through systematic humiliation, fear, pain, starvation, and contempt. Kurt Möbius, a former Police Battalion member who served in Chelmno, had this to say when testifying in 1961:

> I believed the propaganda that all Jews were criminals and subhumans and that they were the cause of Germany's decline after the First World War. The thought that one should disobey or evade the order to participate in the extermination of the Jews did not therefore enter my mind at all.[29]

In this example of the total inversion of the humane order, Möbius found *not* killing the Jews unthinkable. This is Goldhagen's point. The willingness of such as Möbius to act pitilessly towards any within the category 'Jew' indicated how the anti-Semitic belief system was reproducing itself by constituting the very identity of these Germans. Goldhagen, Browning, Lifton and a host of others demonstrate beyond question the willingness of large numbers of Germans of this period to engage in genocide. There is little evidence to hand to suggest that after the war the perpetrators felt remorse or retrospective sympathy for what they did to their victims.

The willingness to obey orders was not born of fear. There is no extant example of a German suffering any serious consequence for refusing to kill a Jew.[30] There are examples of Germans violating other forms of order, indicating that they were not the automatons that post-war defences might suggest. Goldhagen contends that the critical factor in the willingness to kill the Jews was the perpetrator's conception of them, what they believed them to be. His dismissal of the centrality of other types of explanation echoes that of Browning:

> Coercion, obedience to authority, social psychological pressure, self-interest, and displacement of responsibility onto others are explanations, according to their own logic, that are applicable equally and as unproblematically to the perpetrators of the Holocaust as they are to explaining, say, why bureaucrats today would help to implement a policy regarding air quality that they might think is misguided.[31]

Racism in the context of war or its threat headed Browning's list as we saw above and is also that endorsed by Goldhagen:

> The one explanation adequate to these tasks holds that a demonological anti-semitism, of the virulent racial variety, was the common structure of the perpetrator's cognition and of German society in general. The German perpetrators, in this view, were assenting mass executioners, men and women who, true to their own eliminationist antisemitic beliefs, faithful to their cultural antisemitic credo, considered the slaughter to be just.[32]

Towards the end of *Hitler's Willing Executioners*, Goldhagen considers what Hobbes had to say on the natural flow of sympathy for people who suffer great wrongs and he asks what blocked the natural flow of German compassion for Jews. This is an example of the assumed link between empathy and sympathy which I introduced earlier in this essay. His own argument would support the idea that sympathy animates empathy only when favoured by particular beliefs. When, as with

Nazism, a radical revolutionary inversion of a humane moral order succeeds in fanning to dominance already existing beliefs about a social category like that of 'Jew', and when the social mechanisms for constructing and controlling individual minds, identities and worldviews are used to reproduce these ideas throughout social consciousness, then the effects will also be revolutionary, and revolting.

Pitilessness and sympathy are psychological children of historical circumstance. Notwithstanding the awfulness of the twentieth century, there are signs for optimism when a longer-term view is taken. Beliefs about the repulsiveness of deliberately causing suffering to other humans and to other living things are robust in the contemporary world, as Charles Taylor argues. Theodore Zeldin also sounds a positive note when he writes that 'For a whole century, humanity has been finding reasons for showing compassion to those who commit stupid or even horrible crimes; the law is everywhere becoming more merciful.'[33]

One could be forgiven, however, for feeling that there is a Manichean struggle going on between beliefs that favour alleviating the suffering of others and beliefs that couldn't care less. Michael Ignatieff is right in thinking that it is a fact of our species that 'we possess the faculty of imagining the pain and degradation done to other human beings as if it were our own' and that this is the secular defence of human rights.[34] What is needed in addition, however, is that we are brought *to care* that the pain of others should not be deliberately caused nor be allowed to continue where it could be alleviated. Sympathetic empathy for all categories of human being as a feature of national and personal identities is the only guaranteed antidote to recurring pitilessness. History suggests that this is a quixotic aspiration. Is it futile to hold on to it and try to change History's mind?

Notes

1 L. Wispé, *The Psychology of Sympathy*, New York, Plenum Press, 1991, p. 163.
2 C. R. Browning, *Ordinary Men: Reserve Police Battalion 101 and the Final Solution in Poland*, New York, Harper Perennial, 1993, and D. J. Goldhagen, *Hitler's Willing Executioners: Ordinary Germans and the Holocaust*, London, Abacus, 1998.
3 P. L. Harris, *Children and Emotion: The Development of Psychological Understanding*, Oxford, Basil Blackwell, 1989, Chapter 4.
4 Ibid., p. 87.
5 W. Damon, *The Moral Child: Nurturing Children's Natural Moral Growth*, New York, The Free Press, 1988, p. 18.
6 C. Zahn-Waxler, M. Radke-Yarrow, and R. C. King, 'Child Rearing and Children's Prosocial Initiations towards Victims of Distress', *Child Development*, 1979, 50, 319–30. For comprehensive accounts of the research in this area see M. Radke-Yarrow, C. Zahn-Waxler and M. Chapman, 'Children's Prosocial Dispositions and Behavior' in E. M. Hetherington (ed.), *Handbook of Child Psychology, Volume 4: Socialization, Personality and Social Development*, 4th edn, New York, Wiley, 1983. Also see N. Eisenberg and

R. A. Fabes, 'Prosocial Development', and E. Turiel, 'The Development of Morality' in N. Eisenberg (ed.), *Handbook of Child Psychology*, 5th edn, *Volume 3: Social Emotional, and Personality Development*, New York, John Wiley & Sons, 1998.

7 J. Dunn, 'The Beginnings of Moral Understanding: Development in the Second Year' in J. Kagan and S. Lamb (eds), *The Emergence of Morality in Young Children*, Chicago, The University of Chicago Press, 1987, Chapter 2.

8 J. Dunn and P. Munn, 'Sibling Quarrels and Maternal Intervention: Individual Differences in Understanding and Aggression', *Journal of Child Psychology and Psychiatry*, 1986, 27, 583–95.

9 Dunn, 'Beginnings of Moral Understanding', p. 103.

10 F. Heider, *The Psychology of Interpersonal Relations*, New York, Wiley, 1958, Chapter 11.

11 J. Kagan, *The Nature of the Child*, New York, Basic Books, 1984.

12 P. Padfield. *Himmler: Reichsführer-SS*, London, Papermac, 1995, pp.351–2.

13 Goldhagen, op. cit., p. 271.

14 Wispé defines sympathy as 'an increased awareness of the suffering of others and the urge to alleviate it', op. cit., p. 91.

15 T. Zeldin, *An Intimate History of Humanity*, London, Minerva, 1995, p. 243.

16 H. Tajfel, *Differentiation between Groups: Studies in the Social Psychology of Intergroup Relations*, London, Academic Press, 1978, p. 50.

17 E. Staub, *The Roots of Evil: The Origins of Genocide and Other Group Violence*, New York, Cambridge University Press, 1989.

18 C. Browning, op. cit., pp.72–3.

19 Ibid., p. 189.

20 E. Staub, 'The Evolution of Evil', *Theory & Psychology*, 8, 5, October 1998, p. 703.

21 Ibid., p. 704.

22 Ibid.

23 Ibid., p. 705.

24 Goldhagen, op. cit., pp. 28–9.

25 Ibid., p. 7.

26 Ibid., p. 9.

27 Ibid., p. 167.

28 Ibid., p. 175.

29 Ibid., p. 179.

30 Ibid., pp.379, 430 and Browning, op. cit., p. 170.

31 Goldhagen, op. cit., p. 392.

32 Ibid., pp. 392–3.

33 T. Zeldin, *An Intimate History of Humanity*, p.252.

34 M. Ignatieff, 'Human Rights: The Midlife Crisis', *The New York Review of Books*, 20 May 1999, p. 60. He further asks 'Why do we need the idea of God in order to believe that human beings should not be beaten, tortured, coerced, indoctrinated, or in any way sacrificed against their will? These intuitions derive from our own experience of pain and our capacity to imagine the pain of others.'

10

SUFFERING, RADICAL DISLOCATION AND THE LIMITS OF MORAL RESPONSIBILITY

> In all this, self-condemnation strikes us as quite unfair . . . . This guilt seems to subsume the individual victim-survivor rather harshly to the evolutionary function of guilt in rendering us accountable for our relationship to others' physical and psychological existence. This experience of guilt around one's own trauma suggests the moral dimension inherent in all conflict and suffering.
>
> (Robert Jay Lifton, *The Broken Connection: On Death and the Continuity of Life*, 1983, p.172)

If certain ideas which constitute social and personal identities underpin phenomena of pitilessness or compassion, then the same is true for guilt, shame and blame. These negative emotions inhere in ways of appraising human conduct and cannot be understood without understanding the ideas fuelling these appraisals. Cultural psychological accounts of perpetrators and of victims are alike in this respect. Analogous to the role of genes in human lives, individuals are simultaneously the users and the vehicles for the perpetuation of ideas about themselves and their worlds.

The ephemerality of our notions of inside and outside, and the direction with which our preoccupations change from internal to external or from external to internal, are most acutely in play during pain and suffering, on the negative side, or during love and aesthetic or mystical experiences on the positive side. To put it succinctly but crudely, pain and suffering direct attention 'inwards' whereas love and art direct attention 'outwards'. If all experience is a dynamic and variable interaction between the constitutive powers of subjectivity (how things are for me) and intentionality (the focus of my subjectivity), then suffering can be characterised as an intensification of the subjective with a corresponding diminution of the objective and the non-self. Love or aesthetic experiences of art, on the other hand, are intensifications of the powers of the intentional object to shape subjective experience in novel ways.

Negative absorption characterises suffering whereas positive absorption typifies love and the aesthetic. In Chapter 11 I will consider positive absorption and its role in experiences of art that are judged to be 'moving'. Here I want to explore the relationship between this idea of suffering as negative absorption, and the recognition that there can be devastating consequences for individual psychology of having to sequentially occupy and survive within radically opposed moral orders. I take my examples from the testimonies of Holocaust survivors and from victims of torture, and focus in particular on the phenomena of self-blame and survivor guilt in relation to what I want to call the 'space of responsibility'.

There is a kind of moral paradox at the heart of cruelty and suffering. Oppressors with maximum power over others routinely assume minimum responsibility for their actions, whereas their victims, with minimal power over theirs, often assume subsequently devastating responsibility for their inactions. The self-apprehension of victims is strikingly moral. The words 'should have', 'could have', 'enough' and 'maybe' recur throughout the interviews given by survivors of traumatic oppression, and in their writings. 'I felt guilty for many years that maybe I should have run back and tried to get her with me or stay with her. Maybe I didn't do enough to stay together' or 'I had survivor guilt for years. I could never forgive myself . . . I had good connections in Auschwitz . . . but I didn't do enough to save my brother' or 'I'm guilty all my life. I'm guilty I didn't save my father, my mother, my sister. I feel guilty. I could have made Aryan papers for them' or 'I don't feel like I suffered enough.'[1] Wishing that they had or had not done something, judging that they had not done enough or could have done more are the hooks on which the self-blame of survivor guilt is hung.

From a locative understanding of self, there can be no greater examples of dislocation and its consequences for selfhood than the experiences of those who find themselves on the receiving end of genocidal or quasi-genocidal actions, or who become victims of torture, or who suffer profound physical injury such as paralysis. From a position of normality there is a disorienting transition into profound abnormality and, for survivors, a difficult and challenging second relocation into a new post-traumatic world. Making sense of these translocations and transformations of self and world is always done in a particular time and place, from, that is, a particular point of view. It is a narrative task, a recasting of self often in imaginary dialogue with interlocutors speaking from within the memory of the person.

Those who have lived through dreadful experiences know at first hand how their selves are bounded and contained by the thinkable and the unthinkable. Their subsequent struggles with themselves tell us something deeply important about the values that they are desperately trying to regain or reaffirm or perpetuate in the very act of punitively applying them to themselves. Even if they can be said to be unreasonable in their treatment of themselves – in their self-blame and guilt – one can discern a logic which is actually a defence of the very standards by which they harshly judge themselves to have failed. Few perpetrators, it would appear, make or are in a position to make this particular defence. This implicit acknowledgement of the centrality of moral dignity for selfhood is a profound legacy painfully bequeathed to us in the psychological suffering of survivors of this kind. In this chapter I would like to offer some reflections on aspects of this legacy.

Take the Holocaust or Shoah experiences first. The moral order of Nazism was a complete inversion of the ideals of a humane moral order. 'Hardness' and 'pitilessness' were good; compassion, sympathy and ideals of universal benevolence were signs of weakness and thus bad. Notwithstanding a period of acclimatisation to humiliation, deprivation and violence, the moment of entry to the camp system was sudden and unprecedented. Primo Levi is one of many who have described the wretched, totally disoriented state of those who arrived on the ramp at Auschwitz where, in dense moments, a merciless world shattered the expectations of those who were formed by and operated according to the norms of a humane one.[2]

The moment of trauma is one for which we are by definition unprepared. It catches us by surprise and we cope with it at that moment with the reflexes with which we happen to be already equipped. Usually, these reactions are utterly incommensurate with the atrocious scale of what confronts us. Cathy Caruth observes that

> . . . trauma is not locatable in the simple violent or original event in an individual's past, but rather in the way that its very unassimilated nature – the way it was precisely *not known* in the first instance – returns to haunt the survivor later on.[3]

The ignorance that defines trauma is the ignorance of its victim. The subsequent pain of self-blame and guilt which some survivors, especially those who have lost children and other close relatives, inflict upon themselves has everything to do with what they did not know or did not do but which, in retrospect, they think they ought to have known or could have done. Spaces of responsibility have as their boundaries words like 'should', 'could', 'maybe' and 'enough'.

The totality of the traumatic experience at the moment of its occurrence squeezes out the possibility of fully grasping it at that time. The nightmares, flashbacks and other repetitive phenomena that can follow are understood as *post hoc* attempts to cope with the trauma. But the temporal disjunction of the traumatic event and the survivor's reflection upon it leaves it always beyond reach, dooming the sufferer to ineffectual repetition and incessant pain. This is a Freudian explanation of the repetitiveness of post-traumatic symptoms. In trauma, as

Caruth puts it, 'the outside has gone inside without any mediation'.[4] Consider these traumatic events which I take from Lawrence Langer's powerful *Holocaust Testimonies*.[5] Langer built his investigation of the selves, memories and narratives of 'former victims' (preferred to 'survivors') on the Fortunoff Video Archive for Holocaust Testimonies established at Yale University in 1982.

Arriving on the infamous selection ramp in Auschwitz ('left' to immediate death, 'right' for work and temporary life) Anna G. observed a ten-year-old girl refusing to go left after selection. The SS held down the terrified little girl as she scratched and kicked and screamed to her mother nearby not to let them kill her. Anna G. saw an SS man ask the young mother if she wished to go to the left with her daughter. She said No! Anna G. was horrified and at that time 'blamed' the young mother for not choosing to accompany her terrified little girl to death. When her own daughter was born ten years later Anna G. began having nightmares that involved reliving that awful moment on the ramp, but this time her own daughter was the screaming girl.[6] Minutes into the vile inverted world of Auschwitz, was 'blame' the appropriate feeling towards the young mother?

To protect her infant during a selection for work in the Kovno ghetto in 1942 Bessie K. wrapped it in a bundle and tried to sneak it by the Germans. The baby cried and they took it away never to be seen again. What else could she have done in those circumstances? Recalling this forty years later in, as Langer describes it, 'a numb and trancelike voice', Bessie K. says 'I think all my life I have been alone.' She had remarried a most understanding man and had two daughters but had not spoken of this event for most of their lives together as 'I did not want to admit that this had happened to me.' She goes on to say that 'I wasn't even alive; I wasn't even alive. I don't know if it was by my own doing, or it was done, or how, but I wasn't there. But yet I survived.'[7] How is personal responsibility to be assessed in a case like this?

The situations in which people found themselves, situations deliberately constructed by the Nazis, were such as to so curtail choice and action and to so present the remaining options that their victims continued to apply standards of humane conscience to themselves for courses of action that were actually outside their own powers of control. Their own powers of control were largely restricted to their reactions and not to their actions. But, as we observed above, reactions to traumatic events come impotently after they have been seared into their survivors. The result is the anguish of victims blaming themselves for what they had done or not done when in fact they had all but minimal control over how they were to choose, and practically none over what they were to choose between. What remained in their control to some extent were their own attitudes to their decisions and indecisions. The moral space in which they assumed responsibility was not commensurate with the utter powerlessness of the actual space in which they found themselves, a space deliberately constructed to remove all power and personhood from them and from those they loved or admired.

Take another story from the point of entry into Auschwitz. Abraham P. arrived at that place on a train from Hungary with his parents and four brothers. They were totally disoriented when they arrived. At the selection his parents were sent to the left (death) and the four brothers were sent to the right. Not knowing the significance of this, Abraham P. recalls the following: 'I told my little kid brother, I said to him, "*Solly, gey tsu Tate un Mame* [go to Poppa and Momma]." And like a little kid he followed – he did. Little did I know that I sent him to the crematorium. I am . . . I feel like I killed him.'[8] An act of fraternal and familial concern in that context had these unforeseen and murderous consequences, and Abraham P., as a recently arrived representative of the humane tradition in that contrary world, blames himself for the rest of his life.

Or take the testimony of Moses S. for an action that has consequences beyond all expectation and which therefore allocates responsibility to the victims from a scale incredible by 'normal' standards. Two boys shared a bunk and one asked the other to mind his bread while he went to the latrine. Upon return he found that the boy had eaten his bread. He reports this to the Kapo who says to the boy who stole the bread 'You took away his life. Right?' The boy replies that he will return it in the afternoon. The Kapo says No! and takes the boy outside. Moses S. continues: 'He took the fellow outside. "Lie on the floor." He put a piece of *Brett* [a small board or plank] on his neck and with his boots [Moses S. imitates the action with his hands and feet] – bang! on his neck. *Fertig!* [finished!].'[9]

In our world how should the complaining boy feel? In *that* world how should responsibility be allocated? Are the two worlds commensurate? If not, what are the consequences of applying the standards of one to the actions of the other? And what are the consequences for self-knowledge and self-respect? The social reality of the camps was such that the conversation creating that reality was totally under the control of those who ran the camps, and so too were the powers which inevitably were formative of the inmates' selves. The tracks for their becoming were laid for them, and inexorably these tracks led into what Primo Levi called the 'grey zone', the zone in which a moral lessening (by the standards of the pre-camp world) was a necessary condition of survival, allied to sheer luck. Lawrence Langer, introducing his *Art from the Ashes*, writes:

> Western civilization has always prided itself on achieving the thinkable. When Hitler and his cohorts corrupted this vision by making the morally and physically *unthinkable* thinkable, and then practical, possible and finally *real*, they not only stained the idea of civilization, but infected the vaunted sources of its pride.[10]

Something is perpetuated every time an individual or group of individuals experiences guilt, shame or blame. That something is a moral ideal, a valued belief about how one should behave together with an emotional commitment to that belief. These moral ideals are building blocks of social and personal identity, as we saw with the work of Charles Taylor in Chapter 4. They are like boundary walls which contain 'the selves we truly are'. We *are* what they contain. To knock them down, or to have them knocked down, is to destroy or to experience the destruction of self. They shape what is thinkable or unthinkable, desirable or utterly undesirable for us to do. If we fail to do what seems desirable, or do or are forced to do what is undesirable, then we will experience guilt, shame and blame. These negative emotions are the containing cognitions' methods of self-protection, the guardians of their means of reproduction. It is on the borders of their appropriateness that we see the extent of the power of these constitutive moral ideals. Those borders are most visible in conditions of extreme coercion and its aftermath.

Lawrence Langer, counterpointing Charles Taylor's analysis of the *making* of the modern identity, presents his reflections on memory and the Holocaust as an exploration of the *unmaking* of the modern identity. If agency and self-responsibility are the signatures of the modern self, the testimonies of those who survived the Holocaust — and of the many other instances of extreme oppression — tell us what it is like to exist stripped of a sense of agency. Langer is right to maintain that the 'diminished self' must also find a place in our investigations of self and identity. Taylor's spatial metaphor for identity as an orientation 'in moral space' is one, observes Langer, which assumes

> that the existence of frameworks always allows one to find deep in the psyche a gyroscope that insures moral balance. But . . . circumstances in ghettos and camps were deliberately and systematically designed by the Nazis to destroy the functioning of that gyroscope.[11]

Taylor, it must be said in his defence, is quite aware of how human agency can be destroyed in such circumstances, as we can see from this comment:

> Thus, if I were forced by torture or brainwashing to abandon these convictions by which I define my identity, I would be shattered, I would no longer be a subject capable of knowing where I stood and what the meanings of things were for me, I would suffer a terrifying breakdown of precisely those capacities which define a human agent.[12]

Lawrence Langer's conclusion is nonetheless compelling:

What are we to learn from this interlude in history, during which moral intuitions so often were useless because physical and psychological constraints like hunger, illness, fear, despair, and confusion created an unprecedented nonethical environment immune to the promptings of these intuitions? One of the unavoidable conclusions of unreconciled understanding is that we can inhabit more than one moral space at the same time . . . and feel oriented and disoriented at the same time.[13]

In this simultaneous occupancy of two utterly antagonistic moral spaces may lie a logic for that 'illogical sense of responsibility' felt by so many survivors.[14] The role of pain, physical and psychological, is a key part of understanding the limits of agency and hence of self-responsibility. Those brought down to the torturers' cellar or herded onto the selection ramp at Auschwitz, like others in similar awful situations, know intensely the confusion of simultaneously occupying two utterly conflicting moral spaces.

Jean Améry, who committed suicide in 1978, was tortured by the Gestapo in Fort Breendonk in Belgium in 1943 and judged torture to be 'the most horrible event a human being can retain within himself'.[15] His core conclusion about the effects of torture on its victims is that they are dispossessed of the fundamental sense of their bodies as their homes and, with that, they are simultaneously dispossessed of the world as a trustworthy place to be:

> Whoever has succumbed to torture can no longer feel at home in the world. The shame of destruction cannot be erased. Trust in the world, which already collapsed in part at the first blow, but in the end, under torture, fully, will not be regained. . . . It is *fear* that henceforth reigns over him.[16]

He recalls his 'corporeality' being forced upon him by the first blows of his torturer and speaks of the complete transformation of the body into flesh. 'The tortured person is only a body,' writes Améry, and pain 'is the most extreme intensification imaginable of our bodily being.'[17] Pain is pain and, there being nothing more to say, it marks the communicative limits of language. The impact of the deliberately inflicted pain of torture is indelible. The tortured person stays tortured.

Améry's torturers were not, in his judgement, sexual sadists. Their fuel was power and the expansion of themselves as they brutally colonised the receding self-spaces of their victim. Améry did not know the real names of his Resistance colleagues and so could tell the Gestapo nothing more than the aliases he knew. Yet despite his acute understanding of the self-annihilating impact of prolonged, deliberately inflicted agony he still berates himself and speculates that had he known their real names 'I would be standing here now as the weakling I most likely am, and as the traitor I potentially already was.'[18] The width of an alias is all that separates him from total self-abnegation. In terms of his identity's boundaries, to be a 'traitor' or a 'weakling' or not 'a real man' is unthinkable. To be brought close to the dismantling of these boundaries by agonising pain and fear contaminates his sense of himself with an ensuing sense of humiliation, shame, self-blame and guilt. This suffering is the legacy of torture even for those who understand the dynamics of the inevitable diminution of self entailed by agony.

Elaine Scarry's analysis of the structure of torture echoes that of Améry. In parallel with Taylor and Langer on the making and unmaking of identity, Scarry's focus is on the making and unmaking of the correlative world and for this she draws on many sources including accounts of torture in the 1970s documented by Amnesty International.[19] She builds on the insight of survivors of torture that pain negates language and reduces utterance to a scream. In these self-diminished moments are to be found the clearest instances of negative absorption, where self and pain are one mutually constituting event, where agony expands to occupy the full space of subjectivity, where there is no intentional object because the unity of self and pain is the be-all and end-all of those hours, days, weeks.

Pain destroys language, forcing the suffering person to revert to a state prior to language where the scream or the groan or the wail is rooted. Scarry notes how our contemporary understanding of consciousness pivots on its intentionality. We always perceive something, think something, feel something. Damasio, for example, argues that our core consciousness is probably constructed in pulses occasioned by objects of attention, and that the seeming continuity of core consciousness has to do with the immensely rich range of intentional objects which are constantly available to the construing brain. Such objects, both in their powers to co-constitute consciousness and to move conscious persons beyond the boundaries of their own bodies into an external world shared with others, are vehicles for self-expansion. In rich experiences, such as aesthetic experiences of art, they enable experiences of positive absorption as we will see in Chapter 11. Extreme pain however, in stark and unique contrast, has no referential content, no object, no expansionary possibilities for self. This is why pain, in Scarry's view, resists objectification in language.[20]

The purpose of torture is to unmake the self by unmaking the body through pain and fear. In Scarry's terms the structure of torture is the structure of unmaking. Central to the uncreating of the victim's self is the threat to his or her sense of identity of seeking release from pain in what the circumstances are likely to construe as an act of betrayal. Loyalty to comrades, ideals, beliefs was, prior to capture and torture, part of the armature of the person's identity and sense of themselves. The desire for release from agony is construed as weakness.

The correlation between agony, humiliation, and self-diminution on the one hand and acts of 'betrayal' and confession on the other again raises vital questions about the nature of the body in pain and the claims of moral responsibility. Extracting 'confessions', however implausible, helps torturers and their masters justify what they do. 'Confessing', however falsely and fantastically, further diminishes the victim and copper-fastens their sense of being overwhelmed, not least by their own 'weakness'. A profound destruction of self is the risk taken by opponents, real or inadvertent, of torturing regimes. The amplification of that risk can be further assisted in the aftermath of torture by the self-blame and corroding humiliation of the victims, and by the construal of their reactions to the pain as blameworthy by their comrades.

If pain and suffering are the borderlands of such opposing moral spaces, what understanding of their dynamics would alter how moral responsibility is to be allocated in such circumstances? Scarry reminds us of what happens when a dentist's drill hits an exposed nerve: we 'see stars'.[21] The image conveys how the pain obliterates for those moments all the contents of consciousness. Those we love, our names, our concerns, all are absent for those moments. Being non-existent for us we cannot during those moments be said to be capable of 'betraying' them, assuming such a word applied, since we cannot be true or false to that which does not exist. What part has individual moral responsibility to play when the individual's world has ceased to be as an intentional object, pain having fully occupied consciousness and driven out the rest of the person's world? Guilt, shame, blame come *after the event*, when the torture has stopped, when the moral space occupied by the victim before this happened has been reinstated and is now self-punitively applied. This is part of what I understand Jean Améry to have meant when he wrote that the victim of torture 'stays tortured'.

Scarry observes how, in the process by which intense pain destroys a person's self and world, that destruction is experienced *spatially* 'as either the contraction of the universe down to the immediate vicinity of the body or as the body swelling to fill the entire universe'.[22] It is pain that destroys world, self and language in the first instance. 'Confession' and 'betrayal' with their self-recriminations are second-tier agents of destruction.

In the framework of Antonio Damasio's neurological account of consciousness and self, we could say that the losses of self, world and language for the duration of the pain are radical deformations of core consciousness and core self, whereas the subsequent losses of self-regard and reputation are sustained by extended consciousness and autobiographical self and especially by conscience.[23] Since extended consciousness and autobiographical self are founded on core consciousness and core self, any radical alteration of the latter is likely to significantly alter the former and to have definite implications for the reflexive operations of conscience.

Scarry argues that torturers work to make their victims complicit in their own unmaking. There are two strands to the type of torture that is other than the totally vindictive infliction of pain for its own sake, one physical and the other verbal. The ostensible reason for the torture is the torturers' need to have 'a question' answered. The question is the proffered motive for the torture, 'an answer' from the victim its ostensible purpose. The victim's answer is construed by all, including the victim, as 'a betrayal'.

Understood like this, the need to have the question answered is used by the torturers to justify what they do, and extracting an answer is a further means of discrediting the victim. This scenario inverts the moral reality of torture, diminishing the responsibility of the torturers and increasing that of the victims. By shifting attention away from the physical reality of torture towards the verbal, argues Scarry, one begins a move towards accommodating the torturers and masking the moral awfulness of what they do. What they do is to use 'the prisoner's aliveness to crush the things that he lives for'.[24] The question is an act of wounding, the answer a scream. That is the reality of torture.

The victims are conveyed to the point of self-betrayal on a self-annihilating stream of pain. They are systematically dismantled as agents while simultaneously being required to be agents in some respects.

> Despite the fact that in reality he has been deprived of all control over, and therefore all responsibility for, his world, his words, and his body, he is to understand his confession as it will be understood by others, as an act of self-betrayal. In forcing him to confess or, as often happens, to sign an unread confession, the torturers are producing a mime in which the one annihilated shifts to being the agent of his own annihilation.[25]

It is clear why pain and suffering of these kinds test the nature of moral responsibility's centrality to personal identity.

The impact of torture coupled with the fact of being betrayed by another is rather like multiplying two potent causes of isolation. When, coupled with the torture, it is you who are construed as the betrayer, by others but especially by yourself, the impact on self is devastating. Torture is deeply intimate, erasing the public and the private, the inside and the outside, the now and the then. Often it is sexual in nature and marries the extremity of vulnerability with the limits of humiliation. Erik Erikson developed the idea that a primary foundation of 'basic trust' is laid early in the life of a developing self, and fundamentally shapes our attitudes to the world as it unfolds before us.

In particular, the capacity to hope is rooted in the dynamics of basic trust. Sexual abuse, torture and profound betrayal corrode basic trust. That is what Jean Améry meant when he wrote of no longer being able 'to feel at home' in the world after torture. The same point is made by Inger Agger in *The Blue Room* when she writes of sexual abuse and torture as violating three of the most fundamental requirements for basic trust: the belief that the world is a benevolent and fair place; that life has meaning; and that I have worth.[26] That assault is a form of demoralisation, which when spelt out means a dismantling of the moral bases of identity.

When one is betrayed one is left, as Aaron Hass writes, 'feeling exceedingly alone. The boundary between I and the Other becomes impermeable, perhaps for ever.'[27] When you are the 'betrayer' – notwithstanding the doubtfulness of its possibility given the analysis above of the transformation of consciousness that occurs with prolonged and extreme pain – that division occurs within yourself. You no longer trust yourself. No longer trusting yourself, you cease to hope. Ceasing to hope, something profoundly human in you dies. You are literally a broken person, riven by a major faultline for which you hold yourself responsible.

The dislocations of torture and sexual abuse are like major cracks in a pane of glass, distorting light and view and verging on the shattered. This is well understood by the theory of torture, and is one of its explicit aims. Shame and guilt may be seen to rest on a lie or on a misconstrual of responsibility when it is understood that victims are forced to powerlessly occupy two radically antagonistic moral spaces with the ensuing radical disorientation that this entails. At the level of individual psychology, however, that is probably of little comfort to those whose whole being has been so profoundly assaulted and damaged. Yet at the collective level of cultural psychological understanding, perhaps there is another function for profound moral pain such as this.

A logical condition for the apportionment of responsibility is that people be deemed in control of the circumstances governing their actions. Conversely, if a person has no control over these circumstances and is effectively powerless to act (though not necessarily powerless to shape their private *reactions*) then they cannot be held to be responsible for their actions and even less so for their inactions. In such conditions their behaviour becomes the instrument of a more powerfully compelling agency, and it is that agency which should logically be held morally accountable. Of course a person in such circumstances could refuse to be used in this way and try to endure the consequences of this refusal. This *caveat* is necessary since the reply often given by soldiers who commit atrocities is that they were acting under the compulsion of orders. In the case of victims the problem, as we have seen, is that though powerless they assume responsibilities incommensurate with their position and with its possibilities for moral action.

From an individual psychological perspective that burdensome assumption of responsibility may indeed seem unreasonable and illogical. From a social and cultural perspective, however, something else can be seen to be going on, something which makes the post-traumatic suffering of guilt and self-blame at least intelligible and, I would venture, morally productive. This is something which would harmonise with the cultural evolutionary thinking of Richard Dawkins or Daniel Dennett just as it would with the humanistic perspective of Charles Taylor. It is a cultural psychological concern with the ways in which the processes of individual psychology are recruited for the perpetuation of self-making and world-making *ideas*, in this case ideas of what it is morally desirable to be.

We observed earlier how words like 'maybe', 'should have', 'could have', and 'enough' dominated the thoughts of many former victims. We heard the admirable Jean Améry, who in addition to the trauma of Gestapo torture at Fort Breendonk survived subsequent incarceration in Auschwitz, speak of himself as living in the shadow of his potential to be a 'weakling' or 'traitor'. I take these articulations of self-understanding as emblematic of the experiences of probably millions more in the twentieth century.

Implicit in each such account is some ideal of 'more' that could have been done or endured. This is where the metaphor of a 'space of responsibility' comes into play. 'Enough' means adequate or sufficient to satisfy a need or desire. Doing enough means fully filling the space of possibility or responsibility; not doing enough means falling short of this, and 'falling short' implies 'being less'. Being less than the requirements of those ideals which constitute our selves is not likely to leave us feeling as good about ourselves as would be the case if our actions coincided with the limits specified by the ideal.

What determines the adequacy with which we personally occupy such spaces if not some idea of what we ought to do, and such ideas are the moral ideals which constitute our worlds and our identities. For most of us most of the time such ideals are supplied to us. They are shared by others independently of us, and they carry on after us. Ideals as ideas have lives of their own with their own dynamics of self-perpetuation. They are the property of a community of common interest or understanding. Individual members of the community are, analogical to genes, carriers of ideas as identity-forming ideals.

These ideals are instantiated in our make-up as felt articulations of understanding. They shape our neurology in ways that profoundly influence our feelings and our actions, our conceptions of the world and its requirements of us. We do what 'feels' right and we resist doing what 'feels' wrong. The nature of our psychology rewards us with good feelings (pride, happiness) when we behave in accordance with the prescriptions of the ideal, and it punishes us when we resist or transgress the dictates of the ideal (guilt, blame, shame).

These are social emotions, shared with and determined by others. If on fulfilling or failing to fulfil an ideal I felt nothing either way, then I would be a dead end for the perpetuation of that ideal. As St John, in The Book of Revelation, wrote to Laodicea: 'I know that you are neither cold nor hot. How I wish you were either one or the other! But because you are lukewarm, neither hot nor cold, I am going to spit you out of my mouth.'[28]

Even if I transgress that ideal — however unreasonably I judge myself by the standards of logical or legal responsibility — and suffer guilt, blame or shame as a consequence, from a cultural psychological perspective my feelings are likely to favourably influence the perpetuation of the idea that is instantiated in my negative feelings. I may suffer but I do so because I am shaped to care in this way, and caring in this way I add to the likely perpetuation of my shaping ideal. My feelings, whether of pride or guilt, are bodily and psychological resources recruited by ideas for their own perpetuation. This is why phenomena of such huge social and political import as pitilessness and compassion, blame and approbation, cannot be understood outside a cultural psychological framework.

In the cases of Anna G., Bessie K., Abraham P., Jean Améry, and the millions of others for whom they stand, what can be said about the nature of the ideals which their twofold pain (the period of trauma and its aftermath) implicitly endorses? First, that they are ideals that always beckon us further than the place in which we now find ourselves. Otherwise, comparatives like 'more' would not apply. Some rare individuals do exemplify the outer limits of the ideal and themselves come to stand *as* ideals. Jean Améry mentions the great leader of the French Resistance, Jean Moulin, who did have the knowledge to destroy the whole movement but who endured torture to the death without disclosure.

Secondly, they are ideals of solidarity and love, self-transcending ideals which require that one should be for the well-being of others, especially those for whom you bear special responsibility such as your children, parents, family members, comrades. While such an analysis of the dynamics of victim suffering may be of little comfort to those tormented by their own feelings in the aftermath of trauma, there is a form of redemption at the cultural level for the ideals that constitute these sufferings of particular individuals. An echo of this might be heard in one of Nelly Sachs's Holocaust poems when those yet to be born address those who suffered so terribly and refer to themselves as 'future lights for your sorrow'.[29]

Making this part of a common understanding might in some small way in times to come render the moral suffering of others in similar circumstances easier to bear. That common understanding would include a trusting sympathy for those forced across borders into worlds that are 'unfeelable' except by those who have been there. It would know that radical ruptures in the contexts of lives, such as those we have discussed here, leave their victims with narratives of construal which simply don't match the demands they face. It would, however, also understand that the continued application of these moral narratives by victims to their own actions, however irrelevant they may be made to seem by the dynamics of the oppressing context, is part of a continuing struggle for a humane moral order. Forms of humane conscience are ideals it is far better for human beings to have than not to have as governing elements of themselves, despite the price they exact.

Notes

1 A. Hass, *The Aftermath: Living With The Holocaust*, Cambridge, Cambridge University Press, 1995, Chapter 2.
2 P. Levi, *The Drowned and the Saved*, London, Abacus, 1988, p. 42.
3 C. Caruth, *Unclaimed Experience: Trauma, Narrative, and History*, Baltimore, The Johns Hopkins University Press, 1996, p. 4.
4 Ibid., p. 59.
5 L. Langer, *Holocaust Testimonies: The Ruins of Memory*, New Haven, Yale University Press, 1991.
6 Ibid., pp. 12–13.
7 Ibid., p. 49.
8 Ibid., pp. 185–6.
9 Ibid., p. 27.
10 L. Langer (ed.), *Art from the Ashes: A Holocaust Anthology*. Oxford, Oxford University Press, 1995, p. 7.
11 Langer, *Holocaust Testimonies*, p. 200.
12 C. Taylor, *Human Agency and Language: Philosophical Papers 1*, Cambridge, Cambridge University Press, 1985, p. 35.
13 Ibid., p. 201.
14 A. Hass, op. cit., p. 29.
15 J. Améry, 'Torture', in Langer (ed.), *Art from the Ashes*, p. 122. See also J. Améry, *At the Mind's Limits: Contemplations by a Survivor on Auschwitz and Its Realities*, trans. Sidney Rosenfeld and Stella P. Rosenfeld, New York, Schocken, 1986.
16 Améry in Langer (ed.), *Art from the Ashes*, p. 136. For a discussion of how the normal enfolding aspects of rooms and domestic objects are recruited as accessories to torture see E. Scarry, *The Body in Pain: the Making and Unmaking of the World*, Oxford, Oxford University Press, 1985, pp.38–45. For an intriguing extension of domestic architecture as a metaphor for the intertwining of women's lives and abuse see I. Agger, *The Blue Room: Trauma and Testimony among Refugee Women: A Psycho-Social Exploration*, London, Zed Books, 1994.
17 Ibid., p. 131.
18 Ibid., p. 133.
19 Scarry, op. cit.
20 Ibid., p. 5.
21 Ibid., p. 30.
22 Ibid., p. 35.
23 A. Damasio, *The Feeling of What Happens: Body and Emotion in the Making of Consciousness*, New York, Harcourt Brace & Co., 1999.
24 Scarry, op. cit., p. 38.
25 Ibid., p. 47.
26 Agger, op. cit., pp. 13–14.

27 Hass, op. cit., p. 183.
28 The Book of Revelation, 3.15.
29 N. Sachs, 'Chorus of the Unborn' in L. Langer (ed.), *Art from the Ashes: A Holocaust Anthology*, p. 644.

11

BEING MOVED

Art, self and positive absorption

There is a miserable material[istic] and barbarian notion according
to which a man cannot be in two places at once; as though he were
a *thing*! A word may be in several places at once, [e.g.,] *six*, *six*,
because its essence is spiritual; and I believe that a man is no whit
inferior to the word in this respect. . . . But that he truly has this
outreaching identity – such as a word has – is the true and exact
expression of the fact of sympathy, fellow feeling – together with
all unselfish interests, – and all that makes us feel that he has an
absolute worth.

(C. S. Peirce, in V. M. Colapietro, *Peirce's Approach to the Self*,
1989, p. 103)

If the pain of deliberately inflicted torture epitomises negative absorption, then
the expansion of self that occurs in aesthetic experiences of art typifies its antithesis, positive absorption. Agony and art share the similarity that both can entail
absorbing experiences. The radical difference between the two is vectoral. The
coming back into being of the 'I' after an aesthetic experience of art has qualities
of expansiveness, of incorporating something good that was until recently other
than oneself. It has a quality of self-transcendence.

'Coming to' or 'coming back to oneself' after torture is a return to a tortured
self, a self that won't leave self alone, a broken self from which self cannot escape,
self as a container of pain, loathing, hate, grief, humiliation, alienation, anxiety. It
has a quality of immanence in which you *are* the very feelings you would wish not
to be. In aesthetic experiences of art, on the other hand, you cultivate the creation of feelings that you desire to *be*, at least for a short duration. In one, pain
crowds out the intentional object and reduces subjectivity to a homogeneous,
simple state of agony. In the other the subject willingly and trustingly cedes
control of experience to the constructive powers of the intentional object and the
result is a highly desirable passage of self-expansion.

These are the contrasting limits of negative and positive absorption. Positive
absorption opens up; negative absorption radically shuts down. There is a sense in

which the arts are inventions for taking us 'out of our selves', but inventions that depend for their power on our willingness to allow ourselves to be self-forgetful, albeit for relatively brief periods of time, and open to being emotionally re-formed during those periods. What is involved in these periods of aesthetic or positive absorption and what sorts of roots in childhood might such a capacity for experience have? How might these questions advance our understanding of what it is to be moved while listening to music, watching a film or play, dancing or gazing at a picture? Can 'being moved' be understood as 'relocation'?

I find that much that is stimulating in contemporary psychology, neurology, cognitive science and aesthetics is prefigured in John Dewey's lifelong preoccupation with the relationships between the biological and the cultural. His entire *œuvre* is a meditation on the nature of 'experience' for which, late in his life, he realised that he should have substituted the word 'culture'. That is why in what follows I return to Dewey as yet another source for a cultural psychology of self, this time in relation to art.

Many poets, artists, musicians and writers who have reflected on experiences of art have noted the centrality of one particular feature. They have spoken of it in terms of 'being lost in' or 'caught up in' or 'being one with' or 'being absorbed in' the work of art. Dewey insists in his *Art as Experience* that

> the uniquely distinguishing feature of esthetic experience is exactly the fact that no such distinction of self and object exists in it, since it is esthetic in the degree in which organism and environment cooperate to institute an experience in which the two are so fully integrated that each disappears.[1]

Dewey thinks of absorption in terms of the self's *surrender* in the aesthetic construction of the object. Perception and its object progressively and mutually constitute each other within aesthetic experience. In a way that Dewey or William James would have welcomed, Damasio and others are now beginning to spell out how such mutual construction is achieved neurologically. Positive absorption is not, of course, exclusive to aesthetic experience nor to the arts. It is an ideal, according to Dewey, for all experience 'when the desires and urgencies of the self are completely engaged in what is objectively done'.[2]

Mihaly Csikszentmihalyi's concept of 'flow' as a form of 'optimal experience' has many elements of what I am calling positive absorption.[3] Flow is partly characterised by the absence of self-scrutiny. Writing of a climber completely wrapped up in what he is doing, Czikszentmihalyi says that 'There is no way for anything or anybody to bring into question any other aspect of his self.' He goes on to observe that 'loss of self-consciousness does not involve a loss of self, and certainly not a loss of consciousness, but rather, only a loss of consciousness *of* the self'.[4] People capable of being intensely engaged in an activity become part of 'a system of action' greater than themselves. Such experiences are rated as highly satisfying.

My understanding of absorption requires a conception of experience as constituted by the interactive relationship of self and object. Absorption is a quality of that relationship. In aesthetic experiences of art, there is a 'rhythm of surrender and reflection'.[5] Absorption refers to the initial phase of the 'total overwhelming impression', a pre-reflective phase where people give themselves over to the power of the object, exercising minimal control over the nature and direction of the experience. This is of necessity a brief experience, lasting as long perhaps as it takes to savour the smell of an orange, to use an image offered by Kenneth Clark. It may be followed by reflective experiences where answers are sought to questions of what, how and why concerning the previous phase. This reflective phase may lead the person to re-attend to the object and perhaps to participate in a fuller and more elaborate experience. This is why Dewey describes the process as a rhythm. For him, aesthetic absorption is active participation in the formation of experience, where self constructs the object and the object self in mutually determinative ways.

Apart from passing references, psychologists and philosophers of art and of aesthetic experience have rarely offered detailed analyses of this phenomenon which seems to lie at the heart of such experiences. Perhaps this is because descriptions of aesthetic absorption face a particular difficulty for reasons which Rudolf Arnheim identified. In reflecting upon what happens when 'the dynamics of the art product engulfs the self of the performer, creator or beholder, that is, when the actor *becomes* Othello', Arnheim concludes that

> A psychology of the self does not yet exist that is subtle enough to describe the precise difference between situations in which the self acts as an autonomous perceiver of a dynamic state and those in which the self is the very center of such a state.[6]

In other words, an appropriate theory of self must be available to support any description of aesthetic absorption if it is to deal adequately with the transformation of the autonomous, detached perceiver of an art object into that of a subject intimately engaged with and centred in 'the world' of the art work.

Some psychoanalytic theorists of art have followed certain suggestive ideas in Freud's work and have tried to relate the experience of aesthetic absorption to what is taken to be fusional qualities of experience inherent in the infant's relation with its mother. However, this linking of infancy or childhood with the later developed capacity for aesthetic absorption is not exclusive to psychoanalytically inclined writers. Throughout Dewey's aesthetics are scattered references to the foundational nature of certain qualities of childhood experience for adult aesthetic experience.

Although the idea is never developed in Dewey's work, there is a clear recognition that aesthetic experience has its own developmental psychological history. Dispersed throughout his aesthetics we find suggestive intuitions concerning the roots of such experience. We find him asserting that 'through the phases of perturbation and conflict, there abides *the deep-seated memory of an underlying harmony* [my emphasis] the sense of which haunts life like the sense of being founded on a rock.'[7] Dewey quotes from George Eliot's *The Mill on the Floss* to make the point:

> These familiar flowers, these well-remembered bird notes, this sky with its fitful brightness, these furrowed and grassy fields, each with a sort of personality given to it by the capricious hedge, such things as these are the mother tongue of our imagination, the language that is laden with all the subtle inextricable associations the fleeting hours of our childhood left behind them. Our delight in the sunshine on the deep-bladed grass today might be no more than the quaint perception of wearied souls, if it were not for the sunshine and grass of far-off years, which still live in us and transform our perception into love.[8]

Later, when discussing the idea of 'transferred values', Dewey echoes George Eliot when he writes: ' "Transferred values" of emotions experienced from a childhood that cannot be consciously recovered belong to them. Speech is indeed the mother tongue.'[9] Dewey locates the origins of experiences which have a 'mystic aspect of acute surrender' (what I am now calling aesthetic absorption) in early relations with a person's surrounding world. It involves 'resonances of dispositions' which are acquired in those earlier relations, but which are now outside the range of conscious recovery and so cannot become the objects of intellectual thought.[10] The loss and recovery of union with the world are central themes pervading Dewey's thinking, and in this connection he accords a particularly important functional role to art.

Here again we meet Dewey's preoccupation with questions of the continuity of experience. His sense of the continuities of culture and biology is radical. He sees the prefiguration of art in the processes of living itself. Something of artistic process can be learnt from watching a bird building a nest or a spider its web because in all such activities there is a dynamic organised transaction of creature and world. The distinctive feature of man is his *consciousness of the relations found in nature*. Just as the bird's building of its nest is an expansion of its life, so is man's making of art an expansion of his life. But what man does in making art, and in appreciating and enjoying it, is to restore consciously, and thus on the plane of meaning, the union of sense, need, impulse and action characteristic of the live creature. The intervention of consciousness adds regulation, power of selection, and redisposition. Thus it varies the arts in ways without end.[11]

As I understand him, Dewey does not mean by 'restoration' the simple reinstitution of an earlier state but rather that of a disposition. States are transitory and open to relatively rapid change. Dewey's concern is with 'forces and structures that endure through change'.[12] His idea of continuity

> excludes complete rupture on one side and mere repetition of identities on the other: it precludes reduction of the 'higher' to the 'lower' just as it precludes complete breaks and gaps. The growth and development of any living organism from seed to maturity illustrates the meaning of continuity.[13]

The continuity of the less complex with the more complex is the primary postulate of Dewey's naturalistic theory of logic. So, when Dewey writes of the restorative powers of art, he is referring not, I believe, to the restoration of states but to the restoration of forms of relationship. In this, he is very much in harmony with contemporary understanding of memory. In the case of the developmental origins of aesthetic absorption this is a promising line of inquiry. The implication is that we should examine early forms of relating for possible prototypes of later more mature capacities for aesthetic absorption. This is precisely what certain psychoanalytic studies of aesthetic experience do, and for which they claim Dewey's support.

Dewey continually emphasises that experience is not 'something that occurs exclusively inside a self or mind or consciousness, something self-contained and sustaining only external relations to the objective scene in which it happens to be set. . . .'[14] All experience is constituted by and resides in interaction. Reflective analysis can introduce distinctions into the 'psychological phase' of experience, distinctions such as sense, emotion, imagination, idea and so on. But these are not distinctions which are given experientially; they are 'different aspects and phases of a continuous, though varied interaction of self and environment'.[15] The arts, as experiences, remove conflicts between such 'divisions'. 'Hence,' writes Dewey, 'the extraordinary ineptitude of a compartmentalised psychology to serve as an instrument for a theory of art.'[16] Psychoanalysis offers perhaps the only sustained account of aesthetic absorption in psychology. However, we need to ask whether that account is the offspring of just the sort of compartmentalised psychology which Dewey explicitly warns against.

Apart from Freud and his speculations about the infantile roots of 'the oceanic feeling',[17] the names associated with this particular approach to understanding aesthetic absorption are those connected with Object Relations theory, notably Donald Winnicott, Margaret Mahler and Ellen Spitz. Spitz in particular argues that aesthetic absorption involves the re-availability from early infancy of experiences of being fused with or merged with the mother. Her claim is that

> This symbiotic state of early infancy, prior to differentiation between inside and outside, 'I' and 'not-I', corresponds to the 'oceanic state' described by Freud, the 'original self' by Jung, the 'true self' by Winnicott, and the 'ideal state of self' described by Mahler. It is a pleasurable state dependent upon the active, almost complete adaptation by the mother to her infant's needs, which then creates within the child an illusion of magical omnipotence.[18]

She goes on to say that

> The sense of fusion that the infant experiences with the 'all good' mother who exists as a part of self, and his accompanying sense of wellbeing and pleasure, are analogous to what some philosophers have identified as aesthetic pleasure, aesthetic emotion, the privileged moment, or the sense of beauty.[19]

I suspect that this is a mistaken analogy.[20]

Whatever the merit of psychoanalytic intuitions concerning the nature of the relationship between infantile experience and adult 'oceanic feeling', or between infantile experience and aesthetic absorption, the psychoanalytic language framing these intuitions misleads, I believe. Yet the question of how to think about the continuity of early childhood experience, especially preverbal experience, with later experience remains.

Spitz's analogical account of aesthetic absorption as being 'like symbiotic fusion in that encounters with the beautiful may temporarily obliterate our sense of inner and outer separateness' melts away as soon as one tries to phenomenologically apprehend this 'sense of inner and outer separateness' or tries to imagine what its 'obliteration' might feel like.[21] That the boundaries of 'inside' and 'outside' can be temporarily erased in certain art experiences is true as will be apparent in Chapter 12. My problem is with the idea that this is specifically connected to the psychoanalytic idea of symbiotic fusion. The heart of Spitz's analysis of aesthetic absorption is that it is 'the re-availability to us, during moments of creativity or responsiveness in the arts, of aspects of our preoedipal life, with its pleasurable sense of merging and union'.[22] But granting, for the sake of argument, both the existence and the endurance of such a sense, and granting also the possibility of its psychological 're-availability' in moments related to the arts, this still would not explain aesthetic absorption.

This is because explanations like this don't say what such re-available senses of infantile experiences of 'merging and union' *do*, other than to carry with them a pleasant emotional tone. Why should it be such a sense of symbiotic fusion, rather than any other, that becomes reavailable in aesthetic situations? To conjure up a 'desire for fusion' (or a 'restoration' of the mother's body as described by Adrian Stokes[23]) which would be satisfied by aesthetic experiences of art does not get us anywhere. It certainly does not explain absorption as it occurs in aesthetic experience.

Dewey's ideas about the powers of art to restore 'consciously, and thus on the plane of meaning, the union of sense, need, impulse and action characteristic of the live creature' reject an understanding of this restoration as the simple re-institution of a previous state.[24] Restoration for Dewey is not re-availability in the sense underpinning Spitz's account. The restoration concerns forms of relationship, not of states. One can also see that Dewey's references to the origins of aesthetic experience are sometimes phylogenetic, sometimes ontogenetic.[25] When ontogenetic they refer to childhood rather than to infancy, and they centre on 'speech as the mother tongue'. His example from George Eliot pertains to a time in childhood when objects already have their own existence, when perception is capable of delighting in the details of the world that can, with language, give form to imagination.

Dewey's understanding of absorption, as a feature of aesthetic experience, involves the surrender or complete engagement of the self 'in what is objectively done'. Were we to follow the trail of intuitive clues left by Dewey, we would attend to the idea of forms of relating as they develop in the post-infantile, early childhood period of development. We should pay special attention to ways of thinking about the early childhood development of self, since without such an understanding we cannot say much about the development of the capacity to surrender or completely engage the self.

To reject the re-availability account of aesthetic absorption is not to deny the relevance of early childhood experience for later aesthetic experiences. That relevance may be as straightforward as Matisse's insistence on the need to look on the world as though for the first time with the eyes of a child, or it may be as complex as object relations theorists suggest in that the form of aesthetic experience may be linked to forms of infant experience. My point is simply that a better account of aesthetic absorption is needed than that currently available from re-availability proponents.

Donald Winnicott's ideas on transitional objects, especially as used by Ellen Spitz, seem to me to pinpoint a particular difficulty. To put this as succinctly as possible, my view is that this early stage of development requires a descriptive language not of self–other *differentiation*, as preferred by psychoanalytically oriented writers, but of self–other *constitution*. I want to suggest that self and other emerge from a process of construction *after* this state of infantile undif-ferentiation. This stage of undifferentiation is not itself the merging of self and other, as presumed by so many psychoanalytically inclined authors. I suggest that the problem is one of emergence and not one of merging. A similar sort of criticism is offered by Lorenzer and Orban who point to the untenability of arguing for objects that are 'transitional' when those realities supposedly bridged by such objects, namely 'the self' and 'the world', have not yet come into being.[26] Their position, parallel to the one I am proposing, is that self and other do not constitute Winnicott's 'intermediate area of experiencing' but are instead constituted after it.

The phenomenology of making a new type of object, or of formulating a new idea about the world, is difficult to describe without appropriate metaphors. It may be thought to involve the sense of a 'space between' the maker and the world in which the object or idea 'takes shape', before standing autonomously in the objective world. Once there, it acts to define the boundaries of its maker just as its own boundaries, as made object or idea, are clearly perceptible to other observers.

If the present reading of Winnicott is correct, then this is the sort of meaning which he wants the idea of 'potential space' to have, especially as it applies to infantile 'transitional objects'. And if it makes sense to speak of a 'location' for cultural experience[27] – and it is not clear that it does – then this is where Winnicott locates play and cultural activity. The experience of the small child 'lost' in play is retained, he felt, in the intense experiencing that belongs to the arts, to religion and to imaginative living, as well as to creative scientific work. But how can very early experiences of being 'lost' in activity be retained or made re-available? Is this the best description of the continuity between earlier and later experiences of absorption, or is the similarity due to the exercise of similar functions albeit at different times throughout the lifespan?

A formulation in terms of 'inner' and 'outer' reality which interposes a third 'intermediate' realm does not have much appeal. Such a formulation will neces-sarily favour the idea that some sort of 'merging' occurs, with its correlative separations, whereas my Deweyan conception favours instead a language of emergence. I have already observed that the language of union and separation has a ready appeal when we attempt to describe the sequence by which something emerges from the private meanings of its maker, perhaps an artist, into the meanings of the public world. To be seduced by this language of description, however, is to be led like Winnicott to theorise in terms of *transitions*, whereas the language of emergence will lead to theorisation in terms of *transformations*.

In short, the problem becomes that of transformations *of* subject–object relations, rather than transitions *between* subject and object. Instead of there being two worlds with a third world of illusion in between, there is the one ongoing, complex, transmuting world of experience. This preserves the heuristic value of Winnicott's intuitions, but within a more satisfactory framework.

When writing about the problem of 'becoming Othello' in 1966, Arnheim was not confident that the necessary theory of self was then available. The emerging cultural psychology of self, underpinned by neuroscientific theories of self like that of Damasio, offers hope that the sort of theory of self anticipated by Arnheim to deal with such complex phenomena may now be nearer to hand.

Recall Dewey's assertion above that absorption lies at the heart of aesthetic experience, during which no distinction exists between self and object. The source of any such distinction would be the self, more specifically the subject 'I'. My argument so far has been that Dewey's intuitions concerning the restorative powers of art do not refer to the idea that states are restored or made re-available, but rather that a harmony of a degree which does not ordinarily exist between forms of relating is what is restored. The general forms of relating include perceiving, thinking symbolically, and imagining, each with its own types of point of view.

Perhaps aesthetic absorption has to do with alternations in successive types of point of view? Perceptual points of view facilitate the minimally differentiated self–object relationship described by Dewey as the distinguishing feature of aesthetic experience. But it can be objected that the phenomenon of being 'lost in thought' is a form of absorption which relies upon no shift between thinking and perceiving, but which occurs within acts of symbolic thinking or imagining. I can, for instance, become minimally self-aware in thinking my way through a conceptual problem in much the same way as I do during the absorption phase of aesthetic experience.

The answer to this objection involves the psychological role of 'I' in subjectivity, its functions and the circumstances which invite or demand its deployment. It seems reasonable to suggest that I am at my most self-aware when I can use 'I' fluently. This has to do with I's indexical function as a pronoun in defining a location for the speaker or thinker which is distinct from that of other persons. In one sense, it is only a person capable of correctly deploying 'I' who can most fully know that he or she is not somebody or something else. It is as an I that a person takes up a stance over and against the not-I. In certain phases of perceiving there can seem to be a virtual merging or fusing of the subject's perceptual position with the 'that' which is perceived. During the sort of absorption that occurs in intellectual absorption when we are 'lost' in the activity of thinking there is not, I want to suggest, some merging of self or position with the intellectual content. What there is, instead, is *a non-deployment of I*.[28]

In other words, there is not just the presence of a new self-thought unity, but in addition there is the absence of I-predicated thoughts. And the reason for this is that there is no need for them, at least not until such time as a new situation requires them, whether for reasons of an intrapersonal or interpersonal kind. Only when there is a need to identify the source or ownership of thinking – to answer questions, to add significant events to the narrative of oneself, or in some other way to reflect upon oneself – will the deployment of I-thoughts become psychologically necessary.

If this formulation has merit, it points the way to an economical description of aesthetic absorption in particular and of positive absorption in general. I can judge that I have been absorbed only from a state in which I am not now absorbed, but am self-aware. It must always be a backward look from a point in the stream of experience that allows me to say that I was aesthetically absorbed. If I come to understand that such forms of experience can be deliberately brought about I may look to the prospect of being so absorbed again in the future. When that time comes I am likely to be quite aware of what I am doing when I sit down in front of my chosen picture, for example, and begin to gaze at it.

It will be as I gaze that I slowly 'enter' the picture's 'world' and the phase of aesthetic absorption begins. After a period of time I become more self-aware and find myself thinking about the picture or about my reaction to the picture, or whatever. Both the before and after states require the deployment of 'I' with its attendant form of self-consciousness. The 'percipient' or 'absorbed' state did not, but it did deploy its own point of view which, being temporarily freed of involvement with the indexical I, acquired a mobility which allowed it to 'occupy' the picture or, in Deweyan terms, to co-construct the experience which is the picture. This period of occupation is the period of aesthetic absorption.

In this formulation, it is the absence of the conditions demanding the deployment of I that enables the phase of aesthetic absorption to occur. Situations which, while making many rigorous demands upon participating selves, do not include among them prominent demands for the person as 'I' to assert his or her position, distinctiveness or responsibilities, seem to be the types of situation which we call absorbing. Aesthetic and artistic situations are like this, and aesthetic absorption understood as self-forgetfulness is, among other things, a consequence of not having to deploy that particular form of self-centring or self-location which attends the deployment and use of 'I'. This is an economical description of aesthetic absorption. Yet, superficially at least, it seems less at ease with Dewey's comments on memories from childhood than do the psychoanalytic accounts I have mentioned.

Throughout Dewey's aesthetics there are references to the importance of early memories for aesthetic experiences of art. There is, as we have seen, the 'deep-seated memory of an underlying harmony the sense of which haunts life like the sense of being founded on a rock',[29] and the ' "Transferred values" of emotions experienced from a childhood that cannot be consciously recovered. . . .'[30] He also refers experiences which have a 'mystic aspect of acute surrender' back to a person's early relations with the world.[31]

The union to which Dewey is referring is this:

> With the realization (of harmony), material of reflection is incorporated into objects as their meaning. Since the artist cares in a peculiar way for the phase of experience in which union is achieved, he does not shun moments of resistance and tension. He rather cultivates them, not for their own sake but because of their potentialities, bringing to living consciousness an experience that is unified and total.[32]

Dewey is here underlining the distinctive powers of people in general, but of artists in particular, to consciously pay attention to the dialectic of equilibrium and disequilibrium which humans have with their world. Artists care for the solution that unifies experience as an end in itself, whereas scientists use solutions as means of moving on and solving other problems. But more significant for our present discussion is Dewey's observation that 'the material of reflection' is what gives objects like art objects their meaning by being incorporated into them. This is the union that Dewey is talking about.

Dewey's own account of absorption depends upon recognising that certain changes of intentionality are accompanied by changes of subjectivity. He writes:

> [B]ut absorption in a work of art so complete as to exclude analysis cannot be long sustained. There is a rhythm of surrender and reflection. We interrupt our yielding to the object to ask where it is leading and how it is leading there.[33]

This involves a sequence of intentional shifts with corresponding transformations of point of view.

Dewey continually reminds us that speech is the mother tongue. Psycho-analysts are right to stress the foundational importance of the early pre-linguistic phase of life for our later, symbolically saturated lives. But that phase is mostly beyond conscious recall. This preverbal world is predominantly a perceptual-motor world, one in which the young child comes to experience the world first as it 'feels', before in time coming to construct it 'consciously and in the level of meaning'. The perceptual mode of intentionality developmentally grounds the later developing imaginative and symbolic modes, just as in Damasio we saw that the proto-self and core self are the foundations for the later developing autobiographical self. These are certainly like rocks on which extended conscious life is founded. No doubt all sorts of early events recur as kinds of memory and fantasy throughout later life. But as sources of description for aesthetic absorption such explanations seem to me to be unnecessary.

If, however, this was all one could say to describe the dynamics of aesthetic absorption, it would be a rather thin description. What I have offered so far is an account of the negative conditions for absorption. It identifies some of the core skills of self which are *not* involved. There remains the question of what does or can go on during aesthetic absorption in the absence of these controlling and organising functions. In their absence, or attenuation, other functions of self are allowed freer play, as Matisse testifies. My approach to describing the interplay of these other functions is to focus on the idea of the 'centredness' of self, on the sense, that is, of being a centre within a dynamic, always changing forward-moving field of experience. This owes much to Rudolf Arnheim's Gestalt psychological conception of a field. Present moments of experience are always part of such a forward flow. It is in this context that the experience of 'being moved' in art can be refined.

As centres within our own moving fields of experience, we relate or refer things to ourselves and feel that the field of experience has us as its centre. We do this with most control when we deploy 'I' in our thinking or speaking. It is in acts of self-location or in acts of assuming responsibility or ownership that the psychological function of the pronoun 'I' is most evident. But when we daydream, or move along unselfconsciously with the flow of thought or fluent physical action, we are conscious in a differently centred way than when we deploy 'I'. The difference has to do with the relationship of centredness and control. The organisation of novels, paintings, films or sonatas greatly influences the nature of their being apprehended as 'places' in which reading, looking or listening persons find themselves centred. Aesthetic absorption is connected to the shifting senses that accompany our being recentred in new fields of experience, and from the processes whereby one sense of being centred or located transmutes into another.[34]

It takes time to develop our various aptitudes for being origins of perception and action, not the least of which is our ability to master personal pronouns with their possibilities of grammatically structured relations with our worlds.[35] These ways of being centred are intimately connected to feeling and emotion as aspects of aesthetic experience. Our involvement in aesthetic experiences of art is one of active participation. Learning how to participate includes acquiring cognitive skills of reading and symbol-manipulation, social skills of making-believe, empathising, caring, and critical skills of comparing and judging. A major developmental feature of the ability to participate in and to benefit from the arts, as forms of cultural meaning, is the associated phenomenology of feeling.

Emotion and movement derive from the same etymological Latin root *movere*. Emotion is thus understood as a form of movement, as a 'strong agitation of the feelings'. If a work of art strongly engages our feelings then we say that we are moved by it. This is most likely to occur when our control of the situation is minimised, as during phases of absorption. Can we say anything more about the engagement of feeling and the movement of self during and after aesthetic absorption? The American philosopher of art, Kendall Walton, offers some interesting ideas on this question.[36]

When I experience outrage, fear or love while watching a play, there is an emphatic difference between these feelings and their counterparts which I might feel when confronted with similar events in my own daily life. In the first instance it would be utterly inappropriate for me to act upon my feelings (since this is *only* a play) whereas in the latter case it may be quite inappropriate for me not to act. In the case of the play the events are fictional and the feelings I have are what Walton would call quasi-emotions, whereas in my own life they are 'real' feelings entailing, as an intrinsic part of their reality, dispositions to act in relevant and appropriate ways.

Walton connects these different capacities and their development to childhood games of make-believe. He introduces the idea of representations as things whose social function is to serve as props in games of make-believe. They prompt us to imagine. A prop is something which generates further imaginings. Walton argues that 'Participants in games of make-believe, being at once reflexive props and imaginers, imagine of the actual representing actions that they are instances of their doing things, and they imagine this from the inside.'[37] Being reflexive props in their own games, participants then generate fictional truths about themselves. For example, the sticks in their hands are spears and they are Roman legionnaires. Fictional worlds are comprised of fictional truths. Representational works of art, like games of make-believe, generate fictional worlds. How do we feel as fictional occupants of fictional worlds?

Walton introduces the idea of a quasi-feeling or a quasi-emotion. A quasi-pity for Willy Loman in Arthur Miller's *Death of a Salesman* involves no inclination to commiserate with Willy Loman nor to help him. Quasi-feelings are detached from the motivation to act which is appropriate to the full form of that feeling. Actual feelings of pity, for instance, require the belief that someone in distress is in need of comfort and that I should experience the inclination to help them; quasi-feelings of pity do not. Quasi-feelings

> ought to be constellations of sensations or other phenomenological experiences characteristic of real emotions, ones that the appreciator who 'pities Willy Loman' or 'admires Superman,' for instance, shares with people who really pity or admire real people.[38]

Walton distinguishes 'work-worlds' from 'game-worlds'. Game-worlds are expansions of work-worlds and include the appreciator.

Armed with these ideas, Walton develops the idea that adult experiences of art are rooted in childrens' games of make-believe. The limits of this analogy are in the different levels of involvement. Children are physically involved in their games, whereas the restrictions on the possibility of physical participation by adults when they look at pictures or plays shift the emphasis away from physical to psychological participation. Psychological participation in the game-worlds of art entails that it will be fictional that the appreciator has thoughts and feelings, opinions and attitudes concerning what he or she sees or reads about. But if these feelings are fictional why should we take them seriously?

Why do we care about Emma Bovary? Walton says that we don't. What we do care about is the experience of fictionally caring, and what we are interested in are the games in which it is fictional that we follow the fortunes of the likes of Emma. Representations like this serve as props in games of make-believe in which we participate. But why bother to participate in games like this or to engage in imaginative activities generally? Psychologists typically answer in terms of opportunities to try out new roles, to empathise with those in such roles. They argue that such roles provide an outlet for dangerous or socially unacceptable emotions, or that they assist us in working out disturbing or unpleasant features of ourselves, or that they give us practice in dealing with situations we might actually face.

What of the relationship between feeling, art and aesthetic absorption? Walton argues that immersion is not equally part of all appreciation. He writes:

> That experience is perhaps the aim of much 'romantic' art, broadly speaking, but works of certain other kinds shun it as sentimental excess, deliberately 'distancing' the appreciator from the fictional world. Representations sometimes hinder even the imaging of what is fictional. In doing so they effectively undercut appreciators' roles as reflexive props.[39]

He goes on to argue that

> Appreciation is not, in general, to be identified with participation, still less with the kind of participation that constitutes being 'caught up in a story'. But as far as the representational aspects of appreciated works are concerned, the notion of participation is fundamental; appreciation not involving participation is nevertheless to be understood in terms of it.[40]

The feelings we have when we are moved by a work of art are no less real for being incomplete quasi-feelings shorn of their connections to action. People actively engage with art objects to produce works of art. This work that art does has its own dynamism and momentum. In the Deweyan view of art *as* experience, we could say that our being moved occurs when, inhibiting the dynamic controlling thrust of our own subjectivity by not deploying 'I' or by not responding to conditions which invite the deployment of 'I', we are carried along by the momentum of the fictional or depicted or musical 'worlds' into which we dock as readers, spectators, or listeners. It is rather like two streams of consciousness intersecting, interweaving, only to subsequently diverge again. A text's narrative momentum, for example, temporarily becomes mine, its thoughts and images mine, the succession of its ideas the succession of mine.

Although brief in duration, phases of absorption during aesthetic experiences of art, and phases of positive absorption generally, are singularly densely packed with possibilities for the expansion of self. The willing vulnerability that is their precondition greatly increases the likelihood that the person's temporary relocation will not return them to the beginning of their journey, but will rather have moved them, even if ever so slightly, elsewhere.

Notes

1 John Dewey, *Art as Experience*, New York, Capricorn Books G. P. Putnam's Sons, 1958, p. 249.
2 Ibid., p. 240.
3 Mihalyi Csikszentmihalyi, *Flow: The Psychology of Optimal Experience*, New York, Harper Perennial, 1991.
4 Ibid., p. 64.
5 Ibid., p. 144.
6 Rudolf Arnheim, *Toward a Psychology of Art*, Berkeley, University of California Press, 1966, p. 318.
7 Dewey, op. cit., p. 17.
8 Ibid., p. 18n.
9 Ibid., p. 240.
10 Ibid., pp. 28–9.
11 Ibid., p. 25. This is an elaborated description of what G. H. Mead called the manipulative phase of the act.
12 Ibid., p. 323. For a contemporary analysis of states and dispositions see Richard Wollheim, *The Thread of Life*, Cambridge, Cambridge University Press, 1984.
13 John Dewey, *Logic: The Theory of Inquiry*, London, George Allen & Unwin, 1938, p. 23.
14 Ibid., p. 246.
15 Art as Experience, p. 247.
16 Ibid., p. 248.
17 Ciarán Benson, *The Absorbed Self: Pragmatism, Psychology and Aesthetic Experience*, London, Harvester Wheatsheaf, 1993, Chapter 3.
18 Ellen Spitz, *Art and Psyche*, New Haven, Yale University Press, 1985, p. 141.
19 Ibid.
20 Benson, op. cit., Chapter 3.
21 Spitz, op. cit., p. 142.

22 Ibid.

23 See E. Wright, *Psychoanalytic Criticism*, London: Methuen, 1984, p. 85.

24 Dewey, *Art as Experience*, p. 25.

25 Ibid., p. 18.

26 See A. Lorenzer and P. Orban, 'Transitional objects and phenomena: socialization and symbolization' in S. A. Grolnick and L. Barkin, eds. *Between Reality and Fantasy: Transitional Objects and Phenomena*, New York, Jason Aronson, 1978, p. 479.

27 D. Winnicott, 'The Location of Cultural Experience,' in *Playing and Reality*, Harmondsworth: Penguin, 1974, Chapter 7.

28 A fuller discussion of this can be found in Benson, op. cit., Chapters 4–6.

29 Dewey, op. cit., p. 17.

30 Ibid., p. 240.

31 Ibid., p. 28.

32 Ibid., p. 15.

33 Ibid., p. 144.

34 Benson, op. cit., Chapter 6.

35 Ibid., Chapter 5. See also R. Harré and G. Gillett *The Discursive Mind*, London, Sage, 1994, and P. Mühlhäusler and R. Harré, *Pronouns and People: The Linguistic Construction of Social and Personal Identity*, Oxford, Basil Blackwell, 1990.

36 K. Walton, *Mimesis as Make-Believe: On the Foundations of the Representational Arts* Cambridge, Mass., Harvard University Press, 1993.

37 Ibid., p. 213.

38 Ibid., p. 251.

39 Ibid., p. 274.

40 Ibid., p. 275.

12

POINTS OF VIEW AND NONE

Visual art and the location of self

> The idea of the Boddhisattva, one who comes back and entices
> others on the journey, is to some degree the task of the artist. . . .
> This is where I began to appreciate an art that could be a non-
> vicarious act, a seeing whose subject was your seeing.
>
> (J. Turrell, *Air Mass*, 1993)

In December 1994 in the Ardèche in south-east France another extraordinary
gallery of cave paintings was discovered. The paintings in the Chauvet Cave
include the oldest authenticated paintings in the world and were created by the
Cro-Magnon people. The oldest radiocarbon dates are 32,410 ± 720 BP.[1] These
findings indicate that the paintings were made in a timespan of 1,300 years
centred on 31,000 years ago.

When the discovery of the cave was first reported in the press, a comment
made by the English archaeologist, Professor Clive Gamble, struck a chord with
me. Noting that art had a social role from the beginning, he went on to say that
'It was used to solve the problem of who belonged where, and of what roles a
person had to fulfil in order to ensure groups and tribes could survive in a tight,
hard way of life.'[2]

Some of the activities that we now call 'art' were an integral part of culture at
that time. But that was not the point of resonance for me in his comment; my
attention was on the problem to which he referred, the problem of belonging
somewhere. He had in mind that the roots of art had to do with the need to
create initiation ceremonies, to formulate rituals, to demarcate social roles, to
settle territorial disputes, and so on. I'm sure this is part at least of the social
origins of art. But I want to again take this problem of location, and to look at
some of its constituting constructs, notably the binaries inside/outside and here/
there.

There are different types of 'place' or 'space' or 'world' in which 'you' can
be. By 'be' I mean to focus in particular on how it is for you, on your subjectivity
as understood by philosophers like Thomas Nagel and Richard Wollheim, and on

how this is constituted by your interrelations with the 'spaces' or 'fields' or 'worlds' in which you happen to be.[3] As the system which is you-in-a-world changes, as it does from moment to moment, day to day and month to month, so too does your subjectivity change, which in turn is a way of saying that 'you' change. Another concept is needed here, which is the Siamese twin of location, and that is the idea of a point of view.

Our conceptual toolkit now includes the ideas of location, subjectivity, point of view, place, inside/outside and here/there to which I want to add the concept of boundary. Armed with these concepts, I now want to introduce certain experiences deliberately enabled by art, particularly concerning how we think and feel about the inside/outside of ourselves. I will conclude with a speculation about the neuropsychological underpinnings of what I will be calling the 'no point of view phenomenon'.

For the sake of economy and focus in what follows, I will restrict myself to the visual arts as one cultural field of experience. Within the visual arts I will focus primarily on ways in which artists have constructed spectators' points of view, and secondarily on experiences of light and position in art which favour certain experiences of transcendence. When speaking of experiences that they call aesthetic or religious, people regularly report a blurring of the boundaries of self, or a subservience of self to some notion of the good which is greater than the individual self, or a non-engagement or non-deployment – as I argued in Chapter 11 – of a controlling element of self, namely the personal pronoun 'I'.

I sympathise with Richard Wollheim's call to re-psychologise the theory of pictorial meaning. Wollheim's recruitment of psychology, and his theory of meaning, are reminiscent of the great American Pragmatic philosopher John Dewey.[4] For Wollheim, pictorial meaning is triadic. It is located in the mental states of artists, the way in which this causes them to paint, and the experience that an informed and sensitive spectator can be expected to have on looking at their pictures.[5]

I would want to add that the concept of art is open to unbounded change in its technologies, and in its capacities to shape and require new forms of psychological participation and experience.

Forms of art and forms of consciousness constitute each other. Dewey argues that the work of art is not the art object. It is the joint creation of the art object or event and the active, recreating spectator. The totality of this collaboration is the work that art objects and their recipients jointly do. Art is essentially relational. It is experience. A full aesthetic experience has the structure of 'An' experience, argues Dewey. The spectator's being at any point is contingent on where in the flow of the experience he or she is, on where, that is, he or she is positioned in the unfolding work that is art *as* experience. This is the aesthetic theoretical context for what follows.

We have already met many of the words for 'location' and 'being located' in English. They include up/down, front/back, above/below, inside/outside, on/off, here/there, towards/away and now/then. Between them, these constructs form one set of coordinates for psychological location within the perceptual-motor field. This includes our sense of being spatially and temporally located.[6] A second set of coordinates, essential to being a self and a person, locates a self in relation to other selves within social and moral fields. Here, key constructs are I/you, us/them, is/is not, have/not have, yours/mine, and for/against.

Central to both sets of constructs and their relevant fields is the further idea of a 'boundary' as somewhere or something at which one pole of a construct ends and another begins, where for example our 'inside' ends and the 'outside' begins. With here/there or up/down, for instance, there is the idea that the boundary is spatial. But at what point does 'there' experientially become 'here'? And what is the nature of the boundary between 'you' and 'me', or 'me as I now am' and 'me as I then was', say ten years ago? These questions draw in many different branches of psychology, philosophy, neurology, and linguistics.

The ways in which we think and speak of ourselves, and of our positions in the various aspects of the world, are permeated by our use of metaphors based on our language for physical location. Among many other classes of metaphor, Lakoff and Johnson highlight the role of what they call 'orientational metaphors' in shaping how we think of things.[7]

Take the construct up/down as just one example of how the linguistic structure of our psychological lives borrows from the constructs of physical location. Happy is up but sad is down ('My spirits *rose*' or 'My spirits *sank*'); conscious is up but unconscious is down (we say 'Wake *up*' but 'He *fell* asleep'); health and life are up but sickness and death are down ('Lazarus *rose* from the dead' but 'He *fell* ill'); being in control is up but being subject to control is down ('She has control *over* me' but 'He is *under* my control'); good is up but bad is down ('Things are looking *up*' but 'It's been *downhill* since she left'); virtue is up but depravity is down ('She has *high* standards' but 'That was a *low* trick'); rational is up but emotional is down ('The discussion *fell* to the emotional level but I *raised it back up* to the rational plane'); one goes up to heaven but down to hell; and so on. Lakoff and Johnson show how all of these metaphors, and many others, are coherently grounded in experience of one kind or another, physical, social, cultural. We know something from developmental psychology about how children come to learn the language of literal location and then to metaphorically transpose this to ways of making sense of their own psychology, and that of others.[8]

The arts are the most accomplished metaphorical realm created by human beings. Becoming 'part' of such experiences, or being enrolled as co-constructors of them, depends on the inventiveness of artists and of their traditions. Within the visual arts, 'entry' to the world of a work has relied on ideas and practices of perspective and perspective-creation. I want to distinguish four kinds of perspectival entry: any point of view, a defined point of view, one's own point of view, and no point of view. These I take to be, very roughly, successive emphases in the history of Western art, partly dependent for their emergence on technological developments. My interest, as will be apparent shortly, is in a particular contemporary 'no point of view' experience and its implications. My extremely brief treatment of the first three cases should therefore be read as background and context for this fourth case.

Medieval artworks create a pictorial space that is 'flat', without engaging 'depth'. Medieval cosmology and medieval art are intimately linked, as Margaret Wertheim argues.[9] Space and time were understood as being heterogeneous and discontinuous. Below, here on earth and above the stars matched regions of Hell, human life, and Heaven. Danté magisterially mapped them in *The Divine Comedy*. Pre-linear perspectival pictures make no demands on spectators' viewing positions other than that the picture should be visibly in front of them. Within limits of visibility, any point of view will do since the structure of the picture does not anticipate and require a particular viewing position.

The psychological engagement of the spectator, however intense it may be in other respects, does not privilege where the spectator is. The picture does not have the sort of 'depth' which requires a particular 'point of entry,' and the correlative experience, at least as we view it today, can be characterised by a quality of 'distance' and 'otherness' compared with what followed the development of linear perspective. Prior to linear perspective the construction of pictorial space depended on cues such as interposing one figure before another, relative size, and so on. We can only guess at the detailed psychology of how they felt to be seen at that time.[10]

The development of linear perspective is not unrelated to emerging ideas of space as unified and continuous. The technology of linear perspective enabled the making of perceptually compelling virtual spaces into which spectators could be temporarily relocated. It is a technology that requires a defined point of view for optimal experience, one that defines in advance where the viewer should be. It creates that pictorial 'doubleness' which formed the antithesis for so much art in the twentieth century, what Richard Wollheim has called the 'twofoldness' of pictures.[11]

We can look 'into' pictures to see what they are 'about', but we can also withdraw that attention and refocus on qualities of the pictorial surface. From the Renaissance to the twentieth century 'looking in' was the dominant mode of psychological participation in pictorial art. There was an optimum point of entry for this 'looking in', one which was predetermined by the pictorial composition itself. That was the picture's point of view.

We may have a literal perceptual point of view, which has to do with our position in space. We metaphorically extend the phrase to cover our positioning on issues of understanding, morality and social standing. In the always changing flow of consciousness it is useful to think of 'my point of view' generically, as meaning something like the coherent succession of types of point of view which characterise a particular phase of my stream of consciousness.

In experiences of art a visual point of view can be recruited to serve other types of point of view, such as favoured forms of feeling, or moral orientations of a church or political movement, for example. The geometry of linear perspective enables the artist, in addition to creating a powerful illusion of depth, to feed this into the narrative of the painting so that the spectator's eye may be drawn to some central character or action, or perhaps for concealing particular allusions in the work.[12]

The power of this technique is greater even than this since the compelling visual appearance of the new pictorial space changes its relationship with the actual space in which the spectator begins looking at the picture. Artists like Andrea Mantegna recognised this in a work like *St James Led to Execution* (1454–7) and began to explore ways of deliberately linking virtual and actual space in order to create new psychological experiences.

Viewers of this picture feel themselves to be located at a point on the bottom of the picture plane, where the shield of the man standing to the right of the arch touches the ground. Yet their line of sight must be tilted upwards, so powerful is their feeling of being placed at its centre of projection. Kubovy has analysed how Mantegna used his understanding of perspective to create a discrepancy between the direction of the spectator's gaze (upwards) and the direction implicit in the orientation of the picture plane (horizontal). The psychological result is 'a vibrantly tense work full of foreboding.'[13] Leonardo, on the other hand sometimes, as in *The Last Supper*, used perspective to elevate the spectator to a very high centre of projection which induces a feeling of 'spiritual uplift'.

Modernist artists fully understood the technology of linear perspective, its achievements and its expressive exhaustion. This understanding is the basis for my distinction between the 'any point of view' of pre-linear perspective images and the 'own point of view' of twentieth-century Modernism. In Modernist work, it is the 'looking at' facet of the twofoldness of pictures that is required of the spectator rather than 'looking in'. But that 'looking at' requires a subject with a degree of choice about looking and interpreting which is radically different to that of a medieval worshipper before an icon. Modernist work requires autonomous spectators in self-conscious possession of their own points of view. That is the crucial difference in the psychology recruited by medieval pictorial flatness as against Modernist two-dimensionality. One might rather grandly suggest that refusal of depth and redundancy of point of view go together in an epoch of unified space–time.

This cursory review of how Western art has deployed understanding of view-

points – 'any', 'defined', 'own' – allows me to introduce a deployment that strikes me as particularly interesting, and perhaps culturally symptomatic, but for which I would resist the description postmodern. This is the idea of 'no point of view' and its experiential effects and uses. Part of its interest has to do with the quintessentially modern preoccupation with 'interior space' and the 'interior depths' of self, and part of it with questions of personal boundaries, of where 'you' end and something else begins.

In each of my three previous cases the art with which self engages is object-based, imagistic, or else thematises surface qualities, and invites the deployment of a focused attention and some point of view or other. What, though, is the quality of subjectivity when there is no object, no imagery, and no point of view? The strikingly innovative work of the American artist James Turrell allows us to address this question. Turrell's sophisticated work with light itself creates highly distinctive experiences which utilise the twofoldness of perception in contrast to the twofoldness of the pictorial.

For over sixty years psychologists have been interested in what are called *Ganzfelds*. These are total visual fields of uniform light but with no visible image or object. In the ordinary world, experiences of anything like a total visual field of uniform light are extremely rare. Real-world examples of something like a *Ganzfeld* would be what explorers call Arctic 'white-outs' or what pilots rarely experience in a total envelope of fog.

From the 1930s onwards, Gestalt psychologists like Wolfgang Metzger and Kurt Koffka experimented with *Ganzfelds*.[14] In the 1950s and 1960s the American psychologist J. J. Gibson and his co-workers further explored the psychology of total visual fields and came to the conclusion that what was to be seen was nothing in the sense of no-thing.[15] It was rather like looking at the sky in which there is no object and no distance. This 'empty medium' reduced perception to very basic levels.

Locating ourselves in space, it should be remembered, is achieved by relating ourselves to other objects in terms of relative distance. Parallel to this research were inquiries into sensory deprivation and the experiences of disorientation and dislocation which result from being deprived of such stimulation.[16] These types of experience intrigued Turrell. Born in Los Angeles in 1943, he trained as a psychologist before becoming an artist. His utilisations of his observations on seeing are among the most astute available.

With some exceptions such as art which depends wholly on touch, the visual arts self-evidently depend on sight and light. Most often this light is reflected light: reflected from pictures, sculptures, buildings. It may also be translucent, as with stained glass. Light is central to the evolution of life. The brain itself, it is speculated, originated in light-sensitive organs. At every level of human life, even for those born blind, light is centrally important.

Even the congenitally blind can in their own way visualise. Their brains are the outcomes of an evolution of seeing even if they cannot see. Susanna Millar, in her book on understanding and representing space in blind and sighted children, tells of a young and ardent soccer fan of her acquaintance who is blind and who had regularly listened to commentaries on football matches but who visualised the pitch as having one goalpost in the middle, into which both sides kicked the ball.[17]

There is no tangible barrier blocking an actor on a stage from seeing the audience: stage light is the barrier. There is no physical barrier blocking our seeing the stars during daytime: sun lighting the atmosphere is the barrier. Diminish the light and the audience and stars become visible. These examples introduce the ideas underpinning Turrell's work. Light is his medium, and making available for attention the act of seeing is his aim. There is no object in his work, in the sense of something solid, other than the constructions which frame the experiences of the viewers. There is no image because Turrell deliberately wants to avoid associative, symbolic thought. There is no focus or particular place to look. As he says himself, in his works 'You are looking at you looking.'[18]

As examples I will refer to two works in particular. One is called *Air Mass*, but my main focus is his *Ganzfeld Sphere* which he constructed in the National Sculpture Factory in Cork, Ireland in 1996. The *Ganzfeld Sphere* is a real sphere into which the viewer is inserted lying on a tray in a procedure that is similar to having a body-scan. Once the spectator is inside the sphere, lying flat and looking upwards, a technician manipulates the internal lighting of the sphere. As far as is possible there are no visible reference points nor features upon which to focus. The spectator has the experience of being surrounded by light of different hues and changing at different tempos. The experiential result is remarkable.

By removing all possible reference points bar one's own nose, which is a prominent but normally unnoticed protuberance in our field of vision, such feelings as come from the body lying on a hard surface and some ambient sound, Turrell creates a unique type of experience which challenges our sense of being located. He then enlists a whole series of psychological phenomena using light of different hue and rhythm which are otherwise difficult to observe and feel in the complex flux of ordinary experience.

A sample of illustrative reflections from spectators on their own experiences will indicate what is involved in experiencing the *Ganzfeld* phenomenon. I selected these from over 400 in the Visitors' Book in order to show that there is consensus on Turrell's having achieved his role as Bodhisattva. They also highlight the orientational language which people spontaneously use to describe their experiences, and in particular the alterations in the experiences to which the inside/outside and here/there constructs apply.

First let me take the issue of body boundaries, our sense of where we end and the rest of the world begins. Turrell's *Ganzfeld Sphere* makes uncertain our senses of here and there, of inside and outside. He does this, as I have said, with no imagery or symbols upon which to focus and take our bearings. He induces the experiences with fields of light alone, partly by what is there and partly by excluding what is normally there. These are a sample of the comments left by individual participants which I give to illustrate experiential correlates of 'no point of view':

'Sometimes I didn't know whether my eyes were closed or open.'
'I really felt as if the roof of the dome was the outer membrane of my eyes.'
'I felt the colours inside my head, rather than around me.'
'The chamber took over my mind. I entered it and it entered me.'
'What I thought most interesting was the sensation that I had closed my eyes
   when I had not, my eyes at times felt paralysed, great after images like seeing
   into your own retina, from the inside.'
'sense of time vanishes as well as immediate sense of location.'
'felt like being my eyes.'
'I kind of wasn't aware of colour but more of me looking. I couldn't tell if I had
   my eyes open.'
'seeing the colours behind your eyes amazing.'
'Very much a fascinating experience of colour in my head.'
'becoming one great blob of red, soaking in baths of colour.'
'You feel as if the light was inside you.'
'at start of flashes I saw my eyes looking at me.'
'the sensation of being behind my eyelids.'
'felt as if I had no body and no limits.'
'feeling as if your eyes were closed and you were inside your body.'
'You don't get into a colour you become a colour.'
'A journey into and out of the body.'
'After a while I can't tell where the colour ends & I begin . . . I don't know if my
   eyes are open or closed. It feels more like feeling than seeing.'
'An experience into looking at the looking.'
'a feeling of dreaming and being lifted out of myself.'
'it's like it's actually inside your head as if you're blind and this is what you see
   on the inside.'
'You lose yourself totally.'

Whereas the focus of traditional pictorial art is on what is seen, Turrell's express intention and achievement, as is evident from the testimonies above, is to enable the act of seeing itself to be foregrounded. The import of this is a challenge to our common-sense notions of location, boundary and point of view at a very basic level.

Visual perception includes a feeling of the body as we see, and that bodily feeling is larger than seeing alone. Synaesthesia, which has to do with the inter-relations of the senses, is one aspect of this. In the case of the *Ganzfeld Sphere* we have repeated reports of the tangibility and touchability of the light as though the senses of the skin were recruited as part of the act of seeing:

> *'You forget time and space in the sphere. I feel the cold of the blue and the heat of the red.'*
>
> *'Dreaming with open eyes. Feelings of cold and deep blue sea.'*
>
> *'The first time I have ever truly experienced the weight of colour, without any other reference to shape, form, etc.'*
>
> *'The intense reds were so heavy I felt I couldn't raise myself at all. They seemed so close to me & dangerous. The blues were such a relief from the pressure that the sphere seemed a thousand miles high.'*
>
> *'he seems to achieve a solidity of light that can seem quite suffocating.'*
>
> *'chewable light.'*
>
> *'Curious sensations of colour actually touching your skin . . .'*
>
> *'Very interesting experiences ranging from being disconnected & floating to an actual pressure on my eyeballs — very physical in parts and very ethereal in others, mortality.'*
>
> *'Solid colour touched me.'*
>
> *'the colours were really almost touchable . . .'*

The experiential effects of being in the *Sphere* were frequently described as calming, relaxing, womb-like, uplifting, meditative and so on.

Perhaps the most dramatic examples of the use of linear perspective to achieve somewhat analogous effects of uplift are those works on ceilings which incorpor-ate the actual architecture of the building into the picture itself. The artistic intention in such works is to merge the spectator's sense of location in actual space with the virtual space of the picture. This engages the spectator as a partici-pant in the narrative depicted. This is a technique known as *quadratura*. The domes of churches and the ceilings of stately building offer outstanding examples of this.

Domes and the concept of heaven are intimately connected. As the art historian John Shearman points out, there is

> an unbroken tradition from antiquity (that) a vault or a dome, as built architecture, is a symbol of Heaven — a symbolism expressed in language . . . — and the decoration of the symbolic structure nearly always charac-terizes it as Heaven in one way or another.[19]

200

This relationship of sky, dome and heaven continues to be powerful in our thinking. Even though our sense of the sky above us as a domed half-sphere is itself an illusion, its compelling role in the creation of an art in the service of the religious remains as powerful as ever. I offer two examples to illustrate how a changing art reflects a changing psychology and understanding of transcendence.

Fra Andrea Pozzo painted his *St Ignatius Being Received into Heaven* (1691–4) on the hemi-cylindrical ceiling of the Church of Sant' Ignazio in Rome. The complex perspective of this extraordinary ceiling works optimally from a definite point of view marked on the floor by a yellow marble circle. At that point, and looking straight up, the spectator has the powerful sense of the accessibility of this particular heaven. Your sense of location as you look up is of being a part of two continuous worlds, one the actual architectural space you now occupy, and the second the virtual heavenly space into which you are gazing. Were you a believer in the late seventeenth century, this is where you would have hoped to be carried after death.

To our eyes this Baroque extravaganza might seem to be, as we say with unusual aptness, over the top. So much has changed since then in beliefs, values and art. But still the connection of vaults, domes, sky and Heaven remains intact in church designs, even in the late twentieth century. Contrast Pozzo's ceiling with Turrell's church designs for Italy or for the Greek islands of Santorini and Hydra (1988–9). These designs, it seems to me, are still part of the tradition of *quadratura*, but they show how changed is the contemporary spiritual tradition and the experiences it expects art to create.

As with his other work, there is no object or imagistic focus for attention in Turrell's church designs. What is there is changing light. Turrell's designs literally incorporate light from the sky itself using apertures in the roof, and apply ideas developed in smaller-scale work like *Air Mass* (1993).[20] As day turns to night or night to day, and against an internal illumination perhaps of yellowish halogen lights, the light in the apertures changes remarkably. Sometimes it takes on the visible texture of blue-black velvet and completely changes one's sense of where the sky is. 'Here' and 'there' become unhinged from each other, as do the senses of what is inside and outside the walls framing the aperture. The point I want to make, using what I have already said about the subjective psychological aspects of participating in these types of work, is that the nature of religious feeling, as revealed by the contrast between Pozzo and Turrell, is remarkably changed.

Pozzo relies on a specific iconography well understood by the spectator, and on controlled and specific forms of perspective which bring the spectator away from his or her mundane reality into a manifestly different other world 'up there'. Turrell, on the other hand, uses no symbols at all, offers nothing to focus on and works to dissolve the felt distinction between 'in here' and 'out there'. The resulting meditative consequences for the viewer have to do with becoming one with what is there in a rather Zen-like way.

The move away from a collective form of religious being to a more emptied, private and personal type is signified by the different psychologies involved. And quite different epiphanies are entailed. For one, looking up means looking at another better world to which we aspire by being good members of the Church. For the other, looking up involves being returned to 'within' oneself, seeing nothing other than indeterminately placed but almost tangible natural light. The consequence is, most commonly, a profound sense of meditative calmness. This change in type of experience has much to do with the rise of individualism and subjectivism in Western culture, and their shaping of the forms of self-interpretation that feed into the making of the modern self.

I want to conclude speculatively by suggesting that some aspects of Antonio Damasio's theory of the types of neural representation underpinning conscious-ness might possibly add to an explanation of the phenomena which James Turrell has made so impressively his own. Again, I concentrate on what I am calling the 'no point of view phenomenon'.

Merleau-Ponty wrote that 'My body is the fabric into which all objects are interwoven.'[21] This is the same basic idea which Damasio develops using con-temporary neurological insights. Neurologists and neuropsychologists have specu-lated for some time that there are neural networks underpinning a foundational body-self, or neuromatrix or neural self. Damasio elaborates the notion of a 'neural self' or 'proto-self' and outlines its significance for locating what happens to us, whether within the boundaries of our bodies or outside them.[22] He sug-gests that the brain evolved in the first instance, as a means of 'Representing the outside world in terms of the modification it causes in the body proper, that is, representing the environment by modifying the primordial representations of the body proper whenever an interaction between organism and environment takes place'.[23]

These representations are distributed over several regions of the brain and are coordinated by neuron connections, in which the musculoskeletal frame and skin play, in Damasio's view, an important role. This map of the body is dynamic and constantly renewed. If this is valid, it would mean that we should think of most physical interactions with the environment as happening at a place within the body boundary since sense organs exist at a location within the body boundary, such as seeing at the eyes.

Signals from the 'outside' in this physical sense are always double. There is the seeing of something as a non-body signal, but there is also a body signal which comes from a place in the skin where the special signal entered, such as the eyes in the head. Therefore in addition to seeing what you see, you feel-yourself-seeing with your eyes. Visual perception would be 'a feeling of the body as we see'.[24] However, unless things go wrong and demand attention, as for example when we feel pain, perception of the body generally remains in the background.

Turrell's work with experiences of light plays with just that doubleness of perception which is the focus of Damasio's ideas on body-representations in the brain. For Turrell, it is the feeling of seeing itself which is the focus of his work. On the other hand, the psychology of Renaissance perspective was very much about the other aspect of doubleness, situating the spectator the better to see what was there to be seen. In much Modernist painting, the particular doubleness in play was not that 'seeing itself' as against 'that seen' but rather 'looking at' rather than 'looking into', a play with surface qualities having eschewed those of virtual depth. Where spectators feel themselves to be is very different in each type of art.

As the body is represented in the structure of the brain, 'symbols' of the body may be used 'as if' they were current body signals. The pain of phantom limbs after amputation is a case in point. What are called 'as-if loops' in the brain have great significance for our understanding of how we locate ourselves and our feelings. This is again relevant for any consideration of the emotional dimensions of experiences of art. But the general point is that these representations of our body are vital to our sense of how and where we are and that they change, review and renew from moment to moment.[25]

Just how complex this is takes an effort of imagination. For almost every second of our lives and especially of our waking lives – 2,207,520,000 seconds in a life of three score and ten! – what we see and hear and feel is changing. With every movement of the eyes, head and body there is a change in our perceptual point of view and in what we perceive. With every movement forward the world recedes out of sight behind us. Normally none of this incessant change causes us problems. Our world remains relatively constant, stable and seamless, as does our sense of ourselves as points of reference to which all around us is referred. From a neuropsychological perspective, the felt constancy of our point of view must be rooted in an endlessly renewed, but relatively stable, series of biological states, and this must lie at the heart of our ability to orient and locate ourselves perceptually in the world.

We still have little idea of how our distinctively human subjectivity and consciousness emerge. Damasio's suggestion is

> that subjectivity emerges . . . when the brain is producing not just images of an object, not just images of organism responses to the object, but a third kind of image, that of an organism in the act of perceiving and responding to an object. I believe the subjective perspective arises out of the content of the third kind of image.[26]

He goes on to argue that subjectivity is produced by 'successive organism states, each neurally represented anew, in multiple concerted maps, moment by moment, and each anchoring the self that exists at any one moment'.[27]

Could it be that Turrell has isolated phenomenologically, and exploited aesthetically, representations of this third kind, 'images of the organism in the act of perceiving' precisely by his elimination of the object and hence of a point of view? Are the experiences of seeing-ourselves-seeing, which the *Ganzfeld Sphere* enables, the psychological manifestation of Damasio's representations of the organism in the act of perceiving? If this is what Turrell has succeeded in doing, then could his phenomenological dissolution of the operative boundaries of routine categories like inside/outside and here/there result from creating conditions – no object and therefore no correlative point of view – in which this representation of the person in the act of seeing is quarantined from the other putative types of representation comprising our sense-of-self-in-the-world, namely 'representations of the object of perception' and 'representations of organismic responses to an object'? Psychology has much to learn from artistic practices.

Notes

1 Chauvet, J.-M., Deschamps, E. B., and Hillaire, C., *Dawn of Art, The Chauvet Cave: The Oldest Known Paintings in the World*, New York, Harry M. Abrams, 1996, p.122.
2 *The Observer*, London, 22 January 1995.
3 For this view of subjectivity see R. Wollheim, *The Thread of Life*, Cambridge, Cambridge University Press, 1984, and T. Nagel, *Mortal Questions*, Cambridge, Cambridge University Press, 1979.
4 C. Benson, *The Absorbed Self: Pragmatism, Psychology and Aesthetic Experience*, London, Harvester Wheatsheaf, 1993.
5 R. Wollheim, *Painting as an Art*, London, Thames & Hudson, 1987, p. 44.
6 J. Paillard (ed.), *Brain and Space*, Oxford, Oxford University Press, 1991.
7 G. Lakoff and M. Johnson, *Metaphors We Live By*, Chicago and London, The University of Chicago Press, 1980, Chapter 4. See also their recent book, *Philosophy in the Flesh: The Embodied Mind and its Challenge to Western Thought*, New York, Basic Books, 1999, for a development of these ideas.
8 E. Winner, *The Point of Words: Children's Understanding of Metaphor and Irony*, Cambridge, Mass., Harvard University Press, 1988.
9 M. Wertheim, *The Pearly Gates of Cyberspace: A History of Space from Dante to the Internet*, London, Virago, 1999.
10 A. Damasio, *The Feeling of What Happens: Body and Emotion in the Making of Consciousness*, New York, Harcourt Brace & Company, 1999.
11 Wollheim, op. cit. For a discussion of this in relation to perception see I. Rock, *Perception*, New York, Scientific American Library, 1995, Chapter 4.
12 M. Kubovy, *The Psychology of Perspective and Renaissance Art*, Cambridge, Cambridge University Press, 1986, p. 6.
13 Ibid., p. 148.
14 W. Metger, 'Optische Untersuchungen am Ganzfeld, 11. Zur Phänomenologie des

homogenen Ganzfelds', *Psychologische Forschung*, 13, 1930, 6–29. Also see K. Koffka, *Principles of Gestalt Psychology*, New York, Harcourt, Brace and Company, 1935. For an excellent discussion of this work in relation to Turrell see C. Adcock, *J. Turrell, The Art of Light and Space*, Berkeley, University of California Press, 1990, Chapter 7.

15 J. J. Gibson, *The Ecological Approach to Visual Perception*, Boston, Houghton Mifflin, 1979. See also L. L. Avant, 'Vision in the Ganzfeld', *Psychological Bulletin*, 64, 1965, 246–58.

16 See J. Vernon, *Inside the Black Room: Studies of Sensory Deprivation*, Harmondsworth, Penguin, 1966.

17 S. Millar, *Understanding and Representing Space: Theory and Evidence from Studies with Blind and Sighted Children*, Oxford, Clarendon Press, 1994, p. 177.

18 Ibid., p. 26.

19 J. Shearman, *Only Connect: Art and the Spectator in the Italian Renaissance*, Princeton, NJ, Princeton University Press, 1992, pp.151–2. Only in 1798 with Goya's decoration of the dome of San Antonio de la Florida in Madrid where the saint's activities on earth are emphatically depicted is this tradition significantly broken in the Christian context.

20 See Adcock, op. cit., pp.130–2 and 240 n. 13.

21 M. Merleau-Ponty, *Phenomenology of Perception*, translated by C. Smith, London, Routledge & Kegan Paul, 1981, p. 235.

22 A. Damasio, *Descartes' Error: Emotion, Reasoning and the Human Brain*, London, Picador, 1995. Other ideas on neural representational bases of self may be found, for example, in R. Melzack, 'Phantom limbs, the self and the brain: The D. O. Hebb Memorial Lecture', *Canadian Psychology*, 1989, Jan., Vol. 30, (1), 1–16.

23 Damasio, op. cit., p. 230

24 Ibid., p. 232

25 Ibid., p. 235

26 Ibid., p. 243

27 Ibid., p. 235.

13

INDIVIDUAL AND NATIONAL
IDENTITY

Analogy, symbiosis and artistic process

What is Life? Life is the Nation. The individual must die anyway
. . .

(A. Hitler quoted in A. Beevor, Stalingrad, 1999, p. 392)

The man who enjoys marching in line and file to the strains of
music falls below my contempt; he received his great brain by
mistake – the spinal cord would have been amply sufficient. This
heroism at command, this senseless violence, this accursed bom-
bast of patriotism – how intensely I despise them.

(A. Einstein, I Believe, 1940, p. 71)

Explanations offered by a cultural psychology of self and identity will most likely
be of the 'cases and interpretations' kind rather than of 'laws and instances'. They
will, to borrow Clifford Geertz's memorable phrase, look 'less for the sort of
thing that connects planets and pendulums and more for the sort that connects
chrysanthemums and swords'.[1] Such connections are symbolic, implicative,
socially constructed and diverse. The interpretations which psychology itself
makes, like those it studies, are creations rather than revelations. Harré further
reminds us that 'they are creations only if they become reality-creating interpretations, that is become the interpretations used by most people'.[2] The culturally
distinctive features of a people are the ways in which their interpretations of the
world channel how they act in it. This sense of themselves as a distinct people is
part of the foundation for what is called national identity.

Symptoms of national identity are the types of choice which people consistently make in particular circumstances: which side to fight for in times of territorial conflict, which football team to cheer to victory, whom to seek out as
company when in exile in expectation of an easy affinity with those who share
certain common understandings and orientations with oneself. With whom and
where, to put it simply, do we 'feel at home' or 'belong'? It is in this apparently

simple feeling of belonging with 'us' and 'here' rather than with 'them' and 'there' that so much of the awfulness and advantage of nationalism resides.

Roger Hausheer observes that Isaiah Berlin, unusually for a liberal thinker on nationalism, identifies 'belonging' as a feeling which is fundamental for human being. Following Herder and the Romantics, Berlin stresses this deep need to be a member of a continuous cultural and historical community rooted in its own land. Hausheer puts it like this:

> If Berlin is right, then the need to acquire and express one's identity through such a community is a universal need just as imperious as the need for food or for shelter: deprivation may not prove immediately fatal, but in the long run it will wreak havoc.[3]

The possibility of a 'national' identity is only as old as the emergence of nations. It is with the historical formation of nations that the possibilities of collective identification with the nation emerge. Historians are divided on the chronology of the emergence of nations and nationalism. 'Modernists' like Eric Hobsbawm, John Breuilly, Ernest Gellner and Benedict Anderson, for example, argue that the modern political sense of nationality developed in the late eighteenth and early nineteenth centuries.[4]

More recently, historians of the Middle Ages have challenged this location of the origins of nations and nationalism, and have argued instead for a much earlier source. Adrian Hastings, for instance, while acknowledging that nationalism spread with vigour from the period in the late eighteenth century identified by modernist historians, argues that England is historically the prototype of both a nation and a nation-state in a way that is 'detectable already in Saxon times by the end of the tenth century'.[5]

Nationalisms are also woven with other coincident elements of identity such as religion, language and ethnicity, which over the last two hundred years have given rise to various forms of cultural nationalism. Take Ireland as an example, 'Europe's most continuously active nationalist volcano', as Hastings describes it.[6] In Ireland's case the pieces in the jigsaw are Catholicism and Protestantism, the languages of Irish and English, and a melding of the Celtic, Viking, Norman, English and Scottish races. Tom Garvin argues that the power of nationalism as a principle of solidarity derives from 'its intellectual emptiness, which permits it to marry with older loyalties, with democracy, communism, facism, racism, religion and with various economic systems. Nationalism is ideologically agnostic, and as friendly to modernisation as it is to cultural traditionalism.'[7]

Anthony Smith offers an historical sociology of national identity in which he explicitly links the ideology and movement of nationalism with the multidimensional concept of national identity, which he treats as a collective cultural phenomenon.[8] As a modernist, he argues that nationalism is the most compelling identity myth of the modern world with its origins in eighteenth-century Europe.[9] Leaving to one side the contention between modernist and medievalist arguments for the roots of nations and nationalism, Smith's definition of a nation has clarity. He identifies five elements of national identity linked to his definition of a nation as 'a named human population sharing an historic territory, common myths and historical memories, a mass, public culture, a common economy and common legal rights and duties for all members'.[10]

This complex concept is incapable of reduction to a single element. It is wider than the concept of the 'state' which refers exclusively to public institutions. In addition to its economic and other functions, national identity fulfils some explicitly social-psychological purposes. Through mass education it socializes members as 'nationals and citizens' by paying special attention to ideals of cultural authenticity and unity. This it does by facilitating identification with the nation as an ideal in the active construction of its members' selves. Nationalism from this perspective can be understood as, in Charles Taylor's sense, a constitutive good forming a central orienting part of individual selves. Smith argues that

> The new concept of the nation was made to serve as a time–space framework to order chaos and render the universe meaningful by harnessing pre-modern mass aspirations and sentiments for local and familial attachments; herein lay a vital part of the wide appeal of an otherwise abstruse ideology and language.[11]

Individuals constituted nationalistically in this way can readily sacrifice their own lives and those of others on the altar of patriotism. They become living instances of the ideal. With its repertoires of shared values, symbols and traditions, national identity bonds individuals, classes and interest groups together under the superordinate category of the nation. This is a potent way of assisting individual selves to locate and define themselves in the wider world.

It becomes as unthinkable, for example, that they should betray their nation as that they should betray their family. It also becomes thinkable that they should kill or otherwise harm the enemies of the nation. It is in such contexts, for example, that my enemy's enemy can become my friend as happened in both World Wars when a diverse group of European nationalists, including Irish republican elements, looked to Germany as a potential source of military support just as Britain looked to the Pinochet dictatorship for support in its conflict over the Falklands with the then Argentinian dictatorship.

The relationship between personal and national identity is both analogous and symbiotic. They share key features, and each feeds off the other. The psychology of persons and nations is all of a piece. Pre-existing processes of national identity shape and become part of the selves of citizens, and those citizens in turn become, as it were, individual 'carriers' of that identity insofar as it has become part of themselves. The individual citizen's self is 'distributed' through the collectively held ideals which constitute his or her national identity.[12] If we adopt the perspective of a cultural evolutionary psychologist, we will identify all the constituting ideas of nationalism as memes, or more simply as ideas. Their power derives both from the extent to which they have shaped the autobiographical selves of individuals, and also from the proportion of a population whose selves have been significantly shaped in this way. Daniel Dennett's observations on the relation of memes and difference are relevant here:

> The haven all memes depend on reaching is the human mind, but a human mind is itself an artifact created when memes restructure a human brain in order to make it a better habitat for memes. The avenues for entry and departure are modified to suit local conditions, and strengthened by various artificial devices that enhance fidelity and prolixity of replication: native Chinese minds differ dramatically from native French minds, and literate minds differ from illiterate minds.[13]

Differences between peoples in the ways in which they conduct their lives are, like many of the similarities between them, due to the nature of the ideas with which their minds and selves are made, and to the role of those ideas in shaping and guiding their decisions, plans and actions. In what ways can the organisation of national identity be understood as being like that of individual personal identity? This is the analogical question. And in what ways does each type of identity shape and influence the other? This is the issue of symbiosis.

I want to address these questions using the understanding of self as we have seen it emerge in earlier chapters. There we encountered conceptions of self like that of Antonio Damasio. His proto-self, core self and autobiographical self form a hierarchy and correspond respectively to systems of non-conscious integration, focused consciousness in the present moment, and consciousness which extends over past, present and future. This further involves distinctions between consciousness and self-consciousness, and between conscious and non-conscious functioning.

A second repertoire of three distinctions — developed by Harré, Bruner and others — conceives of selves as situated perspectives functioning as reference points (ways of being centred), as agents or originators of action accompanied by variable feelings of power, and as more or less coherent and stable by virtue of narrative powers which produce versions of autobiography appropriate to the demands of particular times and circumstances. Of especial importance for issues of responsibility – with its ancillary phenomena of pride, blame, remorse and guilt – is the possibility of self-creation which depends on particular means of self-interpretation, and on the powers and permissions necessary to use them.

There is also the dialogical dimension of self, the fact of its always being constructed and maintained in relation to an object or an 'Other'. I have developed the idea that a primary function of the psychological system which we call self is to locate and orient persons in whatever field of experience they happen to find themselves. Finally there is the idea of self as always being 'a work in progress' in a way that is strikingly similar to artistic work in progress. National identity formation, maintenance and development is also like artistic process and is, moreover, substantially the product of artistic effort in that, if Adrian Hastings is correct, it requires the existence of a body of written vernacular literature for its emergence. Hastings generalises Eugen Weber's view of France as 'the nation not as a given reality but as a work-in-progress'.[14]

A nation's history as it tells it to itself is always, like an individual's autobiography, unfinished. Nonetheless, it is that operating version of its history in its current version that defines the nation, signposts its current decision-making, determines the concerns which become the centre of preoccupation from which it relates to its world, configures its relations to the 'Others' in that world, and shapes a sense of its own powerfulness or powerlessness, victimhood and grievance. No one who listened to Radovan Karadzic during the Serb onslaught on Bosnia could doubt the role of his epic but mythic retelling of the 1389 Battle of Kosovo in creating and fomenting the Serbian sense of themselves as historic victims, against all the evidence to the contrary. Literature played its role in this outburst of murderous nationalism just as it has done elsewhere. In the view of Karadzic and his followers, this self-story justified their aggression as a religious struggle towards a 'national rebirth' of the Serbs.[15]

These ideas sustain the plausibility of the claim that there are analogical and symbiotic relationships between individual and national identity, and the ancillary claim that the arts can play a role in the formation of national identity parallel to the one which they can play in the amplification of personal identity. Pursuing the analogy may help orient us towards points of symbiotic connection between personal and national identities. It may also suggest how an understanding of both forms of identity as 'works in progress' leads us to look towards artistic creativeness for aspects of their origination. In what follows, I will use Ireland as the main source of my examples given both its significance as an instance of nationalism and, as Hastings also points out, its curious neglect in modernist theories of nationalism.[16]

It is striking how often discussions of the emergence of nationalism rely on extending the language of consciousness and self-consciousness to the abstraction 'nation'. 'A nation is a far more self-conscious community than an ethnicity', writes Hastings.[17] He writes of Ireland 'sprouting a kind of consciousness which may most appropriately be described as nationalism' during the catastrophes of the seventeenth century.[18] For Ernest Gellner 'Nationalism is not the awakening of nations to self-consciousness; it invents nations where they do not exist – but it does need some pre-existing differentiating marks to work on . . . '[19] Declan Kiberd in his magisterial exploration of the role which literature plays in inventing Ireland, has memorably wondered whether, in the complex relations of the two countries, Ireland came to function as England's unconscious.[20]

We even find a conception of a 'proto-nation' functioning in ways suggestive of Damasio's proto-self. It occurs in Hastings's discussion of the central importance of writing for the emergence of a coherent national self-consciousness.[21] Considering the sense in which texts can produce peoples, Hastings argues that 'A community, political, religious, or whatever, is essentially a creation of human communication and it is only to be expected that the form of the communication will determine the character of the community.'[22] Hastings dates the beginning of vernacular literature of Europe – literature in local languages rather than the 'universal' languages of Latin and Greek – to early Christian Ireland and to Wales before the end of the sixth century. Vernacular literatures became widespread in Western Europe before the year 1000. With their growing utility in religion, government and education came the creation, 'almost by necessity', of rudimentary integration which suggests a 'proto-nation'.

This written literature in certain vernacular languages began to create the cultural psychological foundations for the emergence of nations. Languages that remained oral characterised ethnicities but they failed to engender nations. Analogous to the neural proto-self which functions to integrate vital functions and to maintain equilibrium outside the consciousness of the person, so the proto-nation, formed by written vernacular literature, began to create a centre of organisation which in time enabled the emergence of modern self-conscious nations. Hastings identifies the translation of the Bible into the vernacular as having potently and decisively contributed to the emergence of national consciousness. The Bible hinges on the idea of the Jewish people as the Chosen People and thereby provides the original model of the nation. A text with a powerful image of unity, translated into a people's 'own' language, in time came to engender an image of even more comprehensive and ideal unity, the nation.

This image of the nation is formed metaphorically. One such metaphor used by Lakoff and Johnson is that of Nation as Person.[23] It is this metaphor which allows discussion of a nation's 'interests', where the health of a person maps onto the health of a nation, or personal strength onto national military strength. Regarding foreign policy, the nation is understood as a person in a world community of nations, some of whom are neighbours, some friendly, others hostile

211

and so on. Some nations are mature and adult which in national terms means industrialised, while others are 'backward', developing or even 'rogue'.

A more pervasive metaphor, judging by the literature on nations and nationalism, is the Nation as Family. This would in fact seem to be the primary metaphor for nationalism, and the one underpinning that sense of belongingness identified as so essential by Isaiah Berlin and others. The nation is the homeland, the motherland or the fatherland. Its language is the mother tongue. Fellow citizens are brothers and sisters. Citizenship is a birthright. Irredentism aims to reunite the family by 'redeeming' those members outside the present boundaries of the nation.

The frequently occurring idea of a long-gone 'Golden Age' parallels that of a lost childhood, and the urge to national regeneration is act of restoration of that unity which has been lost. Ethnic rebirth, as we have seen with the Serbs, can become an aim of war. To achieve nationhood is then to become adult, and consequently to be eligible to become part of the family of nations. All nations have a name like a family. Those who live next to us are neighbours. Those who are not family are not one of us, and are therefore 'them', those whose interests may well not be 'ours', and whether they are or not, we don't assess our relationships with them by granting primacy to their best interests. We look after our own. Family comes first. It becomes unthinkable for this to be otherwise.

Family is the crucible in which self is forged. Whether directly by incorporation or indirectly by rebellion, the family and its associates (the church to which the family belongs, the schools it chooses for its children, its various loyalties in politics and play) supply and edit the self-constituting narratives available to its offspring, and powerfully influence the structuring of their identities. One's name, one's sense of where one is placed in the affections and distances that make up the constellation of the family, the impact of being male or female, older or younger, emotionally open or secretive, responsible or irresponsible, these and many other constructs are variously available within a family for the construction of self. The nation as family works similarly for those it takes to be its own.

Perhaps the strongest force for the construction of national identity is the humanly inescapable capacity for distinctions and difference-making. The negating powers of self-definition, in telling us what we are not or ought not to be, simultaneously tell us what we are and what we should aspire to be. The thinkable and unthinkable acts which constitute personal identity have their kin in the construction of national identity. Each of the now nearly hundreds of nations and nationalisms throughout the world will have their own particularities and their own competing stories, but in the intricacies of one may be discerned the intricacies of many. The simultaneity of creating what is while specifying what is not, is covered within the field of self studies by the concepts of 'dialogicality' or 'transaction', and 'the Other'.

212

Differentiation is the ubiquitous companion of meaning-making. This helps us understand the ways in which the clusters 'I/we' and 'here' differentiate in practical detail from 'you/them' and 'there'. Only in processes of sharing, and participation in common purpose, can the boundaries of these sets blur, overlap, reconfigure or merge. This is part of what happens in alliances or federations of nations. 'Others' need not be enemies. As Theodore Zeldin comments, 'Animosity against enemies has been a steadfast substitute for positive goals in life.'[24]

The 'Other' is that in dialogue with which I define my own identity. I think of myself as being that which the 'Other' is not, and each 'we' does the same. But this is why the Other is inescapably a constituent part of me. This dynamic is central to the formation of nationhood, nationalism, and national identity. Historians like Hastings think of early forms of the idea of nation, such as arose in England, as giving rise to subsequent movements of nationalism with associated national identities. Once historically on the scene, however, like other powerful creative ideas, nationalism reproduces itself. Over the last two centuries, nationalism as an ideology has given rise to nations in a process that reverses in significant ways the directions of construction evident in its historical precedents.

England has been Ireland's great 'Other'. Ireland's nationalism, it could be argued, is a consequence of England's. The strands of their interconnection are so complex and shifting that it is only in the work of the most insightful historians, writers and artists that the eddies and swamps, flows and refluxes, dams and currents can be discerned. John Hutchinson argues that 'if it is through the historian one learns of the national destiny, the paradigmatic figure of the national community is the artist'.[25] If France is a work in progress for Eugen Weber, Ireland's England and England's Ireland are two terms constantly redefining and reconstructing themselves.

If art helps to create the concepts of nation and nationalism by furthering its self-consciousness as an actual or potential nation, then a few comments on the changing nature of art will be helpful here. The idea of invention unites the concepts of art and national identity. Benedict Anderson, wishing to avoid the possible association of invention with falsification, prefers the ideas of 'imagining' and 'creation'. He writes that 'all communities larger than primordial villages of face-to-face contact (and perhaps even these) are imagined'.[26] Anderson goes on to say that the nation is imagined as limited in its boundaries, sovereign in its freedom, and communal in that the nation, irrespective of deep internal social divisions and inequalities, 'is always conceived as a deep horizontal comradeship'.[27]

These same concepts of imagination, creation and invention characterise contemporary notions of art. The arts have come to play a variety of powerful roles in the formation and maintenance of national identities just as they have played parallel roles in the subversion of certain editions of identity. For the sake of brevity, I will use the metaphor of the mirror to contrast two conceptions of the arts and of their functions.

The first view, heavily indebted to Plato and Aristotle and powerfully employed by the Romantics, thinks of art as mimetic or imitative, as a mirror to nature. It favours 'realistic', representational forms of art which are thought to objectify something already existing. They facilitate epiphanic revelations which connect us to a reality of great significance, we feel, but which would otherwise remain inaccessible.[28] Concepts of resemblance and illusion underpin this understanding of art, where the subject of depiction as it is portrayed facilitates the epiphany.

The contrasting modernist view thinks of art as a semiotic process which actively constitutes realities rather than simply reflecting them. In essence, art makes the mirror, what you see in it and, to a degree, you as you see it. At the heart of this is the idea of the arts as symbol systems, or more loosely as languages, with which meanings are made rather than found.[29] As an ever-strengthening social institution in the modern liberal democratic moral order, art has aspired to an independence and autonomy from the constraints of other moral institutions, such as religious institutions, which would have been inconceivable to pre-Modern artists and writers.

To sharpen the focus of this analysis let me now take Ireland as the case to which to apply some of these ideas. We can pose the problem of the psychological functioning of art in the formation of the modern Irish national identity at two separate levels. First, there was the clash, for want of a better formulation, between pre-Modern and Modernist conceptions of art within the moral order of the newly emerging Catholic Nationalist state from 1922 to perhaps as far as the early 1980s. There are also the much less contentious changes in art and its relations to society which are characteristic of late-twentieth-century Ireland. Finally, there is the question of the contribution of particular artists, art forms and artworks to the formation and transformation of the Irish national identity.

These contrasting conceptions of art suggest two questions concerning the relationship of art and Irish national identity. In what ways did the arts serve the aims of other social institutions in the formation of the modern Irish national identity, and in what ways did art assume for itself the task of constructing a new Irish national identity, despite the wishes of other institutions such as the Catholic Church? That art and artists played the roles both of collaboration and of subversion of versions of Irish national identity is evident in the cultural history of modern Ireland.[30] Invention of realities for imaginative use was the means by which this was done.

The case can be made that the arts played a powerful role in creating the imagined community of a unified Catholic nationalist Ireland, divided by colonisers for eight hundred years and only winning back that long-lost freedom in the third decade of the twentieth century. Many songs, stories and films attest to that. But broaden the scope and one would have to consider the Protestant unionist identity in relation to the concept of 'Irishness' just as one would have to examine the role of the arts in the social-psychological construction of the Protestant nationalist identity or for that matter the internationalist tendencies of socialist identity formations.

Historians identify a variety of cultural nationalisms at play in the early forma-tion of the modern Irish nation which we may take as possible sources for dimen-sions of Irish national identity. One centred on the Gaelic League as led by Douglas Hyde (a Protestant) which sought to de-Anglicise Irish culture and to place the Irish language at the heart of Irish nationhood. Among other things this involved the construction of an ideal ancestral Gaeldom which became the inspira-tion for Ireland's 'old tradition of nationhood' in the 1916 Proclamation of the Irish Republic promulgated by the rebel leaders during their Easter Rising. A second cultural nationalism revolved around the Irish Literary Renaissance led by William Butler Yeats (a Protestant). But the foundation here was the English language. A third was the cultural nationalism exemplified by the journalist D. P. Moran which was 'Catholic, populistic and suspicious of Protestants' (leaders of the other two schools). For them 'Irish' meant 'Irish Catholic of Gaelic Stock'.[31]

The proportionate part played by the nationalistic triad of race, language and religion in the aspiration to invent an Irish identity varied according to the brand of cultural nationalism in question. The cultural and social history of modern Ireland is to a considerable degree a history of their mutual jostling. The Yeatsian form was much more sympathetic to the central formative role and importance of the arts in Irish life than was that of D. P. Moran, as well as being more liberal and complex. Kiberd says of Yeats's project that it was 'to Catholicize the all-too-Protestant Ireland of his youth, and to Protestantize the all-too-Catholic Ireland of his age'.[32]

Accompanying this array of cultural nationalisms is an equally rich palette of political ones. 'In the Irish case', observes Tom Garvin,

> the blood-sacrifice romanticism of Pearse has to compete with the democratic liberal-Catholic synthesis invented by Daniel O'Connell, the guerrilla militarism of the IRA, the socialist republicanism of Connolly, a still-extant Anglo-Irish patriotism, a simple affection for land and com-munity and the formula offered by the Republic of Ireland, a mixture of O'Connellist democratic pragmatism disguised by the iconography derived from the insurrectionist tradition; Irish nationalists have many stories to select from. Similar multi-layered traditions exist elsewhere.[33]

The version of cultural nationalism espoused by such as D. P. Moran, however, was politically the more successful in the early decades of modern Ireland and powerful in stemming the acknowledged social-psychological power of the arts as developed within the tradition of modernism. Traditionalists saw modernism as corrupting of what they construed as traditionally valuable and therefore as essential to the restoration of a 'true' Irish identity. From a contemporary perspective, we may view this as an attempt at inventing that identity rather than as a restoration. Their spirit was especially antagonistic to the experimental, internationalist, Modernism best typified by James Joyce.

In *A Portrait of the Artist as a Young Man* Joyce writes:

> I will tell you what I will do and what I will not do. I will not serve that in which I no longer believe whether it call itself my home, my fatherland or my church; and I will try to express myself in some mode of life or art as freely as I can and as wholly as I can, using for my defence the only arms I allow myself to use – silence, exile, and cunning.[34]

Not terms of endearment to a cultural nationalist of the D. P. Moran kind! Joyce sought in his way to 'forge in the smithy of my soul the uncreated conscience of my race'. Modernism, especially in literature and the visual arts, clearly understood the powers of its various languages to create realities in the most literal sense, and as such posed a sharp and emphatic threat to traditional certainties with their traditional conflicts. This is why the modern spirit came to be thought of as 'unhoused' with Ulysses the wanderer as an emblem.

Joyce's *Ulysses* is constructed in a manner resonant of modern constructivist theories of self. It is a narrative of home and homelessness, a narrative of multiple voices and multiple streams of consciousness, of anxieties about self-definition embodied in the particularities of a single day in June 1904 with a wandering Irish Jew as hero and his errant wife Molly Bloom's exploration of the unconscious and of desire as the affirmation of life. Of *Finnegans Wake* Malcolm Bradbury has written that it 'was the book that spoke abstractly to the great Modernist task both of breaking down an old language and myth, and constructing a new and self-made one that made the art of fiction the art of language itself'.[35]

In terms of the arts and Irish national identity, as elsewhere in Europe of the early to mid-twentieth century, the question was not simply which myths would be preferred elements of national identity, but which understanding of art and language as means of myth-making the political and ecclesiastical powers would allow or promote.

For the early part of the history of newly independent Ireland the traditional view held sway but in recent decades, with the onset of a global mass culture,

Modernist and Postmodernist traditions have gained ascendancy as the tradition-ally rigid authoritarianism of the Catholic Church in particular has waned. In the prose of another great Irish Modernist writer, Samuel Beckett, as Kiberd observes, 'All forms of authority . . . induce irresponsibility.'[36] Released from authority, Beckettian characters survive 'handsomely'. This theme of responsibil-ity in the Irish national identity is played out between the authoritarianism of Catholicism and the conscientious freedom of Protestantism. O'Casey, a Protestant, identifies self-responsibility in his plays as a Protestant virtue.[37]

Again, as can be discerned in Kiberd's work, there is a further relationship in the organisation of the versions of Irish national identity between differing emphases on the scope of obedience to the Church Fathers (a happily powerful nominal positioning within the Nation as Family metaphor) and self-responsibility, their constructions within Catholicism and Protestantism, their mappings onto masculine and feminine stereotypes, their significance in English stereotypes of Catholic Ireland, and the influences of the elements of this stereo-type on the ways in which Catholic Nationalism came to construct its own self-image. Take what Kiberd has to say about the ways in which Ireland came to function as not-England for the English during the Victorian period:

> Victorian imperialists attributed to the Irish all those emotions and impulses which a harsh mercantile code had led them to suppress in themselves. Thus, if John Bull was industrious and reliable, Paddy was held to be indolent and contrary; if the former was mature and rational, the latter must be unstable and emotional; if the English were adult and manly, the Irish must be childish and feminine. In this fashion, the Irish were to read their fate in that of two other out-groups, women and children; and at the root of many an Englishman's suspicion of the Irish was an unease with the woman or child who lurked within himself.[38]

The political implications of this characterisation were that the Irish were incapable of self-government just as, to the Victorian male, women and children were also incapable of rational self-determination. This was an attitude towards women shared by many Irish leaders of post-independent Ireland. Irish national identity of that time was strongly yet ambivalently male. An example to indicate that ambivalence could be the role of women in Irish poetry which is described by the poet Eavan Boland. Her autobiographical account of becoming an Irish woman poet argues that women were so positioned within the realities of Irish poetry as to be marginal as poets but central as a type of woman. 'The idea of the defeated nation being reborn as a triumphant woman was central to a certain type of Irish poem. Dark Rosaleen, Cathleen ni Houlihan. The nation as woman; the woman as national muse.'[39]

Boland objects to the simplification of women in Irish poetry. Fusion of the national and the feminine in the service of a romantic nationalism are for her weaknesses of Irish poetry. This ostensible centrality of woman to the idea of nation depended upon her being put there by men, rather than on any acknowledgement that she could put herself there and exercise the power within the nation that this would imply. Boland's narrative of herself as an Irish woman becoming an Irish woman poet who wished to form her own relation with the idea of nation exemplifies the importance for self-realisation of gaining some control of language within the national discourse. This in turn means controlling interpretation which itself lies at the heart of the creation of social realities. This sense of having 'found one's voice' involves the complex integration of the many conflicting voices that compose self. Again the parallel of national self-realisation and that of individual self is striking and symbiotic.

Control of the languages available for self-construction, opportunities to become fluent in them, and permissions to use them, are central to the construction of national identity, just as they are to personal identity. What those in control of political power within a nation regard as dangerous to its health is indicative of their governing concept of the nation. Again, using an example from the relationship of the state to art, we can point to processes of censorship, or the eschewing of censorship, as a significant indicator of control and the ideals it is taken to protect.

Though far from unique, Irish censorship was narrowly puritan by European standards and hit Irish writers in particular with a special vehemence. Enacted as the Censorship of Publication Act in 1929 it was designed to effectively control the distribution of British newspapers and publications.[40] It aimed to shape, by defence mechanisms of exclusion, the mass public culture of the new Ireland in line with a particular ideal of national purity. That purity of national self was most endangered by its 'Others', England and the non-Catholic world. The means of corruption were written representations and visual depictions. A board of five men appointed by the Minister for Justice and answerable only to him operated under a blanket of virtual secrecy.

The parallels with the psychological defense mechanisms of suppression and denial are striking. The intended policy of isolating Irish citizens from practically anything that dealt significantly with their erotic lives and sexuality through state censorship of publications and films was born of a paternalistic authoritarianism which sought to 'protect' the populace from 'harmful' products, for which read representations and depictions of sexuality. The psychology of the power relations implicit here, the ideas justifying their deployment, and the end towards which these measures were directed, can be interpreted as attempts to control the ways in which Irish people interpreted their own sexuality and in doing so constructed it. By the 1950s, a lay Catholic action group, the Knights of

Columbanus, was 'in virtual control' of the Censorship Board.[41] As such, one can interpret the practices of Irish censorship as one very obvious way in which powerful cultural forces sought to control particular formative sources of self, notably its sexual dimensions. Even Margaret Mead's works on *Growing up in New Guinea, Coming of Age in Samoa*, and *Male and Female* were banned!

This then allowed the state to shape what it regarded as desirable forms of sexual self-understanding through the education system, the Catholic Church and the family. Such official curricula, and the powerful hidden curricula that shadow them, have aptly been described as instruments for the creation of minds.[42] Control of school curricula can therefore have powerful national consequences.

The backhanded compliment to the arts was that their power was acknowledged and, arguably, exaggerated and oversimplified. The legislation was liberalised to some effect in 1967 and again with the passing of the Health (Family Planning) Act, 1979. But in the nearly forty years of its full operation most Irish writers of significance were banned thereby denying the Irish people access to crucial forms of national self-exploration and self-definition. Also banned were very many great non-Irish artists and writers.

The principal effect of this, in the views of writers like Liam O'Flaherty and Samuel Beckett, was to turn Ireland into an 'intellectual and moral wasteland'.[43] Now, of course, these writers are the heroes of that time. Irish national identity has gone through a number of liberalising editions since then. Authoritarianism with its secretive ways has become profoundly unpopular. In a world where satellite and internet technologies are redefining the nature and boundaries of communities the implications for the potentially waning powers of national politicians to control the formation of identities are profound and unprecedented.

A final comment. The sentimentality of nationalistic art suggests one of its greatest dangers. As Garvin argues, 'Nationalist and unionist fundamentalists in Ireland are united in one thing: twin collective addictions to self-sentimentalisation.'[44] Sentimentality is repetition, a closed loop of feeling. It involves an attitude to art as the occasion for activating emotion already familiar to the person and desired by them for that very reason. The work of art, and it need not be a good one, functions as a trigger for feelings tied to other purposes. It is the repetition of the experience in a near reflex way that is the purpose of the music or poem or whatever.

Required habits of feeling can be harnessed to songs and images for purposes of control as well as for purposes of solidarity. Anthems, ballads, flags, stories, films, and so on can be created as instruments of manipulation just as they can be as embodiments of memory or as celebrations of survival. In Eavan Boland's terms, the psychology of sentimentality would be linked to 'arts of reassurance', to the protective sense that not only need people not change but that change itself is undesirable, indeed potentially a betrayal of self. It is here that the familiarity of the traditional has the edge on the avant-garde, since it pits the known against the unknown.

George Steiner has written that 'To read well is to take great risks. It is to make vulnerable our identity, our self-possession.'[45] But to read well depends upon being educated well, and again we return to a central problem for a cultural psychology of art and national identity. This is the nature of the institutional sources of a nation's selves and the degree to which they value and encourage self-criticism. Jerome Bruner argues that 'The importance of narrative for the cohesion of a culture is as great, very likely, as it is in structuring an individual life.'[46] That is why the arts are so central to the formations of identity, and that is why it is in the source and nature of narrative forms, with their powers to make meanings, that the symbiotic relationship of personal and national identity finds its common source and sustenance.

Notes

1 See C. Geertz, *Local Knowledge: Future Essays in Interpretive Anthropology* (2nd edn), London, Fontana Press, 1993, p. 19.
2 R. Harré, *Social Being: A Theory for Social Psychology*, Oxford, Basil Blackwell, 1979, p. 237.
3 Isaiah Berlin, *The Proper Study of Mankind: An Anthology of Essays*, eds. H. Hardy and R. Hausheer, London, Pimlico, 1998, p. xxxiii.
4 See, for example, E. J. Hobsbawm, *Nations and Nationalism since 1780*, Cambridge, Cambridge University Press, 1990; J. Breuilly, *Nationalism and the State* (2nd edn), Manchester, Manchester University Press, 1993; E. Gellner, *Nations and Nationalism*, Oxford, Blackwell, 1983; Benedict Anderson, *Imagined Communities: Reflections on the Origins and Spread of Nationalism*, London, Verso, 1991.
5 Adrian Hastings, *The Construction of Nationhood: Ethnicity, Religion and Nationalism*, Cambridge, Cambridge University Press, 1997, p. 5.
6 Ibid., p.220.
7 T. Garvin, *Mythical Thinking in Political Life: Reflections on Nationalism and Social Science*, Dublin, Maunsell, 2000, p. 73.
8 A. D. Smith, *National Identity*, London, Penguin, 1991.
9 Smith's position is this: 'But if by nationalism we wish to designate ideologies and movements that presuppose a world of nations, each with its own character, and a primary allegiance to the nation as the sole source of political power and the basis of world order, then we shall be hard put to find movements inspired by such ideals in the ancient, or medieval worlds, let alone in ancient Egypt.' (Ibid., pp.46–7)
10 Ibid., p. 14.
11 Ibid., p. 78.
12 J. Bruner, *Acts of Meaning*, Cambridge, Mass., Harvard University Press, 1990.
13 D. Dennett, *Darwin's Dangerous Idea: Evolution and the Meanings of Life*, New York, Simon & Schuster, 1995, p. 365.

14 Hastings, op. cit., p. 26.
15 Ibid., Chapter 5 on 'The South Slavs'.
16 Hastings, op. cit., p. 95.
17 Ibid., p. 3.
18 Ibid., p. 82.
19 E. Gellner, *Thought and Change*, London, Weidenfeld and Nicholson, 1964, p. 169.
20 D. Kiberd, *Inventing Ireland: The Literature of the Modern Nation*, London, Jonathan Cape, 1995, p. 29.
21 Hastings, op. cit., pp.20–2.
22 Ibid., p. 20.
23 G. Lakoff and M. Johnson, *Philosophy in the Flesh: The Embodied Mind and its Challenge to Western Thought*, New York, Basic Books, 1999, pp. 533–5.
24 T. Zeldin, *An Intimate History of Humanity*, London, Minerva, 1995, p. 215.
25 See J. Hutchinson and A. D. Smith (eds), *Nationalism*, Oxford, Oxford University Press, 1994, p. 123.
26 Anderson, op. cit. p. 6.
27 Ibid., p. 7.
28 See C. Taylor, *Sources of the Self: The Making of the Modern Identity*, Cambridge, Mass., Harvard University Press, 1989, p. 419.
29 See N. Goodman, *Ways of Worldmaking*, Hemel Hempstead, Harvester Wheatsheaf, 1978; U. Eco, *A Theory of Semiotics*, London, Macmillan, 1977; and R. Barthes, *Elements of Semiology*, trans. A. Lavers and C. Smith, New York, Hill and Wang, 1967.
30 See T. Brown, *Ireland: A Social and Cultural History*, London, Fontana, 1985; C. Barrett, 'Irish Art and Nationalism', *Studies*, LXIV, Winter 1975 and J. Lee, *Ireland 1912–1985: Politics and Society*, Cambridge, Cambridge University Press, 1989.
31 C. Cruise O'Brien, *Passion and Cunning: Essays on Nationalism, Terrorism and Revolution*, London, Simon and Schuster, 1988, p. 194.
32 Kiberd, op. cit., p. 451.
33 See Garvin, op. cit., p. 48.
34 J. Joyce, *A Portrait of the Artist as a Young Man*, ed. Seamus Deane, London, Penguin, 1992, p. 269.
35 M. Bradbury, *The Modern World*, London, Penguin, 1989, p. 176.
36 Kiberd, op. cit., p. 460.
37 Ibid., p. 422.
38 Ibid., p. 30.
39 E. Boland, 'Outside History', *The American Poetry Review*, March–April 1990, p. 42.
40 J. Carlson, ed., *Banned in Ireland*, London, Routledge, 1990, p. 3.
41 E. Bolster, *The Knights of Columbanus*, Dublin, Gill and Macmillan, 1979.
42 See E. Eisner, *Cognition and Curriculum: A Basis for Deciding What to Teach*, London, Longman, 1982 and H. Gardner, *The Unschooled Mind: How Children Think and How Schools Should Teach*, London, Fontana, 1993.
43 Carlson, op. cit.
44 Garvin, op. cit., p. 15.
45 G. Steiner, *Language and Silence: Essays 1958–1966*, London, Penguin, 1969, p. 29.
46 J. Bruner, *The Culture of Education*, Cambridge, Mass., Harvard University Press, 1996, p. 40.

14

PSYCHOLOGIES OF MATURITY

Development or destination?

> The understanding gained in examining a life itself comes to per-
> meate that life and direct its course. To live an examined life is to
> make a self-portrait. Staring out at us from his later self-portraits,
> Rembrandt is not simply someone who looks like that but one who
> also sees and knows himself *as* that, with the courage this requires.
> (R. Nozick, *The Examined Life: Philosophical Meditations*,
> 1989, pp.12–13)

Positivist psychology misses the moral point of human being. Such an approach
to human mentality cannot account for the important things like self or self-
creation, like moral identity or the variable, incessantly evolving worldviews that
gestate and nurture forms of human psychology which are manifest in how
people live their lives or participate politically. Its profound ignorance or ignoring of history and culture leaves it with a desiccated puppet of a creature that
reacts more than acts. This Procrustean psychology ignores the creative consequences for living of critical self-examination. Thankfully, psychology is return-
ing to Alexander Pope's view that 'The proper study of Mankind is Man', and
man is intrinsically rooted in time and place or, rather, in place-times. Even
psychologists who are adamantly opposed to the hegemony of positivism in their
discipline, and who struggle to free themselves from this way of construing
human being, can show in their work the consequences of themselves being
ahistorical and acultural in their thinking.

The question of what psychology has to say about 'the good life' works like a
diagnostic test for this disciplinary malignancy. To the words 'whole', 'full',
'good', 'complete', 'integrated', 'unified', 'fully functioning', 'self-actualised',
'self-realised', 'self-fulfilled', 'positively mentally healthy' add 'mature' (from
maturitas meaning 'ripeness') and you have a fairly complete lexicon of psychological terms to name the ideal end-state of individual human development.
Every good parent and teacher, every educational system, every counsellor and
psychotherapist must have, even implicitly, an ideal (that is, an idea whose realisation it would be good to commit oneself to) of what a successful outcome of

222

their work with another person would be. From this it may be but a short step to outlining what an ideal state of human development in general might be, often with precepts to follow for achieving it. The popular psychology sections of bookshops are full of offers of assistance in this area. But the individualistic assumptions underpinning much of this literature on psychological self-help are often startlingly naive.

Charles Taylor identifies, as we have seen, the idea of 'radical reflexivity' as being central in the development of the modern identity. This involves an attending to myself as the agent of my own experience, as an 'I' who takes ownership of what I do. Bruner deploys this idea as meta-narrative, a form of reflection on my life which unifies into one story, *my* story, the many stories that make up my life. Psychologists of different schools, psychoanalytic and humanistic in particular, ask questions about the ideal 'perfected' self. These inquiries may be in response to the demands of clinical situations, where a description of mental health is needed, or to familial and educational demands where there is a requirement for standards of what good child-rearing or good educational formation might be. In this essay I want to ask whether cultural psychological conceptions of self can help to place in critical context the grounds for the 'ideals' of self proposed by some from these schools of psychology. How important for self-realisation or self-fulfilment is the sort of reflection required by the idea of self as narrative? In particular, is psychology proposing itself as a moral source for contemporary lives?

Radically reflecting upon yourself is a form of self-consciousness. It involves symbolically objectifying yourself as an idea, with a view perhaps to changing some aspect of yourself. It deploys skills of selection and comparison, of questioning and evaluation. Culturally supplied narratives of the good life such as biographies, autobiographies, memoirs, novels, psychological case histories of 'successful' personal development, religious homilies, propagandistic political exhortations, and so on can act as local guides to local standards of good self-reflective and self-narrating practice.

Self-reflection or meta-narration is not easy. At a much more mundane level, most people run easily without giving it a moment's thought. However, once they begin to think about their running as they are running, they may begin to lose their rhythm and perhaps even to stumble. Self-consciousness disrupts many skilled activities like rocks in a stream disrupt the flow of the water.

Many a shy, self-conscious person walking in a very public space – up the aisle of a church, for example – has a dread of exactly this sort of thing happening because they are preoccupied with imagining how they look to others. They imaginatively occupy what they take to be the perspective of 'the other' on themselves while simultaneously acting as themselves. Since construing themselves as the object of others' attention is an imaginative production of their own

223

making, it is fair to say that it is they themselves who get in their own way. Their attention is divided and their formerly automatic skill loses its fluency. This is reminiscent of Ogden Nash's centipede who was

> . . . happy, quite,
> Until a toad, for fun,
> Enquired which leg came after which
> Which brought his mind to such a pitch
> He lay bewildered in the ditch
> Forgetting how to run.

We can seem to be adept at doing something until such time as we think about how we are doing it. When the toad of self-reflection questions the harmony of the many stories on whose legs we move through life, we too can become as confused and immobilised as the centipede. Where to start? Which event was the more important? Which led to what? Could the movement of my life have been made more satisfying? Why did I take this direction and not that? and so forth. Self-doubt is a necessary condition for self-change. Radical self-reflection employs tools which are supplied in the first instance, as Paul Ricoeur reminds us, by our culture:

> And an examined life is, in large part, one purged, one clarified by the cathartic effects of the narratives, be they historical or fictional, conveyed by our culture. So self-constancy refers to a self instructed by the works of a culture that it has applied to itself.[1]

Using these tools can change what we are and do, and how well or badly we do it. Think of Toad as the urge to meta-narrative in a life (possibly in the guise of Bruner's 'Trouble') with Centipede as the unexamined life moving along its path. Successful self-examination polishes the initial centipede-like confusion into a story of a life chosen as against a life merely led. The idea that an unexamined life is not worth living is at least as old as Socrates. Examining your life and creating its narrative structure is the path to owning it, to making it *yours* in contrast to the unexamined life which simply unfolds but cannot be said to be chosen. It ensures that your life feels continuously and constantly yours. The stance of cultural psychology is very much a product of modernity. It conflicts with certain theocratic or totalitarian accounts of human life where obedience to a dominant authority rather than individual choice is the regulating ideal for important decision-making.

Cultures of the latter kind want obedient characters, not unfettered authors of their own stories, as the Salman Rushdie affair illustrates, or the fate of the arts and academic freedom under Hitler and Stalin. What would be missing from a psychological account of the 'good' or 'full' life, or the 'mature' or 'true' self, that did not explicitly take into account the *constitutive* powers of language, narrative, and moral sources when trying to describe such a self and the shape of its life?

The 'view from nowhere', to use Thomas Nagel's characterisation of the ideal scientific perspective, is radically distorted when the idea of a completely developed life is the focus of inquiry. At this level, all psychological perspectives on what constitutes a desirable pattern of human development are morally and locally contingent. There is no aboriginal or 'true' self to which we can turn for guidance.

The idea of a 'true' and a 'false' self recurs in both psychoanalytic thinking (for example Donald Winnicott) and humanistic psychological theorising (Carl Rogers and the 'Human Potential Movement', for instance). It has philosophical sources of support in the work of Rousseau and Kant, and voices of opposition from Hegel and Dewey. 'New Age' psychologies are particularly fond of this idea of a true self 'deep down' which simply needs to be massaged or conjured out into the open. Such views tend to assume that man is 'innately good' and comes to be led astray by society. The 'Anti-Psychiatry Movement' of the 1960s and 1970s shared this view of the malevolence of society without necessarily sharing this view of self. R. D. Laing could pungently comment that 'Society highly values its normal man. It educates children to lose themselves and to become absurd, and thus to be normal.'[2]

Cultural psychology argues that we understand ourselves to be who we are through the richness or poverty of the languages of expression which we come to acquire. We emerge from and become who we are over many years through transactions with our families, churches, schools, friends, enemies, books, films, governments and others. A task for psychology is to explain how these transactions lead to a fabricated world of individualized subjectivity within the world of networked minds and collectivized subjectivity which is our culture. The self to whom we may be true is a self whose very being is collective, so that to be true to oneself invariably means being true to something other than oneself. A psychology which fails to recognise this in its formulation of an ideal of maturity occludes a crucial part of the picture.

A now familiar *caveat* once again needs emphasis. This does not imply that every self and every horizon of meaning within which it takes its stand is equally good and admirable. A blandly tolerant relativism is not an inevitable outcome of this way of thinking. There are still grounds to favour some versions of the good, and some types of self, as being far preferable to others. As Richard Rorty says, in a review of Charles Taylor's book *The Ethics of Authenticity*, 'But fellow-feeling degenerates into self-indulgent cant and political frivolity when we forget that some cultures, like some people, are no damn good: they cause too much pain, and so have to be resisted (and perhaps eradicated) rather than respected.'[3] The excessive infliction of pain and suffering is becoming a touchstone of societal quality.

With this declaration of position in mind, together with its ancillary cautions, we can now examine some ideas of 'maturity' in psychology. The word 'maturity' is used to indicate the completion of some process. Stage theories are especially fond of calibrating the developmental chronology of maturity. We speak of physical, intellectual, sexual or emotional maturity. The ages for each maturing process may not coincide as when, advising against child marriage in Western cultures, we disengage the idea of sexual maturity from that of emotional maturity. We place more value on the latter, with its implications for freedom of choice and personal fulfilment, and the dignity associated in Western eyes with having that freedom. Connected to this is our high valuation of being educated, economically viable and independent. When the word 'maturity' is extended to high-level abstractions like 'person' or 'self' its applicability becomes stretched and poses a number of serious problems.

At the heart of these lurks the idea of 'human nature'. If there is substance to the idea of a common human nature then this should give us our lead in describing what its ripening or maturity would entail. How similar and how different are the peoples of the world? We tend to notice differences between people within our own communities more quickly than similarities, and with people from another nation or race the tendency is to notice similarities between them perhaps more quickly than differences. Compared to genetically close primates such as chimpanzees, however, human beings are universally very alike. Within narrow bands of difference we are physically similar in structure, have similar physiologies, laugh and cry, think and talk, desire and fear.

Does this fact of genetic similarity help us determine what human nature might be? In terms of the separate trajectories of development mentioned above the answer is yes. In any culture a child of four who cannot speak, or walk, or who avoids everyone, or who cries incessantly or who clings to mother as though his life depended on it, would be a cause of concern. If by the middle to late teens there was no sign of sexual maturing there might also be cause for concern. For speaking, forms of thinking, relating, sexuality, and so on there are, notwithstanding local variability and differences of convention, broadly agreed standards of maturity to be applied universally. If this was all there was to the idea of human nature then agreement might be easy enough to reach on what it and its fulfilment are. But not surprisingly the situation is more complex than this.

That few per cent genetic difference between ourselves and chimpanzees marks an incalculable difference between what we can do and what they can do, between what we are and what they are. Somewhere in that genetic difference is our capacity to symbolise, from which derives the open-ended possibility of our endlessly creating and recreating common worlds of meaning. The shape of our lives may be very like those of others who share our framework of meaning and very different from those who live within different horizons of meaning. This is the territory of narrative identity and its moral sources, and it is here that difficulties with the ideas of 'a human nature' and its mature form arise. The danger is that a specification of what a mature, ideal or desirable self looks like would always be local, ethnocentric, theocentric or ideological in some way. Ideas of self and of self-fulfilment are discursively constituted within horizons of meaning, as we have seen in the work of Bruner, Taylor, Harré and others. This is where a sharply questioning Toad can wreak havoc with conventional assertions about maturity that claim universal application.

Ideals of self-development and their application to the maturity of particular people are, to a significant degree, moral judgements. Judgements across time and culture on whether a life was 'good' or 'full' may not be commensurate with the moral sources within whose horizons that self developed and located itself. In their own lives, and in the judgement of their communities, the self-realisation of Achilles or Ulysses would be described and evaluated very differently to that of Jesus or Muhammad, which in turn would be quite different to that of Freud or Woody Allen.

Some psychologists try to avoid the moral dimension by asserting that a universal ideal of maturity accompanies a universal conception of self. On this particular tendency, cultural psychology casts a cold eye. Abraham Maslow, for instance, believed that his idea of self-actualization transcended nationalism, class and caste:

> I have described my self-actualizing subjects as transcending nationalism. I could have added that they also transcend class and caste. This is true in my experience even though I would expect a priori that affluence and social dignity are apt to make self-actualization more probable.[4]

He later writes that

> my prediction or guess about the future of the normality idea is that some form of theory about generalized, species-wide, psychological health will soon be developed, which will hold for all human beings no matter what their culture and no matter what their time.[5]

This is ahistorical, acultural psychology in full self-confident flight despite the camouflage of historical references.

At the heart of Maslow's position is the belief that man has 'an essential nature of his own' with universal needs that are 'good or neutral rather than evil'. On the basis of these assumptions Maslow goes on to claim that

> full health and normal and desirable development consist in actualizing this nature, in fulfilling these potentialities, and in developing into matur- ity along the lines that this hidden, covert, dimly seen essential nature dictates, growing from within rather than being shaped from without.[6]

'Good' is what assists the actualisation of this nature, 'bad' is what thwarts or hinders it. Maslow believed that he was talking about a human nature discovered by modern psychology, including psychoanalysis. The contrary view is that what he took to be a true universal human nature was in fact the desirable lineaments of the modern self as it has been shaped and constituted by the forces of modern- ity. This latter view sees what Maslow and others take as given elements of human nature, there to be 'discovered', as instead cultural-historical achieve- ments or constructions. These constituted aspects of self are contingent and open to significant change.

A second point of difference comes into play when we ask how we are to think about the social use of this knowledge of 'human nature' and its optimal devel- opment. On Maslow's view social policies which take the optimal self- development of their citizens as an aim are merely unmasking and enabling to unfold what is already there 'within'. Here psychology would function as a mid- wife. On the other, cultural psychological view, optimal development of selves as a societal goal is not a following of a natural 'discovered' path but rather a moral- political commitment to forming some types of self as opposed to others. On this view, psychology functions not as a midwife to what is already there in embryo, but more as a collaborator in the construction of a cultural ideal. These are radically different roles with quite different responsibilities.

In each position psychology is recruited to further an ideal of self- development. The difference is that this ideal is actually rooted in psychology as its source in the Maslow perspective, although not in the way Maslow might think. Either way, psychology can become an active player in the shaping of a culture's ideal selves. Gordon Allport in his account of the 'mature personality' suggests as much when he writes that 'It would be sounder ethics and sounder psychology to encourage the development of human potentialities in all six direc- tions [characterising the mature personality as he understands it] from childhood to the end of life.'[7]

Allport is much more sophisticated than Maslow in his recognition that the constituents of the 'mature personality' are culturally bounded and ethically shaped. He explicitly restricts his portrait of the mature person to the modern Western consensus on what constitutes soundness, health or maturity.[8] This difference between Maslow and Allport is crucial since each grounds the moral source of the ideal of self-development differently. Maslow would defend his ideal on 'empirical' psychological grounds, Allport on cultural, ethical grounds.

This is not an arcane academic distinction. For the last thirty or so years, Anglo-American culture has seen the development of a large industry of self-development and self-improvement largely underpinned by the Maslow-type position. The products of this industry are radically individualistic and could be argued to shape and strengthen those same forces of individualism and subjectivism which gave rise to them. Psychology has provided a substantial proportion of these guides to self-meaning.

I am not suggesting that there are no good ideas here, nor that psychology at this high level of life as it is lived has no role to play in advising on the practices of contemporary living. I am arguing that the reasons and the authority for both the advising and the advice lie in other territory than simply psychology, and that psychology's own narrative of self-understanding is often too restricted to understand this. In a word, psychology of this sort is naive of the political, philosophical and moral underpinnings of itself.

So what are some of these ideals of self-development that psychologists have talked of? I will present a series of pen-pictures from within psychology for comparative purposes and will then return to the question of their implicit moral context. In 1954 Abraham Maslow published his account of what he called 'self-actualizing people'. This became widely influential, especially with the 1960s 'counter-culture', and moved from the realm of psychological description into that of a 'Recipe for Fulfillment'. It was one of the texts used to support what came to be known as the 'Me-generation' of the 1960s and 1970s. The book in which it first appeared, *Motivation and Personality*, was revised in 1970 which was also the year of Maslow's death.

Maslow selected from among people known to him, and from public and historical figures, a sample of those whom he, together with some others, judged to be exemplars of 'self-actualization'. He borrowed this idea of self-actualisation from the organismic theorist Kurt Goldstein who held that the motive to realise all of one's potentialities was the central motive in people. Hence the idea of the 'Human Potential Movement' as it later developed. The numbers in the study were small, the method of selection questionable, but the idea quickly gained currency. Among the named people included in his study were Abraham Lincoln, Thomas Jefferson, Albert Einstein, Eleanor Roosevelt, William James, Aldous Huxley, Fritz Kreisler, Pablo Casals, Martin Buber, John Keats, George William Russell (A. E.), Pierre Renoir and Walt Whitman.

Maslow formed the following general impression of these 'self-actualized', psychologically healthy people. They were unusually efficient at perceiving reality, were spontaneous because they were continually open to the possibilities of experience, were independent in their judgements, could lose themselves in their work, had 'democratically' structured personalities, were tolerant, flexible and open to other people, could genuinely identify with other people and were sympathetic and affectionate, had deep but selective personal relationships, were self-sufficient with a need for privacy, accepted themselves, were strong, were concerned with ethical and 'ultimate' questions, and had a subtle unhostile sense of the humorous in human life.

In short, they were creative people who brought their own distinctive individuality to bear on whatever they did. None of this meant that they were without flaws or conflicts or that they were particularly happy. But they were individuals very much in charge of their own lives, actualising their own potentialities. Maslow formed the following conclusion, one close to Charles Taylor's when he argues that modernity has settled on the life of the artist as an ideal model for the modern identity: 'My feeling is that the concept of creativeness and the concept of the healthy, self-actualizing, fully human person seem to be coming closer and closer together and may perhaps turn out to be the same thing.'[9]

Desirable though this sort of person might be, it is just one possible type of psychological structure. What determines whether you get this sort of personality structure rather than another? If you believe in a universal human nature inexorably unfolding along a predetermined path of psychological development, then you won't agree with the assertion that this is not a description of an untrammelled human nature finding at last its full expression in the freedom of a liberal Western democracy. Nor will you be happy with the claim that what you have with Maslow's 'self-actualising person' is the sort of human development favoured and needed by this sort of societal organisation. The proposition that all such descriptions of 'maturity' are contingent will be controversial.

To illustrate what this means consider a relevant but narrower range of psychological ability, the ability to make moral judgements. Inspired by the cognitive-developmental theories of Jean Piaget, Lawrence Kohlberg charted what he took to be a developmental profile of the cognitive ability to make moral judgements.[10] For this he worked empirically but within the theoretical framework of Piaget. He assumed that judging what was the best thing to do in particularly difficult moral dilemmas was a function both of age and by extension of cognitive ability. This ability developed systematically with age, according to Piaget, reaching its mature stage somewhere in mid-adolescence. Moral judging was therefore a cognitive ability and cognitive abilities were universally similar.

Kohlberg formulated a developmental schedule of six sub-stages combined into three main stages which he called the pre-conventional, the conventional and the post-conventional. The highest and latest achieved level was the post-conventional and represented the highest level of cognitive functioning as it came to be applied to issues of moral dilemmas and judgements. In effect, this last and 'highest' stage involved taking responsibility oneself for finding a solution to the presenting dilemma by, for instance, formulating your own principle of right and wrong for this situation and applying it. If law and conscience clash, conscience should have precedence if you are at the highest level, Stage 6.

Rom Harré offers what I believe is a convincing critique of the assumptions underlying the judgement that this highest level is the 'highest' because it represents superior cognitive achievement. Its relevance here is in showing how a more focused ability, such as the idea of a highest cognitive 'level' of moral judgement, may itself be a variable cultural construction. Harré distinguishes what he calls 'moralities of conation' from 'moralities of cognition'.[11] In a morality of conation the call upon you is to find the strength or 'will-power' to do what you know to be right, and you know what is right because the legitimate authorities – the clergy, for example – have told you. You have been reared in the knowledge of the given rules of right and wrong and your moral task within the horizons of this world is not to make up your own criteria for right and wrong but to have the 'strength of character' to obey. Many, particularly theocratic, cultures exemplify moralities of conation. Moralities of cognition, in contrast, are those where the possibilities of different options to moral questions are open, where debate and dialogue are the means of resolving dilemmas, where the individual is raised to actively think about and take personal responsibility for her or his actions in many areas of moral choice. This sort of morality characterises the secular thinking of Western liberal democracies.

Supposing you carried out a Kohlberg-type study using his moral dilemmas in, say, Qom in Iran or in Mea Shearim in Jerusalem or in the Curia in the Vatican, and found that the level of reasoning underpinning people's moral judgements was largely at level 4, the stage of conventional moral reasoning where to be judged 'good' is to fulfil your duties. Would you conclude that the mullahs or rabbis or priests were cognitively retarded? After all, they would probably not be expected to endorse an individualistic as against an authoritarian approach to moral judgement.

As it happens, the empirical studies of moral judgement using Kohlberg's criteria yield fuzzy results but educationalists have adopted this stage framework as a working guide for 'developing' their pupils' 'cognitive abilities' with a view to 'advancing' their moral judgements. The point of this critique is that the assumption of universality of one type of moral judgement is ethnocentric. The same point can be made of Maslow's self-actualising person. What is in question is not differences in 'levels' of moral judgement or self-actualisation or psychological health, but differences in formative moral orders. Different moral orders favour different moralities and different qualities of self in their members.

The issue is not whether forms of self-development like those characterising Maslow's self-actualised people are undesirable. It is that their desirability is not to do with what psychology has shown to be good but rather to do with our favouring one form of life, and its associated ways of constructing its members, over another. What psychology 'finds' in these cases are the effects on self-construction of more fundamental social-political dynamics.

Maslow's ideal clearly manifests elements of the modern identity as analysed by Taylor. The centrality of love and work (Freud's succinct answer to the question of good development was *Lieben und arbeiten*, the ability to love and work), of tolerance and compassion, of democracy and plurality, of self-sufficiency and self-acceptance, of disengaged reason as in the detached and humorous grasp of the real, and at the heart of it all a recognition of the coincidence of self and creativity. From a narrative perspective this places the modern ideal of self in the author's chair and makes the task of living fully a task of individualising one's creation of oneself (a view favoured by Jung). Maslow thought that his self-actualisers found the philosophic basis for their values in their acceptance of the nature of self and society. This, as cultural psychology argues, begs the question of which society and which version of self.

Lest it be thought that Maslow is alone in this pen-picture of what we might now call the contemporary Western ideal we can see that there is a wider consensus for this idea. The parallels between the construction of self and a work of art are also made within the field of discursive psychology. Harré and Gillett maintain that

> The ideal is a psychological life with the character of an artistic project and not merely a stream of experiences and responses to stimulation. Of such a life we might say that it has meaning in the same sense as a work of art has meaning.[12]

Carl Rogers shares Maslow's assumption about the fundamental 'goodness' of human beings, and offers this ideal of the fully functioning person.[13] Such a person would function 'freely in all the fullness of organismic potentialities', be dependable in being realistic, self-enhancing, socialised and appropriate in his behaviour, creative, ever-changing, 'always discovering himself and the newness in himself in each succeeding moment of time'. This person would be totally open to experience (no distorting inhibitions or defences), live in the present, and would find 'their organism' a trustworthy means of arriving at the most satisfying behaviour in each existential situation because they could trust what 'felt right'. Again we have this implicit identification of full functioning with the ideal of the artist creatively drawing on inner resources. Rogers's highly individualistic description makes no serious theoretical mention of other people, nor of meaning and the ways in which it is negotiated. While supportive of Maslow's description it is less complete, but it has had wide influence notably in the world of education and has also formed the basis of curricula for self-formation.

Gordon Allport synthesised existing pictures for his own description of the 'mature personality' in 1961.[14] Such people had 'an extended sense of themselves', were compassionate and could relate warmly to other people, were emotionally secure and self-accepting, had a realistic grasp of the world and of their own abilities, could objectify themselves with insight and humour, and had developed a 'unifying philosophy of life'. Quite how in line with Taylor's analysis of the modern self is Allport's earlier characterisation of the mature person can be seen from his concluding remarks:

> No society holds together for long without the respect man shows to man. The individual today struggles on even under oppression, always hoping and planning for a more perfect democracy where the dignity and growth of each personality will be prized above all else.[15]

For Erik Erikson's lifespan approach to development the completeness of self involves our way of dying which is intimately linked to our way of living. The ideal psychic state with which to resolve the crisis of old age is to integrate all that has gone before into an acceptance of death as part of the process of life. Erikson suggests that 'healthy children will not fear life if their elders have integrity enough not to fear death'.[16] This obviously relates to our beliefs about death and its aftermath and here we are back to the issue of moral sources and the psychological processes of narrative thinking and of self as a meta-narrative construction. A unifying philosophy of life and the struggle to integrate one's life (despair being the psychological state of failure to do this, in Erikson's view) both presuppose narrative abilities and narrative forms.

Narratives of self and dying are intrinsic parts of the process of self-completion. How to die well involves telling oneself about how to die or not to die, and trying to shape one's dying accordingly. In this it matters whether the local custom insists on dying being private and hidden or public and shared. Harré's theory of social being maintains that the contemporary practice of removing the moment of death from a public and social milieu militates against the dying person's ability to complete his character by 'making a good death'. He argues that in other epochs the management of dying was socially much more satisfactory.[17]

Work like Erikson's is based on the idea that a life develops by adapting to the demands made upon it, whether at biologically or socially determined milestones of development. These demands vary from historical time to historical time and from one culture to another. Each critical period within an individual life requires a successful adaptation; otherwise, subsequent adaptations may be put at risk. The criteria for overall success or failure emerge from within a culture. The 'best' life in an honour culture would be the most glorious and famous, in a religious culture the saintliest, in a contemporary achievement-oriented culture the most creative and original, and so on.

This raises the question of function: What purpose is served by becoming a mature sort of person such as the kind outlined above? The answer may be in terms of a need for respect or justification in one's own eyes or those of others; to enable us to die well precisely because we have achieved a sense of completeness and conclusion relatively uncontaminated by regret. The particular narrative form which is our self and its life may have an intrinsic order which impels our story towards just this sort of closure. A Christian woman will want a Christian way of dying with its particular script for dignity and peace, whereas an atheist will want her way of dying with its own rituals of dignity. A man with a heavy weight of historical guilt like Albert Speer, who understands that the impulsion to self-respect arises in and from the respect of others, has a particularly challenging task in rendering his story complete and satisfactorily closed.[18]

This question of function could lead us to shy away from the monolith of a single all-encompassing maturity and to speak instead of forms of maturity. Anthony Storr reminds us of the very considerable difficulties with social relations exhibited by the likes of Newton, Wittgenstein or Kafka, for example, and yet their lives were ones of great and original richness in terms of the work they did and left to the world.[19] A worthwhile life may not coincide with a full life (Mozart, Schubert and Keats died very young), nor a good life with a worthwhile one (Wagner or Picasso may not have been especially admirable at the personal level but their achievements were immense). Yeats was clear in posing the tension between 'perfection of life' and 'perfection of work'. The worthwhileness of the millions of ordinary lives that are realised anonymously can only be reckoned on their own terms and within the terms of the cultures that give rise to those lives and are sustained and perpetuated by them. Asking 'For what?' after terms like full, complete, worthwhile, good and so on is an insurance against oversimplification. The fact is that selves may be realised in as many ways as stories can be well ended. Whether the realisation is admirable is always another question.

Finally, to return to the question of psychology and its role in specifying the manifest of a well-developed self. It may be a bit like Picasso's answer to the criticism that his portrait of Gertrude Stein did not look like her which was to the effect that it would. The relationship of psychology to society is not that of a neutral observer but rather that of a contributing player. Psychology's descriptions of ideal self-development may not be universally true as of now but conceivably could become so.

The reasons for this would not be because psychology had scientifically tapped into some universal script for self-development, as Maslow hoped, but rather that the sort of social-political order which gave rise to the modern identity had become globalised. One could use Allport's description of the mature personality or Kohlberg's of post-conventional moral judgement as frameworks for educational policies of self-development but the justification for doing so would not be psychological in the end but moral and political.

There is a great economic, demographic, environmental and cultural turbulence in the contemporary world. It may be that it will become universally psychologically satisfying to be the sort of person described as ideal by the psychologies above because liberal capitalist Western-style democracies are winning the struggle for global domination. The form of the modern Western identity would then be the shape of a global identity. Only in such speculative circumstances would a universal psychology of 'maturity', as Allport envisaged it, make sense and then only secondarily for psychological reasons. The globalisation of this type of psychological discourse would be a conquest not a finding.

If that global conquest was based on notions of human rights then it would be a benign conquest. Certainly the conditions for achieving self-fulfilment of the kind outlined above include, as Alan Gewirth argues, effective human rights to freedom and well-being, coupled with the sort of reasonableness that recognises that other people must also have these same rights.[20] Psychology, when it questions how lives ought to be led, needs to become a more self-critical and sophisticated player in this world theatre. It has a role to play as cultural critic, but only to the extent that it becomes aware of the ways in which its 'findings' can be refractions of its own culture.

If human action and its governance is the central problem for psychology then, from the perspective of navigating human worlds, aspirations and ideals function like destinations guiding actions and keeping them generally on track. Ideals are essential, but we should know where they come from. For this the lesson is simple: always be thankful for the attentions of a troublesome Toad.

Notes

1 P. Ricoeur, *Time and Narrative*, Vol. 3, trans. K. Blamey and D. Pellauer, London, The University of Chicago Press, 1988, p. 247.

2 R. D. Laing, *The Politics of Experience and The Bird of Paradise*, Harmondsworth, Penguin, 1970, p. 24.

3 Rorty's review appeared in the *London Review of Books*, 8 April 1993, p. 3.

4 A. Maslow, *Motivation and Personality* (2nd edn), New York, Harper & Row, 1970, p. xxi.

5 Maslow, op. cit., pp. 268–9.

6 Ibid., p. 269.

7 G. Allport, *Pattern and Growth in Personality*, London, Holt, Rinehart and Winston, 1970, p. 307.

8 Ibid., p. 276.

9 A. Maslow, *The Farther Reaches of Human Nature*, Harmondsworth, Pelican, 1973, p. 59.
10 L. Kohlberg, *The Meaning and Measurement of Moral Development*, Worcester, Mass.: Clark University Press, 1980.
11 R. Harré, *Personal Being*, Oxford, Blackwell, 1983, Chapter 9.
12 R. Harré and G. Gillett, *The Discursive Mind*, London, Sage, 1994, p. 143.
13 C. Rogers, *Freedom to Learn*, Columbus, Ohio, Charles E. Merrill, 1969.
14 Allport, op. cit., Chapter 12.
15 Ibid., p. 573.
16 E. H. Erikson, *Childhood and Society*, Harmondsworth, Penguin, 1969, p. 261.
17 R. Harré, *Social Being* (2nd edn), Oxford, Blackwell, 1993, p. 218.
18 G. Sereny, *Albert Speer: His Battle with Truth*, London, Macmillan, 1995.
19 A. Storr, *Solitude*, London, Harper Collins, 1994.
20 A. Gewirth, *Self-Fulfillment*, Princeton, NJ, Princeton University Press, 1998, p. 215.

CONCLUSION

NAVIGATING HUMAN WORLDS

> It may sound paradoxical, but if we want to sustain the planet into
> the future, the first thing we must do is to stop taking advice from
> nature. Nature is a short-term Darwinian profiteer.
>
> (R. Dawkins, *The Observer*, London, 21 May 2000, p. 21)

> And this is of course the difficult job, is it not; to move the spirit
> from its nowhere pedestal to a somewhere place, while preserving
> its dignity and importance; to recognize its humble origin and
> vulnerability, yet still call upon its guidance.
>
> (A. Damasio, *Descartes' Error*, 1996, p. 252)

From where should we seek advice about our future if not from nature? Where
else if not from culture, which is to say from the meanings which we ourselves
make. That is the thrust of this book. If self is the locative, navigational system
that I have argued for, simultaneously containing its world and being contained by
it, then how can we think about this question of navigating our futures, whether
encountered or fabricated by our own actions? Our paths 'through' life are sometimes found, sometimes forged. The biological origins of self may seem humble
from the vantage point of full-blown, creative, moral consciousness, but those
humble roots are dazzlingly complex.

Taking Damasio's framework for the structure of developed human selfhood –
a hierarchical integration of proto-self, core self and autobiographical self – it is
clear that the operations of proto-self and core self systems are largely under the
automatic control of the brain in its body. The shaping and control of autobiographical self, however, while dependent on the constantly self-renewing
foundations of proto-self and core self, is significantly a matter of learning. Learning in this sense is another word for the kinds of change that are instigated by
non-genetic forces such as the instructions and influences of other people, or by
the powers of choice, and the range of their applicability, which develop within
the repertoire of skills which come to constitute a person. Here is the proper
domain of a cultural psychology of self, as I have argued.

Within that domain lies the very best and the very worst of human being. The
changing fields of the arts, law, science and morality share it with brutality,

egoism, oppression and greed. All can be illuminated by a cultural psychology, provided that that psychology respects the complexity of its subject matter, and acknowledges its own need to draw on other disciplines like philosophy, history, neuroscience, anthropology, sociology and cultural criticism. It must think synoptically, developing arguments as well as conducting investigations.[1] Cultural psychology must also understand its own unavoidable rootedness in its own times and places.

This is not an argument for a facile relativism where one judgement is as good as the next. Evidence must back argument, and the rules for the construction of both must be part of a community of understanding. However, it is to say that there is an inescapably imaginative dimension to cultural psychology once it begins to contribute to the bigger questions like those that preoccupy activists of many kinds seeking ways forward for the human race. 'Finding a place in the world,' writes Jerome Bruner, 'for all that it implicates the immediacy of home, mate, job, and friends, is ultimately an act of imagination.'[2]

To understand how people find their places in their worlds, we must understand how they imagine them, and themselves as part of them. That requires that we understand the ideas that constitute narratives of self and group. Since not very many people invent the ideas by which they live and fabricate their lives, the implication is that we must understand the sources, histories, and shifting implications for action, of those received ideas which most significantly shape human lives across time and place. Studying the genealogy of significant ideas must form an important strand of the cultural psychology of self, as should inquiries into the specific roles that apparently similar ideas play out under the influence of historically and culturally different configurations, fields, contexts, situations, networks, or 'spaces of the possible'.

Ideas which function as destinations are the sorts often called ideals. It is by the lights of ideals that we judge any particular navigation, individual or collective, to have been successful or not. To navigate is to have a destination in mind, to plan a course which will take one to that terminus, and to be able to control and adapt along the way according to the various obstacles and advantages encountered. Of course, to start with any prospect of success one must first know where one is in the here and now.

This book has dealt with navigation at two levels. It has outlined some of the directions being taken by the emerging grouping called cultural psychology, and it has given examples of how cultural psychology might itself explore the conditions governing how individuals and groups think about shaping and controlling the journeys that are their lives. A cultural psychology can articulate an understanding of what particular people, and specific groups, take to be desirable courses of navigation, and the criteria by which they evaluate them. A relevant primary metaphor, as we were reminded in the beginning of this book by Lakoff and Johnson, is that 'Purposes are Destinations'.

The freedom to formulate purposes is therefore of particular significance. Freedom, as I understand it, is a function both of skills, and of the permission and encouragement to use those skills. Greater freedom is a consequence of greater skilfulness. Being 'free to' break the rules of music, for example, is a freedom open only to those who can already play music well. Enlargement of freedom in any area follows upon the development of skills in that area, or upon the lifting of forces constraining existing skills. Diminution of freedom, in contrast, occurs when skills are lost or their operation curtailed. This applies to the kinds of skill that constitute selves as the sorts of selves they are.

Taking control of one's own life by objectifying and understanding it, and becoming responsible for one's actions, require very high-level skills. Being able to assume moral responsibility for one's own actions, and being free to shape the configuration and direction of one's own conduct, requires that one be skilful in responsibility-taking, and that one be permitted and encouraged to do so. We considered this in Chapter 8. This comes in part from believing that one has a right to the dignity that comes from respecting, and having respected, one's own bodily and psychological integrity, and from membership of a community that shares this belief. There is much work to be done in articulating the relationship between the kind of freedom enabled by such understanding and the practicalities of trying to live well.

An underlying theme throughout the book has been that freedom, responsibility, meaning and creativity are deeply interconnected, as are their institutional counterparts, morality, art and science. A role for philosophy is to articulate the bigger picture in which these connections come into focus and become visible. Each of these concepts of freedom, responsibility, meaning and creativity kicks into play when we consider the existential imperative that faces every human being – however cruelly diminished the scope for freely, creatively, self-responsibly living their particular lives might be – namely, how to lead their lives well. Asking how people think about living their lives well is another way of inquiring how they navigate their lives within the particular human worlds that contain them.

The complication attending the navigation of human worlds is this: that the destinations we find ourselves thinking attractive, and the courses we plot to get there, are partly of our own making. Therein lies the source of their moral dimension. Choice, and its correlate 'freedom', are built into the fabric of selfhood. The nature of being a self, in the developed sense of a self-constituting meaning-maker enmeshed in worlds or webs fabricated by and with other self-constituting narrators, crucially involves skills in moving into, through, around, and out of such worlds, albeit always and inescapably into yet other worlds of meaning. Until, that is, the biological processes sustaining selfhood cease working and we die. After that, the continued existence of selves is symbolic and endures in the memories of others still living.

Our biology makes possible what we can do: our cultures, and ourselves as cultured, make possible how we do it. The style of our actions depends upon the ways in which we make sense of our needs, desires and concerns. The skills available to us to make such meanings, help shape our imagined purposes or destinations. Imagining such destinations enables us to construct a frame within which we can get our bearings. The direction and degree of control we have over our lives is a function of how effectively we can imagine ends, care about them, and marshal resources to get there.

For most of us most of the time, means and ends are suggested by local traditions and disciplined by local conventions. The ways of doing things, including ways of thinking about them, that comprise any such tradition are tools that have been forged in the past for problems encountered in the past. Their current applicability depends on the degree to which presently confronted problems are similar to those which gave rise to the earlier solutions. Collective human meaning-making is inherently restless and incessantly changing. Consequently, this dynamic can be as ruthless and as impatient with traditional modes of navigation as the Darwinian world of nature can be with maladapted organisms. Successful living requires flexibility and adaptability.

The difference between physical and cultural worlds is one of imagination. We can imagine our cultural worlds differently and, in doing so, we can acquire new powers of navigation, new directions, new destinations, new cares and complacencies, new feelings and inclinations within new frames of meaning. Acquiring control over life-courses requires self-understanding which writers like Sternberg and Spear-Swerling also identify as the key to personal navigation.[3] They also seem to approach my understanding of self as a locative system in believing that personal navigation involves 'a person's total configuration of the self with respect to the self, and also all the people and events in one's life'.[4] Formulating one's own story is a key navigational strategy, as we saw in Chapter 3.

The concept of 'self', at its most useful, should be crafted at a level of abstraction sufficient to integrate the extraordinary complexity of elements and connections that characterise this human universal. My argument has been that a fundamental function of self, so conceptualised, is to constantly and reflexively establish people's present positions, to stabilise their senses of themselves as part of current situations, to project an imagined future (including, perhaps, the possibility of a reinterpreted past), to evaluate desirable and undesirable aspects of that imagined future according to current desires and ideals, and to plan appropriate navigational strategies and tactics. The degree to which people can rely on their feelings is a key part of this story of self, as we saw in Chapter 7.

The cultural psychology of self is part of the more general human project of understanding ourselves, our changing worlds, and of wondering how best to live in them. Its deeper imperatives, I believe, are inescapably moral. While remaining fully open to the ever-refining insights of neuroscience, the cultural psychology of self is itself fundamentally an interpretive rather than a natural science. This is because the subjects of its investigations are self-making, self-transforming, self-interpreting, self-locating creatures – us.

Notes

1 C. Geertz, *Available Light: Anthropological Reflections on Philosophical Topics*, Princeton, NJ, Princeton University Press, 2000, p. 207.
2 J. Bruner, *The Culture of Education*, Cambridge, Mass., Harvard University Press, 1996, p. 41.
3 R. J. Sternberg and L. Spear-Swerling, 'Personal Navigation' in M. Ferrari and R. L. Sternberg (eds), *Self-Awareness: Its Nature and Development*, New York, The Guilford Press, 1998, p. 227.
4 Ibid., p. 233.

BIBLIOGRAPHY

Adcock, C., *J. Turrell: The Art of Light and Space*, Berkeley, University of California Press, 1990.

Agger, I., *The Blue Room: Trauma and Testimony among Refugee Women*, London, Zed Books, 1994.

Alderson, P., *Children's Consent to Surgery*, Buckingham, Open University Press, 1993.

Allport, G., *Pattern and Growth in Personality*, London, Holt, Rinehart & Winston, 1970.

Alwin, D. F., 'From obedience to autonomy: Changes in traits desired in children, 1924–1978', *Public Opinion Quarterly*, 1988, 52, pp. 33–52.

Améry, J., 'Torture' in L. Langer (ed.), *Art from the Ashes*, Oxford, Oxford University Press, 1995.

—— *At the Mind's Limits: Contemplations by a Survivor on Auschwitz and Its Realities*, trans. S. Rosenfeld and S. P. Rosenfeld, New York, Schocken, 1986.

Amnesty International, 'Child Soldiers', International Secretariat, 18 November 1999.

Amsterdam, A. G. and Bruner, J., *Minding the Law: How Courts Rely on Storytelling, and How Their Stories Change the Ways We Understand the Law – and Ourselves*, Cambridge, Mass., Harvard University Press, 2000.

Anderson, B., *Imagined Communities: Reflections on the Origins and Spread of Nationalism*, London, Verso, 1991.

Anderson, J., 'Child development: An historical perspective', *Child Development*, 1956, 27, pp. 181–96.

Aries, P., *Centuries of Childhood*, Harmondsworth, Penguin, 1973.

Arnheim, R., *Toward a Psychology of Art*, Berkeley, University of California Press, 1966.

Auden, W. H. et al., *I Believe: The Personal Philosophies of Twenty-Three Eminent Men and Women of Our Time*, London, George Allen and Unwin Ltd, 1947.

Austin, J. L., *How to Do Things with Words*, Oxford, Clarendon Press, 1962.

Avant, L., 'Vision in the Ganzfeld', *Psychological Bulletin*, 64, 1965, pp. 246–58.

Bakhtin, M. M., *The Dialogic Imagination: Four essays by M. M. Bakhtin*, ed. M. E. Holquist, trans. C. Emerson and M. E. Holquist, Austin, University of Texas Press, 1981.

Baron-Cohen, S., *Mindblindness: An Essay on Autism and Theory of Mind*, Cambridge, Mass., The MIT Press, 1997.

Barrett, C., 'Irish Art and Nationalism', *Studies*, LXIV, Winter 1975.

Barthes, R., *Elements of Semiology*, trans. A. Lavers and C. Smith, New York, Hill and Wang, 1967.

—— *A Barthes Reader*, ed. S. Sontag, London, Cape, 1982.

Beevor, A., *Stalingrad*, London, Penguin, 1999.

Benson, C., *The Absorbed Self: Pragmatism, Psychology and Aesthetic Experience*, London, Harvester Wheatsheaf, 1993.

Berlin, I., *The Proper Study of Mankind: An Anthology of Essays*, (eds) H. Hardy and R. Hausheer, London, Pimlico, 1998.

Billig, M., *Freudian Repression: Conversation Creating the Unconscious*, New York, Cambridge University Press, 1999.

Blake, W., *William Blake: A Selection of Poems and Letters*, ed., J. Bronowski, Harmondsworth, Penguin, 1978.

Bloom, P. et al. (eds) *Language and Space*, Cambridge, Mass., MIT Press, 1996.

Boland, E., 'Outside History', *The American Poetry Review*, March–April 1990, p. 42.

Bolster, E., *The Knights of Columbanus*, Dublin, Gill and Macmillan, 1979.

Borstelman, L. J., 'Children before psychology: Ideas about children from antiquity to the late 1800s' in W. Kessen (vol. ed.), *History, Theory and Methods*, vol 1. of P. H. Mussen (ed.), *Handbook of Child Psychology* (4th edn), New York, Wiley, 1983.

Bourdieu, P., *Outline of a Theory of Practice*, Cambridge, Cambridge University Press, 1977.

Bradbury, M., *The Modern World*, London, Penguin, 1989.

Breuilly, J., *Nationalism and the State* (2nd edn), Manchester, Manchester University Press, 1993.

Brodkey, H., 'Passage into non-existence', *Independent on Sunday*, London, 11 Feb. 1996, p. 10.

—— *This Wild Darkness: The Story of My Death*, London, Fourth Estate, 1996.

Bronfenbrenner, U., *The Ecology of Human Development*, Cambridge, Mass., Harvard University Press, 1979.

Brown, T., *Ireland: A Social and Cultural History*, London, Fontana, 1985.

Browning, C. R., *Ordinary Men: Reserve Police Battalion 101 and the Final Solution in Poland*, New York, Harper Perennial, 1992.

Bruner, J., *In Search of Mind: Essays in Autobiography*, London, Harper & Row, 1983.

—— *Actual Minds, Possible Worlds*, Cambridge, Mass., Harvard University Press, 1986.

—— *Acts of Meaning*, Cambridge, Mass., Harvard University Press, 1990.

—— 'The Autobiographical Process', *Current Sociology*, 43, 2/3 (Autumn 1995).

—— 'Self Reconsidered: Five Conjectures', Paper presented to the Annual Meeting of the Society for Philosophy and Psychology, State University of New York at Stony Brook, 8 June 1995.

—— *The Culture of Education*, Cambridge, Mass., Harvard University Press, 1996.

Bruner, J. and Kalmar, D. A., 'Narrative and metanarrative in the construction of self', in M. Ferrari and R. Sternberg (eds), *Self-Awareness: Its Nature and Development*, New York, Guilford, 1997.

Bruner, J. and Lucariello, J., 'Monologue as narrative recreation of the world' in K. Nelson (ed.), *Narratives from the Crib*, Cambridge, Mass., Harvard University Press, 1989.

Budd, M., *Wittgenstein's Philosophy of Psychology*, London, Routledge, 1989.

Bullock, A., *Hitler and Stalin: Parallel Lives*, London, Fontana, 1993.

Cahan, E., Mechling, J., Sutton-Smith, B. and White, S. H., *Children in Time and Place: Developmental and Historical Insights*, Cambridge, Cambridge University Press, 1993.

Cairns, E., *Children and Political Violence*, Oxford, Blackwell, 1996.

Carlson, J., (ed.) *Banned in Ireland*, London, Routledge, 1990.

Caruth, C., (ed.) *Trauma: Explorations in Memory*, Baltimore, The Johns Hopkins University Press, 1995.

—— *Unclaimed Experience: Trauma, Narrative, and History*, Baltimore, The Johns Hopkins University Press, 1996.

Casey, E. S., *Getting Back into Place: Toward a Renewed Understanding of the Place-World*, Bloomington, Indiana University Press, 1993.

—— *The Fate of Place: A Philosophical History*, Berkeley, University of California Press, 1998.

Chang, J., *Wild Swans: Three Daughters of China*, London, Flamingo, 1993.

Chauvet, J. M., Deschamps, E. B. and Hillaire, C., *Dawn of Art: The Chauvet Cave: The Oldest Known Paintings in the World*, New York, Harry M. Abrams, 1996.

Clark, A. and Karmiloff-Smith, A., 'The Cognizer's Innards: A Psychological and Philosophical Perspective on the Development of Thought.' *Mind & Language, Vol. 8, 1994, pp. 487–519.*

Colapietro, V. M., *Peirce's Approach to the Self*, Albany, NY, State University of New York Press, 1989.

Colby, A. and Damon, W., *Some Do Care: Contemporary Lives of Moral Commitment*, New York, Free Press, 1992.

Colby, A. and W. Damon, 'The Uniting of Self and Morality in the Development of Extraoradinary Moral Commitment' in G. G. Noam and T. E. Wren (eds), *The Moral Self*, Cambridge, Mass., The MIT Press, 1993.

Cole, M., *Cultural Psychology; A Once and Future Discipline*, Cambridge, Mass., Harvard University Press, 1996.

Coles, R., *The Moral Life of Children*, Boston, Atlantic Press, 1986.

Cotlow, L., *In Search of the Primitive*, London, Robert Hale, 1967.

Cox, M. V., *The Child's Point of View*, Brighton, The Harvester Press, 1986.

Cox, R. (ed.), *Shaping Childhood: Themes of Uncertainty in the History of Adult–Child Relationships*, London, Routledge, 1996.

Cruise O'Brien, C., *Passion and Cunning: Essays on Nationalism, Terrorism and Revolution*, London, Simon & Schuster, 1998.

Crystal, D., *The Cambridge Encyclopedia of Language*, Cambridge, Cambridge University Press, 1989.

Csikszentmihalyi, M., *Flow: The Psychology of Optimal Experience*, New York, Harper Perennial, 1991.

Damon, W., *The Moral Child: Nurturing Children's Natural Moral Growth*, New York: The Free Press, 1988.

Damasio, A., *The Feeling of What Happens: Body and Emotion in the Making of Consciousness*, New York, Harcourt Brace & Co., 1999.

—— *Descartes' Error: Emotion, Reason and the Human Brain*, London, Papermac, 1996.

Dawkins, R., *The Selfish Gene*, Oxford, Oxford University Press, 1976.

De Beauvoir, S., *Force of Circumstance*, London, Penguin, 1968.

Dennett, D., *Darwin's Dangerous Idea: Evolution and the Meanings of Life*, New York, Simon & Schuster, 1995.

—— *Consciousness Explained*, London, Allen Lane The Penguin Press, 1991.

—— 'The Origin of Selves', *Cogito*, 1, 1989, pp. 163–73.

—— 'Why Everyone is a Novelist', *Times Literary Supplement*, 16–22 Sept. 1988, pp. 1016, 1028–29.

Dewey, J., *Art as Experience*, New York, Capricorn Books G. P. Putnam's Sons, 1958.

—— *Logic: The Theory of Inquiry*, London, George Allen & Unwin, 1938.

Donald, M., *Origins of the Modern Mind: Three Stages in the Evolution of Culture and Cognition*, Cambridge, Mass., Harvard University Press, 1991.

Donaldson, M., *Human Minds: An Exploration*, London, Allen Lane, 1992.

Dunn, J., 'The Beginnings of Moral Understanding: Development in the Second Year' in J. Kagan and S. Lamb (eds), *The Emergence of Morality in Young Children*, Chicago, The University of Chicago Press, 1987.

Dunn. J. and Munn, P., 'Sibling Quarrels and Maternal Intervention: Individual Differences in Understanding and Aggression', *Journal of Child Psychology and Psychiatry*, 1986, 27, pp. 583–95.

Eakin, P. J. *How Our Lives Become Stories: Making Selves*, Ithaca, Cornell University Press, 1999.

Eco, U., *A Theory of Semiotics*, London, Macmillan, 1977.

Einstein, A., in W. H. Auden et al. *I Believe: The Personal Philosophies of Twenty-Three Eminent Men and Women of Our Time*, London, George Allen & Unwin, 1947.

Eisenberg, N. and Fabes, R. A., 'Prosocial Development' in *Handbook of Child Psychology*, (5th edn), Volume 3: *Social Emotional and Personality Development*, ed. N. Eisenberg, New York, John Wiley & Sons, 1998.

Eisner, E., *Cognition and Curriculum: A Basis for Deciding What to Teach*, London, Longman, 1982.

Elder, G. H. et al., *Children in Time and Place: Developmental and Historical Insights*, Cambridge, Cambridge University Press, 1993.

Erikson, E. H., *Childhood and Society*, Harmondsworth, Penguin, 1969.

Fauconnier, G., *Mappings in Thought and Language*, Cambridge, Cambridge University Press, 1997.

Ferrari, M. and Sternberg, R. L. (eds), *Self Awareness: Its Nature and Development*, New York, The Guilford Press, 1998.

Feyerabend, P., *Killing Time: The Autobiography of Paul Feyerabend*, Chicago, The University of Chicago Press, 1995.

Feynman, R., *What Do YOU Care What Other People Think*, New York, Bantam, 1988.

Flavell, J. H., Shipstead, S. G. and Croft, K., 'What young children think you see when their eyes are closed', *Cognition*, 8, 1980, pp. 369–87.

Frankfurt, H., 'On the Necessity of Ideals' in G. G. Noam and T. E. Wren (eds), *The Moral Self*, Cambridge, Mass., MIT Press, 1993.

Frith, U., 'A New Look at Language and Communication in Autism', *British Journal of Disorders of Communication*, 24, 1989, pp. 123–50.

Freud, S., *The Complete Introductory Lectures on Psychoanalysis*, trans. and ed. J. Strachey, London, George Allen & Unwin, 1971.

Gardner, H., *The Unschooled Mind: How Children Think and How Schools Should Teach*, London, Fontana, 1993.

—— *Frames of Mind: The Theory of Multiple Intelligences*, London, Paladin Books, 1985.

—— *The Mind's New Science: A History of the Cognitive Revolution*, New York, Basic Books, 1985.

Garvin, T., *Mythical Thinking in Political Life: Reflections on Nationalism and Social Science*, Dublin, Maunsell, 2000.

Gazzaniga, M. S., Ivry, R. B. and Mangun, G. R., *Cognitive Neuroscience: The Biology of the Mind*, New York, W. W. Norton & Co., 1998.

Geertz, C., *Available Light: Anthropological Reflections on Philosophical Topics*, Princeton, NJ, Princeton University Press, 2000.

—— *Local Knowledge: Further Essays in Interpretive Anthropology* (2nd edn), London, Fontana Press, 1993.

Gellner, E., *Nations and Nationalism*, Oxford, Blackwell, 1983.

—— *Thought and Change*, London, Weidenfeld and Nicholson, 1964.

Gergen, K., *Realities and Relationships: Soundings in Social Construction*, Cambridge, Mass., Harvard University Press, 1994.

Gewirth, A., *Self-Fulfillment*, Princeton, NJ, Princeton University Press, 1998.

Gibson, J. J., *The Ecological Approach to Visual Perception*, Boston, Houghton Mifflin, 1979.

Glover, J., *I: The Philosophy and Psychology of Personal Identity*, London, Penguin Books, 1989.

Goldhagen, D. J., *Hitler's Willing Executioners: Ordinary Germans and the Holocaust*, London, Abacus, 1998.

Goodman, N., *Ways of Worldmaking*, Hemel Hempstead, Harvester Wheatsheaf, 1978.

Hardyment, C., *Dream Babies: Child Care from Locke to Spock*, London, Cape, 1983.

Harré, R., *The Singular Self: An Introduction to the Psychology of Personhood*, London, Sage, 1998.

—— 'Discursive Psychology' in J. A. Smith, R. Harré and L. Van Langenhove (eds), *Rethinking Psychology*, London, Sage, 1995.

—— *Social Being* (2nd edn), Oxford, Basil Blackwell, 1993.

—— 'Language Games and Texts of Identity', in J. Shotter and K. Gergen (eds), *Texts of Identity*, London, Sage, 1989.

—— *Personal Being*, Oxford, Basil Blackwell, 1983.

Harré, R., and Gillett, G., *The Discursive Mind*, London, Sage, 1994.

Harré, R and Parrott, W. G., *The Emotions: Social, Cultural and Biological Dimensions*, London, Sage, 1996.

Harris, P. L., *Children and Emotion: The Development of Psychological Understanding*, Oxford, Basil Blackwell, 1989.

Hass, A., *The Aftermath: Living with the Holocaust*, Cambridge, Cambridge University Press, 1995.

Haste, H., 'Moral responsibility and moral commitment: The integration of affect and cognition' in T. Wren (ed.), *The Moral Domain: Essays in Ongoing Discussion between Philosophy and the Social Sciences*, Cambridge, Mass., The MIT Press, 1990.

Hastings, A., *The Construction of Nationhood: Ethnicity, Religion and Nationalism*, Cambridge, Cambridge University Press, 1997.

Heider, F., *The Psychology of Interpersonal Relations*, New York, Wiley, 1958.

Herman, J., *Trauma and Recovery*, New York, Basic Books, 1992.

Hjort, M. and Laver, S. (eds), *Emotion and the Arts*, Oxford, Oxford University Press, 1997.

Hobsbawm, E. J., *Nations and Nationalism since 1780*, Cambridge, Cambridge University Press, 1990.

Holland, D., Lachinotte, W. Jr., Skinner, D. and Cain, C., *Identity and Agency in Cultural Worlds*, Cambridge, Mass., Harvard University Press, 1998.

http: //www. child-soldiers. org/

Humphrey, N., *A History of the Mind*, London, Chatto & Windus, 1992.

Husserl, E., *Husserl: Shorter Writings*, (eds) P. McCormick and F. Elliston, Notre Dame, Ind., University of Notre Dame Press, 1981.

Hutchinson, J. and Smith, A. D. (eds) *Nationalism*, Oxford, Oxford University Press, 1994.

Hwang, C. P. et al. (eds), *Images of Childhood*, Mahwah, NJ, Lawrence Erlbaum, 1996.

Ignatieff, M., 'Human Rights: The Midlife Crisis', *The New York Review of Books*, 20 May 1999, p. 58.

Iser, W., *The Act of Reading: A Theory of Aesthetic Response*, London, Routledge & Kegan Paul, 1978.

Jakobson, R., *Russian and Slavic Grammar: Studies, 1931–1981*, (eds) L. Waugh and M. Halle, The Hague, Mouton, 1984.

James, W., *Essays in Radical Empiricism*, London, Longman's, Green & Co., 1912.

Jaynes, J., *The Origin of Consciousness in the Breakdown of the Bicameral Mind*, Boston, Houghton Mifflin Company, 1976.

Jenkins, R., *Social Identity*, London, Routledge, 1996.

Joyce, J., *A Portrait of the Artist as a Young Man*, ed. Seamus Deane, London, Penguin Books, 1992.

Kagan, J., *The Nature of the Child*, New York, Basic Books, 1984.

—— 'Is there a self in infancy?' in M. Ferrari and R. J. Sternberg (eds), *Self-Awareness: Its Nature and Development*, New York, The Guilford Press, 1998.

Kagan, J. and Lamb, S. (eds)., *The Emergence of Morality in Young Children*, Chicago, The University of Chicago Press, 1987.

Kessen W., 'The American child and other cultural inventions' in F. S. Kessel and A. W. Siegel (eds), *The Child and Other Cultural Inventions*, Houston Symposium, No. 4, New York, 1983.

Kiberd, D., *Inventing Ireland: The Literature of the Modern Nation*, London, Jonathan Cape, 1995.

Kissinger, H., *The White House Years*, London, Weidenfeld and Nicolson, 1979.

Kitwood, T., *Concern for Others: A New Psychology of Conscience and Morality*, London, Routledge, 1990.

Koffka, K., *Principles of Gestalt Psychology*, New York, Harcourt, Brace and Company, 1935.

Kohlberg, L., *The Meaning and Measurement of Moral Development*, Worcester, Mass., Clark University Press, 1980.

Kojima, H., 'Japanese Concepts of Child Development from the Mid-17th to the Mid-19th Century', *International Journal of Behavioral Development*, 1986, 9, pp. 315–19.

Kolak, D. and Martin, R. (eds), *Self and Identity: Contemporary Philosophical Issues*, New York, Macmillan, 1991.

Kubovy, M., *The Psychology of Perspective and Renaissance Art*, Cambridge, Cambridge University Press, 1986.

Laing, R. D., *The Politics of Experience and The Bird of Paradise*, Harmondsworth, Penguin, 1970.

Lakoff, G. and Johnson, M., *Metaphors We Live By*, Chicago and London, The University of Chicago Press, 1980.

—— *Philosophy in the Flesh: The Embodied Mind and its Challenge to Western Thought*, New York, Basic Books, 1999.

Lamb, M. E., Sternberg, K. J., Hwang, C.-P. and Broberg, A. G. (eds), *Child Care in Context: Cross-Cultural Perspectives*, Hillsdale, NJ, Lawrence Erlbaum, 1992.

Langer, L., *Holocaust Testimonies: The Ruins of Memory*, New Haven, Yale University Press, 1991.

—— (ed.), *Art from the Ashes: A Holocaust Anthology*, Oxford, Oxford University Press, 1995.

Langer, S., *Mind: An Essay on Human Feeling*, Volume 1, Baltimore, The Johns Hopkins University Press, 1970.

Lazarus, R. S., *Emotion and Adaptation*, New York, Oxford University Press, 1991.

Lee, J., *Ireland 1912–1985: Politics and Society*, Cambridge, Cambridge University Press, 1989.

Lemaire, A., *Jacques Lacan*, trans. D. Macey, London, Routledge & Kegan Paul, 1979.

Levi, P., *The Drowned and the Saved*, London, Abacus, 1988.

Levine, R., *A Geography of Time: The Temporal Misadventures of a Social Psychologist*, New York, Basic Books, 1997.

Lifton, R. J., *The Broken Connection: On Death and the Continuity of Life*, New York, Basic Books, 1983.

—— *The Nazi Doctors: A Study in the Psychology of Evil*, London, Papermac, 1986.

Linde, C., *Life Stories: The Creation of Coherence*, Oxford, Oxford University Press, 1993.

Lorenzer, A. and Orban, P., 'Transitional Objects and Phenomena: Socialization and Symbolization' in S. Grolnick and L. Barkin (eds), *Between Reality and Fantasy: Transitional Objects and Phenomena*, New York, Jason Aronson, 1978.

Luria, A. R., *Human Brain and Psychological Processes*, New York, Harper and Row, 1966.

Magris, C., *Danube: A Sentimental Journey from the Source to the Black Sea*, London, Collins Harvill, 1990.

Maslow, A., *Motivation and Personality* (2nd edn), New York, Harper & Row, 1970.

—— *The Farther Reaches of Human Nature*, Harmondsworth, Pelican, 1973.

McCarthy, C., *The Crossing*, London, Picador, 1995.

McDermott, J. J. (ed.), *The Writings of William James*, New York, The Modern Library, 1968.

Mead, G. H., *Mind, Self and Society*, Chicago, University of Chicago Press, 1934.

Melzack, R., 'Phantom limbs, the self and the brain: The D. O. Hebb Memorial Lecture', *Canadian Psychology*, 1989, January, Vol. 30 (1), pp. 1–16.

Merleau-Ponty, M., *Phenomenology of Perception*, trans. C. Smith, London, Routledge & Kegan Paul, 1981.

Metger, W., 'Optische Untersuchungen am Ganzfeld, 11. Zur Phänomenologie des homogenen Ganzfelds,' *Psychologische Forschung*, 13, 1930, pp. 6–29.

Milgram, S., *Obedience to Authority: An Experimental View*, New York, Harper and Row, 1975.

Millar, S., *Understanding and Representing Space: Theory and Evidence from Studies with Blind and Sighted Children*, Oxford, Clarendon Press, 1994.

Milner, B., 'The Memory Defect in Bilateral Hippocampus Lesions', *Psychiatric Research Reports* 11, 1959, pp. 43–58.

Milton, J., *Poetical Works*, ed. D. Bush, London, Oxford University Press, 1966.

Mühlhäusler, P. and Harré, R., *Pronouns and People: The Linguistic Construction of Social and Personal Identity*, Oxford, Basil Blackwell, 1993.

Murray, L. and Andrews, L., *The Social Baby*, London, The Children's Project, 2000.

Mussen, P. H. (ed.), *Handbook of Child Psychology* (4th edn), New York, Wiley, 1983.

Myers, G. E., *William James: His Life and Thought*, New Haven, Yale University Press, 1986.

Nagel, T., *Mortal Questions*, Cambridge, Cambridge University Press, 1979.

—— *The View from Nowhere*, Oxford, Oxford University Press, 1986.

Neisser, U., 'Five Kinds of Self-Knowledge', *Philosophical Psychology*, 1, 1, 1988, pp. 35–59.

Neisser, U. and Jopling, D. A. (eds), *The Conceptual Self in Context: Culture, Experience, Self-Understanding* (Emory Symposium on Cognition, 7), Cambridge, Cambridge University Press, 1997.

Nelson, K. (ed.), *Narratives from the Crib*, Cambridge, Mass., Harvard University Press, 1989.

Noam, G. G. and Wren, T. E. (eds), *The Moral Self*, Cambridge, Mass., The MIT Press, 1993.

Nozick, R., *The Examined Life: Philosophical Meditations*, New York, Simon and Schuster, 1989.

Oatley, K. and Jenkins, J. M., *Understanding Emotions*, Oxford, Blackwell, 1996.

Oatley, K. and Johnson-Laird, P. N., 'Towards a cognitive theory of emotions', *Cognition and Emotion*, 1987, Vol. 1, pp. 29–50.

Olson, D., *The World on Paper*, Cambridge, Cambridge University Press, 1994.

Padfield, P., *Himmler: Reichsführer-SS*, London, Papermac, 1995.

Paillard, J. (ed.), *Brain and Space*, Oxford, Oxford University Press, 1991.

Pearce, J., 'Consent to Treatment during Childhood: The Assessment of Competence and the Avoidance of Conflict', *The British Journal of Psychiatry*, 1994, 165, pp. 713–16.

Pinker, S., *How the Mind Works*, London, Allen Lane The Penguin Press, 1997.

Pollock, L. A., *Forgotten Children: Parent-child relations from 1500 to 1900*, Cambridge, Cambridge University Press, 1983.

Prost, A. and Vincent, G., *A History of Private Life:* Vol. 5, *Riddles of Identity in Modern Times*, Cambridge, Mass., Belknap Press, 1991.

Proust, M., *Remembrance of Things Past*, New York, Chelsea House, 1987.

Radke-Yarrow, M., Zahn-Waxler, C. and Chapman, M., 'Children's Prosocial Dispositions and Behaviour' in E. M. Hetherington (ed.), *Handbook of Child Psychology*, Volume 4: *Socialisation, Personality and Social Development*, New York, Wiley, 1983.

Ramsay, F., 'General Propositions and Causality' in *The Foundations of Mathematics and other Logical Essays*, London, 1931, p. 238.

Ricoeur, P., *Time and Narrative* Vol. 3, trans. K. Blamey and D. Pellauer, London, The University of Chicago Press, 1988.

Robinson, D. N., *Wild Beasts and Idle Humours: The Insanity Defense from Antiquity to the Present*, Cambridge, Mass., Harvard University Press, 1996.

Rock, I., *Perception*, New York, Scientific American Library, 1995.

Rogers, C., *Freedom to Learn*, Columbus, Ohio, Charles E. Merrill, 1969.

Rorty, R., 'Review of The Ethics of Authenticity', *The London Review of Books*, 8 April 1993.

Sachs, N., 'Chorus of the Unborn' in L. Langer (ed.), *Art from the Ashes: A Holocaust Anthology*, Oxford, Oxford University Press, 1995, p. 644.

Sacks, O., *An Anthropologist on Mars: Seven Paradoxical Tales*, London, Picador, 1995.

—— *The Man Who Mistook His Wife for a Hat*, London, Picador, 1986.

Said, E., *Out of Place: A Memoir*, London, Granta Books, 1999.

Salgado, S., *Migrations: Humanity in Transition*, New York, Aperture Foundation, 2000.

Scarry, E., *The Body in Pain: The Making and Unmaking of the World*, Oxford, Oxford University Press, 1985.

Schank, R. C. and Abelson, R. P., *Scripts, Plans, Goals and Understanding: An Inquiry into Human Knowledge Structures*, Hillsdale, NJ, Erlbaum, 1977.

Schlink, B., *The Reader*, London, Orion, 1998.

Sereny, G., *Albert Speer: His Battle with the Truth*, London, Macmillan, 1995.

Seymour, W., *Remaking the Body: Rehabilitation and Change*, London, Routledge, 1998.

Shearman, J., *Only Connect: Art and the Spectator in the Italian Renaissance*, Princeton, NJ, Princeton University Press, 1992.

Shore, B., *Culture in Mind: Cognition, Culture, and the Problem of Meaning*, Oxford, Oxford University Press, 1996.

Shotter, J. and Gergen, K. (eds), *Texts of Identity*, London, Sage, 1989.

Shweder, R., *Thinking through Cultures: Expeditions in Cultural Psychology*, Cambridge, Mass., Harvard University Press, 1991.

Singer, E., *Child-Care and the Psychology of Development*, London, Routledge, 1992.

Smith, A., *The Theory of Moral Sentiments*, Oxford, Oxford University Press, 1976.

Smith, A. D., *National Identity*, London, Penguin, 1991.

Smith, M. and Kollock, P., *Communities in Cyberspace*, London, Routledge, 1998.

Sobchack, V., *The Address of the Eye: A Phenomenology of Film Experience*, Princeton, NJ, Princeton University Press, 1992.

Speer, A., *Inside the Third Reich*, London, Cardinal, 1975.

Spitz, E., *Art and Psyche*, New Haven, Yale University Press, 1985.

Spitz, R., *The First Year of Life: A Psychoanalytic Study of Normal and Deviant Development*, New York, International Universities Press, 1965.

Stainton Rogers, R. and Stainton Rogers, W., *Stories of Childhood: Shifting Agendas of Child Concern*, London, Harvester Wheatseaf, 1992.

Staub, E., *The Roots of Evil: The Origins of Genocide and Other Group Violence*, New York, Cambridge University Press, 1989.

—— 'The Evolution of Evil', *Theory & Psychology*, 8, 5, October 1998, p. 703.

Steiner, G., *Language and Silence: Essays 1958–1966*, London, Penguin, 1969.

Stewart, I. and Cohen, J., *Figments of Reality: The Evolution of the Curious Mind*, Cambridge, Cambridge University Press, 1997.

Stigler, J. W., Shweder, R. A. and Herdt, G. (eds), *Cultural Psychology: Essays on Comparative Human Development*, Cambridge, Cambridge University Press, 1990.

Storr, A., *Solitude*, London, Harper Collins, 1994.

Storry, M. and Childs, P. (eds), *British Cultural Identities*, London, Routledge, 1997.

Stuart, F., *Black List, Section H*, London, Penguin, 1996.

Styron, W., *Darkness Visible*, London, Picador, 1991.

Sutherland, S., *Breakdown*, St Albans, Granada, 1977.

Tajfel, H., *Differentiation between Groups: Studies in the Social Psychology of Intergroup Relations*, London, Academic Press, 1978.

Taylor, C., *Human Agency and Language: Philosophical Papers 1*, Cambridge, Cambridge University Press, 1985.

—— *Sources of the Self: The Making of the Modern Identity*, Cambridge, Mass., Harvard University Press, 1989.

—— *The Ethics of Authenticity*, Cambridge, Mass., Harvard University Press, 1991.

Tomasello, M., *The Cultural Origins of Human Cognition*, Cambridge, Mass., Harvard University Press, 1999.

Tuan, Y., *Space and Place*, Minneapolis, University of Minnesota Press, 1976.

Turiel, E. 'The Development of Morality' in *Handbook of Child Psychology* (5th edn), Volume 3: *Social Emotional and Personality Development*, ed. N. Eisenberg, New York, John Wiley & Sons, 1998.

—— *Mind in Society: The Development of Higher Psychological Processes*, eds M. Cole, V. John-Steiner, S. Scribner and E. Souberman, Cambridge, Mass., Harvard University Press, 1978.

Turrell, J., *Air Mass*, London, The South Bank Centre, 1993.

Valsiner, J., *Culture and the Development of Children's Action: A Cultural-Historical Theory of Developmental Psychology*, New York, Wiley, 1987.

—— *Human Development and Culture: The Social Nature of Personality and its Study*, Lexington, Mass., Lexington Books, 1989.

Vernon, J., *Inside the Black Room: Studies of Sensory Deprivation*, Harmondsworth, Penguin, 1966.

Vygotsky, L., *Thought and Language*, Cambridge, Mass., The MIT Press and Wiley, 1962.

Walton, K., *Mimesis as Make-Believe: On the Foundations of the Representational Arts*, Cambridge, Mass., Harvard University Press, 1993.

Wertheim, M., *The Pearly Gates of Cyberspace: A History of Space from Dante to the Internet*, London, Virago, 1999.

White, S. H. and Siegel, A. W., 'Cognitive Development in Time and Space', In B. Rogoff and J. Lave (eds), *Everyday Cognition: Its Development in Social Context*, Cambridge, Mass., Harvard University Press, 1984.

WHO Family and Reproductive Health and Division of Emergency and Humanitarian Action, 'The Impact of Armed Conflict on Children: A Threat to Public Health', Geneva, *WHO*, July 1996, p. 54.

Wilson, R. A. and Keil, F. C. (eds), *The MIT Encyclopedia of the Cognitive Sciences*, London, The MIT Press, 1999.

Winner, E., *The Point of Words: Children's Understanding of Metaphor and Irony*, Cambridge, Mass., Harvard University Press.1988.

Winnicott, D., *Playing and Reality*, Harmondsworth: Penguin, 1974.

Wispé, L., *The Psychology of Sympathy*, New York, Plenum Press, 1991.

Wittgenstein, L., *Philosophical Investigations* (2nd edn), eds G. E. M. Anscombe and R. Rhees, trans. G. E. M. Anscombe, Oxford, Basil Blackwell, 1958.

Wollheim, R., *The Thread of Life*, Cambridge, Cambridge University Press, 1984.

—— *Painting as an Art*, London, Thames & Hudson, 1987.

Wolpert, L., *Malignant Sadness: The Anatomy of Depression*, London, Faber and Faber, 1999.

Woodhead, M. et al. (eds), *Becoming a Person*, London, Routledge, 1991.

Wright, E., *Psychoanalytic Criticism*, London, Methuen, 1984.

Zahn-Waxler, C., Radke-Yarrow, M. and King, R. C., 'Child Rearing and Children's Prosocial Initiations towards Victims of Distress', *Child Development*, 1979, 50, pp. 319–30.

Zaner, R. M., *The Problem of Embodiment: Some Contributions to a Phenomenology of the Body* (2nd edn), The Hague, Martinus Nijhoff, 1971.

Zeldin, T., *An Intimate History of Humanity*, London, Minerva, 1995.

Zelizer, V. A. R., *Pricing the Priceless Child: The Changing Value of Children*, New York, Basic Books, 1985.

INDEX

Abraham P. 165, 173

Achilles 227

absorption 127; aesthetic 176–90, 193; negative 162, 176; positive 162, 176–90

adolescence 135

aesthetic absorption *see* absorption

agency 20, 56, 57, 60, 84, 90, 94, 166; and language 174; moral 133, 134, 136, 141, 144

Agger, Inger 170–1

Alderson, Priscilla 140, 141

Allen, Woody 227

Allport, Gordon 228, 229, 233, 235

Alzheimer's disease 99

Améry, Jean 167, 169, 170, 172, 173

Amnesty International 139, 168

Anderson, Benedict 207, 213

Anderson, Terry 125–6, 129

Anna G. 164, 173

anosognosia 35, 36

anthropology 219, 220, 243

anti-Semitism *see* Jews

Arbib, Michael 34, 43

Aries, Philippe 136, 144

Aristotle 6, 214

Arnheim, Rudolf 178, 184, 187, 190

art 71, 82, 127, 128, 161, 176, 177, 180, 189, 190, 239; as experience 87, 193; expressive 82, 84, 85, 101; and identity 213–20; and light 197, 200, 201, 205; as metaphor 194, 195, 214; perspectives 195, 196, 203, 204;

self-surrender 177, 178, 186, 187; social origins of 192, 204

attention: directing 161, 168; seeking 138; sharing 142, 143

attitudes, of others 148

Auschwitz 163–5; *see also* Holocaust

authority 217, 219, 224

autism 145

autobiographical self 18, 60, 93, 94, 97, 123, 209; *see also* narrative identity

Bakhtin, M. 62, 72

Baron-Cohen, Simon 141–3, 145

Barthes, Roland 55, 58

Beckett, Samuel 217, 219

beliefs 73, 74, 83, 122

belonging 206–7

Benson, C. 29

Berlin, Isaiah 83, 85, 207, 212, 220

Berthoz, A. 43

Bessie K. 164, 173

betrayal 168–72

Bible 211

bicameral mind 16, 74–80, 85, 86, 132

bilaterality 14

Billig, M. 58

Blake, William 144, 145

blame: attributing 148, 161; self 162, 164, 166, 168, 169, 171, 210

blindness 197, 198; and self 20, 96, 142, 205

body: morphology 7; and self 4, 6, 7, 8, 22, 23, 95
Boland, Eavan 217, 218, 219, 221
boundaries, of self 8, 10, 19, 132, 134, 181, 183, 184, 193, 194, 199
Bradbury, Malcolm 216
brain damage: and feeling 106, 107, 109–11; and self 35–41
brain function, and self 31–44
Brand, Cabell 135
Breuilly, John 207
Brodkey, Harold 101
Browning, Christopher 147, 153, 154, 158
Bruner, Jerome ix, x, xi, xiii, 3, 4, 11, 14, 17, 21, 28, 29, 30, 46, 50–53, 55–7, 59–62, 71, 83, 88, 93, 122, 123, 128, 129, 140, 143, 209, 220, 227, 240, 243
Buber, Martin 229
Bullock, Alan 47, 57, 124, 129
Burke, Kenneth 52

Cahan, E. 130
Cardozo, Judge 140
caring 150, 159
Caruth, Cathy 163, 164
Casals, Pablo 229
Casey, Edward xi, xii, xiii, 3, 6, 8, 9, 14, 15, 22–3, 29, 103, 116, 122
categorisation 25
cave paintings 192; see also art
censorship 218, 219
centredness 60, 61, 94, 113, 187
Chang, J. 60, 62, 70, 72
changes, self 122–5, 129, 161–74; and trauma 56–7, 124–6, 162, 163
children 130–145; assertiveness 138; attention-seeking 138; attention-sharing 142, 143; autism 142; competencies 138–41, 145; consent to surgery 140, 141, 145; decision-making 140; empathy 149, 150; expectations 138; mindblindness 141, 142; mindreading 141, 142; mothering 149, 150; pitilessness 139, 141, 150; responsibility 137–41, 144, 147, 148; and roots of aesthetic absorption

180–4; sibling rivalry 149, 160; as soldiers 139, 140, 145; sympathy 150; teasing 149; wisdom 141
choice xii, 133, 241; radical 135
Clark, Kenneth 178
cognition see thinking
cognitive neuroscience 17, 32, 34, 36, 42, 169, 202, 205, 243
Cohen, J. 15, 125, 129, 130
Colby, Anne 133, 135, 136, 144
Cole, Michael 11
compassion 127, 134, 144, 146; in children 141
confabulation 40, 41
conflict, internal 107
conscious awareness 42
consciousness 76, 80, 84, 113, 174; collective 116; continuity of 41, 50, 112, 179, 180; core 111, 112, 121, 123, 168, 169, 202, 209; extended 112, 123; and feeling 113; individual 116; location of 75; self- 94, 223; stream of 82, 112, 190, 196; subjective 80
container metaphor 79
Cox, Maureen 97
creativity 82, 83, 230
cruelty see pitilessness
Csikszentmihalyi, Mihaly 177, 190
cultural psychology 11, 12, 13, 17, 18, 21, 49, 53, 54, 100, 105, 107, 116, 122, 123, 224, 227, 240, 243; defining 15; historical perspective 136–8, 144, 147, 148, 151, 159, 207
culture x; location of 191; and self 4, 11, 12, 13, 54, 57, 177; theory of 143

Da Vinci, Leonardo 196
Damasio, Antonio xi, 12, 13, 14, 19, 31, 33–7, 43, 76, 88, 90, 97, 101, 103, 105–10, 112, 116, 117, 122, 127, 168–9, 177, 184, 186, 202–4, 209, 239
Damon, William 130, 133, 135, 136, 137, 141, 144, 145, 159
Darwin, Charles 15, 86
David (brain damaged man) 39, 40, 109, 110, 111

Dawkins, Richard 54, 58, 73, 172, 239
de Beauvoir, Simone 49
deceit 80
Demos, John 115, 117
denial 218
Dennett, D. 15, 28, 29, 30, 40, 54, 59, 86, 100, 172, 209
depression 48, 58, 83
Descartes 43, 68, 69, 101, 103, 116
desires, second order 134, 135
development 222, 223, 225, 228, 229; adolescence 135; complete 233; ideals of 229, 230, 232, 234; infant 19, 20; moral 137, 149; of personhood 94, 95; self 18; *see also* maturity
Dewey, John 8, 28, 85, 87, 90, 116, 117, 177–80, 182, 184–6, 190, 191, 193, 225
dialogic self 62, 72
disgust 147, 154
dislocation *see* changes
disorientation 103, 104
Donaldson, Lord 141
Donaldson, Margaret 19, 20, 29
dualism 5, 79
Dunn, Judy 149, 160
Durr, Virginia 136
dying 233, 234

ecological self 18, 19, 20, 22
education, culture of 145, 221, 243
ego 88
Einstein, Albert 206, 229
Eliot, George 179, 182
Eliot (brain damaged man) 107, 108, 109
emotions: and goals 114; and morality 150; as pathfinders 103–16, 123; quasi 188, 189; recursive nature of 148; of responsibility 147, 150; and social control 115
empathy: in children 149, 150; inhibition of 151, 152, 155, 159; *see also* sympathy
Erikson, Erik 170, 233, 236
evil, origins of 160
evolution 15; biological 142; cultural 54, 59, 73, 74, 86, 129

expression 71, 82
eye-direction detector (EDD) 141, 142
eyes, as location of self 19, 20, 23, 29, 34, 35

familiarity 103, 104, 109, 113, 121
family 212
feelings *see* emotions
felt thinking 106
Fenyman, R. 31
Feyerabend, Paul 72
F. H. (brain damaged man) 39, 40
flow *see* absorption, aesthetic
Fraiberg, Selma 19–20
Frankfurt, Harry 133, 134, 135, 136, 144
free will 83
freedom 81, 100, 133, 241; limits to 134, 135
Freud, Sigmund 18, 47, 49, 88, 101, 178, 180, 181, 227, 232
Frith, Uta 96
fulfillment, self 81, 82, 87, 229; *see also* development
full life *see* good life
fusion, symbiotic *see* oceanic feelings

Gage, Phineas (brain damaged man) 107, 108, 109
Gamble, Prof. Clive 192
Ganzfeld Sphere xii, 197, 198, 199, 200, 204
Gardner, H. 29
Garvin, T. 215, 219
Gazzaniga, M. 42, 43, 44
Geertz, Clifford xiii, 3, 206
Gellner, Ernest 207, 211, 221
genocide 155–58; and responsibility 156, 162, 164, 165, 167
geotropic statural referential 34
Gergen, Ken 53
Gewirth, Alan 235, 236
Gibson, J.J. 197
Gillett, G. 100, 101, 191, 232, 236
Gillick Competence 140
Gillick, Mrs 140
Glover, Jonathan 73, 74, 83, 84, 85
gods *see* verbal hallucinations

Goebbels, J. 24
Goethe, J. W. von 70
golden age 212
Goldhagen, Daniel 147, 148, 153, 155, 156, 157, 158
Goldstein, Kurt 229
good 61–4; *see also* moral identity
good life 66, 128, 222, 223, 225, 227, 232, 234
Greg (brain damaged man) 37–40
guilt 133, 147, 148, 151, 155, 161, 162, 166, 168, 169, 171, 210, 234

hallucinations *see* verbal hallucinations
harmony 185, 186
Harré, Rom xi, 11, 14, 17, 20, 21, 53, 58, 61, 62, 72, 73, 85, 89, 90, 91, 92, 94, 97–100, 115, 116, 117, 122, 123, 191, 206, 209, 227, 231–3, 236
Hass, Aaron 171, 174
Haste, Helen 136
Hastings, Adrian 207, 210, 211, 213, 220
Hausheer, Roger 207
health, psychological 227–31
Heaney, S. 45
Heaven 7, 129, 200, 201
Hegel, G. W. F. 225
Heider, Fritz 150
Herder, J. G. 207
Herdt, Gilbert 11
here/there binary 7–10, 19, 20, 192, 193, 198, 199, 213
Himmler, Heinrich 24, 151
history, personal 81; *see also* narrative identity
Hitler, Adolf 47, 126, 129, 147, 153, 155, 157, 158, 165, 206, 225
H. M. (brain damaged man) 23, 109
Hobbes, T. 158
Hobsbawm, Eric 207, 220
Holland, Dorothy 131
Holocaust 74, 147, 151, 156, 157, 158, 162, 163, 164, 166, 175; *see also* Jews
Homer's *Iliad* 77, 79, 81
honour 65, 133
horizon 62, 65

human nature 226, 227, 228, 230, 236
Human Potential Movement 225, 229
human rights *see* rights, human
Humphrey, Nicholas 51, 52, 57, 58
Husserl, E. 9, 22, 29
Hutchinson, John 213
Huxley, Aldous 229
Hyde, Douglas 215

I, use of xii, 5, 6, 27, 97, 98, 99, 184, 185, 187, 190, 193, 194, 213
ideals 134, 144, 172–4, 240
identification 142
identity: maintaining 135; modern 70, 71, 86; national 126, 128, 206–20; personal 85, 89, 101, 128, 133, 206–20; social 89, 101; *see also* narrative identity
Ignatieff, Michael 67, 72, 159, 160
Iliad see Homer's *Iliad*
individualism 64, 133, 202, 229, 232
individuation 82; *see also* self-actualization
information processing 17, 18, 21, 22
inner depths, of self 68, 71, 82
inner speech 76, 92
inside/outside binary 192, 193, 198, 199
integration, of self 56, 135, 233
integrity 134
intentional agents 143
intentionality 123
intentionality detector (ID) 141, 142, 143
internalization 68
internet 93
intersubjectivity 91, 114
Ireland 210–19, 221
Iser, Wolfgang 55

Jakobson, Roman 52, 101
James, Henry 56
James, William 22, 23, 29, 41, 50, 51, 83, 84, 86, 95, 98, 99, 105, 121, 177, 229
Jaynes, Julian xi, 14, 16, 74–81, 85, 86, 100, 122, 132
Jefferson, Thomas 229
Jenkins, J. 114, 116

Jenkins, R. 101
Jews, treatment of 24, 147, 148, 151, 154, 156–9; *see also* genocide
Jimmie (brain damaged man) 39, 40
Joan of Arc 78
Johnson, M. xi, 8, 10, 11, 15, 17, 25–8, 30, 34, 35, 75, 122, 194, 204, 211, 241
Johnson-Laird, P. N. 113, 114, 116
Joyce, James 71, 216, 221
Jung, C. G. 181, 232

Kafka, F. 234
Kagan, Jerome 29, 150
Kalmar, D. 53, 55, 56, 58
Kant, I. 70, 98, 225
Karadzic, Radovan 54, 210
Keats, John 229, 234
Kersten, Felix 151
Kiberd, D. 215, 217, 221
Kissinger, Henry 48, 58
Kitwood, T. 146
Koffka, Kurt 197
Kohlberg, Lawrence 230, 231, 235, 236
Korsakoff syndrome 39
Kosslyn, Stephen 34
Kreisler, Fritz 229
Kubovy, M. 196

Lacan, Jacques x, xiii
Laing, R. D. 225, 235
Lakoff, G. xi, 8, 10, 11, 15, 17, 25–9, 30, 34, 35, 75, 122, 194, 204, 211, 241
Langer, Lawrence 164–6, 168
Langer, Susanne 93, 104, 105, 109, 112, 116
language: and agency 144; autism 101; baby-talk 95; controlling function 86; and feelings 73, 79; games 73, 85, 92; inner speech 76, 92; and pain 168; private 92; pronouns 88–101; and self 18, 22, 23, 24, 73, 88–101, 191, 218, 221; sign 96; writing 77, 79, 86, 102
Lazarus, R. S. 113, 116
Lenin, V. 126

Leonardo 196
Levi, Primo 163, 165
liberty, concepts of 86
Lifton, Robert Jay 158, 161
Linde, Charlotte 97
linguistic binary 10
literature 216, 217, 221; vernacular 211
location ix, xii, 3, 4, 193, 194; psychology of 5, 6, 10, 11, 194
locational self (Lakoff and Johnson) 27–8
locative system, self as xi, xii,; 3, 4, 11, 17, 26–8, 61, 73, 99, 121, 123, 134, 239
Locke, John 69
logic 190
Lorenzer, A. 183, 191
love 161, 173, 179, 232; attachment 114; caregiving 114; sexual 114
Luria, A. R. 114, 117

McCarthy, C. 16, 45
Mahler, Margaret 18, 181
Mantegna, Andrea 196
Maslow, Abraham 227, 228, 229, 230, 232, 234, 235
mastery, of self 68
Matisse, H. 182
maturity 225–8, 230, 234–5; threshold 141; *see also* development
Mead, G. H. 27, 30, 78, 96
Mead, Margaret 219
meaning: of life 220; location of 72; theory of 193
meaningfulness 69, 81, 227, 242
mechanisms 61
memes 54, 59, 73, 74, 129, 209
memory 58, 123, 180; loss 29, 40
Merleau-Ponty, M. 8, 22, 28, 34, 36, 202, 205
metaphor 25–7; of architecture 174; container 79; event-structure 26; mirror 214; moving-time 26; multiple selves 28; of nations 211, 212; orientational 194; primary 25; spatial 130; subject-self 27, 28; time-orientation 26, 35
Metzger, Wolfgang 197

Millar, Susanna 198
Miller, Arthur 188
Miller, Jonathan 39, 43
Milner, Brenda 23, 29, 109
Milton, J. 129
mind: discursive 101, 102, 236; embodied
    221; emergent 129, 130
mindblindness 141, 142, 145
mind-space 76, 80, 88
Möbius, Kurt 157, 158
modernism 214, 216, 217
monologue 58
Montaigne, M. E. de 70
moral compass 151
moral exemplars 136
moral identity 59–71, 126, 127, 130–45,
    166, 167; developing 137, 149, 159, 160;
    dismantling 171
moral judgment 230, 231
Moran, D. P. 215, 216
Moses S. 165
Moulin, Jean 173
moved, being see absorption, aesthetic
Mozart, W. A. 234
Munn, P. 149
myth 216, 220

Nagel, Thomas 21, 89, 101, 192, 225
names 95
narrative identity 21, 27, 28, 29, 37, 41, 42,
    45–57, 70, 123, 227, 235; and life crises 56,
    57; life stories 102; meta- 52, 54, 60, 67, 71;
    structure 52, 112, 224; see also
    autobiographical self
nationalism 207–17, 219, 220, 221;
    transcending 227
nature–nurture debate x
navigation 105, 121, 134, 240, 242
Neisser, Ulric 17–22, 28, 29
neuroscience see cognitive neuroscience
Newton, Sir Isaac 234
Noam, G. G. 130, 144
non-deployment of I 184–5
novels 70; see also art

Nozick, R. 222

O'Flaherty, Liam 219
Oatley, K. 113, 114, 116
obedience 144, 158, 224
object relations theory 181, 183, 184
oceanic feelings 180–82
Orban, P. 183, 191
other 212, 213
outgroups, treatment of 147, 152, 153, 155; see
    also Jews
ownership 51, 52, 91, 92, 224

Paillard, Jacques 33–4, 35, 43
pain 167, 168, 169, 173; and self-diminution
    168, 169
Parrott, W. G. 115, 116, 117
patriotism 206
Peirce, C. S. 176
Penfield, Wilder 78
perceptual binary 10, 200
perception: bodily 43, 203; visual 200, 202–5
personhood, developing 94, 95, 235
perspective 5, 193, 196, 197, 201, 202, 204
Piaget, J. 18, 26, 230
Picasso, P. 234
Pinochet, A. 208
pitilessness 127, 134, 144, 151, 154, 157; of
    children 139, 141, 150; and compassion
    146–59, 161; origins of 160; and
    responsibility 144, 158
place xi, 6, 7, 29, 103; and mind 129;
    structuring 9; -world xiii; 116; see also
    location
place–time 6, 9, 18
Plato 68, 214
play 183; make-believe 187, 188, 189, 191
poetry 144, 145, 173; Irish 217, 218; see also art
point of view see perspective
Pope, Alexander 222
Pozzo, Fra Andrea 201
practices 61
pride 147, 148, 151, 210
privacy 49, 50

private language argument 92
pronouns 88–102
Propp, Vladimir 52
proto-self 12, 19, 111, 121, 123, 202, 209, 211
Proust, Marcel 49, 58
psychological symbiosis *see* symbiosis, psychological
psychology: Gestalt 9, 197, 205; new age 225; positivist 222; social 220
psychotherapy 48
punctual self 69
purpose 241

questioning 90, 91

racism 158
radical reflexivity *see* reflection
Ramsay, Frank 73, 85
ratchet theory 143
reason 26, 68, 106, 107, 109
reflection, self- 178, 180, 186, 223, 224
regulatory self 60
religion 65, 66, 71
relocation xi, xii, 122, 123
remorse 147, 210
Renoir, Pierre 229
Renouvier, C. B. 83
responsibility xii, 122, 126, 130–45, 210; and authority 217, 219, 224; of children 137–41, 147, 148; criminal 139; moral 127, 169, 171; other 131, 132; self- 75, 80, 81, 86, 122, 126, 127, 131–3, 136, 166; space of 162, 164, 172
restoration 179, 180, 182, 184
Ricoeur, Paul 46, 47, 52, 57, 224
rights, human 67, 72, 85, 122, 160, 235
Robinson, D. N. 129
Rogers, Carl 105, 225, 232, 236
Roosevelt, Eleanor 229
Rorty, Amelie 52, 235
Rorty, R. 121, 225–6
Rousseau, J.-J. 70, 225
rules, following 72

Rushdie, Salman 224
Russell, George William 229

Sachs, Nellie 173, 175
Sacks, Oliver 37, 39, 40, 43, 44
Said, Edward 125, 129
St Augustine 68, 69
St John 172
Sakharov, Andrei 133
Salgado, Sebastiao 122, 129
Sartre, J.-P. 135
scaffolding 140
Scarry, Elaine 168, 169–70
Schlink, B. 146
Schubert 234
second-order desires 134
self: absorbed 190; -accounting 57; -actualization 84, 229–31, 236; -awareness 57, 185, 243; -belief 84; collective 126; conceptual 18, 21; -consciousness 94, 223; -control 79; -creation 73–85; definitions of 89, 90; doubt 224; extended 18, 21; false 225; function of 4; ideal 181; in infancy 19, 29, 57, 58; interpersonal 18, 20; inwardness of 81; -justification 149; -knowledge 18, 135, 137, 242; original 181; phenomenon of 4; private 18, 21; regulatory 60; -respect 126; -responsibility *see* responsibility, self-; -surrender 177, 178, 186, 187, (*see also* absorption, aesthetic); symbolic 242; true 225; *see also* proto-self
self/not self *see* boundaries, of self
sensory deprivation 197
sentimentality 219
sexual abuse 171
sexuality 218, 219
Seymour, Wendy 124
shame 147, 148, 151, 161, 166, 168, 169, 171
shared-attention mechanism (SAM) 141, 142
Shearman, John 200
Shore, Brad 11
Shweder, Richard 11, 15
Smith, Adam 127, 129
Smith, Anthony 207, 208

Socrates 224

somatic marking 109

space: and brain 43; history of 204; and place 14

space–time 6, 7, 9, 18

spatial relations 25

Spear-Swerling, L. 242

Speer, Albert 29, 48, 49, 50, 58, 234, 235

Spitz, Ellen 181, 182, 190

Spitz, René 95

stability, of self 50, 122, 125

Stalin, J. 47, 126, 129, 225

Staub, Ervin 154, 155, 156, 157, 160

Stein, Gertrude 234

Stein, J. F. 43

Steiner, George 220

Stern, Daniel 20

Sternberg, R. J. 242

Stewart, I. 15, 125, 129, 130

Stigler, James 11

Storr, Anthony 234, 236

story *see* narrative identity

Strachey, James 88

Stuart, F. 49, 58

subjectivism 64

subjectivity 64, 123, 127, 161, 193, 202–4, 227

subjunctivizing reality 55

suffering 161–74

suppression 218

survivor guilt 162

Sutherland, Stuart 48, 58

symbiosis, psychological 95, 140, 209

symbolism 5, 10, 17, 28, 54, 186, 227; of domes 200, 201

sympathy 146, 147, 152, 156, 159; in children 150; definition 160; psychology of 146, 159; *see also* compassion *and* empathy

Tajfel, Henri 153, 160

Taylor, Charles xi, 14, 53, 57, 59–72, 74, 81, 82, 99, 123, 131, 134–6, 159, 166, 168, 172, 208, 221, 223, 225, 227, 230, 232, 233

Thatcher, Margaret 88

theory of mind mechanism (ToMM) 141–3

thinkable 157, 158, 162, 208, 212; *see also* unthinkable

thinking: development of 86, 145; and feeling 106, 112; out loud 92; paradigmatic 51

Todorov, Tzvetan 52, 55

Tóibín, Colm 49

Tomasello, Michael xiii, 11, 15, 142, 143, 145

torture 162, 167–71, 174

Tourette's Syndrome 23

transcendence, of self *see* absorption, aesthetic

transferred values 179, 185

transient global amnesia 112, 113

transitional objects 182, 183

Trapp, Major 154

trauma 124, 125, 126, 162, 163

Trevarthen, Colwyn 20

trust, basic 167, 170, 171

Tuan, Yi-Fu 7, 14, 103, 116

Turrell, James xii, 127, 192, 197–204

Ulysses 227

unconscious, and self 47, 48, 49

understanding, self 135, 137, 242; development of 159

unthinkable 133, 134, 150, 162, 166, 208, 212; *see also* thinkable

verbal hallucinations 76–80

voices *see* verbal hallucinations

Vygotsky, Lev 54, 76, 77, 92, 94, 101, 140

Wagner, W. R. 234

Walton, Kendall 188, 189, 191

Wearing, Clive 39

Weber, Eugen 210

Wertheim, M. 14, 195

White, Hayden 52

Whitman, Walt 229

Winnicott, Donald 181–3, 225

Wispé, Lauren 146, 159, 160

Wittgenstein, Ludwig 73, 92, 101, 104

Wollheim, Richard 192, 193, 195, 204

Wolpert, L. 48, 58
work, ability to 232
World Health Organisation 139
worlds: game- 188, 189; human 16; work-
   188
Wren, T. E. 130, 144
writing, invention of 77, 79

Yeats, William Butler 215
Yevtushenko, Y. A. 153

Zahn-Waxler, Carolyn 149, 159
Zeldin, Theodore 93, 101, 153, 159, 213,
   221
Zen 202

0845 473837

07732182 0901